COLLINS

PORTUGUESE GEM DICTIONARY

Portuguese-English
English-Portuguese

N. J. LAMB, M.A.
Senior Lecturer in Portuguese and Spanish
University of Liverpool

COLLINS
LONDON AND GLASGOW

GENERAL EDITOR: J. B. FOREMAN

First Published 1964

Latest Reprint 1974

CONTENTS

ISBN 0 00 458661 1

PRINTED IN REAT BRITAIN

BY COLLINS CLEAR-TYPE PRESS

FOREWORD

The compiler's aim has been to produce a clear, compact and up-to-date pocket dictionary. To achieve clarity, avoiding a mere accumulation of undifferentiated words, much use has been made of explanatory terms in brackets. In making a dictionary of this size, the problem of selection of words is acutely difficult but it is hoped that no vital, essential term has been omitted.

I am profoundly indebted to my friend and colleague, Dr. Firmino de Deus Crespo, who responded so ungrudgingly and cheerfully to my many demands on his patience in the task of elucidating meanings. I wish also to express my thanks to his successor at Liverpool, Dr. Luís M. P. Alonso for his assistance in the final stages.

N. J. L.

PREFÁCIO

Tentei fazer um dicionário claro e actualizado. Para conseguir tal fim, evitando o mero amontoado de palavras não diferanciadas entre si, inseri entre parênteses muitos termos explicativos. Ao fazer um dicionário deste tamanho, o problema da escolha das palavras é particularmente difícil mas espero não ter omitido qualquer palavra essencial.

Estou profundamente agradecido ao meu colega e amigo, Dr. Firmino de Deus Crespo, que sempre atendeu generosamente e de boa vontade todos os pedidos que dirigi à sua colaboração paciente na tarefa de esclarecer o sentido de tantas palavras. Aproveito a oportunidade para exprimir os meus cordiais agradecimentos também ao sucessor do Dr. Crespo em Liverpool, Dr. Luís M. P. Alonso, pelo seu auxílio nos preparativos finais.

N. J. L.

ABBREVIATIONS
ABREVIATURAS

abbrev.	abbreviation	abreviatura
acad.	academic	académico
adj.	adjective	adjectivo
adv.	adverb	adverbio
anat.	anatomical	anatómico
approx.	approximately	aproximadamente
archit.	architecture	arquitectura
art.	article	artigo
astr.	astronomy	astronomia
bot.	botany	botânica

Braz.	Brazilian	Brasileiro
chem.	chemistry	química
coll.	colloquial	coloquial
com.	commerce	comércio
conj.	conjunction	conjunção
eccl.	ecclesiastical	eclesiástico
elect.	electricity	electricidade
eng.	engineering	engenharia
espec.	especially	especialmente
f.	feminine noun	substantivo feminino
fig.	figurative	figuaritivo
geog.	geography	geografia
gir.	slang	gíria
interj.	interjection	interjeição
leg.	legal	legal
m.	masculine noun	substantivo masculino
mf.	masculine *or* feminine noun	substantivo masculino *ou* feminino
maths.	mathematics	matemática
mech.	mechanics	mecânica
med.	medical	médico
mil.	military	militar
min.	mineralogy	mineralogia
mus.	music	música
naut.	nautical	náutico
orni.	ornithology	ornitologia
paint.	painting	pintura
photo.	photography	fotografia
pl.	plural	plural
poet.	poetic	poético
polit.	political	político
pop.	popular	popular
Port.	Portuguese	Português
pr.	pronoun	pronome
prep.	preposition	preposição
print.	printing	tipografia
relig.	religion	religião
s.	noun	substantivo
s/adj.	noun and adjective	substantivo e adjectivo
sl.	slang	gíria, calão
theat.	theatre	teatro
U.K.	United Kingdom	Inglaterra
U.S.A.	United States	Estados Unidos
usu.	usually	usualmente
va.	transitive verb	verbo transitivo
vn.	intransitive verb	verbo intransitivo
vr.	reflexive verb	verbo reflexo
zool.	zoology	zoologia

SPELLING

The spelling throughout is that adopted in the Portuguese-Brazilian Agreement on Orthography of 1945. This spelling is now the standard form in Portugal, but in Brazil there are still some variations: e.g. the circumflex accent (^) is more widely used (e.g. **êste, êsse, pôrto,** etc.), and it frequently indicates a close vowel where Portugal has an open vowel (e.g. **bônus, cômodo**; in Portugal, **bónus, cómodo**); **c**, when silent, is omitted before a consonant (e.g. **ato** in place of Portugal's **acto, ação** in place of **acção**). In both Portugal and Brazil a word containing **oi** may have an alternative form in **ou**: **coisa—cousa; tesoiro—tesouro; toiro—touro.**

PRONUNCIATION

The pronunciation given in the first section of this dictionary is the pronunciation of Portugal, not of Brazil. In general, Brazilian pronunciation seems clearer to the English ear than that of Portugal: for example, in Brazil the unstressed vowels 'a' and 'e' (represented in the 'figured pronunciation' here by the letters 'ă', 'ĕ') are less slurred, less 'obscure', than in Portugal, and final 'e' is more distinct. No transcription into English symbols can represent with complete accuracy the complexities of Portuguese sounds. The transcription or 'figured pronunciation' used here can serve only as an approximation.

N.B.—In the 'figured pronunciation' the syllables are separated by hyphens (except after the stressed syllable); the stress is to be placed on the syllable immediately preceding the acute accent mark ('): e.g. **estilo** [ish-tee'loo], where the stress falls on the syllable 'tee'.

Vowels and Diphthongs

Symbol	*Symbol represents approximately the following English sounds*
[ah]	long, open *a*, as in 'father, rather'.
[ar]	long, open *a* plus strong trilled *r*, as in 'starry'.
[a]	short *a* as in 'patted, lap'.
[ă]	slurred, obscure *a* as in 'sofa, China, about'. (But this sound is more open and distinct in Brazil.)
[air]	as in 'hairy', with strong *r*.
[ay]	as in 'stay, play', but without the final glide; a pure vowel, not a diphthong.
[ay-ee]	*ay* as in 'play' plus a rapidly pronounced *ee*; roughly equivalent to *ey* in the interjection 'hey!'
[e]	as in 'bet, gem'.

[e'oo] *e* as in 'bet' plus a rapidly pronounced *oo*.
[ĕ] an obscure *e* as in 'token, fallen'. (More open and clearer in Brazil.)
[ee] as in 'meet, seen'.
[i] as in 'bit'.
[ish] as in 'dish'.
[o] short, open *o* as is 'top', potter'. (For Americans, the sound is roughly that of *a* in 'walk. talk'.)
[oh] close *o*; a pure 'o' as in Northern English 'most, rope'.
[oh-ee] the close, pure *o* plus rapidly spoken *ee*; like *owy* in 'showy'.
[oo] as in 'moon'.
[or] as in 'sorrow', but with strong *r*.
[ow] as in 'how, cow'.
[oy] as in 'boy'.
[ȳ] *y* as in 'style, my'.

Consonants

[b], [f], [k], [l], [m], [n], [p], [sh], [t], [v], [w], [y], [z], as in English.
[d] as in English but rather softer between two vowels (though not as soft as in Spanish).
[g] as in 'get, go'.
[kw] as in 'bookworm', or the *qu* in 'queen'.
[ly] like *li* in 'million'.
[ny] like *ny* in 'canyon', or *ni* in 'onion'.
[r] a stronger, more trilled *r* than in English; closer to Scottish *r*.
[s] hard *s* as in 'so, sip'.
[zh] like *s* in measure'.
[*n*] This symbol represents the nasalized sounds, which are, however, weaker than in French. Thus [ee*n*] represents a nasalized [ee]; [ow*n*] is a nasalized [ow]; [a*n*] is a nasalized [a], close to English 'an' in 'bank'

THE PORTUGUESE ALPHABET

A [ah]
B [bay]
C [say]
D [day]
E [e]
F [ef]
G [zhay; gay]
H [ă-gah']
I [ee]
J [zho'tă]
L [el]
M [em]
N [en]
O [oh]
P [pay]
Q [kay]
R [e'ri]
S [es]
T [tay]
U [oo]
V [vay]
X [sheesh]
Z [zay]

Ç [say sĕ-dee'lyă]
K [ka'pă]
W [vay doo'ploo; vay doo-brah'doo]
Y [ee gray'goo; eep'see-lon]

PORTUGUESE - ENGLISH DICTIONARY

a [ă] *prep.* to, at, in.
aba [ah'bă] *f.* brim (of hat); tails (of coat).
abade [ă-bahd'] *m.* abbot.
abadessa [ă-bă-de'să] *f.* abbess.
abadia[ă-bă-dee'ă] *f.* abbey.
abafadiço [ă-bă-fă-dee'soo] *adj.* sultry, stifling.
abafar [ă-bă-far'] *va.* t o stifle, smother; to hush up (a case, incident).
abaixar [ă-bȳ-shar'] *va.* to lower.
[under, below.
abaixo [ă-bȳ'shoo] *adv.* down,
abalado [ă-bă-lah'doo] *adj.* shaken; loose.
abalançar [ă-bă-la*n*-sar'] *va.* to weigh; to swing; *vr.* to rush on.
abalar [ă-bă-lar'] *va.* to shake; *vn.* to run away, go off.
abalizado [ă-bă-lee-zah'doo] *adj.* eminent, notable; marked out (of boundary, channel).
abalo [ă-bah'loo] *m.* shock, disturbance.
abalroar [ă-bal-roo-ar'] *vn.* to collide.
[to shake.
abanar [ă-bă-nar'] *va.* to fan;
abandonar [ă-ba*n*-doo-nar'] *va.* to abandon, give up, leave.
abandono [ă-ba*n*-doh'noo] *m.* abandonment, desertion; destitution.
abarcador [ă-băr-kă-dohr'] *m.* monopolist.
abarcar [ă-băr-kar'] *va.* to monopolize; to embrace (with one's ambition, vision); to contain, include.
abarrotar [ă-bă-roo-tar'] *va.* to fill up, glut.
abastado [ă-băsh-tah'doo] *adj.* wealthy, well-off.
abastamento [ă-băsh-tă-me*n*'too] *m.* supply, supplies.
abastança [ă-băsh-ta*n*'să] *f.* abundance, plenty.
abastecer [ă-băsh-tĕ-sayr'] *va.* to supply, provide.
abastecimento [ă-băsh-tĕ-see-me*n*'too] *m.* supply, supplies, provisions, stock; supplying; refuelling (of aeroplane).
abater [ă-bă-tayr'] *va.* to knock, (pull, cut, shoot) down; to humble.
abatido [ă-bă-tee'doo] *adj.* dejected, depressed.
abatimento [ă-bă-tee-me*n*'-too] *m.* depression; allowance, discount.
abcesso [ăb-se'soo] *m.* abscess.
abdicação [ăb-dee-kă-sow*n*'] *f.* abdication.
abdicar [ăb-dee-kar'] *vn.* to abdicate; *va.* to abandon, renounce (rights, etc.).
abecê [ah-bay-say'] *m.* alphabet, ABC.
abeirar [ă-bay-ee-rar'] *vn.* to approach.
abelha [ă-bay'lyă] *f.* bee; — mestra, queen-bee.
abençoar [ă-be*n*-soo-ar'] *va.* to bless; to praise.

aberração [ă-bĕ-ră-sow*n*'] *f.* aberration; error.
aberta [ă-bair'tă] *f.* opening, gap; break (in clouds, bad weather).
aberto [ă-bair'too] *adj.* open; frank, candid.
abertura [ă-bĕr-too'ră] *f.* opening; hole, aperture.
abeto [ă-be'too] *m.* fir-tree.
abismado [ă-beezh-mah'doo] *adj.* astounded, stupefied; lost (in thought, amazement, etc.).
abismar [ă-beezh-mar'] *va.* to astound, amaze.
abismo [ă-beezh'moo] *m.* abyss, chasm; depths.
abjecção [ăb-zhe-sow*n*'] *f.* abjection, degradation.
abjecto [ăb-zhe'too] *adj.* abject.
abjuração [ăb-zhoo-ră-sow*n*'] *f.* abjuration, recantation.
abjurar [ăb-zhoo-rar'] *va.* to abjure, forswear.
abnegação [ăb-nĕ-gă-sow*n*'] *f.* abnegation, self-sacrifice.
abnegar [ăb-nĕ-gar'] *va.* to renounce.
abóbada [ă-bo'bă-dă] *f.* arched roof, vault.
abóbora [ă-bo'boo-ră] *m.* vegetable marrow; pumpkin.
abolição [ă-boo-lee-sow*n*'] *f.* abolition; extinction.
abolir [ă-boo-leer'] *va.* to abolish, annul.
abominação [ă-boo-mee-nă-sow*n*'] *f.* abomination; abhorrence.
abominar [ă-boo-mee-nar'] *va.* to abominate, detest.
abonar [ă-boo-nar'] *va.* to be a surety for; to guarantee.
abono [ă-boh'noo] *m.* guarantee; bail; bonus.
abordar [ă-boor-dar'] *va.* to attack, to board (ship); to broach (subject); to accost (person).
aborrecer [ă-boo-rĕ-sayr'] *va.* to detest, abhor, hate; to weary, bore; *vr.* to grow weary, bored.
aborrecido [ă-boo-rĕ-see'doo] *adj.* annoyed; bored, weary; wearisome, boring; disliked, detested.
aborrecimento [ă-boo-rĕ-see-me*n*'too] *m.* dislike, aversion; boredom, tediousness.
abortar [ă-boor-tar'] *vn.* to miscarry; to fail, come to nothing (of schemes).
aborto [ă-bohr'too] *m.* miscarriage, abortion; monster.
abotoar [ă-boo-too-ar'] *va.* to button; *vn.* to bud.
abraçar [ă-bră-sar'] *va.* to embrace, clasp, hug; to include.
abraço [ă-brah'soo] *m.* embrace, hug; warm greetings (in letters).
abrandar [ă-bra*n*-dar'] *va.* to soften, mollify; to mitigate; to slow down (speed).
abranger [ă-bra*n*-zhayr'] *va.* to comprise, include.
abrasar [ă-bră-zar'] *va.* to burn; *vr.* to be consumed (with passion).
abre-latas [a-brĕ-la'tăsh] *m.* tin-, can-opener.
abreviação [ă-brĕ-vee-ă-sow*n*'] *f.* abridgement.
abreviar [ă-brĕ-vee-ar'] *va.* to abbreviate, abridge, shorten.
abreviatura [ă-brĕ-vee-ă-too'ră] *f.* abbreviation.
abrigar [ă-bree-gar'] *va.* to shelter, cover, protect.
abrigo [ă-bree'goo] *m.* shelter, cover, protection.
abril [ă-breel'] *m.* April.
abrir [ă-breer'] *va.* to open; to unfold; to unfasten; to switch on (light); to turn on (tap).
abrogação [ă-broo-gă-sow*n*'] *f.* abrogation, repeal.

abrogar [ă-broo-gar'] *va.* to repeal, abrogate.
abrolho [ă-broh'lyoo] *m.* thistle; thorn; *pl.* (*fig.*) difficulties.
abrupto [ă-broop'too] *adj.* steep, rugged.
ábside [ab'seed] *f.* apse.
absolutismo [ăb-soo-loo-teezh'moo] *m.* absolutism.
absoluto [ăb-soo-loo'too] *adj.* absolute.
absolver [ăb-sohl-vayr'] *va.* to absolve, acquit.
absorção [ăb-soor-sow*n*'] *f.* absorption.
absorto [ăb-sor'too] *adj.* amazed, absorbed.
absorver [ăb-soor-vayr'] *va.* to absorb, consume, imbibe.
abstémio [ăbsh-te'mee-oo] *adj.* abstemious.
abstenção [ăbsh-te*n*-sow*n*'] *f.* abstention.
abster-se [ăbsh-tayr'sĕ] *vr.* to abstain, refrain.
abstinência [ăbsh-tee-ne*n*'-see-ă] *f.* abstinence, self-denial.
abstracção [ăbsh-tra-sow*n*'] *f.* abstraction; omission; absence of mind.
abstrair [ăbsh-tră-eer'] *va.* to abstract, remove; *vr.* to become thoughtful.
absurdo [ăb-soor'doo] *adj.* absurd, stupid; *m.* absurdity.
abulia [ă-boo-lee'ă] *f.* lack of will; apathy.
abundância [ă-boo*n*-da*n*'see-ă] *f.* abundance, plenty.
abundante [ă-boo*n*-da*nt*'] *adj.* abundant, plentiful, copious.
abundar [ă-boo*n*-dar'] *vn.* to abound in; to be rich in, full of.
abusar [ă-boo-zar'] *va.* to abuse; to revile; to misuse; to take undue advantage of.
abuso [ă-boo'zoo] *m.* abuse; misuse.
abutre [ă-boo'trĕ] *m.* vulture.
acabado [ă-kă-bah'doo] *adj.* perfect, faultless; finished; old, worn-out.
acabar [ă-kă-bar'] *va.* to finish, end, conclude; — **com** to finish off, put an end to; — **de** to have just.
acabrunhado [ă-kă-broo-nyah'doo] *adj.* downcast.
acabrunhar [ă-kă-broo-nyar'] *va.* to depress, distress.
acaçapar-se [ă-kă-să-par'sĕ] *vr.* to cower, crouch.
academia [ă-kă-dĕ-mee'ă] *f.* academy.
académico [ă-kă-de'mee-koo] *m.* academician; *adj.* academic.
acalmar [ă-kal-mar'] *va.* to calm, soothe, appease, pacify.
acalorado [ă-kă-loo-rah'doo] *adj.* heated; excited.
açambarcar [ă-sa*n*-băr-kar'] *va.* to monopolize, buy up.
açamo [ă-să'moo] *m.* muzzle.
acampamento [ă-ka*n*-pă-me*n*'too] *m.* camp.
acampar [a-ka*n*-par'] *vn.* to camp.
acanhado [ă-kă-nyah'doo] *adj.* shy, bashful, timid.
acanhamento [ă-kă-nyă-me*n*'too] *m.* shyness.
acantonar [ă-ka*n*-too-nar'] *va.* to billet (troops).
acariciar [ă-kă-ree-see-ar'] *va.* to caress, fondle.
acarretar [ă-kă-rĕ-tar'] *va.* to cart, transport; to cause.
acaso [ă-kah'zoo] *m.* chance, fortune, hazard, luck; *adv.* **por** —, by chance.
acatamento [ă-kă-tă-me*n*'-too] *m.* respect, deference.
acatar [ă-kă-tar'] *va.* to respect, revere; to accept, respect (order, etc.).
acautelar [ă-kow-tĕ-lar'] *va.* to caution; *vr.* to beware of; to take care.
acção [ah-sow*n*'] *f.* action; activity; deed; battle; lawsuit;

stock, share (*com.*); plot (of play); — de graças, thanksgiving.
accionado [ă-see-oo-nah'doo] *adj.* set in motion, worked by, driven by; *m.pl.* gestures.
accionamento [ă-see-oo-nă-me*n*'too] *m.* drive, driving action (of machine).
accionar [ă-see-oo-nar'] *va.* to drive, work (machine); to sue (*leg.*); *vn.* to gesticulate.
accionista [ă-see-oo-neesh'tă] *m.* shareholder.
acções [ah-soy*n*sh'] *f.pl.* shares, stock (*com.*)
aceder [ă-sĕ-dayr'] *vn.* to accede, agree.
aceitação [ă-say-ee-tă-sow*n*'] *f.* acceptance; approbation.
aceitar [ă-say-ee-tar'] *va.* to accept; to agree to.
aceite [ă-say'eet] *m.* acceptance (*com.*); *adj.* acceptable; agreed, admitted.
aceito [ă-say'ee-too] *adj.* accepted, acceptable; admitted.
aceleração [ă-sĕ-lĕ-ră-sow*n*'] *f.* acceleration.
acelerar [ă-sĕ-lĕ-rar'] *va.* to accelerate; to expedite.
acenar [ă-sĕ-nar'] *vn.* to beckon; to make a sign; to nod.
acender [ă-se*n*-dayr'] *va.* to light (fire, lamp, etc.); to switch on (light); to set on fire; to excite, inflame.
acento [ă-se*n*'too] *m.* accent; stress; tone.
acentuação [ă-se*n*-too-ă-sow*n*'] *f.* accentuation; accent; stress.
acentuar [ă-se*n*-too-ar'] *va.* to accentuate; to stress, emphasize; to mark with an accent.
acepção [ă-sep-sow*n*'] *f.* acceptance (of meaning of a word).
acepipes [ă-sĕ-peepsh'] *m. pl.* hors d'oeuvres; delicacies; tit-bits.
acerbar [ă-sĕr-bar'] *va.* to embitter, exacerbate.
acerbo [ă-sayr'boo] *adj.* harsh, bitter, cruel, sharp.
acerca de [ă-sayr'kă dĕ] *prep.* about, concerning.
acercar [ă-sĕr-kar'] *va.* to approach, place near, bring near; *vr.* to approach.
acérrimo [ă-se'ree-moo] *adj.* pertinacious, obstinate, stubborn; very bitter.
acertado [ă-sĕr-tah'doo] *adj.* correct, exact; sensible.
acertar [ă-sĕr-tar'] *vn.* to hit the mark; to be right; *va.* to set right (clock, etc.).
acervo [ă-sayr'voo] *m.* heap.
aceso [ă-say'zoo] *adj.* lit, alight, lighted; on fire; excited.
acessível [ă-sĕ-see'vel] *adj.* accessible.
acesso [ă-se'soo] *m.* access, admittance; fit (of coughing, anger, etc.); por —s, by fits and starts.
acessório [ă-sĕ-so'ree-oo] *adj.* accessory, additional; *m.* accessory, addition; *m.pl.* accessories, fittings.
acetona [ă-sĕ-toh'nă] *f.* nail varnish remover; acetone.
achacoso [ă-shă-koh'zoo] *adj.* sickly, ailing.
achado [ă-shah'doo] *m.* find, discovery; *adj.* found.
achanar [ă-shă-nar'] *va.* to level, to make even; to remove difficulties.
achaque [ă-shak'] *m.* (chronic) ailment; vice.
achar [ă-shar'] *va.* to find, come across, discover, find out; to think, believe; *vr.* to feel (health); to be; to find oneself.
achatar [ă-shă-tar'] *va.* to flatten; to squash.
achega [ă-shay'gă] *f.* assistance; addition.

achegar [ă-shĕ-gar'] *va.* to draw, bring near.
acidentado [ă-see-den-tah'-doo] *adj.* uneven, irregular, rough, broken (ground); chequered (life).
acidental [ă-see-den-tal'] *adj.* accidental, unexpected.
acidente [ă-see-dent'] *m.* accident.
acidez [ă-see-daysh'] *f.* acidity; sourness.
ácido [ah'see-doo] *m.* acid; *adj.* acid, sour, tart.
acima [ă-see'mă] *adv.* above; up; *prep.* — de, above, beyond, over; mais —, higher up; pela rua —, up the street.
acinte [a-seent'] *m.* spite, malice.
acirrar [ă-see-rar'] *va.* to irritate, provoke; to incite, stir up.
aclamação [ă-klă-mă-sown'] *f.* acclamation; applause, cheers.
aclamar [ă-klă-mar'] *va.* to acclaim; to applaud, cheer.
aclaração [ă-klă-ră-sown'] *f.* clarification, explanation.
aclarar [ă-klă-rar'] *va.* to clarify, explain, make clear; *vr.* to clear up, brighten.
aclimatação [ă-klee-mă-tă-sown'] *f.* acclimatization.
aclimar [ă-klee-mar'] *va.* to acclimatize.
aço [ah'soo] *m.* steel; sword.
acocorar-se [ă-koo-koo-rar'-sĕ] *vr.* to squat, crouch.
açoitar [ă-soh-ee-tar'] *va.* to whip, scourge, lash.
acolá [ă-koo-lah'] *adv.* over there, yonder.
acolhedor [ă-koo-lyĕ-dohr'] *adj.* welcoming, hospitable.
acolher [ă-koo-lyayr'] *va.* to receive, admit (somebody); to welcome; *vr.* to shelter, take refuge.
acolhimento [ă-koo-lyĕ-men'-too] *m.* reception; shelter; welcome.
acólito [ă-ko'lee-too] *m.* [acolyte.
acometer [ă-koo-mĕ-tayr'] *va.* to attack, assault; to undertake (a task).
acometida [ă-koo-mĕ-tee'dă] *f.* assault, attack, onslaught.
acometimento [ă-koo-mĕ-tee-men'too] *m.* attack; attempt; attack, fit (*med.*).
acomodação [ă-koo-moo-dă-sown'] *f.* accommodation.
acomodar [ă-koo-moo-dar'] *va.* to accommodate; *vr.* to fit in with, adapt oneself to.
acompanhamento [ă-kon-pă-nyă-men'too] *m.* retinue, suite; accompaniment (*mus.*).
acompanhar [ă-kon-pă-nyar'] *va.* to accompany, go with, escort; to keep company; to accompany (*mus.*).
aconchegado[ă-kon-shĕ-gah'-doo] *adj.* snug, cosy; tucked in.
acondicionamento [ă-kon-dee-see-oo-nă-men'too] *m.* packing, wrapping; air-conditioning.
acondicionar [ă-kon-dee-see-oo-nar'] *va.* to condition; to pack, wrap; to arrange.
aconselhar [ă-kon-sĕ-lyar'] *va.* to advise.
acontecer [ă-kon-tĕ-sayr'] *vn.* to happen, occur, come about.
acontecimento [ă-kon-tĕ-see-men'too] *m.* event, incident.
açor [ă-sohr'] *m.* goshawk.
acordar [ă-koor-dar'] *va/vn.* to wake(n), awake(n); *vn.* to agree. [(*mus.*).
acorde [ă-kohrd'] *m.* chord
acordeão [ă-koor-dee-own'] *m.* accordion.
acordo [ă-kohr'doo] *m.* agreement; de —, agreed; in agreement.
açoreano [ă-soo-ree-ă'noo] *m.*

native of the Azores; *adj.* of the Azores.
acostumado [ă-koosh-too-mah'doo] *adj.* accustomed; used to.
acostumar [ă-koosh-too-mar'] *va.* to accustom, familiarize; *vr.* to get used to.
acotovelar [ă-koo-too-vĕ-lar'] *va.* to nudge; to jostle.
acre [a'krĕ] *adj.* bitter, pungent; acrid (smoke); harsh.
acreditar [ă-krĕ-dee-tar'] *va.* to believe; to put faith in; to warrant; to credit (*com.*); to accredit (ambassador, etc.).
acrescentar [ă-krĕsh-sen-tar'] *va.* to add; to augment.
acréscimo [ă-kresh'see-moo] *m.* increase; rise; addition.
acrimónia [ă-kree-mo'nee-ă] *f.* acrimony.
acrisolar [ă-kree-zoo-lar'] *va.* to refine, assay (metals); to purify, test.
acrobata [ă-kroo-bah'tă] *m.* [acrobat.
acta [ah'tă] *f.* record, minutes.
activar [a-tee-var'] *va.* to speed up; to set in motion.
actividade [a-tee-vee-dahd'] *f.* activity; agility.
activo [a-tee'voo] *adj.* active; diligent; agile, nimble; *m.* assets, credit balance.
acto [ah'too] *m.* act; action; **—continuo**, immediately afterwards; **no mesmo —**, simultaneously.
actor [a-tohr'] *m.* actor.
actriz [a-treesh'] *f.* actress.
actuação [a-too-ă-sow*n*'] *f.* action, activity; pressure, influence.
actual [a-too-al'] *adj.* present; actual, direct, effective.
actualidade [a-too-ă-lee-dahd'] *f.* presen t time; *f.pl.* news.
actualizar [a-too-ă-lee-zar'] *va.* to modernize; to realize.
actuar [a-too-ar'] *vn.* to act; *va.* to put into action; to influence. [actuary.
actuário [a-too-ah'ree-oo] *m.*
açúcar [ă-soo'kar] *m.* sugar.
açucareiro [ă-soo-kă-ray'ee-roo] *m.* sugar-bowl; sugar manufacturer, refiner.
açucena [ă-soo-say'nă] *f.* white lily.
açude [ă-sood'] *m.* weir, dam.
acudir [ă-koo-deer'] *vn.* to go to help; to respond; to retort.
açular [ă-soo-lar'] *va.* to set (dogs) on; to provoke.
acumulação [ă-koo-moo-lă-sow*n*'] *f.* accumulation.
acumulador [ă-koo-moo-lă-dohr'] *m.* accumulator.
acumular [ă-koo-moo-lar'] *va.* to accumulate, amass, store up.
acusação [ă-koo-ză-sow*n*'] *f.* accusation, charge.
acusar [ă-koo-zar'] *va.* to accuse; to reveal (faults, etc.); **— a recepção**, to acknowledge receipt.
acústica [ă-koosh'tee-kă] *f.* acoustics. [slash.
acutilar [ă-koo-tee-lar'] *va.* to
adaga [ă-dah'gă] *f.* dagger.
adaptação [ă-dap-tă-sow*n*'] *f.* adaptation.
adaptar [ă-dap-tar'] *va.* to adapt. [cellar.
adega [ă-day'gă] *f.* wine-
adejar [ă-dĕ-zhar'] *va.* to flap (wings); to flutter.
adelgaçar [ă-del-gă-sar'] *va.* to attenuate; to thin down, dilute; to taper off.
adentro [ă-de*n*'troo] *adv.* inside, indoors. [adherent.
adepto [ă-dep'too] *m.* follower,
adequado [ă-dĕ-kwah'doo] *adj.* adequate, appropriate.
adereçar [ă-dĕ-rĕ-sar'] *va.* to adorn.
adereço [ă-dĕ-ray'soo] *m.* adornment, finery.

aderir [ă-dĕ-reer'] *vn.* to adhere; to stick.
adernar [ă-dĕr-nar'] *vn.* to heel over (*naut.*).
adesão [ă-dĕ-zow*n*'] *f.* adhesion; support.
adesivo [ă-dĕ-zee'voo] *m.* adhesive tape, sticking plaster; *adj.* adhesive.
adestrado [ă-dĕsh-trah'doo] *adj.* skilful, skilled.
adestrar [ă-dĕsh-trar'] *va.* to train, to instruct.
adeus [ă-day'oosh] *interj.* good-bye; dizer —, to say good-bye, to bid farewell to.
adiamento [ă-dee-ă-me*n*'too] *m.* adjournment; postponement.
adiantado [ă-dee-a*n*-tah'doo] *adj.* advanced; fast (watch, clock).
adiantar [ă-dee-a*n*-tar'] *va.* to advance; to put on, forward (watch, clock).
adiante [ă-dee-a*n*t'] *adv.* forward, onward; mais —, further on.
adiar [ă-dee-ar'] *va.* to postpone, adjourn, delay.
adição [ă-dee-sow*n*'] *f.* addition; sum.
adicionar [ă-dee-see-oo-nar'] *va.* to add.
adicto [ă-deek'too] *adj.* addicted, inclined, devoted.
adido [ă-dee'doo] *m.* attaché.
aditamento [ă-dee-tă-me*n*'-too] *m.* addition, increase.
adivinhação [ă-dĕ-vee-nyă-sow*n*'] *f.* fortune-telling, divination; guessing.
adivinhar [ă-dĕ-vee-nyar'] *vn.* to guess; to divine.
adivinho [ă-dĕ-vee'nyoo] *m.* fortune-teller; soothsayer.
adjacente [ăd-zhă-sent'] *adj.* adjacent.
adjudicação [ăd-zhoo-dee-kă-sow*n*'] *f.* grant, award (of works contract, etc.); decision (*leg*).
adjudicar [ăd-zhoo-dee-kar'] *va.* to allot, to award.
adjunto [ăd-zhoo*n*'too] *adj.* joined, attached; *m.* assistant, associate.
administração [ăd-mee-nish-tră-sow*n*'] *f.* administration; management, directorate; board; office; ministry.
administrador [ăd-mee-nish-tră-dohr'] *m.* administrator; director, manager; — de falências, trustee.
administrar [ăd-mee-nish-trar'] *va.* to administer, govern, manage.
admiração [ăd-mee-ră-sow*n*'] *f.* wonder, admiration; ponto de —, exclamation mark.
admirado [ăd-mee-rah'doo] *adj.* astonished, surprised.
admirar [ăd-mee-rar'] *va.* to admire; *vr.* to be astonished at, wonder at; não admira, no wonder!
admirável [ăd-mee-rah'vel] *adj.* admirable.
admissão [ăd-mee-sow*n*'] *f.* admission; admittance.
admitir [ăd-mee-teer'] *va.* to admit; to receive.
admoestação [ăd-moo-ĕsh-tă-sow*n*'] *f.* admonition.
admoestar [ăd-moo-ĕsh-tar'] *va.* to admonish, reprove.
adoçar [ă-doo-sar'] *va.* to sweeten; to soften; to pacify, assuage, mitigate; to smooth.
adoecer [ă-doo-ĕ-sayr'] *vn.* to fall ill; to suffer from; *va.* to make ill.
adolescente [ă-doo-lĕsh-se*n*t'] *mf/adj.* adolescent.
adopção [ă-do-sow*n*'] *f.* adoption.
adoptar [ă-do-tar'] *va.* to adopt.
adoração [ă-doo-ră-sow*n*'] *f.* adoration, worship.

adorar [ă-doo-rar'] *va.* to adore, worship.
adormecer [ă-door-mĕ-sayr'] *va.* to lull to sleep; *vn.* to fall asleep.
adornar [ă-door-nar'] *va.* to adorn, ornament, decorate.
adorno [ă-dohr'noo] *m.* adornment, ornamentation, finery.
adquirir [ăd-kĕ-reer'] *va.* to acquire, get.
adrede [ă-drayd'] *adv.* purposely, deliberately.
adro [ad'roo] *m.* church square, open space in front of a church; churchyard.
aduana [ă-doo-ă'nă] *f.* custom(s)-house.
aduaneiro [ă-doo-ă-nay'ee-roo] *adj.* customs; *m.* customs-officer.
adubar [ă-doo-bar'] *va.* to manure; to season, spice (food).
adubo [ă-doo'boo] *m.* manure; dressing (leather); seasoning (food). [flattery.
adulação [ă-doo-lă-sow*n*'] *f.*
adular [ă-doo-lar'] *va.* to flatter; to fawn on.
adulteração [ă-dool-tĕ-ră-sow*n*'] *f.* adulteration, falsification.
adulterar [ă-dool-tĕ-rar'] *va.* to adulterate, falsify.
adultério [ă-dool-te'ree-oo] *m.* adultery.
adulto [ă-dool'too] *m/adj.* adult, grown up.
adusto [ă-doosh'too] *adj.* scorched, parched; sunburnt.
aduzir [ă-doo-zeer'] *va.* to adduce, bring forward.
adventício [ăd-ve*n*-tee'see-oo] *adj.* adventitious; foreign; unusual; *m.* newcomer; foreigner; upstart.
adversário [ăd-vĕr-sah'ree-oo] *m.* adversary, opponent.
adversidade [ăd-vĕr-see-dahd'] *f.* adversity, misfortune.
adverso [ăd-vair'soo] *adj.* adverse, contrary.
advertência [ăd-vĕr-te*n*'see-ă] *f.* warning; advice; note, observation; preface (in book).
advertido [ăd-vĕr-tee'doo] *adj.* prudent; well advised.
advertir [ăd-vĕr-teer'] *va.* to warn, advise; to draw attention to.
advogado [ăd-voo-gah'doo] *m.* lawyer, barrister, advocate.
advogar [ăd-voo-gar'] *va.* to advocate (a cause, etc.); to plead (a case in court).
aéreo [ă-air'ee-oo] *adj.* air, aerial; ataque —, air-raid; via —a, by air, air mail.
aeroporto [ă-air-oh-pohr'too] *m.* airport.
afã [ă-fa*n*'] *m.* eagerness; exertion; anxiety, care.
afabilidade [ă-fă-bee-lee-dahd'] *f.* affability, courtesy.
afadigar [ă-fă-dee-gar'] *va.* to tire (out); *vr.* to tire oneself.
afagar [ă-fă-gar'] *va.* to caress, fondle; to cherish (hopes, etc.).
afamado [ă-fă-mah'doo] *adj.* renowned, famous, celebrated.
afanoso [ă-fă-noh'zoo] *adj.* laborious; painstaking.
afastado [ă-făsh-tah'doo] *adj.* remote, distant, secluded; retired, removed.
afastar [a-făsh-tar'] *va.* to remove; to keep off, away; to deflect; *vr.* to keep away; to deviate; to move away; to withdraw.
afável [ă-fah'vel] *adj.* affable, courteous, genial.
afazer [ă-fă-zayr'] *va.* to accustom.
afazeres [ă-fă-zay'rĕsh] *m.pl.* business, duties, tasks.
afear [ă-fee-ar'] *va.* to disfigure, deface.
afectado [ă-fe-tah'doo] *adj.* conceited, affected.

afectar [ă-fe-tar'] *va.* to affect; to pretend, feign.
afecto [a-fe'too] *m.* affection, fondness; *adj.* affectionate, devoted.
afectuoso [ă-fe-too-oh'zoo] *adj.* affectionate, tender.
afeição [ă-fay-ee-sown'] *f.* affection, fondness, devotion.
afeiçoado [ă-fay-ee-soo-ah'-doo] *adj.* fond of, devoted to; *m.* friend.
afeiçoar [ă-fay-ee-soo-ar'] *va.* to shape, fashion, mould; *vr.* to take a fancy to; to devote oneself to.
afeito [ă-fay'ee-too] *adj.* accustomed, used to.
aferidor [ă-fĕ-ree-dohr'] *m.* inspector of weights and measures.
aferir [ă-fĕ-reer'] *va.* to gauge; to check; to compare.
aferrado [ă-fĕ-rah'doo] *adj.* obstinate, stubborn; firmly attached to.
aferrar [ă-fĕ-rar'] *va.* to grapple; to anchor; to grasp; *vr.* to stick to (opinions, etc.).
afiançar [ă-fee-an-sar'] *va.* to stand bail; to guarantee.
afiar [ă-fee-ar'] *va.* to sharpen.
afilhada [ă-fee-lyah'dă] *f.* god-daughter. [godson.
afilhado [ă-fee-lyah'doo] *m.*
afiliar [ă-fee-lee-ar'] *va.* to affiliate, admit; *vr.* to join.
afim [ă-feen'] *m.* relative, relation; *adj.* similar, akin, related.
afinação [ă-fee-nă-sown'] *f.* refining; tuning (*mus.*).
afinar [ă-fee-nar'] *va.* to refine; to adjust; to tune (*mus.*).
afinco [ă-feen'koo] *m.* tenacity, assiduity.
afinidade [ă-fee-nee-dahd'] *f.* affinity, relationship.
afirmação [ă-feer-mă-sown'] *f.* affirmation; statement.
afirmar [ă-feer-mar'] *va/vn.* to affirm, assert, declare.
afirmativo [ă-feer-mă-tee'-voo] *adj.* affirmative, positive.
afixar [ă-feek-sar'] *va.* to stick, post (notices, bills).
aflição [ă-flee-sown'] *f.* affliction, distress, grief.
afligir [ă-flee-zheer'] *va.* to afflict, distress, grieve; *vr.* to worry about, distress oneself, to fret.
afloramento [ă-floo-ră-men'-too] *m.* outcrop (of coal, etc.).
afluência [ă-floo-en'see-ă] *f.* abundance; great flow (of water, etc.); pressure (of traffic); crowd.
afluente [ă-floo-ent'] *m.* tributary, stream; *adj.* copious.
afluir [ă-floo-eer'] *vn.* to flow, stream, run into; to congregate.
afogar [ă-foo-gar'] *va.* to drown; to suffocate, stifle, choke; to extinguish, put out (fire); *vr.* to drown, be drowned.
afogo [ă-foh'goo] *m.* suffocation; anguish, affliction; haste.
afoito [ă-foh'ee-too] *adj.* bold.
afora [ă-fo'ră] *prep.* except, apart from, save.
aforrar [ă-foo-rar'] *va.* to line (clothes); to save (money); to free (slaves).
afortunado [ă-foor-too-nah'-doo] *adj.* fortunate, lucky.
afronta [ă-fron'tă] *f.* insult.
afrontar [ă-fron-tar'] *va.* to insult, affront, outrage; to confront, face (danger, etc.).
afrouxar [ă-froh-shar'] *va/vn.* to slacken, abate, slow down, loosen.
afugentar [ă-foo-zhen-tar'] *va.* to drive off, put to flight; to banish (care, etc.).
afundar [ă-foon-dar'] *va.* to sink; to deepen (a cavity); *vr.* to sink.
agachar-se [ă-gă-shar'sĕ]

vr. to crouch, squat, stoop.
agarrar [ă-gă-rar'] *va.* to seize, grip, hold, grasp, clutch; *vr.* to cling, hold on to.
agasalhado [ă-gă-ză-lyah'-doo] *adj.* cosy, snug; sheltered.
agasalhar [ă-gă-ză-lyar'] *va.* to shelter, entertain; *vr.* to wrap oneself up.
agasalho [ă-gă-za'lyoo] *m.* shelter, hospitality; warm clothes.
agência [ă-zhen'see-ă] *f.* agency; office.
agenciar [ă-zhen-see-ar'] *va.* to negotiate for; to try to get.
agenda [ă-zhen'dă] *f.* notebook.
agente [ă-zhent'] *m.* agent; — **de** câmbios, stock-broker; — **de** seguros marítimos, underwriter.
ágil [ah'zheel] *adj.* agile, nimble, active, brisk.
agiota [ă-zhee-o'tă] *m.* stock-jobber; money-lender; speculator.
agir [ă-zheer'] *vn.* to act.
agitação [ă-zhee-tă-sown'] *f.* agitation; disturbance.
agitado [ă-zhee-tah'doo] *adj.* agitated, disturbed; restless; rough (sea).
agitar [ă-zhee-tar'] *va.* to agitate, disturb, perturb; to shake (bottle); to stir (liquid, etc.); to swing, wave (arms, etc.); *vr.* to be upset; to get rough (sea).
aglomerar [ăg-loo-mĕ-rar'] *va.* to agglomerate, heap up.
agonia [ă-goo-nee'ă] *f.* agony, anguish; death pangs.
agonizante [ă-goo-nee-zant'] *m.* dying person.
agonizar [ă-goo-nee-zar'] *vn.* to be dying; to agonize.
agora [ă-go'ră] *adv.* now; — mesmo, a moment ago; por —, for the present; *interj.* now!, come!, I don't believe it! ainda —!, here you are at last!
agosto [ă-gohsh'too] *m.* August.
agouro [ă-goh'roo] *m.* omen.
agraciar [ă-gră-see-ar'] *va.* to award, to decorate with (title, medal, etc.).
agradar [ă-gră-dar'] *va.* to please, gratify; *vr.* to like.
agradável [ă-gră-dah'vel] *adj.* pleasant, enjoyable, agreeable.
agradecer [ă-gră-dă-sayr'] *va.* to thank, to be grateful for; não tem que —, not at all!
agradecimento [ă-gră-dĕ-see-men'too] *m.* gratitude; *m.pl.* thanks.
agrado [ă-grah'doo] *m.* pleasure; kindness.
agrário [ă-grah'ree-oo] *adj.* agrarian.
agravar [ă-gră-var'] *va.* to aggravate; *vn.* to lodge an appeal (*leg.*).
agravo [ă-grah'voo] *m.* offence, injury, wrong; appeal (*leg.*).
agredir [ă-grĕ-deer'] *va.* to attack, assault.
agregado [ă-grĕ-gah'doo] *m.* aggregate, sum total.
agregar [ă-grĕ-gar'] *va.* to amass, add.
agremiação [ă-grĕ-mee-ă-sown'] *f.* association.
agressão [ă-grĕ-sown'] *f.* aggression, attack, assault.
agressivo [ă-grĕ-see'voo] *adj.* aggressive, threatening.
agreste [ă-gresht'] *adj.* rural, rustic; wild, uncultivated (country); rough (hide; weather; people).
agrião [ă-gree-own'] *m.* watercress.
agrícola [ă-gree'koo-lă] *adj.* agricultural.
agricultura [ă-gree-kool-too'ră] *f.* agriculture; farming.
agrilhoar [ă-gree-lyoo-ar'] *va.* to chain, put in irons.
agro [ag'roo] *adj.* bitter,

harsh; *m.* cultivated land.
agrupar [ă-groo-par'] *va.* to group.
água [a'gwă] *f.* water; **— doce,** fresh water; **— potável,** drinking water; **— benta,** holy water; **fazer —,** to leak (*naut.*); **à flor de —,** awash; **—s furtadas,** *f.pl.* garret, attic.
aguaceiro [a-gwă-say'ee-roo] *m.* heavy shower; squall.
aguadeiro [a-gwă-day'ee-roo] *m.* water-carrier.
aguar [a-gwar'] *va.* to water; to dilute; to spoil.
aguardar [ă-gwăr-dar'] *va.* to wait (for), await; to expect.
aguardente [a-gwăr-de*n*t'] *m.* brandy.
aguarela [a-gwă-re'lă] *f.* water-colour (*art*).
aguçar [ă-goo-sar'] *va.* to sharpen.
agudeza [ă-goo-day'ză] *f.* sharpness, acuteness; perspicacity, subtlety; witticism.
agudo [ă-goo'doo] *adj.* sharp, keen, acute; witty; penetrating.
agueiro [ă-gway'ee-roo] *m.* [gutter.
aguentar [ă-gwe*n*-tar'] *va.* to tolerate, put up with, stand; to ride out (a storm); to support (wall, etc.).
aguerrido [ă-gĕ-ree'doo] *adj.* warlike, bellicose; courageous.
águia [a'gee'-ă] *f.* eagle.
aguilhada [ă-geel-yah'dă] *f.* goad.
aguilhão [ă-gee-lyow*n*'] *m.* spur, goad; spike; sting (of wasp, etc.); stimulus, incentive.
agulha [ă-goo'lyă] *f.* needle; compass; switch, points (railway, tramlines); steeple (of church); **— ferrugenta,** meddler, intriguer.
agulheiro [ă-goo-lyay'ee-roo] *m.* needle-case; needle-maker; pointsman (railway, tramlines); hole, opening.
agulheta [ă-goo-lyay'tă] *f.* tag (on laces, etc.); nozzle.
ai [ȳ] *interj.* oh!, alas!; **—deles,** woe to them. [way.
aí [ă-ee'] *adv.* there; **por —,** that
aia [ȳ'yă] *f.* nursemaid, nanny; governess.
ainda [ă-ee*n*'da] *adv.* still, yet; even; **— que,** although; **— agora,** just now; **— bem,** fortunately; **— assim,** even so, nevertheless; **— em (por) cima,** over and above; **— quando,** even though.
aipo [ȳ'poo] *m.* celery.
airado [ȳ-rah'doo] *adj.* frivolous, dissolute.
airoso [ȳ-roh'zoo] *adj.* comely, graceful, elegant; decent.
ajeitar [ă-zhay-ee-tar'] *va.* to arrange; *vr.* to adapt.
ajoelhar-se [ă-zhoo-ĕl-yar'sĕ] *vr.* to kneel.
ajuda [ă-zhoo'dă] *f.* help, aid, assistance; grant, subsidy.
ajudante [ă-zhoo-da*n*t'] *m.* assistant; adjutant (*mil.*); server (*eccl.*); **— de campo,** aide-de-camp.
ajudar [ă-zhoo-dar'] *va.* to help, aid, assist; to serve (at Mass); *vr.* to use, employ.
ajuizado [ă-zhoo-ee-zah'doo] *adj.* sensible, wise, discreet.
ajuizar [ă-zhoo-ee-zar'] *va.* to judge; to estimate.
ajuntamento [ă-zhoo*n*-tă-me*n*'too] *m.* assembly.
ajuntar [ă-zhoo*n*-tar'] *va.* to join; to add; to assemble, to collect; to amass (money); to attach (documents, etc.).
ajustar [ă-zhoosh-tar'] *va.* to adjust, fit, fix; to settle (dispute, accounts, etc.); *vr.* to agree (on).
ajuste [ă-zhoosht'] *m.* agreement, settlement; adjustment.

ala [ah'lă] *f.* row, file, tier; aisle; wing (of building, army, etc.).
alagar [ă-lă-gar'] *vn.* to inundate, flood.
alambicado [ă-lan-bee-kah'-doo] *adj.* affected.
alambicar [ă-lan-bee-kar'] *va.* to distil; *vr.* to be affected.
alambique [ă-lan-beek'] *m.* still, retort.
alameda [ă-lă-may'dă] *f.* avenue, grove.
álamo [a'lă-moo] *m.* poplar.
alarde [ă-lard'] *m.* ostentation, boasting; **fazer — de**, to parade, show off, boast of.
alargar [ă-lăr-gar'] *va.* to enlarge, widen, extend; to loosen, slacken (belt, etc.); *vr.* to enlarge on (theme, etc.); **— o passo**, to walk faster.
alarido [ă-lă-ree'doo] *m.* outcry, shout, lamentation.
alarma [ă-lar'mă] *f. or* **alarme** [ă-larm'] *m.* alarm, alert; tumult; outcry.
alastrar [ă-lăsh-trar'] *va.* to scatter, spread; to ballast.
alavanca [ă-lă-van'kă] *f.* lever; crowbar.
albarda [al-bar'dă] *f.* pack-saddle.
albergar [al-bĕr-gar'] *va.* to provide lodging; to shelter.
albergue [al-bairg'] *m.* inn; hospice, shelter.
albornoz [al-boor-nosh'] *m.* burnous; large, hooded cloak.
álbum [al'boon] *m.* album.
alça [al'să] *f.* sights (on rifle); handle, ring.
alcachofra [al-kă-sho'fră] *f.* artichoke.
alçada [al-sah'dă] *f.* jurisdiction, competence.
alcançar [al-kan-sar'] *va.* to reach, arrive at; to obtain; to attain; to overtake; to comprehend; *vn.* to reach; to suffice.
alcance [al-kans'] *m.* reach; power, competence; understanding; range (of gunfire, vision); deficit; **ao — de**, within reach (range) of; **ao — da voz**, within earshot, call; **de grande —**, of great consequence.
alcantil [al-kan-teel'] *m.* crag, precipice.
alcantilado [al-kan-tee-lah'-doo] *adj.* steep, precipitous.
alçapão [al-să-pown'] *m.* trap-door.
alçaprema [al-să-pray'mă] *f.* crowbar; forceps (of dentist).
alçar [al-sar'] *va.* to lift, raise; *vr.* to rise up.
alcateia [al-kă-te'yă] *f.* pack (of wolves, etc.); gang (of thieves, etc.).
alcatrão [al-kă-trown'] *m.* tar; pitch.
alcofa [al-koh'fă] *f.* basket.
álcool [al'koo-ol] *m.* alcohol.
Alcorão [al-koo-rown'] *m.* Koran.
alcoviteiro [al-koo-vee-tay'-ee-roo] *m.* pimp, procurer; *f.* bawd.
alcunha [al-koon'yă] *f.* nick-name.
aldeão [al-dee-own'] *m.* villager; peasant.
aldeia [al-day'yă] *f.* village, hamlet.
aldrava [al-drah'vă] *f.* latch; door-knocker.
alecrim [ă-lĕ-kreen'] *m.* rose-mary.
alegação [ă-lĕ-gă-sown'] *f.* allegation; argument; proof.
alegar [ă-lĕ-gar'] *va.* to allege, maintain, adduce.
alegoria [ă-lĕ-goo-ree'ă] *f.* allegory.
alegrar [ă-lĕ-grar'] *vn.* to cheer up, rejoice, gladden; *vr.* to be glad, rejoice, be delighted.
alegre [ă-le'grĕ] *adj.* cheerful, lively, gay, merry.
alegrete [ă-lĕ-grayt'] *m.* flower-box, -pot.
alegria [ă-lĕ-gree'ă] *f.* joy, merriment, cheerfulness.
aleijar [ă-lay-ee-zhar'] *va.* to cripple; to maim, disable.

aleitamento [ă-lay-ee-tă-men'too] *m.* feeding (of baby); — materno, breast-feeding.
aleitar [ă-lay-ee-tar'] *va.* to feed, suckle (baby).
aleivosia [ă-lay-ee-voo-zee'ă] *f.* treachery, perfidy.
aleivoso [ă-lay-ee-voh'zoo] *adj.* treacherous, perfidious.
além [ah-len'] *adv.* beyond; — disso, besides; — **mar,** overseas.
alemão [ă-lĕ-mown'] *m/adj.* [German.
alentado [ă-len-tah'doo] *adj.* brave, bold; encouraged.
alentar [ă-len-tar'] *va.* to encourage, stimulate.
alerta [a-lair'tă] *adv.* on the alert; *m.* alert.
alfabeto [al-fă-be'too] *m.* alphabet.
alface [al-fas'] *f.* lettuce.
alfacinha [al-fă-seen'yă] *mf.* (*pop.*) native of Lisbon.
alfaia [al-fȳ'yă] *f.* household equipment, furnishings; implements; ornament.
alfaiate [al-fȳ-yaht'] *m.* tailor.
alfândega [al-fan'dĕ-gă] *f.* customs; custom-house.
alfarrabista [al-fă-ră-beesh'tă] *m.* second-hand bookseller.
alfarroba [al-fă-roh'bă] *f.* carob.
alfazema [al-fă-zay'mă] *f.* [lavender.
alferes [al-fair'ĕsh] *m.* second-lieutenant; ensign.
alfinete [al-fee-nayt'] *m.* pin; *pl.* pin-money.
alfombra [al-fon'bră] *f.* [carpet.
alforges [al-forzh'ĕsh] *m.pl.* saddle-bags; provisions.
alforra [al-foh'ră] *f.* mildew.
alga [al'gă] *f.* seaweed.
algaravia [al-gă-ră-vee'ă] *f.* gibberish, gabble; rigmarole.
algarismo [al-gă-reezh'moo] *m.* numeral, figure.
algazarra [al-gă-za'ră] *f.* hubbub, uproar, clamour.
algemas [al-zhay'măsh] *f.pl.* handcuffs; manacles.
algeroz [al-zhĕ-rosh'] *m.* gutter; drain-pipe.
algibeira [al-zhĕ-bay'ee-ră] *f.* pocket.
algo [al'goo] *adv.* somewhat.
algodão [al-goo-down'] *m.* cotton; — **em rama,** cotton-wool.
algoz [al-gosh'] *m.* executioner.
alguém [al-gen'] *pron.* somebody, someone; anybody, anyone.
algum [al-goon'] *adj.* some, any; — tanto, somewhat; de modo —, in no way; definitely not.
algures [al-goo'rĕsh] *adv.* somewhere.
alheio [ă-lyay'yoo] *adj.* somebody else's, another's; of others; foreign, extraneous, remote; *m.pl.* strangers.
alho [a'lyoo] *m.* garlic; — porro, leek; **ser um** —, to be clever, smart.
ali [ă-lee'] *adv.* there.
aliado [ă-lee-ah'doo] *adj.* allied; *m.* ally.
aliança [ă-lee-an'să] *f.* alliance; wedding-ring.
aliar [ă-lee-ar'] *va.* to ally, join, unite; *vr.* to make an alliance; to be joined in marriage.
aliás [ă-lee-ash'] *adv.* besides, moreover; otherwise.
alibi [a'lee-bee] *m.* alibi.
alicate [ă-lee-kat'] *m.* pliers; — de revisor, ticket-punch.
alicerce [ă-lee-sairs'] *m.* foundation, base.
aliciar [ă-lee-see-ar'] *va.* to entice, allure, seduce.
alienação [ă-lee-ĕ-nă-sown'] *f.* alienation, transfer (of title to property); — **mental,** insanity.
alienado [ă-lee-ĕ-nah'doo] *adj.* transferred (property); in-

sane; hospital de —s, lunatic asylum.
aligátor [ă-lee-gah'tor] *m.* alligator, crocodile.
aligeirar [ă-lee-zhay-ee-rar'] *va.* to lighten; to speed up, hasten; to alleviate.
alijar [ă-lee-zhar'] *va.* to jettison, throw overboard.
alimentação [ă-lee-me*n*-tă-sow*n*'] *f.* nourishment; food; nutrition; provisioning.
alimentar [ă-lee-me*n*-tar'] *va.* to feed, nourish; *vr.* — **de**, to live (feed) on.
alimento [ă-lee-me*n*'too] *m.* food, nourishment; — **de gados**, fodder; *pl.* allowance; alimony.
alindar [ă-lee*n*-dar'] *va.* to beautify, embellish.
alínea [ă-lee'nee-ă] *f.* paragraph; sub-heading.
alinhamento [ă-lee-nyă-me*n*'too] *m.* alignment; dressing (of troops on parade).
alinhar [ă-lee-nyar'] *va.* to align; to line up; to adorn.
alinhavar [ă-lee-nyă-var'] *va.* to tack (sewing).
alinho [ă-lee'nyoo] *m.* alignment; tidiness, neatness.
alisar [ă-lee-zar'] *va.* to smooth; to plane.
alistar [ă-leesh-tar'] *va/vr.* to enlist; to recruit; to enrol.
aliviar [ă-lee-vee-ar'] *va.* to lighten, alleviate, soothe.
alívio [ă-lee'vee-oo] *m.* alleviation; relief.
aljava [al-zhah'vă] *f.* quiver.
aljôfar [al-zhoh'far] *m.* seed-pearl.
aljube [al-zhoob'] *m.* prison; dungeon; lock-up.
alma [al'mă] *f.* soul; spirit; fortitude, courage; essence; character; enthusiasm; driving force; — **penada**, ghost; — **de eleição**, salt of the earth.
almanaque [al-mă-nak'] *m.* almanac.
almejar [al-mĕ-zhar'] *va.* to long for, crave.
almirantado [al-mee-ra*n*-tah'doo] *m.* Admiralty.
almirante [al-mee-ra*n*t'] *m.* Admiral.
almíscar [al-meesh'kar] *m.* musk.
almoçar [al-moo-sar'] *vn.* to have lunch.
almoço [al-moh'soo] *m.* lunch, luncheon; **primeiro (pequeno)** —, breakfast.
almocreve [al-moo-krev'] *m.* muleteer.
almofada [al-moo-fah'dă] *f.* pillow; cushion.
almofariz [al-moo-fă-reesh'] *m.* mortar, basin.
almotolia [al-moo-too-lee'ă] *f.* can (for olive-oil, etc.).
alocução [ă-loo-koo-sow*n*'] *f.* allocution, address.
alojamento [ă-loo-zhă-me*n*'-too] *m.* accommodation; lodging; billet (*mil.*).
alojar [ă-loo-zhar'] *va.* to lodge; to billet (*mil.*).
alongar [ă-lo*n*-gar'] *va.* to lengthen; to prolong; to draw out, pull out (leaf of table); to stretch out (arm, etc.).
alpendre [al-pe*n*'drĕ] *m.* porch; shed.
alpestre [al-pesh'trĕ] *adj.* Alpine.
alpinismo [al-pee-neezh'moo] *m.* mountaineering, climbing.
alpista [al-peesh'tă] *m.* bird-seed.
alquebrar [al-kĕ-brar'] *vn.* to weaken; to stoop (through weakness); to break in two (ship).
alqueire [al-kay'eer] *m.* bushel.
alqueive [al-kay'eev] *m.* fallow land.
alta [al'tă] *f.* rise (in prices, etc.); discharge (from hospital).

altaneiro [al-tă-nay'ee-roo] *adj.* haughty, arrogant.
altar [al-tar'] *m.* altar; — **mor,** high altar.
altear [al-tee-ar'] *va.* to raise.
alteração [al-tĕ-ră-sown'] *f.* alteration, change; falsification; disquiet, perturbation; debasing (of coinage).
alterar [al-tĕ-rar'] *va.* to alter, change; to falsify; to disturb; *vr.* to be disturbed; to get angry.
altercação [al-tĕr-kă-sown'] *f.* altercation, quarrel.
alternar [al-tĕr-nar'] *vn/va.* to alternate, take turns.
alternativa [al-tĕr-nă-tee'vă] *f.* alternative.
alternativo [al-tĕr-nă-tee'-voo] *adj.* alternative.
alterno [al-tair'noo] *adj.* alternate, every other.
alteza [al-tay'ză] *f.* highness; sublimity; excellence.
altissonante [al-tee-soo-nant'] *adj.* high-sounding.
altivo [al-tee'voo] *adj.* haughty, arrogant.
alto [al'too] *adj.* high, tall, lofty; loud (voice); important; upper (district, area, etc.); alta noite, dead of night; *adv.* openly, plainly; **por** —, superficially; *m.* height; summit; top; **fazer** —, to halt, stop; *interj.* halt! stop!
alto-falante [al-too-fă-lant'] *m.* loud-speaker; megaphone.
altura [al-too'ră] *f.* height; latitude; time, period, occasion; depth; **estar à — de,** to be equal to (undertaking, etc.).
alugar [ă-loo-gar'] *va.* to let, hire, rent.
alucinação [ă-loo-see-nă-sown'] *f.* hallucination.
alude [ă-lood'] *m.* avalanche.
aludir [ă-loo-deer'] *vn.* to allude, refer to.
aluir [ă-loo-eer'] *va/vn.* to shake; to ruin; to collapse, fall.
alumiar [ă-loo-mee-ar'] *va.* to light, give light to; to enlighten.
aluno [ă-loo'noo] *m.* pupil, student; —**interno,** boarder.
alusão [ă-loo-zown'] *f.* allusion, reference.
alusivo [ă-loo-zee'voo] *adj.* allusive, referring to.
alvará [al-vă-rah'] *m.* decree; licence, certificate.
alvedrio [al-vĕ-dree'oo] *m.* freewill.
alvejar [al-vĕ-zhar'] *va.* to aim [at.
alvenaria [al-vĕ-nă-ree'ă] *f.* masonry.
álveo [al'vee-oo] *m.* river bed.
alvéolo [al-ve'oo-loo] *m.* socket (of teeth); cell (of honeycomb).
alvíssaras [al-vee'să-răsh] *f.pl.* reward.
alvitrar [al-vee-trar'] *va.* to propose, suggest.
alvo [al'voo] *m.* target; *adj.* [white.
alvorada [al-voo-rah'dă] *f.* dawn; reveille (*mil.*).
alvoroçar [al-voo-roo-sar'] *va.* to agitate, stir up, excite.
alvoroço [al-voo-roh'soo] *m.* disturbance, commotion; excitement, enthusiasm.
alvura [al-voo'ră] *f.* whiteness; purity.
ama [ă'mă] *f.* nurse; governess; housekeeper.
amabilidade [ă-mă-bee-lee-dahd'] *f.* kindness, friendliness, amiability.
amachucar [ă-mă-shoo-kar'] *va.* to crush.
amaciar [ă-mă-see-ar'] *va.* to smooth, soften.
amada [ă-mah'dă] *f.* sweetheart; darling.
amador [ă-mă-dohr'] *m.* lover; amateur.
amadurecer [ă-mă-doo-rĕ-sayr'] *va/vn.* to ripen, mature.

amadurecimento [ă-mă-doo-rĕ-see-men'too] *m.* ripeness.
âmago [ă'mă-goo] *m.* core, pith, heart.
amainar [ă-mȳ-nar'] *va.* to furl (sails); *vn.* to abate (storm, etc.).
amaldiçoar [ă-mal-dee-soo-ar'] *va.* to curse, execrate; to swear at. [amalgam.
amálgama [ă-mal'gă-mă] *m.*
amalgamar [ă-mal-gă-mar'] *va.* to amalgamate.
amamentar [ă-mă-men-tar'] *va.* to suckle, nurse.
amaneirado [ă-mă-nay-ee-rah'doo] *adj.* affected.
amanhã [ah-mă-nyan'] *adv.* tomorrow; — de manhã, tomorrow morning.
amanhar [ă-mă-nyar'] *va.* to cultivate, till; to prepare.
amanhecer [ă-mă-nyĕ-sayr'] *vn.* to dawn; *m.* dawn, daybreak.
amanho [ă-mă'nyoo] *m.* cultivation, tillage; preparation; *pl.* tools, implements.
amansar [ă-man-sar'] *va.* to tame; to pacify.
amante [ă-mant'] *mf.* lover.
amanuense [ă-mă-noo-ens'] *m.* clerk.
amar [ă-mar'] *va.* to love.
amarelo [ă-mă-re'loo] *adj.* yellow.
amargar [ă-măr-gar'] *va.* to embitter, make bitter.
amargo [ă-mar'goo] *adj.* bitter; *m.* bitterness.
amargura [ă-măr-goo'ră] *f.* affliction, grief; bitterness.
amarrar [ă-mă-rar'] *va.* to tie up (ship); to make fast, lash.
amarrotar [ă-mă-roo-tar'] *va.* to crumple (up).
amassar [ă-mă-sar'] *va.* to knead; to mix.
amável [ă-mah'vel] *adj.* kind; pleasant, likeable.
amazona [ă-mă-zoh'nă] *f.* amazon; horsewoman; riding-habit.
ambages [an-bah'zhĕsh] *m.pl.* circumlocution, roundabout phrases; sem —, plainly.
âmbar [an'bar] *m.* amber.
ambição [an-bee-sown'] *f.* ambition; aspiration.
ambicionar [an-bee-see-oo-nar'] *va.* to covet, desire eagerly.
ambicioso [an-bee-see-oh'-zoo] *adj.* ambitious, aspiring.
ambiente [an-bee-ent'] *m.* atmosphere; surroundings.
ambiguidade [an-bee-gwee-dahd'] *f.* ambiguity; double meaning.
ambíguo [an-bee'gwoo] *adj.* ambiguous, doubtful.
âmbito [an'bee-too] *m.* scope, sphere of action; ambit.
ambos [an'boosh] *adj.pl.* both.
ambulância [an-boo-lan'see-ă] *f.* ambulance; field hospital.
ambulante [an-boo-lant'] *adj.* roving, itinerant.
ameaça [ă-mee-ah'să] *f.* threat, menace.
ameaçar [ă-mee-ă-sar'] *va.* to threaten.
amedrontar [ă-mĕ-dron-tar'] *va.* to frighten, intimidate.
amêijoa [ă-may'ee-zhoo-ă] *f.* cockle. [plum.
ameixa [ă-may'ee-shă] *f.*
amêndoa [ă-men'doo-ă] *f.* almond; *pl.* Easter gifts (of sweets).
amendoim [ă-men-doo-een'] *m.* peanut, monkey-nut.
amenidade [ă-mĕ-nee-dahd'] *f.* amenity, pleasantness.
amenizar [ă-mĕ-nee-zar'] *va.* to make pleasant, agreeable.
ameno [ă-may'noo] *adj.* pleasant, agreeable.
americano [ă-mĕ-ree-kă'noo] *m/adj.* American.

amesquinhar [ă-mĕsh-kee-nyar'] *va.* to disparage; to belittle.
amestrar [ă-mesh-trar'] *va.* to train, teach.
amianto [ă-mee-a*n*'too] *m.* asbestos.
amido [ă-mee'doo] *m.* starch.
amigável [ă-mee-gah'vel] *adj.* friendly; amicable.
amígdala [ă-meeg'dă-lă] *f.* tonsil.
amigo [ă-mee'goo] *m.* friend; *adj.* fond of; friendly.
amimado [ă-mee-mah'doo] *adj.* spoiled (child); caressed, petted.
amimar [ă-mee-mar'] *va.* to caress; to pamper.
amistoso [ă-meesh-toh'zoo] *adj.* friendly, cordial.
amiudar [ă-mee-oo-dar'] *va.* to do often, repeat frequently.
amiúde [ă-mee-ood'] *adv.* frequently, often.
amizade [ă-mee-zahd'] *f.* friendship, amity; love.
amnistia [ăm-nish-tee'ă] *f.* amnesty.
amo [ă'moo] *m.* master.
amodorrado [ă-moo-doo-rah'doo] *adj.* sleepy, drowsy.
amoedar [ă-moo-e-dar'] *va.* to mint, coin.
amofinar [ă-moo-fee-nar'] *m.* to harass, torment, vex.
amolar [ă-moo-lar'] *va.* to sharpen, grind; to annoy.
amoldar [ă-mol-dar'] *va.* to mould, fashion; *vr.* to adapt oneself to.
amolecer [ă-moo-lĕ-sayr'] *va.* to soften; to melt.
amolgar [ă-mol-gar'] *va.* to squash, crush; to bend; to dent.
amontoar [ă-mo*n*-too-ar'] *va.* to pile (heap) up.
amor [ă-mohr'] *m.* love; affection, fondness; **— próprio**, conceit; **por — de**, for the sake of; **— perfeito**, pansy.
amora [ă-mo'ră] *f.* mulberry; **— silvestre**, blackberry.
amordaçar [ă-moor-dă-sar'] *va.* to muzzle, gag.
amoroso [ă-moo-roh'zoo] *adj.* loving; affectionate.
amortalhar [ă-moor-tă-lyar'] *va.* to shroud, lay out (corpse).
amortecer [ă-moor-tĕ-sayr'] *va.* to deaden; to break (fall, etc.); to absorb (shock, etc.); to moderate, weaken.
amortecido [ă-moor-tĕ-see'-doo] *adj.* faint, weak.
amortização [ă-moor-tee-ză-sow*n*'] *f.* amortisation; redemption, repayment; **caixa da —**, sinking-fund.
amostra [ă-mosh'tră] *f.* sample, specimen.
amotinar [ă-moo-tee-nar'] *vn.* to mutiny; *va.* to incite to mutiny.
amparar [a*n*-pă-rar'] *va.* to support; to protect, shelter.
amparo [a*n*-pah'roo] *m.* support; protection, shelter.
ampliação [a*n*-plee-ă-sow*n*'] *f.* enlargement, amplification, magnification.
ampliar [a*n*-plee-ar'] *va.* to enlarge, extend, amplify.
amplificação [a*n*-pli-fee-kă-sow*n*] *f.* enlargement, amplification.
amplificar [a*n*-pli-fee-kar'] *va.* to enlarge, amplify.
amplitude [a*n*-plee-tood'] *f.* extent, width, spaciousness.
amplo [a*n*'ploo] *adj.* ample, spacious, wide-ranging; rich.
ampola [a*n*-poh'lă] *f.* blister.
ampulheta [a*n*-poo-lye'tă] *f.* hour-glass.
amputar [a*n*-poo-tar'] *va.* to [amputate.
amuar [ă-moo-ar'] *vn.* to sulk.
amuleto [ă-moo-lay'too] *m.* amulet, talisman.

amuo [ă-moo'oo] *m.* sulking, sulkiness.
anacronismo [ă-nă-kroo-neezh'moo] *m.* anachronism.
anafar [ă-nă-far'] *va.* to fatten.
anais [ă-nÿsh'] *m.pl.* annals.
analfabetismo [ă-nal-fă-bĕ-teezh'moo] *m.* illiteracy.
analfabeto [ă-nal-fă-be'too] *m.* illiterate.
analisar [ă-nă-lee-zar'] *va.* to analyse; to parse (sentence).
análise [ă-nah'leez] *f.* analysis; parsing (of sentence).
analítico [ă-nă-lee'tee-koo] *adj.* analytic(al).
analogia [ă-nă-loo-zhee'ă] *f.* analogy.
análogo [ă-nah'loo-goo] *adj.* analogous; similar.
ananás [ă-nă-nash'] *m.* pineapple.
anão [ă-nown'] *m.* dwarf.
anarquia [ă-năr-kee'ă] *f.* anarchy, lawlessness.
anátema [ă-nah'tĕ-mă] *m.* anathema, excommunication; denunciation, condemnation.
anatomia [ă-nă-too-mee'ă] *f.* anatomy.
anca [an'kă] *f.* haunch; croup; *pl.* hips.
ancho [an'shoo] *adj.* broad, wide; conceited.
anchova [an-shoh'vă] *f.* anchovy.
ancião [an-see-own'] *m.* venerable old man.
ancinho [an-see'nyoo] *m.* rake.
âncora [an'koo-ră] *f.* anchor.
ancoradouro [an-koo-ră-doh'roo] *m.* anchorage.
ancorar [an-koo-rar'] *va/vn.* to anchor.
andadura [an-dă-doo'ră] *f.* gait.
andaime [an-dÿm'] *m.* scaffolding.
andamento [an-dă-men'too] *m.* walking, running, movement; pace; course; progress; tempo, measure (*mus.*).
andar [an-dar'] *vn.* to go, walk, move; to be; — **de gatas**, to go on all fours; — **bem**, to do well; *m.* floor, storey; level (in mine); gait, walk; — **térreo**, ground floor (*Braz.*).
andas [an'dăsh] *f.pl.* stilts.
andor [an-dohr'] *m.* litter.
andorinha [an-doo-ree'nyă] *f.* swallow.
andrajos [an-drah'zhoosh] *m.* rags.
anedota [ă-ne-do'tă] *f.* anecdote, tale.
anel [ă-nel'] *m.* ring; ringlet, curl (of hair); link (in chain).
anelante [ă-nĕ-lant'] *adj.* breathless, panting.
anelar [ă-nĕ-lar'] *va.* to long for, desire; *vn.* to pant.
anelo [ă-ne'loo] *m.* desire, longing.
anexação [ă-nek-să-sown'] *f.* annexation.
anexar [ă-nek-sar'] *va.* to annex; to join.
anexo [ă-nek'soo] *adj.* annexed; joined, linked; *m.* annex.
anfíbio [an-fee'bee-oo] *adj.* amphibious.
anfiteatro [an-fee-tee-ah'troo] *m.* amphitheatre; circle, balcony (theatre).
anfitrião [an-fee-tree-own'] *m.* host.
angariar [an-gă-ree-ar'] *va.* to attract, entice; to angle for; to obtain.
angina [an-zhee'nă] *f.* quinsy, pharyngitis; — **de peito**, heart trouble *or* attack, angina pectoris.
angolano [an-goo-lă'noo] *or* **angolense** *m/adj.* native of, pertaining to, Angola.
angra [an'gră] *f.* creek, inlet, bay.
angular [an-goo-lar'] *adj.* angular; **pedra** —, corner-stone.
ângulo [an'goo-loo] *m.* angle; corner.
angústia [an-goosh'tee-ă] *f.* anguish, anxiety, affliction.

anho [ă'nyoo] *m.* lamb.
anil [ă-neel'] *m.* indigo.
anilha [ă-nee'lyă] *f.* ring; washer (for tap).
animação [ă-nee-mă-sow*n*'] *f.* animation, bustle, liveliness.
animado [ă-nee-mah'doo] *adj.* animated, lively, vivacious.
animadversão [ă-nee-mad-vĕr-sow*n*'] *f.* criticism, censure; hatred, dislike.
animal [ă-nee-mal'] *m.* animal: (*fig.*) blockhead; brute.
animar [ă-nee-mar'] *va.* to encourage, incite, animate; *vr.* to gain confidence; to resolve.
ânimo [ă'nee-moo] *m.* spirit, courage, resolution; intention.
animosidade [ă-nee-moo-zee-dahd'] *f.* animosity.
animoso [ă-nee-moh'zoo] *adj.* courageous, spirited.
aninhar [ă-nee-nyar'] *vn.* to nestle; to snuggle up, down.
aniquilação [ă-nee-kee-lă-sow*n*'] *f.* annihilation.
aniquilar [ă-nee-kee-lar'] *va.* to annihilate, destroy.
anis [ă-neesh'] *m.* aniseed.
aniversário [ă-nee-vĕr-sah'-ree-oo] *m.* anniversary; birthday.
anjo [a*n*'zhoo] *m.* angel.
ano [ă'noo] *m.* year; — **bissexto**, leap-year; — **económico**, financial year; — **lectivo**, academic year; **dia de — bom**, New Year's Day; **dia de —s**, birthday; **fazer —s**, to have a birthday; **um — por outro**, once every few years.
anódino [ă-no'dee-noo] *m.* anodyne; *adj.* insignificant.
anoitecer [ă-noh-ee-tĕ-sayr'] *vn.* to grow dark; **ao —**, at nightfall.
anomalia [ă-noo-mă-lee'ă] *f.* anomaly, irregularity.
anómalo [ă-no'mă-loo] *adj.* anomalous, irregular.
anónimo [ă-no'nee-moo] *adj.* anonymous; **sociedade —a**, joint stock company.
anormal [ă-nor-mal'] *adj.* abnormal.
anoso [ă-noh'zoo] *adj.* old.
anotação [ă-noo-tă-sow*n*'] *f.* note; annotation.
anotar [ă-noo-tar'] *va.* to note down; to annotate; to make notes on.
ânsia [a*n*'see-ă] *f.* anxiety; ardent desire, longing.
ansiar [a*n*-see-ar'] *va.* to desire ardently; to yearn for.
ansiedade [a*n*-see-ĕ-dahd'] *f.* anxiety; desire.
ansioso [a*n*-see-oh'zoo] *adj.* anxious; desirous.
antagónico [a*n*-tă-go'nee-koo] *adj.* antagonistic.
antagonismo [a*n*-tă-goo-neezh'moo] *m.* antagonism.
antagonista [a*n*-tă-goo-neesh'tă] *m.* antagonist.
ante [ant] *prep.* before.
antebraço [a*n*-tĕ-brah'soo] *m.* forearm.
antecâmara [a*n*-tĕ-kă'mă-ră] *f.* antechamber.
antecedência [a*n*-tĕ-sĕ-de*n*'-see-ă] *f.* priority; antecedence.
antecedente [a*n*-tĕ-sĕ-de*n*t'] *m*/*adj.* antecedent; *adj.* previous, preceding.
anteceder [a*n*-tĕ-sĕ-dayr'] *va.* to precede, go before.
antecessor [a*n*-tĕ-sĕ-sohr'] *m.* predecessor; *pl.* ancestors.
antecipação [a*n*-tĕ-see-pă-sow*n*'] *f.* anticipation.
antecipado [a*n*-tĕ-see-pah'-doo] *adj.* in advance.
antecipar [a*n*-tĕ-see-par'] *va.* to anticipate; to forestall; to bring forward.
antemão [a*n*-tĕ-mow*n*'] *adv.* **de —**, beforehand.
antena [a*n*-tay'nă] *f.* antenna, feeler (of insects); spar,

yard (*naut.*); wireless aerial.
antenome [*an*-tĕ-nohm'] *m.* Christian (first) name; title (before name).
anteontem [*an*-tee-*on*'ten] *adv.* the day before yesterday.
antepara [*an*-tĕ-pah'ră] *f.* bulkhead (*naut.*).
anteparar [*an*-tĕ-pă-rar'] *va.* to defend, protect; to stop, check.
anteparo [*an*-tĕ-pah'roo] *m.* screen; rampart.
antepassados [*an*-tĕ-pă-sah'-doosh] *m.pl.* ancestors.
antepor [*an*-tĕ-pohr'] *va.* to put before; to prefer.
anterior [*an*-tĕ-ree-ohr'] *adj.* preceding, former, previous; front (part of house, etc.).
anterioridade [*an*-tĕ-ree-oh-ree-dahd'] *f.* priority, precedence.
anteriormente [*an*-tĕ-ree-ohr-ment'] *adv.* previously.
antes [*an*tsh] *adv.* before; rather; quanto —, as soon as possible.
antessala [*an*-tĕ-sa'lă] *f.* anteroom, ante-chamber.
antiaéreo [*an*-tee-ă-air'ee-oo] *adj.* anti-aircraft.
antídoto [*an*-tee'doo-too] *m.* antidote.
antigamente [*an*-tee-gă-me*n*t'] *adv.* formerly, in the past.
antigo [*an*-tee'goo] *adj.* ancient, old; former.
antigualha [*an*-tee-gwa'lyă] *or* **antigalha**, *f.* antique; junk.
antiguidade [*an*-tee-gwee-dahd'] *f.* antiquity; ancient times; seniority (in employment); *pl.* ancient monuments; antiques.
antílope [*an*-tee'loop] *m.* antelope.
antipatia [*an*-tee-pă-tee'ă] *f.* antipathy, aversion, dislike.
antipático [*an*-tee-pah'tee-koo] *adj.* uncongenial, disagreeable, unpleasant.
antiquado [*an*-tee-kwah'doo] *adj.* antiquated, out of date.
antiquário [*an*-tee-kwah'ree-oo] *m.* antiquarian.
antiquíssimo [*an*-tee-kwee'-see-moo] *adj.* very old, ancient.
antítese [*an*-tee'tĕz] *f.* antithesis.
antojo [*an*-toh'zhoo] *m.* fancy; craving.
antolhos [*an*-to'lyoosh] *m.pl.* eye-shade; blinkers (for horse); fancies, whims.
antologia [*an*-too-loo-zhee'ă] *f.* anthology.
antro [*an*'troo] *m.* cavern.
antropófago [*an*-troo-po'fă-goo] *m.* cannibal.
anual [ă-noo-al'] *adj.* annual, yearly.
anuário [ă-noo-ah'ree-oo] *m.* year-book; annual.
anuidade [ă-noo-ee-dahd'] *f.* annuity, annual payment.
anuir [ă-noo-eer'] *vn.* to assent to.
anulação [ă-noo-lă-sow*n*'] *f.* annulment, cancellation.
anular [ă-noo-lar'] *va.* to annul, rescind.
anunciação [ă-noo*n*-see-ă-sow*n*'] *f.* annunciation.
anunciar [ă-noo*n*-see-ar'] *va.* to announce; advertise.
anúncio [ă-noo*n*'see-oo] *m.* advertisement, notice; announcement.
anuviar [ă-noo-vee-ar'] *va.* to cloud, darken; *vr.* to cloud over; to grow dark.
anverso [*an*-vair'soo] *m.* obverse (side).
anzol [*an*-zol'] *m.* fish-hook; cair no —, to swallow the bait, be tricked.
apadrinhar [ă-pă-dree'nyar] *va.* to act as godfather to; to protect, support, sponsor.

apagado [ă-pă-gah'doo] *adj.* put out, extinguished; dim, dark; faint (letters, etc.).
apagar [ă-pă-gar'] *va.* to put out, extinguish, quench; to switch off (light, etc.).
apaixonado [ă-pȳ-shoo-nah'-doo] *adj.* passionate.
apaixonar [ă-pȳ-shoo-nar'] *va.* to inspire passion; *vr.* to fall passionately in love with; to become impassioned, angry; to become passionately fond of.
apalpar [ă-pal-par'] *va.* to touch, feel; to grope.
apanhar [ă-pă-nyar'] *va.* to catch, grasp, seize; to reap; to gather.
apaniguado [ă-pă-nee-gwah'-doo] *m.* adherent, follower.
apara [ă-pah'ră] *f.* shaving, clipping.
aparador [ă-pă-ră-dohr'] *m.* sideboard; buffet.
aparar [ă-pă-rar'] *va.* to trim, clip, cut (hair, nails, etc.); to prune (fruit-trees); to sharpen (pencil, etc.); to parry (blow); to smooth out. down.
aparato [ă-pă-rah'too] *m.* pomp, pageantry, show.
aparecer [ă-pă-rĕ-sayr'] *vn.* to appear; to turn up.
aparecimento [ă-pă-rĕ-see-me*n*'too] *m.* appearance.
aparelhado [ă-pă-rĕ-lyah'-doo] *adj.* ready, prepared; suited; adorned.
aparelhar [ă-pă-rĕ-lyar'] *va.* to prepare, get ready; to saddle, harness (horse); to rig (ship).
aparelho [ă-pă-ray'lyoo] *m.* preparation; apparatus; equipment; gear, tackle (*naut.*); household effects, utensils; harness; *pl.* tools, instruments.
aparência [ă-pă-re*n*'see-ă] *f.* appearance, aspect.
aparentado [ă-pă-re*n*-tah'-doo] *adj.* related; **bem —**, well connected.
aparentar [ă-pă-re*n*-tar'] *va.* to feign, affect; *vr.* to marry into, become linked with (by marriage).
aparente [ă-pă-re*n*t'] *adj.* apparent, pretended, feigned.
aparição [ă-pă-ree-sow*n*'] *f.* appearance; apparition, ghost.
aparo [ă-pah'roo] *m.* (pen-) nib.
apartado [ă-păr-tah'doo] *adj.* secluded, solitary, separated.
apartamento [ă-păr-tă-me*n*'-too] *m.* separation; seclusion, solitude, isolation; apartment.
apartar [ă-păr-tar'] *va.* to separate, set aside.
aparte [ah-part'] *m.* aside (*theat.*).
apascentar [ă-păsh-se*n*-tar'] *va.* to graze; to feast (one's eyes on, etc.).
apatia [ă-pă-tee'ă] *f.* apathy.
apático [ă-pah'tee-koo] *adj.* apathetic, indifferent.
apavorar [ă-pă-voo-rar'] *va.* to terrify.
apaziguamento [ă-pă-zee-gwă-me*n*'too] *m.* pacification; appeasement.
apaziguar [ă-pă-zee-gwar'] *va.* to pacify, appease; *vr.* to quieten down.
apeadeiro [ă-pee-ă-day'ee-roo] *m.* (railway) halt.
apear [ă-pee-ar'] *va.* to set down; (*fig.*) to dismiss; *vr.* to get off, alight, dismount.
apedrejar [ă-pĕ-drĕ-zhar'] *va.* to stone, pelt with stones.
apegar-se [ă-pĕ-gar'sĕ] *vr.* to adhere, be devoted, cling to.
apego [ă-pay'goo] *m.* attachment; fondness.
apelação [ă-pĕ-lă-sow*n*'] *f.* appeal.
apelante [ă-pĕ-la*n*t'] *mf.* appellant.
apelar [ă-pĕ-lar'] *va.* to appeal.

apelidar [ă-pĕ-lee-dar'] *va.* to name; to summon (*archaic*).
apelido [ă-pĕ-lee'doo] *m.* surname.
apelo [ă-pay'loo] *m.* appeal.
apenas [ă-pay'năsh] *adv.* only; hardly; *conj.* as soon as.
apêndice [ă-pe*n*'dees] *m.* appendix, supplement.
aperceber [ă-pĕr-sĕ-bayr'] *va.* to perceive; to prepare.
apercebimento [ă-pĕr-sĕ-bee-me*n*'too] *m.* perception; preparation; equipment.
aperfeiçoamento [ă-pĕr-fay-ee-soo-ă-me*n*'too] *m.* perfecting; improvement.
aperfeiçoar [ă-pĕr-fay-ee-soo-ar'] *va.* to perfect; to improve.
aperitivo [ă-pĕ-ree-tee'voo] *m.* aperitif, appetizer.
apertado [ă-pĕr-tah'doo] *adj.* tight; narrow; closely packed.
apertão [ă-pĕr-tow*n*'] *m.* (tight) squeeze.
apertar [ă-pĕr-tar'] *va.* to pack together; to grip; to tighten; to squeeze; to press; to cramp; — **a mão,** to shake hands; — **o passo,** to quicken one's step; *vn.* to narrow; to grow more intense; to press.
aperto [ă-payr'too] *m.* pressure; oppression; tightening, squeezing together; restriction; peril; hardship; harshness; urgency.
apesar [ă-pĕ-zar'] *prep.* — **de,** in spite of, despite.
apetecer [ă-pĕ-tĕ-sayr'] *va.* to desire; to covet; to have a taste for.
apetecível [ă-pĕ-tĕ-see'vel] *adj.* tempting, desirable.
apetite [ă-pĕ-teet'] *m.* appetite; desire.
apetitoso [ă-pĕ-tee-toh'zoo] *adj.* appetizing; tempting.
apetrechar [ă-pĕ-trĕ-shar'] *va.* to fit out, equip.
ápice [ah'pees] *m.* summit; apex.
apiedar-se [ă-pee-ĕ-dar'sĕ] *vr.* to pity, have mercy on.
apinhar [ă-pee'nyar] *va.* to press together; *vr.* to crowd together, swarm.
apitar [ă-pee-tar'] *vn.* to whistle.
apito [ă-pee'too] *m.* whistle; hooter (of ship, factory).
aplacar [ă-plă-kar'] *va.* to placate, appease.
aplainar [ă-plȳ-nar'] *va.* to plane; to level (off).
aplanar [ă-plă-nar'] *va.* to smooth, level; to remove (difficulties).
aplaudir [ă-plow-deer'] *va.* to applaud, clap; to approve of.
aplauso [ă-plow'zoo] *m.* applause; praise.
aplicação [ă-plee-kă-sow*n*'] *f.* diligence; application; use.
aplicar [ă-plee-kar'] *va.* to apply; *vr.* to devote oneself to.
aplicado [ă-plee-kah'doo] *adj.* hard-working, industrious.
apocalipse [ă-poo-kă-leeps'] *m.* Apocalypse; (Book of) Revelation.
apodar [ă-poo-dar'] *va.* to taunt, mock; to call (somebody) names.
apoderar-se [ă-poo-dĕ-rar'sĕ] *vr.* to seize, gain possession of.
apodo [ă-poh'doo] *m.* nickname; taunt.
apodrecer [ă-poo-drĕ-sayr'] *va.* to rot, corrupt; *vn.* to rot.
apodrecimento [ă-poo-drĕ-see-me*n*'too] *m.* rottenness, decay, putrefaction.
apogeu [ă-poo-zhay'oo] *m.* summit, height (of success, etc.).
apoiado [ă-poo-yah'doo] *adj.* supported, approved; leaning on; *interj.* hear! hear!; *m.* applause, approval.

apoiar [ă-poo-yar'] *va.* to support, back up; to base; *vr.* to rest on, lean on.
apoio [ă-poh'yoo] *m.* support.
apólice [ă-po'lees] *f.* policy (insurance); certificate; bond.
apologia [ă-poo-loo-zhee'ă] *f.* defence (in speech, writing); eulogy.
apólogo [ă-po'loo-goo] *m.* fable, apologue.
apontador [ă-po*n*-tă-dohr'] *m.* prompter (*theat.*); overseer; (attendance) register.
apontamento [ă-po*n*-tă-me*n*'too] *m.* note; minute; draft.
apontar [ă-po*n*-tar'] *va.* to aim; to point out; to note down; to prompt (*theat.*); *vn.* to begin to appear; to sprout.
apoplexia [ă-poo-ple-see'ă] *f.* stroke, apoplexy.
apoquentar [ă-poo-ke*n*-tar'] *va/vr.* to worry.
aportar [ă-poor-tar'] *vn.* to arrive (ship).
após [ă-posh'] *prep.* after; *adv.* afterwards, after.
aposentado [ă-poo-ze*n*-tah'-doo] *adj.* retired.
aposentar [ă-poo-ze*n*-tar'] *va/vr.* to retire; to lodge.
aposento [ă-poo-ze*n*'too] *m.* room; lodging; apartment.
apossar-se [ă-poo-sar'sě] *vr.* to take possession of.
aposta [ă-posh'tă] *f.* bet.
apostar [ă-poosh-tar'] *va.* to bet; *vr.* to pledge oneself.
apostila [ă-poosh-tee'lă] *f.* marginal note.
apóstolo [ă-posh'too-loo] *m.* apostle.
apóstrofo [ă-posh'troo-foo] *m.* apostrophe.
apotegma [ă-poo-teg'mă] *m.* maxim.
apoucado [ă-poh-kah'doo] *adj.* mean; base.
apoucar [ă-poh-kar'] *va.* to humiliate; to belittle.
aprazar [ă-pră-zar'] *va.* to arrange, appoint, fix (time, place, for meeting); to postpone.
aprazer [ă-pră-zayr'] *vn.* to please.
apreçar [ă-prě-sar'] *va.* to value, price.
apreciação [ă-prě-see-ă-sow*n*'] *f.* appreciation; estimation.
apreciar [ă-prě-see-ar'] *va.* to appreciate, value, esteem.
apreciável [ă-prě-see-ah'vel] *adj.* appreciable; estimable.
apreço [ă-pray'soo] *m.* esteem; consideration; appreciation.
apreender [ă-pree-e*n*-dayr'] *vn.* to apprehend; to seize.
apreensão [ă-pree-e*n*-sow*n*'] *f.* seizure; apprehension; misgiving.
apreensivo [ă-pree-e*n*-see'-voo] *adj.* apprehensive, uneasy.
apregoar [ă-prě-goo-ar'] *va.* to proclaim.
aprender [ă-pre*n*-dayr'] *va.* to learn.
aprendiz [ă-pre*n*-deesh'] *m.* apprentice; beginner; novice.
aprendizagem [ă-pre*n*-dee-zah'zhe*n*] *f.* apprenticeship.
apresentação [ă-prě-ze*n*-tă-sow*n*'] *f.* introduction; presentation; bearing, appearance.
apresentar [ă-prě-ze*n*-tar'] *va.* to introduce, present; to produce, exhibit, show.
apressado [ă-prě-sah'doo] *adj.* hurried, hasty; in a hurry.
apressar [ă-prě-sar'] *va.* to hasten, hurry.
apressurar [a-prě-soo-rar'] *va.* to hurry, hasten.
aprestar [ă-prěsh-tar'] *va.* to equip, fit out, get ready.
aprestos [ă-presh'toosh] *m.pl.* equipment, gear; preparations.
aprisco [ă-preesh'koo] *m.* sheepfold.

aprisionar [ă-pree-zee-oo-nar'] *va.* to capture, imprison.
aprontar [ă-pro*n*-tar'] *va.* to get ready, prepare.
apropriação [ă-proo-pree-ă-sow*n*'] *f.* appropriation.
apropriado [ă-proo-pree-ah'-doo] *adj.* appropriate, suitable.
apropriar [ă-proo-pree-ar'] *va.* to appropriate; to adapt.
aprovação [ă-proo-vă-sow*n*'] *f.* approval; approbation.
aprovar [ă-proo-var'] *va.* to approve; to pass (an examination).
aproveitado [ă-proo-vay-ee-tah'doo] *adj.* thrifty; industrious; well cultivated (land).
aproveitamento [ă-proo-vay-ee-tă-me*n*'too] *m.* profit; advantage.
aproveitar [ă-proo-vay-ee-tar'] *va.* to profit by, take advantage of; to utilize; *vr.* to make good use of, to avail oneself of.
aprovisionar [ă-proo-vee-zee-oo-nar'] *va.* to supply.
aproximação [ă-pro-see-mă-sow*n*'] *f.* approximation; approach.
aproximado [ă-pro-see-mah'-doo] *adj.* approximate.
aproximar [ă-pro-see-mar'] *va/vr.* to approach, draw near; to bring near, together, close; to resemble.
aprumo [ă-proo'moo] *m.* vertical position; assurance.
aptidão [ap-tee-dow*n*'] *f.* aptitude, ability, capacity, fitness; **exame de —,** entrance examination; **— física,** physical fitness.
apto [ap'too] *adj.* apt, fit; suitable; capable, competent.
apunhalar [ă-poo-nyă-lar'] *va.* to stab.
apupar [ă-poo-par'] *va.* to hoot, boo, jeer.
apurado [ă-poo-rah'doo] *adj.* refined, polished, fine, select.
apurar [ă-poo-rar'] *va.* to purify, refine; to perfect; to verify.
apuro [ă-poo'roo] *m.* refinement, elegance; perfecting; want, difficulty, hardship.
aquário [ă-kwah'ree-oo] *m.* aquarium.
aquartelar [ă-kwăr-tĕ-lar'] *va.* to billet.
aquecedor [ă-ke-sĕ-dohr'] *m.* [heater.
aquecer [ă-ke-sayr'] *va.* to heat, warm; to stir up; to irritate; *vr.* to grow warm, hot.
aquecimento [ă-ke-see-me*n*'-too] *m.* heating.
aqueduto [ă-kĕ-doo'too] *m.* aqueduct.
aquém [ah-ke*n*'] *adv.* on this side; **estar — de,** not to come up to.
aquentar [ă-ke*n*-tar'] *va.* to warm, heat; to stir up.
aqui [ă-kee'] *adv.* here; **eis —,** here is, here you have.
aquietar [ă-kee-e-tar'] *va.* to quieten, pacify.
aquinhoar [ă-kee-nyoo-ar'] *va.* to divide up.
aquisição [ă-kee-zee-sow*n*'] *f.* acquisition.
ar [ar] *m.* air; appearance, aspect; **ao — livre,** in the open air.
árabe [ah'răb] *m/adj.* Arab.
arado [ă-rah'doo] *m.* plough.
aragem [ă-rah'zhe*n*] *f.* breeze; **apanhar uma —,** to get a breath of air.
arame [ă-rahm'] *m.* wire; **— farpado,** barbed wire.
aranha [ă-ră'nyă] *f.* spider.
arauto [ă-row'too] *m.* herald.
arbitragem [ăr-bee-trah'-zhe*n*] *f.* arbitration; decision.
arbitrar [ăr-bee-trar'] *va.* to arbitrate; to award, decide.
arbitrariedade [ăr-bee-trah-

ree-ĕ-dahd'] *f.* arbitrariness, capriciousness.
arbitrário [ăr-bee-trah'ree-oo] *adj.* arbitrary.
arbitrio [ăr-bee'tree-oo] *m.* decision, will; ao — **de**, at the disposal of; — **livre**, free-will.
árbitro [ar'bee-troo] *m.* arbitrator, arbiter; referee (sport).
arbusto [ăr-boosh'too] *m.* shrub; bush. [ark.
arca [ar'kă] *f.* chest, coffer;
arcada [ăr-kah'dă] *f.* arcade; dar —**s**, to pant, heave.
arcaico [ăr-kah'ee-koo] *adj.* archaic, antiquated.
arcar [ăr-kar'] *va.* to arch; to bend, bow; — **com**, to shoulder (responsibilities).
arcebispo [ăr-sĕ-beesh'poo] *m.* archbishop.
arco [ar'koo] *m.* arch; bow; — **íris**, rainbow.
ardente [ăr-de*n*t'] *adj.* burning, ardent, fervent.
arder [ăr-dayr'] *vn.* to burn, blaze.
ardido [ăr-dee'doo] *adj.* bold, courageous; burned.
ardil [ăr-deel'] *m.* trick, stratagem.
ardor [ăr-dohr'] *m.* ardour, fervour, zeal; heat.
ardósia [ăr-do'zee-ă] *f.* slate.
árduo [ar'doo-oo] *adj.* arduous, hard.
área [ah'ree-ă] *f.* area.
areal [ă-ree-al'] *m.* sandy beach; sand-bank; sand-pit.
areia [ă-ray'yă] *f.* sand; — **movediça**, quicksand.
arejar [ă-rĕ-zhar'] *va.* to air; *vr.* to get some fresh air.
arena [ă-ray'nă] *f.* arena, ring.
arenga [ă-re*n*'gă] *f.* harangue.
arenoso [ă-rĕ-noh'zoo] *adj.* sandy.
arenque [ă-re*n*k'] *m.* herring.
aresta [ă-resh'tă] *f.* ridge; edge; beard (of corn).
arfar [ăr-far'] *vn.* to pant, gasp for breath; to roll, pitch (ship). [mortar.
argamassa [ăr-gă-ma'să] *f.*
argelino [ăr-zhĕ-lee'noo] *m/adj.* Algerian.
argentino [ăr-zhe*n*-tee'noo] *m.* Argentinian; *adj.* Argentine; silvery, silver.
argila [ăr-zhee'lă] *f.* clay.
argola [ăr-go'lă] *f.* ring; — **da porta**, door-knocker.
argúcia [ăr-goo'see-ă] *f.* subtlety, astuteness.
argueiro [ăr-gay'ee-roo] *m.* trifle; speck of dust, grit.
arguente [ăr-gwe*n*t'] *mf.* accuser. [accused.
arguido [ăr-gwee'doo] *m.*
arguir [ăr-gweer'] *va.* to accuse; *vn.* to argue, plead.
argumentação [ăr-goo-me*n*-tă-sow*n*'] *f.* argument.
argumentar [ăr-goo-me*n*-tar'] *vn.* to argue.
argumento [ăr-goo-me*n*'too] *m.* argument; theme (of play, book, etc.).
arguto [ăr-goo'too] *adj.* acute; sharp, shrill.
ária [ah'ree-ă] *f.* aria; tune.
aridez [ă-ree-daysh'] *f.* aridity.
árido [ah'ree-doo] *adj.* arid.
aríete [ă-ree'ĕt] *m.* battering-ram.
aristocrata [ă-reesh-too-krah'tă] *mf.* aristocrat.
aritmética [ă-reet-me'tee-kă] *f.* arithmetic.
arlequim [ăr-lĕ-kee*n*'] *m.* harlequin, buffoon.
arma [ar'mă] *f.* arm, weapon; — **branca**, cold steel; *pl.* coat of arms; military career; **passar pelas** —, to shoot, execute.
armação [ăr-mă-sow*n*'] *f.* preparation, fitting out; ornamentation; gear, tackle; equipment; framework, structure.

armada [ăr-mah'dă] *f.* fleet, navy. [trap, snare.
armadilha [ăr-mă-dee'lyă] *f.*
armador [ăr-mă-dohr'] *m.* shipowner; ship's outfitter; undertaker; decorator.
armadura [ăr-mă-doo'ră] *f.* armour.
armamento [ăr-mă-men'too] *m.* armament.
armar [ăr-mar'] *va.* to arm; to set (up), prepare; to decorate; to fit out (ship); — **cavaleiro**, to knight; *vr.* to arm oneself, provide oneself with.
armário [ăr-mah'ree-oo] *m.* cupboard; cabinet, chest.
armazém [ăr-ma-zen'] *m.* store, shop; warehouse, storehouse; magazine.
armazenar [ăr-mă-zĕ-nar'] *va.* to store; to hoard.
armistício [ăr-meesh-tee'see-oo] *m.* armistice, truce.
aro [ah'roo] *m.* ring, hoop; rim.
aroma [ă-roh'mă] *f.* scent, aroma, fragrance.
aromático [ă-roo-mah'tee-koo] *adj.* fragrant, aromatic.
arpão [ăr-pown'] *m.* harpoon.
arpéu [ăr-pe'oo] *m.* harpoon; grappling iron. [harpoon.
arpoar [ăr-poo-ar'] *va.* to
arquear [ăr-kee-ar'] *va.* to arch; to gauge (ship).
arquejar [ăr-kĕ-zhar'] *vn.* to pant, gasp.
arqueologia [ăr-kee-oo-loo-zhee'ă] *f.* archaeology.
arquitecto [ăr-kee-te'too] *m.* architect.
arquitectura [ăr-kee-te-too'-ră] *f.* architecture.
arquivar [ăr-kee-var'] *va.* to file, deposit, keep. [chives.
arquivo [ăr-kee'voo] *m.* ar-
arrabaldes [ă-ră-baldzh'] *m.pl.* suburbs, outskirts.
arraia [ă-rȳ'ă] *f.* ray (fish); — **miúda**, mob, rabble.
arraial [ă-ră-yal'] *m.* (village) festival, fête; (*Braz.*) hamlet; encampment (*mil.*).
arraiano [ă-rȳ-ă'noo] *m.* borderer.
arraigado [ă-rȳ-gah'doo] *adj.* ingrained, deep-rooted.
arraigar [ă-rȳ-gar'] *vn.* to take root; *vr.* to settle down.
arrais [ă-rȳsh'] *m.* skipper, captain, master.
arrancada [ă-ran-kah'dă] *f.* dash; sudden pull, jerk; **fazer uma** —, to clear the ground.
arrancar [ă-ran-kar'] *va.* to pull, drag out; to uproot; *vn.* to set off, start; to expire.
arranco [ă-ran'koo] *m.* dash, sudden burst; **—s da morte**, death-pangs.
arranha-céus [ă-ră'nyă se'-oosh] *m.* skyscraper.
arranhadura [ă-ră-nyă-doo'-ră] *f.* scratch. [scratch.
arranhar [ă-ră-nyar'] *va.* to
arranjar [ă-ran-zhar'] *va.* to arrange; to tidy up; to obtain; to manage; to regulate.
arranjo [ă-ran'zhoo] *m.* arrangement; agreement; tidiness.
arras [ah'răsh] *f.pl.* earnest-money, pledge; dowry.
arrasar [ă-ră-zar'] *va.* to demolish, raze, level; to fill to the brim, to overflowing.
arrastado [ă-răsh-tah'doo] *adj.* driven, dragged; dragging; drawn out; wretched; forced (interpretation); drawling (speech).
arrastão [ă-răsh-town'] *m.* drag-net; pull, haul.
arrastar [ă-răsh-tar'] *va.* to drag, haul; to drawl (speech); — **a asa**, to court; *vr.* to drag on; to crawl along.
arrasto [ă-rash'too] *m.* dragging, hauling; **rede de —**, trawl-net.

arrazoado [ă-ră-zoo-ah'doo] *m.* plea; speech; *adj.* reasonable.
arrear [ă-ree-ar'] *va.* to harness; to furnish; to adorn.
arrebatado [ă-rĕ-bă-tah'-doo] *adj.* rapid; violent; enraptured.
arrebatamento [ă-rĕ-bă-tă-men'too] *m.* rapture, ecstasy; rashness; anger.
arrebatar [ă-rĕ-bă-tar'] *va.* to carry off, snatch; to enchant; *vr.* to be carried away (by passion); to fly into a rage.
arrebicado [ă-rĕ-bee-kah'-doo] *adj.* affected; painted (face); gaudy; (*sl.*) dolled up.
arrebique [ă-rĕ-beek'] *m.* affectation; frippery; rouge, make-up, paint.
arrebitado [ă-rĕ-bee-tah'doo] *adj.* perky, saucy; nariz —, snub nose.
arrebol [ă-rĕ-bol'] *m.* red sky.
arrecada [ă-rĕ-kah'dă] *f.* earring.
arrecadação [ă-rĕ-kă-dă-sown'] *f.* collection (of money, etc.); depot, depository.
arrecadador [ă-rĕ-kă-dă-dohr'] *m.* collector; tax collector.
arrecadar [ă-rĕ-kă-dar'] *va.* to collect; to take possession of; to lock up.
arredar [ă-rĕ-dar'] *va.* to remove; to push aside.
arredio [ă-rĕ-dee'oo] *adj.* strayed; solitary.
arredondar [ă-rĕ-don-dar'] *va.* to round (off, out); — uma conta, to give a round sum.
arredores [ă-rĕ-doh'rĕsh] *m.pl.* suburbs, outskirts, surroundings, surrounding district.
arrefecer [ă-rĕ-fĕ-sayr'] *va/vn.* to cool (off, down).
arregaçar [ă-rĕ-gă-sar'] *va.* to turn up, tuck up.
arreganhar [ă-rĕ-gă-nyar'] *vn.* to grin; to show one's teeth (in a grin or snarl).
arreio [ă-ray'yoo] *m.* ornament, adornment; *pl.* harness; trappings.
arrelia [ă-rĕ-lee'ă] *f.* worry, trouble; ill-omen.
arrematar [ă-rĕ-mă-tar'] *va.* to conclude; to buy or sell by auction; to tie in a knot.
arremedar [ă-rĕ-mĕ-dar'] *va.* to mimic, ape.
arremedo [ă-rĕ-may'doo] *m.* mimicry; imitation.
arremessar [ă-rĕ-mĕ-sar'] *va.* to hurl, throw; *vr.* to hurl oneself; to attack, rush at.
arremesso [ă-rĕ-may'soo] *m.* assault, attack; threat; throw.
arremeter [ă-rĕ-mĕ-tayr'] *va.* to attack, assault; to spur on.
arremetida [ă-rĕ-mĕ-tee'dă] *f.* attack, onslaught.
arrendamento [ă-ren-dă-men'too] *m.* lease; letting; rent.
arrendar [ă-ren-dar'] *va.* to let; to rent.
arrendatário [ă-ren-dă-tah'-ree-oo] *m.* tenant; leaseholder.
arrepender-se [ă-rĕ-pen-dayr'sĕ] *vr.* to repent, regret.
arrependimento [ă-rĕ-pen-dee-men'too] *m.* repentance, regret.
arrepiar [ă-rĕ-pee-ar'] *va.* to horrify; to salt (fish); *vr.* to shiver with fright; — caminho, to retrace one's steps.
arrepio [ă-rĕ-pee'oo] *m.* chill, shiver.
arresto [ă-resh'too] *m.* seizure, confiscation, distraint.
arrevesado [ă-rĕ-vĕ-zah'doo] *adj.* difficult, obscure; cross-grained, testy (character).
arrevesar [ă-rĕ-vĕ-zar'] *va.* to turn inside out, upside down.

arriar [ă-ree-ar'] *va.* to lower; *vn.* to yield.
arriba [ă-ree'bă] *adv.* up; água —, upstream.
arribação [ă-ree-bă-sown'] *f.* arrival (in port); ave de —, bird of passage, migratory bird.
arribar [ă-ree-bar'] *vn.* to put into port; to arrive; to recover (in health, fortune).
arrimar [ă-ree-mar'] *va.* to support, prop up; *vr.* to lean against, on. [protection.
arrimo [ă-ree'mo] *m.* support;
arriscado [ă-reesh-kah'doo] *adj.* dangerous, risky; daring.
arriscar [ă-reesh-kar'] *va.* to risk, hazard.
arrobe [ă-rohb'] *m.* syrup (of fruits). [tighten.
arrochar [ă-roo-shar'] *va.* to
arrocho [ă-roh'shoo] *m.* stick (for tightening); cudgel.
arrogância [ă-roo-gan'see-ă] *f.* arrogance.
arrogante [ă-roo-gant'] *adj.* arrogant, proud, haughty.
arrogar-se [ă-roo-gar'sĕ] *vr.* to arrogate, usurp, claim.
arroio [ă-roh'yoo] *m.* brook, stream, rivulet.
arrojado [ă-roo-zhah'doo] *adj.* daring, brave; rash.
arrojar [ă-roo-zhar'] *va.* to hurl; to drag; *vr.* to hurl oneself into, venture on.
arrojo [ă-roh'zhoo] *m.* boldness, daring; —s do mar, wreckage, sea-wrack.
arromba [ă-ron'bă] *f.* lively, noisy tune; coisa de —, astounding, magnificent thing *or* event.
arrombar [ă-ron-bar'] *va.* to break down, into; to force open. [face, confront.
arrostar [ă-roosh-tar'] *va.* to
arrotar [ă-roo-tar'] *vn.* to belch; to boast.
arrotear [ă-roo-tee-ar'] *va.* to clear (ground for cultivation).
arroubamento [ă-roh-bă-men'too] *m. or* **arroubo**, *m.* ecstasy, rapture, bliss; transport (of joy, etc.); flight (of imagination, etc.).
arroz [ă-rohsh'] *m.* rice; **pó** de —, face-powder.
arrozal [ă-roo-zal'] *m.* rice-field. [uproar.
arruaça [ă-roo-ah'să] *f.* riot,
arruamento [ă-roo-ă-men'too] *m.* laying out of streets; alignment of buildings.
arrugar [ă-roo-gar'] *va.* to wrinkle, crease; — **a fronte**, to frown.
arruinar [ă-roo-ee-nar'] *va.* to ruin, demolish.
arrulhar [ă-roo-lyar'] *vn.* to coo (doves); to lull to sleep; to 'bill and coo' (lovers).
arrulho [ă-roo'lyoo] *m.* lullaby; cooing.
arrumar [ă-roo-mar'] *va.* to arrange, put in order; to tidy (up); to stow (cargo); to keep (accounts); *vr.* to secure employment.
arsenal [ăr-sĕ-nal'] *m.* arsenal; dock-yard.
arte [art] *f.* art; skill; astuteness; cunning, artfulness; belas —s, fine arts.
artefacto [ăr-tĕ-fak'too] *m.* manufactured article; artefact.
arteiro [ăr-tay'ee-roo] *adj.* artful, wily.
artelho [ăr-tay'lyoo] *m.* ankle.
artéria [ăr-tair'ee-ă] *f.* artery; thoroughfare, highway.
articulação [ăr-tee-koo-lă-sown'] *f.* joint; articulation, pronunciation.
articulado [ăr-tee-koo-lah'doo] *adj.* jointed; pronounced, articulated; *m.* statement (*leg.*).
articular [ăr-tee-koo-lar'] *va.* to articulate; to pronounce (clearly); to put together.

articulo [ăr-tee'koo-loo] *m.* knuckle, joint; article (of contract, etc.).
artífice [ăr-tee'fees] *m.* artisan, craftsman; inventor.
artificial [ăr-ti-fee-see-al'] *adj.* artificial.
artifício [ăr-ti-fee'see-oo] *m.* artifice, trick; device; craft; fogo de —, fireworks.
artificioso [ăr-ti-fee-see-oh'-zoo] *adj.* artful, crafty; ingenious.
artigo [ăr-tee'goo] *m.* article; section, item, clause; — **de fundo**, leading article.
artilharia [ăr-tee-lyă-ree'ă] *f.* artillery.
artilheiro [ăr-tee-lyay'ee-roo] *m.* gunner, artillery-man.
artimanha [ăr-tee-mă'nyă] *f.* trick, stratagem.
artista [ăr-teesh'tă] *mf.* artist; artiste (professional singer, etc.).
artrite [ăr-treet'] *f.* arthritis.
arvorar [ăr-voo-rar'] *va.* to hoist; *vr.* to set oneself up as.
árvore [ar'voor] *f.* tree; shaft; mast.
arvoredo [ăr-voo-ray'doo] *m.* grove, wood; masts (*naut.*).
ás [ash] *m.* ace.
asa [ah'ză] *f.* wing; handle (of basket, etc.).
ascendência [ăsh-se*n*-de*n*'-see-ă] *f.* ancestry, origins; ascendency.
ascendente [ăsh-se*n*-de*n*t'] *m.* ancestor; ascendency; *adj.* rising, upward.
ascender [ăsh-se*n*-dayr'] *vn.* to rise, ascend.
ascensão [ăsh-se*n*-sow*n*'] *f.* ascent; dia da —, Ascension Day.
ascensor [ăsh-se*n*-sohr'] *m.* [lift, elevator.
asceta [ăsh-se'tă] *mf.* ascetic; hermit.
ascético [ăsh-se'tee-koo] *adj.* [ascetic.
asco [ash'koo] *m.* revulsion, disgust; dar —, to be disgusting, revolting.
asfalto [ăsh-fal'too] *m.* as- [phalt.
asfixiar [ăsh-feek-see-ar'] *va.* to suffocate, choke; to asphyxiate.
asiático [ă-zee-ah'tee-koo] *adj.* [Asian, Asiatic.
asilo [ă-zee'loo] *m.* institution, home (for aged, orphans, etc.); asylum; refuge.
asma [azh'mă] *f.* asthma.
asneira [ăzh-nay'ee-ră] *f.* nonsense, stupid remark.
asno [azh'noo] *m.* ass, donkey.
aspa [ash'pă] *f.* St. Andrew's cross; *pl.* sails (of windmill); inverted commas; quotation marks.
aspecto [ăsh-pe'too] *m.* aspect; [appearance.
aspereza [ăsh-pĕ-ray'ză] *f.* harshness, roughness, severity.
áspero [ash'pĕ-roo] *adj.* harsh, rough, severe.
aspiração [ăsh-pee-ră-sow*n*'] *f.* breathing (in), suction; aspiration.
aspirador [ăsh-pee-ră-dohr'] *m.* suction pipe; vacuum-cleaner.
aspirante [ăsh-pee-ra*n*t'] *m.* [cadet (*mil.*).
aspirar [ăsh-pee-rar'] *va.* to draw in (air); to aspirate (sounds); *vn.* to aspire to.
aspirina [ăsh-pi-ree'nă] *f.* aspirin.
asqueroso [ăsh-kĕ-roh'zoo] *adj.* repulsive, disgusting.
assaltar [ă-sal-tar'] *va.* to assault, attack, assail.
assalto [ă-sal'too] *m.* assault, attack.
assanhar [ă-să-nyar'] *va.* to irritate, infuriate; *vr.* to get furious.
assar [ă-sar'] *va.* to roast.
assassinar [ă-să-see-nar'] *va.* to assassinate, murder.
assassínio [ă-să-see'nee-oo] *m.* murder; assassination.

assassino [ă-să-see'noo] *m.* murderer; assassin.
assaz [ă-sash'] *adv.* sufficiently, enough; quite; rather.
asseado [ă-see-ah'doo] *adj.* clean, spotless, neat.
assear [ă-see-ar'] *va.* to clean, tidy up.
assediar [ă-sĕ-dee-ar'] *va.* to besiege; to importune.
assegurar [ă-sĕ-goo-rar'] *va.* to assure; to ensure.
asseio [ă-say'yoo] *m.* cleanliness, neatness.
assembleia [ă-se*n*-blay'yă] *f.* assembly, meeting.
assemelhar-se [ă-sĕ-mĕ-lyar'sĕ] *vr.* to resemble.
assentada [ă-se*n*-tah'dă] *f.* session, sitting; deposition (*leg.*); **de uma —**, at one sitting.
assentado [ă-se*n*-tah'doo] *adj.* settled, agreed.
assentador [ă-se*n*-tă-dohr'] *m.* razor-strop; recorder, registrar; fitter (*mech.*); bricklayer.
assentar [ă-se*n*-tar'] *va.* to seat; to place, lay; to settle; to sharpen (razor); to note down; **— praça**, to enlist; *vn.* to fit; to go with (patterns, colours, etc.).
assentimento [ă-se*n*-tee-me*n*'too] *m.* assent, consent.
assento [ă-se*n*'too] *m.* seat; site; sediment; prudence.
asserção [ă-sĕr-sow*n*'] *f.* assertion.
assestar [ă-sĕsh-tar'] *va.* to aim, point.
asseverar [ă-sĕ-vĕ-rar'] *va.* to affirm, declare solemnly.
assiduidade [ă-see-doo-ee-dahd'] *f.* assiduousness, assiduity, diligence.
assíduo [ă-see'doo-oo] *adj.* assiduous, diligent.
assim [ă-see*n*'] *adv.* so, thus; **— que**, as soon as.
assimilação [ă-see-mee-lă-sow*n*'] *f.* assimilation.
assimilar [ă-see-mee-lar'] *va.* to assimilate.
assinalado [ă-see-nă-lah'doo] *adj.* famous; marked (out).
assinalar [ă-see-nă-lar'] *va.* to mark (out); *vr.* to become noted, famous.
assinante [ă-see-na*n*t'] *m.* subscriber.
assinar [ă-see-nar'] *va.* to sign; to subscribe to; to fix (a time); to assign.
assinatura [ă-see-nă-too'ră] *f.* signature; subscription.
assistência [ă-seesh-te*n*'see-ă] *f.* audience, those present; attendance, presence; assistance, aid.
assistente [ă-seesh-te*n*t'] *m.* person present; assistant; *adj.* assistant, auxiliary.
assistir [ă-seesh-teer'] *vn.* to be present, attend; *va.* to attend (the sick); to help, assist.
assoar-se [ă-soo-ar'sĕ] *vr.* to blow one's nose.
assobiar [ă-soo-bee-ar'] *vn.* to whistle; *va.* to hoot at, jeer at.
assobio [ă-soo-bee'oo] *m.* whistling; whistle; hiss.
associação [ă-soo-see-ă-sow*n*'] *f.* association; society.
associado [ă-soo-see-ah'doo] *m.* associate, member; partner.
associar [ă-soo-see-ar'] *va.* to associate.
assolar [ă-soo-lar'] *va.* to devastate, lay waste, destroy.
assomar [ă-soo-mar'] *vn.* to appear (at); to look out of, lean out of; *vr.* to grow angry.
assombradiço [ă-so*n*-bră-dee'soo] *adj.* timid, fearful.
assombrar [ă-so*n*-brar'] *va.* to astonish, amaze; to frighten; to shade.
assombro [ă-so*n*'broo] *m.*

amazement; marvel; dread.
assombroso [ă-son-broh'zoo] *adj.* amazing, astonishing.
assomo [ă-soh'moo] *m.* sign.
assorear [ă-soo-ree-ar'] *va/vn.* to silt up.
assumir [ă-soo-meer'] *va.* to assume, take (up, on ,over).
assunção [ă-soon-sown'] *f.* assumption.
assunto [ă-soon'too] *m.* subject, theme, topic; affair, business, matter.
assustadiço [ă-soosh-tă-dee'-soo] *adj.* timid.
assustar [ă-soosh-tar'] *va.* to frighten, startle , scare.
astro [ash'troo] *m.* star, planet; celebrity, 'star'.
astrónomo [ăsh-tro'noo-moo] *m.* astronomer.
astúcia [ăsh-too'see-ă] *f.* cunning, slyness.
astuto [ăsh-too'too] *adj.* cunning, astute, sly.
atacador [ă-tă-kă-dohr'] *m.* attacker; shoe-lace.
atacar [ă-tă-kar'] *va.* to attack, assail; to lace up, do up.
atalaia [ă-tă-lȳ'yă] *f.* watch-tower; sentinel.
atalhar [ă-tă-lyar'] *va.* to intercept, obstruct, stop; to cut short (speech, etc.); *vn.* to take a short cut.
atalho [ă-ta'lyoo] *m.* short cut.
ataque [ă-tak'] *m.* attack.
atar [ă-tar'] *va.* to tie, fasten.
atarefado [ă-tă-rĕ-fah'doo] *adj.* busy.
ataúde [ă-tă-ood'] *m.* coffin.
ataviar [ă-tă-vee-ar'] *va.* to adorn, bedeck, dress up.
atávico [ă-ta'vee-koo] *adj.* atavistic.
até [ă-te'] *prep.* until, till; as far as, up to; *adv.* even; — **à vista,** — **logo,** good-bye, cheerio, see you soon; — **mais não poder,** to the utmost.
atear [ă-tee-ar'] *va.* to kindle, inflame, stir up. [atheist,
ateísta [ă-tay-eesh'tă] *mf.*
atemorizar [ă-tĕ-moo-ree-zar'] *va.* to frighten, terrify.
atenção [ă-ten-sown'] *f.* attention; civility, courtesy; care; *interj.* look out! take care!
atencioso [ă-ten-see-oh'zoo] *adj.* attentive; courteous.
atender [ă-ten-dayr'] *va.* to pay attention to, take note of, attend to; — **à porta,** to answer the door.
atentado [ă-ten-tah'doo] *m.* criminal attack; outrage.
atentar [ă-ten-tar'] *va/vn.* to pay attention to, observe; to make a criminal attack.
atento [ă-ten'too] *adj.* attentive; respectful.
atenuação [ă-tĕ-noo-ă-sown'] *f.* attenuation, diminution.
atenuante [ă-tĕ-noo-ant'] *f.* extenuation, extenuating circumstance (*leg.*); *adj.* extenuating (*leg.*).
atenuar [ă-tĕ-noo-ar'] *va.* to attenuate, diminish; to extenuate (*leg.*).
aterragem [ă-tĕ-rah'zhen] *f.* landing (aeroplane).
aterrar [ă-tĕ-rar'] *va.* to terrify, frighten; to fill in, (cover) with soil; *vn.* to land (aeroplane).
atestado [ă-tĕsh-tah'doo] *m.* testimonial; certificate; affidavit.
atestar [ă-tĕsh-tar'] *va.* to certify, declare.
ateu [ă-tay'oo] *m.* atheist; *adj.* atheistic.
atiçar [ă-tee-sar'] *va.* to poke the fire; to incite, stir up.
atilado [ă-tee-lah'doo] *adj.* intelligent, sensible; conscientious; polished.
atinado [ă-tee-nah'doo] *adj.* shrewd; prudent.

atinar [ă-tee-nar'] *va.* to hit on, guess accurately.
atingir [ă-teen-zheer'] *va.* to attain, reach; to hit; to understand.
atirador [ă-tee-ră-dohr'] *m.* marksman, shot.
atirar [ă-tee-rar'] *va.* to throw; *vn.* to shoot at.
atitude [ă-tee-tood'] *f.* attitude.
atlas [at'lăsh] *m.* atlas.
atleta [ăt-le'tă] *mf.* athlete; champion (of a cause, etc.).
atlético [ăt-le'tee-koo] *adj.* athletic, vigorous.
atmosfera [ăt-moosh-fair'ă] *f.* atmosphere.
atoleiro [ă-too-lay'ee-roo] *m.* marsh, swamp, bog.
átomo [ah'too-moo] *m.* atom.
atónito [ă-to'nee-too] *adj.* astonished, amazed, stunned.
atordoado [ă-toor-doo-ah'-doo] *adj.* stupefied, stunned.
atordoamento [ă-toor-doo-ă-men'too] *m.* stupefaction.
atormentador [ă-toor-men-tă-dohr'] *m.* tormentor, torturer.
atormentar [ă-toor-men-tar'] *va.* to torment, torture.
atrabiliário [ă-tră-bee-lee-ah'ree-oo] *adj.* bad-tempered; spiteful; disagreeable.
atracar [ă-tră-kar'] *va.* to moor; to secure; to accost, assault; *vn.* to come alongside (ship).
atracção [ă-trah-sown'] *f.* attraction, appeal.
atractivo [ă-trah-tee'voo] *m.* attraction; *m.pl.* charms, beauty; *adj.* attractive.
atraente [ă-tră-ent'] *adj.* attractive, charming.
atraiçoado [ă-trȳ-soo-ah'doo] *adj.* treacherous; betrayed.
atraiçoar [ă-trȳ-soo-ar'] *va.* to betray.
atrair [ă-tră-eer'] *va.* to attract, allure, draw.
atrapalhar [ă-tră-pă-lyar'] *va.* to confuse, muddle.
atrás [ă-trash'] *adv.* back, behind; *prep.* — **de**, behind; after.
atrasado [ă-tră-zah'doo] *adj.* late, delayed; slow (clock); backward; behindhand; *m.pl.* arrears.
atrasar [ă-tră-zar'] *va.* to delay; to put back; *vr.* to get into arrears; to fall behind.
atraso [ă-trah'zoo] *m.* delay; backwardness; *pl.* arrears; com —, late.
através [ă-tră-vesh'] *prep.* — de, through; across.
atravessar [ă-tră-vĕ-sar'] *va.* to cross; to pass through, over.
atreito [ă-tray'ee-too] *adj.* subject to, prone to; accustomed to.
atrelar [ă-trĕ-lar'] *va.* to put on a leash; to harness; to yoke; to link, couple; to allure (*fig.*).
atrever-se [ă-trĕ-vayr'sĕ] *vr.* to dare, venture.
atrevido [ă-trĕ-vee'doo] *adj.* bold, daring; insolent.
atrevimento [ă-trĕ-vee-men'too] *m.* boldness, daring; impudence.
atribuição [ă-tree-boo-ee sown'] *f.* attribution; competence; *pl.* rights, powers.
atribuir [ă-tree-boo-eer'] *va.* to attribute, ascribe.
atributo [ă-tree-boo'too] *m.* attribute.
átrio [a'tree-oo] *m.* hall, vestibule; courtyard.
atrito [ă-tree'too] *m.* attrition; friction.
atroar [ă-troo-ar'] *va.* to stun (with noise); *vn.* to roar.
atrocidade [ă-troo-see-dahd'] *f.* atrocity, outrage.
atrofiar-se [ă-troo-fee-ar'sĕ]

vr. to become atrophied, waste away.
atropelar [ă-troo-pĕ-lar'] *va.* to trample on (down, over); to knock down; to run over.
atropelo [ă-troo-pay'loo] *m.* hurry, rush; trampling down.
atroz [ă-trosh'] *m.* atrocious; grievous.
atulhar [ă-too-lyar'] *va.* to fill up, cram.
atum [ă-toon'] *m.* tunny (-fish).
aturado [ă-too-rah'doo] *adj.* constant; diligent.
aturar [ă-too-rar'] *va.* to endure, bear.
aturdido [ă-toor-dee'doo] *adj.* astounded; stunned.
aturdir [ă-toor-deer'] *va.* to astound, stupefy.
audácia [ow-dah'see-ă] *f.* courage, audacity; effrontery, 'cheek'.
audaz [ow-dash'] *adj.* bold, courageous; impudent.
audiência [ow-dee-*en*'see-ă] *f.* session, sitting, hearing; formal reception, audience.
auditor [ow-dee-tohr'] *m.* judge, magistrate; hearer, listener.
auditório [ow-dee-to'ree-oo] *m.* audience; hall, auditorium.
audível [ow-dee'vel] *adj.* audible.
auferir [ow-fĕ-reer'] *va.* to obtain.
auge [owzh] *m.* summit, pinnacle.
augurar [ow-goo-rar'] *va.* to prognosticate, augur.
aula [ow'lă] *f.* class; lecture-room, classroom; dar —, to give a lecture, to take a class.
aumentar [ow-men-tar'] *va.* to increase, enlarge.
aumento [ow'men-too] *m.* increase, rise; expansion.
aura [ow'ră] *f.* breeze; — popular, popular favour.
áureo [ow'ree-oo] *adj.* golden.
auréola [ow-re'oo-lă] *f.* halo.
aurífero [ow-ree'fĕ-roo] *adj.* gold-bearing.
aurora [ow-ro'ră] *f.* dawn.
ausência [ow-zay*n*'see-ă] *f.* absence.
ausentar-se [ow-zen-tar'sĕ] *vr.* to absent oneself, stay away.
ausente [ow-zen*t*'] *adj.* absent; *mf.* missing person.
auspício [owsh-pee'see-oo] *m.* omen; *pl.* auspices, patronage.
austeridade [owsh-tĕ-ree-dahd'] *f.* austerity.
austero [owsh-tair'oo] *adj.* austere; severe, stern.
austral [owsh-tral'] *adj.* southern.
austríaco [owsh-tree'ă-koo] *adj/m.* Austrian.
autenticar [ow-ten-tee-kar'] *va.* to confirm, authenticate.
autêntico [ow-te*n*'tee-koo] *adj.* authentic, genuine.
auto [ow'too] *m.* document (*leg.*); official report; public ceremony; (short) play; (motor-)car; *pl.* proceedings (*leg.*).
autocarro [ow-too-ka'roo] *m.* bus; motor-coach.
autócrata [ow-to'kră-tă] *m.* autocrat.
autóctone [ow-tok'ton] *adj.* indigenous, native, aboriginal.
autógrafo [ow-to'gră-foo] *m.* autograph.
automático [ow-too-ma'tee-koo] *adj.* automatic.
autómato [ow-to'mă-too] *m.* automaton; robot.
automóvel [ow-too-mo'vel] *m.* (motor-)car; (*U.S.A.*) automobile.
autonomia [ow-too-noo-mee'-ă] *f.* self-government, autonomy, home rule.
autónomo [ow-to'noo-moo] *adj.* autonomous; free.

autópsia [ow-top'see-ă] *f.* post-mortem, autopsy.
autor [ow-tohr'] *m.* author; discoverer; creator; perpetrator (of crime); plaintiff (*leg.*). [authorship.
autoria [ow-too-ree'ă] *f.*
autoridade [ow-too-ree-dahd'] *f.* authority, power.
autoritário [ow-too-ree-tah'-ree-oo] *adj.* authoritarian.
autorização [ow-too-ree-ză-sow*n*'] *f.* authorization, permission.
autorizado [ow-too-ree-zah'-doo] *adj.* authorized; reliable.
autorizar [ow-too-ree-zar'] *va.* to authorize; to approve; to legalize.
auxiliar [ow-see-lee-ar'] *va.* to help, assist, aid; *adj.* auxiliary; *mf.* assistant; clerk.
auxílio [ow-see'lee-oo] *m.* help, aid, assistance.
avaliação [ă-vă-lee-ă-sow*n*'] *f.* (e)valuation, estimate.
avaliar [ă-vă-lee-ar'] *va.* to evaluate, estimate; to value; to appreciate (ability, etc.).
avançar [ă-va*n*-sar'] *vn.* to advance; to proceed.
avarento [ă-vă-re*n*-too] *adj.* avaricious, miserly, mean.
avareza [ă-vă-ray'ză] *f.* avarice; meanness.
avaria [ă-vă-ree'ă] *f.* damage.
avariar [ă-vă-ree-ar'] *va.* to damage.
avaro [ă-vah'roo] *m.* miser; *adj.* miserly, avaricious.
ave [ahv] *f.* bird; fowl; — **de rapina**, bird of prey.
aveia [ă-vay'yă] *f.* oats.
avelã [ă-vě-la*n*'] *f.* hazel-nut.
avença [ă-ve*n*'să] *f.* agreement, settlement.
avenida [ă-vě-nee'dă] *f.* avenue.
avental [ă-ve*n*-tal'] *m.* apron.
aventar [ă-ve*n*-tar'] *va.* to air, ventilate; to perceive, foresee; to put forward (an idea, suggestion).
aventura [ă-ve*n*-too'ră] *f.* adventure; venture.
aventurado [ă-ve*n*-too-rah'-doo] *adj.* adventurous, daring; **bem** —, blessed; fortunate, happy; **mal** —, unfortunate, wretched.
aventurar [ă-ve*n*-too-rar'] *va/vr.* to venture, risk.
aventureiro [ă-ve*n*-too-ray'-ee-roo] *m.* adventurer; *adj.* adventurous.
averiguação [ă-vě-ree-gwă-sow*n*'] *f.* inquiry; discovery (of the truth).
averiguar [ă-vě-ree-gwar'] *va.* to ascertain; to investigate.
aversão [ă-věr-sow*n*'] *f.* aversion, dislike.
avesso [ă-vay'soo] *adj.* contrary, opposed to; *m.* wrong side; reverse side; **ao** —, inside out. [ostrich.
avestruz [ă-věsh-troosh'] *m.*
avezar-se [ă-vě-zar'sě] *vr.* to fall into the habit of; to become used to.
aviação [ă-vee-ă-sow*n*'] *f.* aviation; aircraft; air force.
aviado [ă-vee-ah'doo] *m.* (*Braz.*) trader, agent; *adj.* ready; on the way.
aviador [ă-vee-ă-dohr'] *m.* airman, aviator.
aviamento [ă-vee-ă-me*n*'too] *m.* completion, execution (of task, order); despatch (of goods); *pl.* materials, supplies; tools. [plane.
avião [ă-vee-ow*n*'] *m.* aero-
aviar [ă-vee-ar'] *va.* to despatch (goods); to carry out (task); — **uma receita**, to make up a prescription; *vr.* to get ready; to bestir oneself.
avidez [ă-vee-daysh'] *f.* covetousness, avidity.

ávido [a'vee-doo] *adj.* eager, avid; greedy.
avigorar [ă-vee-goo-rar'] *va.* to invigorate.
aviltar [ă-veel-tar'] *va.* to degrade, dishonour; to vilify.
avinagrado [ă-vee-nă-grah'-doo] *adj.* sour, bitter.
avisado [ă-vee-zah'doo] *adj.* wise, prudent, cautious.
avisar [ă-vee-zar'] *va.* to inform; to warn; to advise; *vr.* to think over carefully.
aviso [ă-vee'zoo] *m.* warning; notice, announcement; a meu —, in my opinion.
avistar [ă-veesh-tar'] *va.* to catch sight of, descry; *vr.* to come into view; to have an interview with.
avitualhar [ă-vee-too-ă-lyar'] *va.* to provision.
avivar [ă-vee-var'] *va.* to revive; to stir up; to enliven; to freshen up.
aviventar [ă-vee-ve*n*-tar'] *va.* to revive; to encourage.
avizinhar [ă-vi-zee-nyar'] *va.* to bring close to; *vr.* to approach.
avo [ah'voo] *m.* fraction [(*maths.*).
avô [ă-voh'] *m.* grandfather.
avó [ă-vo'] *f.* grandmother; avós, *m.pl.* grandparents; ancestors.
avoengos [ă-voo-e*n*'goosh] *m.pl.* ancestors, forebears.
avolumar-se [ă-voo-loo-mar'sĕ] *vr.* to grow in volume.
avulso [ă-vool'soo] *adj.* separate; single (copy of journal, etc.).
avultado [ă-vool-tah'doo] *adj.* [large, bulky.
avultar [ă-vool-tar'] *vn.* to bulk large; to increase, spread.
axila [ak-see'lă] *f.* armpit.
azáfama [ă-zah'fă-mă] *f.* hurry, bustle, flurry.
azar [ă-zar'] *m.* bad luck; jogo de —, game of chance.
azedo [ă-zay'doo] *adj.* bitter, acid, irritable, bad-tempered.
azedume [ă-zĕ-doom'] *m.* bitterness, bitter taste; sourness; acrimony, irritability.
azeite [ă-zay'eet] *m.* olive-oil.
azeitona [ă-zay-ee-toh'nă] *f.* olive.
azenha [ă-zay'nyă] *f.* water-[mill.
azeviche [ă-zĕ-veesh'] *m.* jet.
azevinho [ă-zĕ-vee'nyoo] *m.* holly.
azia [ă-zee'ă] *f.* heart-burn, [acidity.
aziago [ă-zee-ah'goo] *adj.* unlucky, ill-omened.
ázimo [ah'zee-moo] *adj.* unleavened.
azinhaga [ă-zee-nyah'gă] *f.* country lane, path.
azinheira [ă-zee-nyay'ee-ră] *f.* holm-oak.
azo [ah'zoo] *m.* opportunity; [pretext.
azote [ă-zot'] *m.* or **azoto,** nitrogen.
azougue [ă-zohg'] *m.* quick-[silver.
azul [ă-zool'] *adj.* blue.
azulejo [ă-zoo-lay'zhoo] *m.* glazed, ornamental tile.

B

baba [bah'bă] *f.* slobber, dribble.
bacalhau [bă-kă-lyow'] *m.* cod, codfish.
bacelo [bă-say'loo] *m.* sprig of vine; newly-planted vine.
bacharel [bă-shă-rel'] *m.* bachelor (academic degree); babbler, prater.
bacia [bă-see'ă] *f.* wash-basin; shaving-bowl; basin (of river, sea).
bacilo [bă-see'loo] *m.* bacillus.
baço [bah'soo] *adj.* dull, tarnished, dark; *m.* spleen (*med.*).
báculo [ba'koo-loo] *m.* staff; crozier (*eccl.*).
badalar [bă-dă-lar'] *vn.* to

clang, ring; to gossip, chatter.
badalo [bă-dah'loo] *m.* clapper (of bell).
baeta [bă-yay'tă] *f.* baize.
bafejar [bă-fĕ-zhar'] *va.* to breathe gently on; to inspire; to favour.
bafio [bă-fee'oo] *m.* musty smell; mould.
bafo [bah'foo] *m.* breath; breeze; favour.
baga [bah'gă] *f.* berry; drop, bead (of sweat).
bagaço [bă-gah'soo] *m.* crushed skins, pips, husks (of fruit, sugar cane, etc.).
bagageiro [bă-gă-zhay'ee-roo] *m.* porter.
bagagem [bă-gah'zhe*n*] *f.* luggage, baggage, bags.
bagatela [bă-gă-te'lă] *f.* trifle, bagatelle.
bago [bah'goo] *m.* grape; grain (of wheat); (*sl.*) 'dough', cash.
baía [bă-ee'ă] *f.* bay.
bailado [bȳ-lah'doo] *m.* ballet; dance.
bailar [bȳ'lar'] *vn.* to dance.
baile [bȳl] *m.* dance, ball.
bainha [bă-ee'nyă] *f.* sheath, scabbard; hem (of dress).
baioneta [bȳ-oo-nay'tă] *f.* bayonet; — **calada,** fixed bayonet.
bairro [bȳ'roo] *m.* district, quarter, ward, suburb.
baixa [bȳ'shă] *f.* decrease, reduction, fall; hollow (of valley); lower part (of town); casualty (in battle); shallow part (of river, etc.); **ter** —, to be dismissed; **dar** —, to retire; to be retired, demobilized (*mil.*).
baixa-mar [bȳ'shă-mar] *f.* low tide.
baixar [bȳ-shar'] *va.* to lower; *vn.* to get off, alight; to come (go) down; to decline.
baixeza [bȳ-shay'ză] *f.* meanness; abjectness.
baixio [bȳ-shee'oo] *m.* shoal.
baixo [bȳ'shoo] *adj.* low; short; mean, vulgar; — **relevo,** bas-relief; *adv.* low, low down; in a low voice; **em** —, below; downstairs; **para** —, down, downwards; **por** — **de,** under, underneath, beneath; *m.* lower part; shallow, shoal; bass (*mus.*).
bala [ba'lă] *f.* bullet; bale (of cotton, paper, etc.).
balada [bă-lah'dă] *f.* ballad.
balança [bă-la*n*'să] *f.* scales, balance.
balançar [ba-la*n*-sar'] *va.* to balance; to weigh (arguments, etc.); *vn.* to rock, sway.
balanço [bă-la*n*'soo] *m.* lurching, swaying, rolling; balance-sheet (*com.*); **dar** —, to audit (accounts); **em** —, uncertain, in the balance.
balão [bă-low*n*'] *m.* balloon.
balaustrada [bă-lowsh-trah'-dă] *f.* balustrade.
balbuciar [bal-boo-see-ar'] *va.* to stutter, stammer; to babble.
balbúrdia [bal-boor'dee-ă] *f.* uproar, bedlam, confusion.
balcão [bal-kow*n*'] *m.* balcony; counter (shop); dress-circle (*theat.*).
balda [bal'dă] *f.* defect, fault.
baldaquim [bal-dă-kee*n*'] *m.* canopy.
baldar [bal-dar'] *va.* to frustrate, baulk.
balde [bald] *m.* bucket, pail.
baldear [bal-dee-ar'] *va.* to wash down, swab down (decks); to decant (liquids); to bail (water); to transfer (goods, passengers).
baldio [bal-dee'oo] *adj.* uncultivated; *m.* waste land.
baleeiro [bă-lee-ay'ee-roo] *m.* whaling-ship; whaler (man or boat).

baleia [bă-lay'yă] *f.* whale.
balido [bă-lee'doo] *m.* bleating.
baliza [bă-lee'ză] *f.* buoy, seamark; sign, mark; post; beacon; goal-posts (football).
balneário [bal-nee-ah'ree-oo] *m.* bathing-place, watering-place, spa.
balofo [bă-loh'foo] *adj.* empty (phrases, etc.), puffed up.
baloiço [bă-loh'ee-soo] *m.* swing; swinging.
balsa [bal'să] *f.* thicket; raft; tub.
bálsamo [bal'să-moo] *m.* balsam, balm.
baluarte [bă-loo-art'] *m.* bulwark, bastion.
bambo [băn'boo] *adj.* slack.
bambolear [ban-boo-lee-ar'] *vn.* to sway, swagger, swing the hips; to reel, totter.
bambu [ban-boo'] *m.* bamboo.
banal [bă-nal'] *adj.* banal, commonplace.
banana [bă-nă'nă] *f.* banana.
banca [ban'kă] *f.* writing-desk; office (of lawyer, solicitor); stake (in card games).
bancada [ban-kah'dă] *f.* row (of seats, benches).
bancário [ban-kah'ree-oo] *adj.* banking, bank.
bancarrota [ban-kă-roh'tă] *f.* bankruptcy; **fazer —**, to go bankrupt.
banco [ban'koo] *m.* bench; bank; **— de areia**, sandbank; **— de coral**, coral reef.
banda [ban'dă] *f.* side; sash; band (*mus.*); **pôr de —**, to put aside.
bandeira [ban-day'ee-ră] *f.* flag, banner, standard, ensign; (*Braz.*) armed pioneer column, armed band.
bandeirante [ban-day-ee-rant'] *m.* (*Braz.*) member of armed band, pioneer, explorer.
bandeja [ban-day'zhă] *f.* tray.
bandido [ban-dee'doo] *m.* bandit, outlaw, highwayman.
bando [ban'doo] *m.* group; faction, band; gang; flock, herd; proclamation.
bandoleira [ban-doo-lay'ee-ră] *f.* bandoleer; sling (for rifle).
bandoleiro [ban-doo-lay'ee-roo] *m.* highwayman, robber, bandit.
bandolim [ban-doo-leen'] *m.* mandolin.
bandurra [ban-doo'ră] *f.* mandolin, guitar (*approx.*).
banha [bă'nyă] *f.* fat, lard.
banhar [bă-nyar'] *va.* to bathe.
banheira [bă-nyay'ee-ră] *f.* bath-tub.
banheiro [bă-nyay'ee-roo] *m.* bath-attendant; beach-guard.
banhista [bă-nyeesh'tă] *mf.* bather.
banho [bă'nyoo] *m.* bath; bathe (in sea); coat, coating (of dye, etc.); **—s de casamento**, banns (of marriage).
banir [bă-neer'] *va.* to banish.
banqueiro [ban-kay'ee-roo] *m.* banker; bank manager.
banquete [ban-kayt'] *m.* banquet.
banzé [ban-ze'] *m.* row, uproar; rowdiness.
baptismo [ba-teezh'moo] *m.* baptism; christening; **nome de —**, Christian name.
baptizar [ba-tee-zar'] *va.* to baptize; to christen; to water (milk, wine).
baque [bak] *m.* thud; (*Braz.*) instant.
baquear [bă-kee-ar'] *vn.* to fall with a thud.
baqueta [bă-kay'tă] *f.* drum-stick.
baraço [bă-rah'soo] *m.* string; rope.
barafunda [bă-ră-foon'dă] *f.* tumult, uproar.
baralhar [bă-ră-lyar'] *va.* to shuffle(cards); to confuse, mix up.

baralho [bă-ra'lyoo] *m.* pack of cards.
barão [bă-rown'] *m.* baron; (*archaic*) great man, hero.
barata [bă-rah'tă] *f.* cockroach.
barato [bă-rah'too] *adj.* cheap, inexpensive; *adv.* cheaply.
barba [bar'bă] *f.* beard; *pl.* whiskers; navalha de —, razor; fazer a —, to s have.
barbaridade [băr-bă-ree-dahd'] *f.* barbarity, cruelty; dizer —s, to talk absolute rubbish.
barbarismo [băr-bă-reezh'-moo] *m.* barbarism.
bárbaro [bar'bă-roo] *adj.* barbarous, savage; rough, crude; *m.* barbarian.
barbatana [băr-bă-tă'nă] *f.* fin.
barbearia [băr-bee-ă-ree'ă] *f.* barber's shop. [barber.
barbeiro [băr-bay'ee-roo] *m.*
barca [bar'kă] *f.* (small) boat; barge; ferry-boat.
barcaça [băr-kah'să] *f.* lighter, barge.
barcagem [băr-kah'zhen] *f.* load, freight; fare, charge.
barco [bar'koo] *m.* boat; ship.
barda [bar'dă] *f.* hedge; fence; heap; em —, in abundance.
bardo [bar'doo] *m.* bard, poet; sheepfold; hedge.
barlavento [bar-lă-ven'too] *m.* windward.
barómetro [bă-ro'mĕ-troo] *m.* barometer.
barqueiro [băr-kay'ee-roo] *m.* boatman; ferryman.
barra [ba'ră] *f.* bar; rod.
barraca [bă-rah'kă] *f.* tent; hut; stall (in market).
barracão [bă-ră-kown'] *m.* shed. [dam; dike.
barragem [bă-rah'zhen] *f.*
barranco [bă-ran'koo] *m.* gorge, ravine, gully.
barreira [bă-ray'ee-ră] *f.* barrier; stockade; clay-pit.
barrete [bă-rayt'] *m.* cap; biretta (*eccl.*).
barrica [bă-ree'kă] *f.* cask.
barricada [bă-ree-kah'dă] *f.* barricade.
barriga [bă-ree'gă] *f.* belly; fazer —, to bulge; — da perna, calf of the leg. [cask.
barril [bă-reel'] *m.* barrel,
barro [ba'roo] *m.* clay; louça de —, earthenware.
barrote [bă-rot'] *m.* beam, rafter.
barulhento [bă-roo-lyen'too] *adj.* noisy, rowdy.
barulho [bă-roo'lyoo] *m.* noise, row.
base [bahz] *f.* basis, foundation; base (*mil.*, *archit.* *etc.*).
basear [bă-zee-ar'] *va.* to base.
basta [bash'tă] *interj.* that's enough; that will do.
bastante [băsh-tant'] *adv.* enough, sufficiently; quite, rather; *adj.* enough, sufficient.
bastão [băsh-town'] *m.* stick; baton (*mil.*).
bastar [băsh-tar'] *vn.* to suffice, be enough.
bastardo [băsh-tar'doo] *m.* bastard; *adj.* bastard, spurious.
bastidor [băsh-tee-dohr'] *m.* embroidery frame; *pl.* wings (*theat.*).
basto [bash'too] *adj.* thick; dense; plentiful.
bastonada [băsh-too-nah'dă] *f.* bastinado; cudgelling.
batalha [bă-ta'lyă] *f.* battle.
batalhão [bă-tă-lyown'] *m.* battalion.
batata [bă-tah'tă] *f.* potato.
batedeira [bă-tĕ-day'ee-ră] *f.* butter-churn.
batedor [bă-tĕ-dohr'] *m.* beater (in hunt); outrider; scout.
batedouro [bă-tĕ-doh'roo] *m.* washing place (at riverside).

bate-estacas [ba-tĕsh-ta'-kăsh] *f.* pile-driver.
bate-folha [ba-tĕ-foh'lyă] *m.* tinker, tinsmith; gold-beater (*archaic*).
bátega [ba'tĕ-gă] *f.* heavy shower.
bater [bă-tayr'] *va.* to beat, strike, hit; to defeat; to knock at (door); to coin (money); — **as palmas**, to clap; — **os pés**, to stamp (one's feet); — **trigo**, to thresh (corn); *vr.* to fight.
bateria [bă-tĕ-ree'ă] *f.* battery; — **de cozinha**, kitchen utensils.
batida [bă-tee'dă] *f.* shooting party; drive, battue; reprimand; **de** —, hastily.
batido [bă-tee'doo] *adj.* beaten; commonplace, trite.
batina [bă-tee'nă] *f.* cassock (*eccl.*); gown (undergraduates, students).
batoque [bă-tok'] *m.* bung, stopper; bung-hole.
batota [bă-to'tă] *f.* fraud, trick.
batuta [bă-too'tă] *f.* baton.
baú [bă-oo'] *m.* trunk.
baunilha [bow-nee'lyă] *f.* vanilla.
bazófia [bă-zo'fee-ă] *f.* swagger, swank; boasting.
beata [bee-ah'tă] *f.* excessively (ridiculously) devout woman; hypocrite; bigot; *adj.* blessed.
beatice [bee-ă-tees'] *f.* bigotry; hypocrisy.
beatificar [bee-ă-tee-fee-kar'] *va.* to beatify.
beatitude [bee-ă-tee-tood'] *f.* blessedness, holiness.
beato [bee-ah'too] *adj.* blessed; happy; hypocritical.
bebedeira [bĕ-bĕ-day'ee-ră] *f.* drunken spree, binge; drunkenness.
bebedice [bĕ-bĕ-dees'] *f.* drunkenness.
bêbedo [bay'bĕ-doo] *adj.* drunk, intoxicated; *m.* drunkard.
bebedoiro [bĕ-bĕ-doh'ee-roo] *m.* water-trough.
beber [bĕ-bayr'] *va*/*vn.* to drink; to swallow; to imbibe.
bebida [bĕ-bee'dă] *f.* drink.
beca [be'kă] *f.* robes, gown.
beco [bay'koo] *m.* alley, lane; — **sem saída**, blind alley, cul-de-sac.
bedelho [bĕ-day'lyoo] *m.* latch.
beiço [bay'ee-soo] *m.* lip; **fazer** —, *or* **beicinho**, to pout.
beiçudo [bay-ee-soo'doo] *adj.* thick-lipped, blubber-lipped.
beijar [bay-ee-zhar'] *va.* to kiss.
beijo [bay'ee-zhoo] *m.* kiss.
beira [bay'ee-ră] *f.* edge, brink, margin; —**s do telhado**, eaves; **à** — **de**, at the side of, beside; on the verge of.
beira-mar [bay'ee-ră mar] *f.* seaside, seashore; **à** —, by the sea; at the seaside.
beleza [bĕ-lay'ză] *f.* beauty, loveliness.
belga [bel'gă] *m*/*adj.* Belgian.
beliche [bĕ-leesh'] *m.* berth; bunk.
belicoso [bĕ-lee-koh'zoo] *adj.* warlike, pugnacious.
beligerante [bĕ-lee-zhĕ-ra*n*t'] *m*/*adj.* belligerent.
beliscar [bĕ-leesh-kar'] *va.* to pinch, nip.
belo [be'loo] *adj.* beautiful, lovely, handsome, fair, fine.
bem [be*n*] *adv.* well; right; very; **ainda** —, very good, excellent; — **que**, although; *m.* good; darling, loved one; **levar a** —, to approve, take in good part; **haver por** —, to see fit to, decree.
bem-aventurança [be*n*-ă-ve*n*-too-ra*n*'să] *f.* blessedness, bliss; *pl.* the Beatitudes.

bem-estar [be*n*-ish-tar'] *m.* comfort; well-being.
bem-me-quer [be*n*-mĕ-kair'] *m.* daisy.
bem-vindo [be*n*-vee*n*'doo] *adj.* welcome.
bem-visto [be*n*-veesh'too] *adj.* well thought of, highly esteemed.
bênção [be*n*'sow*n*] *f.* blessing.
bendito [be*n*-dee'too] *adj.* blessed.
beneficência [bĕ-nĕ-fee-se*n*'-see-ă] *f.* beneficence, kindness, charity.
beneficiar [bĕ-nĕ-fee-see-ar'] *va.* to benefit; to improve; to cultivate (fields); (*naut.*) to overhaul (gear, etc.); to process, clean, prepare (rice, coffee, etc.).
benefício [bĕ-nĕ-fee'see-oo] *m.* benefit; profit; favour, kindness; (*eccl.*) living, benefice.
benéfico [bĕ-ne'fee-koo] *adj.* kind, charitable; beneficial.
benemérito [bĕ-nĕ-me'ree-too] *adj.* worthy, distinguished; *m.* benefactor, worthy servant (of country, humanity, etc.).
beneplácito [bĕ-nĕ-pla'see-too] *m.* consent, approval.
benevolência [bĕ-nĕ-voo-le*n*'-see-ă] *f.* benevolence, good-will.
benévolo [bĕ-ne'voo-loo] *adj.* kind-hearted, benevolent.
benignidade [bĕ-neeg-nee-dahd'] *f.* kindness, benignity.
benigno [bĕ-neeg'noo] *adj.* benign, kind, gentle; pleasant (climate); mild (weather).
benquisto [be*n*-keesh'too] *adj.* well-loved, well-liked.
bens [be*n*sh] *m.pl.* property, possessions, estate; **— de raiz,** real estate.
bento [be*n*'too] *adj.* holy.
benzer [be*n*-zayr'] *va.* to bless.
berço [bayr'soo] *m.* cradle; birthplace; source.
berrar [bĕ-rar'] *vn.* to bellow; to roar.
besta [baysh'tă] *f.* beast; fool, ass, stupid person; **— de carga,** beast of burden.
bestialidade [bĕsh-tee-ă-lee-dahd'] *f.* bestiality, brutality; stupidity.
besuntar [bĕ-zoo*n*-tar'] *va.* to smear.
beterraba [bĕ-tĕ-rah'bă] *f.* beetroot; **açucar de —,** beet sugar.
betume [bĕ-toom'] *m.* bitumen.
bexiga [bĕ-shee'gă] *f.* bladder; *pl.* small-pox; pock-marks (on skin); **—s doidas,** chicken-pox.
bezerro [bĕ-zay'roo] *m.* (yearling) calf; tanned calf-skin.
bibe [beeb] *m.* (child's) pinafore.
biberão [bee-bĕ-row*n*'] *m.* (baby's) feeding-bottle.
bíblia [bee'blee-ă] *f.* Bible.
bíblico [bee'blee-koo] *adj.* biblical.
bibliófilo [bee-blee-o'fee-loo] *m.* book-lover, bibliophile.
bibliografia [bee-blee-oo-gră-fee'ă] *f.* bibliography.
biblioteca [bee-blee-oo-te'kă] *f.* library.
bibliotecário [bee-blee-oo-tĕ-kah'ree-oo] *m.* librarian.
bica [bee'kă] *f.* jet, spout; **estar à —,** to be on the point of, due for.
bicar [bee-kar'] *va.* to peck.
bicha [bee'shă] *f.* worm; leech; snake; queue (of people); bad-tempered woman.
bicho [bee'shoo] *m.* worm, grub; insect; animal; ugly or awkward person; **matar o —,** to wet one's whistle; *pl.* vermin; **ter —s carpinteiros,** to be fidgety.
bicicleta [bee-see-kle'tă] *f.* bicycle.
bico [bee'koo] *m.* beak; (gas) jet; (pen) nib; (needle) point; **— de obra,** difficult task; **calar**

o —, to shut up; andar nos —s dos pés, to tip-toe.
bidé [bee-de'] *m.* bidet; sitz-bath.
biela [bee-e'lă] *f.* piston rod.
biénio [bee-e'nee-oo] *m.* two-year period.
bife [beef] *m.* (beef)steak.
bifurcação [bee-foor-kă-sow*n*'] *f.* division; branching (off); fork (of roads).
bigode [bee-god'] *m.* moustache.
bigorna [bee-gor'nă] *f.* anvil.
bilha [bee'lyă] *f.* jug, jar, pot.
bilhar [bee-lyar'] *m.* billiards; billiard table; billiard hall.
bilhete [bee-lyayt'] *m.* ticket; note; — **de ida**, single ticket; — **de ida e volta**, return ticket; — **postal**, postcard; — **de visita**, visiting-card.
bilheteira [bee-lyĕ-tay'ee-ră] *f.* booking-office, ticket-office; box-office (*theat.*).
bilingue [bee-leeng'] *adj.* bilingual.
bilioso [bee-lee-oh'zoo] *adj.* bilious, liverish.
bílis [bee'leesh] *m.* bile; bad temper.
bilro [beel'roo] *m.* bobbin.
bimensal [bee-me*n*-sal'] *adj.* twice monthly, fortnightly.
binóculo [bee-no'koo-loo] *m.* binoculars; field-glasses; opera-glasses.
biografia [bee-oo-gră-fee'ă] *f.* biography.
biógrafo [bee-o'gră-foo] *m.* biographer.
biólogo [bee-o'loo-goo] *m.* biologist. [screen.
biombo [bee-o*n*'boo] *m.*
biqueira [bee-kay'ee-ră] *f.* toe (of shoe); drainpipe.
birra [bee'ra] *f.* obstinacy, stubbornness; antipathy; **ter — com**, to dislike, detest.
bis [beesh] *interj.* encore!
bisavô [bee-ză-voh'] *m.* great-grandfather.
bisavó [bee-ză-vo'] *f.* great-grandmother.
bisbilhotice [beezh-bee-lyoo-tees'] *f.* gossip, tittle-tattle.
biscoito [beesh-koh'ee-too] *m.* biscuit; bun. [tube.
bisnaga [beezh-nah'gă] *f.*
bisonho [bee-zoh'nyoo] *adj.* inexperienced; *m.* raw recruit.
bispado [beesh-pah'doo] *m.* bishopric.
bispo [beesh'poo] *m.* bishop.
bissexto [bee-sesh'too] *adj.* **ano —**, leap-year.
bisturi [beesh-too-ree'] *m.* scalpel.
bitola [bee-to'lă] *f.* gauge, standard; model.
bivaque [bee-vak'] *m.* bivouac.
bizarria [bee-ză-ree'ă] *f.* gallantry, dash; elegance, gracefulness; pomp.
bizarro [bee-za'roo] *adj.* brave, gallant, dashing; generous; handsome, elegant.
blandícias [bla*n*-dee'see-ăsh] *f.pl.* endearments; caresses.
blasfemar [blăsh-fĕ-mar'] *vn/va.* to blaspheme; to curse.
blasfémia [blăsh-fe'mee-ă] *f.* blasphemy; curse.
blasonar [blă-zoo-nar'] *va/vn.* to boast.
blindado [blee*n*-dah'doo] *adj.* armoured (cars, tanks, etc.).
blindagem [blee*n*-dah'zhe*n*] *f.* armour-plate.
bloco [bloh'koo] *m.* block; (*polit.*) bloc.
bloquear [bloo-kee-ar'] *va.* to blockade.
bloqueio [bloo-kay'yoo] *m.* blockade.
blusa [bloo'ză] *f.* smock; (woman's) blouse.
boa [boh'ă] *adj.* good; **é —**, amazing!, really!; **metido em —s**, to be in a tight spot; **vir**

às —s, to see sense, come round.
boa [boh'ă] *f.* boa constrictor.
boas-vindas [boh'ăzh veen'-dăsh] *f.pl.* welcome; dar as —, to welcome.
boato [boo-ah'too] *m.* rumour.
bobice [boo-bees'] *f.* foolery.
bobina [boo-bee'nă] *f.* bobbin; coil; spool (*photo.*).
bobo [boh'boo] *m.* fool, clown, jester.
boca [boh'kă] *f.* mouth; entrance; opening, hole; **céu da —**, roof of mouth, palate; **à — cheia**, openly, frankly; **— do estômago**, pit (of stomach).
bocado [boo-kah'doo] *m.* morsel, piece, mouthful; short while, short time.
bocal [boo-kal'] *m.* mouth (of jug, etc.); (*mus.*) mouth-piece.
boçal [boo-sal'] *adj.* stupid; boorish; brutish.
bocejar [boo-sĕ-zhar'] *vn.* to yawn.
bochecha [boo-she'shă] *f.* cheek.
boda [boh'dă] *f.* wedding breakfast; wedding reception; wedding; *pl.* wedding anniversary; **— de ouro**, golden wedding.
bode [bod] *m.* goat; **— expiatório**, scapegoat.
bodega [boo-de'ga] *f.* low-grade wine-shop, 'dive'; coarse, disgusting food.
boémio [boo-e'mee-oo] *m.* Bohemian; vagrant.
bofar [boo-far'] *va.* to spew out, vomit; *vn.* to gush out.
bofes [bofsh] *m.pl.* lungs (*pop.*).
bofetada [boo-fĕ-tah'dă] *f.* slap in the face; insult.
boi [boh'ee] *m.* ox; (*pop.*) **pé de —**, die-hard, conservative; **olho de —**, skylight.
bóia [boy'ă] *f.* buoy; **— de salvação**, life-buoy.
boião [boo-yown'] *m.* pot, jar.
boiar [boh-yar'] *vn.* to float; (*fig.*) to hesitate.
boieiro [boh-yay'ee-roo] *m.* herdsman; drover.
bóina [boy'nă] *f.* beret.
bojar [boo-zhar'] *vn.* to bulge, swell out, jut out.
bojo [boh'zhoo] *m.* bulge, protuberance, swelling.
bojudo [boo-zhoo'doo] *adj.* pot-bellied, swollen.
bola [bo'lă] *f.* ball; **— de sabão**, soap-bubble.
bolacha [boo-lah'shă] *f.* biscuit; slap (*pop.*).
bolas [bo'lăsh] *interj.* rubbish! nonsense!; *m.* booby, sap (*sl.*).
bolbo [bohl'boo] *m.* bulb.
boleia [boo-le'yă] *f.* driver's seat; **dar uma —**, to give a lift.
boletim [boo-lĕ-teen'] *m.* bulletin; report; official gazette.
bolha [boh'lyă] *f.* blister; bubble; **ter —**, (*sl.*) to be dotty, cracked.
bolo [boh'loo] *m.* cake; stake (gambling).
bolor [boo-lohr'] *m.* mould; mustiness.
bolota [boo-lo'tă] *f.* acorn.
bolsa [bohl'să] *f.* purse; pouch; stock exchange; scholarship, grant.
bolseiro [bohl-say'ee-roo] *m.* scholarship-holder, scholar.
bom [bon] *adj.* good; fine; healthy, sound; suitable; **de — tom**, fashionable; **ano —**, New Year.
bomba [bon'bă] *f.* pump; bomb, shell; **— de incêndio**, fire-engine.
bombardeamento [bon-băr-dee-ă-men'too] *m.* bombardment, bombing.
bombardear [bon-băr-dee-ar'] *va.* to bombard, bomb, shell.

bombeiro [bo*n*-bay'ee-roo] *m.* fireman.
bombom [bo*n*'bo*n*] *m.* chocolate (sweet).
bombordo [bo*n*-bor'doo] *m.* port, portside.
bonacheirão [boo-nă-shay-ee-rown'] *adj.* kindly, good-natured.
bonança [boo-na*n*'să] *f.* fair, calm weather (at sea); (*fig.*) tranquillity, good fortune.
bondade [bo*n*-dahd'] *f.* goodness, kindness.
bonde [bo*n*'dě] *m.* (*Braz.*) tram.
bondoso [bo*n*-doh'zoo] *adj.* kind-hearted, helpful.
boné [bo-ne'] *m.* cap.
boneca [boo-ne'kă] *f.* doll.
bonina [boo-nee'nă] *f.* daisy.
bonito [boo-nee'too] *adj.* pretty, nice; fine; *m.* striped tunny.
bónus [bo'noosh] *m.* bonus; special allowance; reduced rate.
boquiaberto [boh-kee-ă-bair'too] *adj.* open-mouthed, gaping.
boquilha [boo-kee'lyă] *f.* cigarette-holder.
borboleta [boor-boo-lay'tă] *f.* butterfly.
borbotar [boor-boo-tar'] *vn.* to gush out; to bubble.
borbulha [boor-boo'lyă] *f.* blister; bubble (on boiling liquid).
borbulhar [boor-boo-lyar'] *vn.* to gush out, flow out; to bubble (when boiling).
borco [bohr'koo] *m.* de —, upside down (of glass, jug, etc.), face down (of persons).
borda [bor'dă] *f.* edge; rim; bank (of river); pela — fora, overboard; à —, alongside.
bordado [boor-dah'doo] *m.* embroidery.
bordão [boor-dow*n*'] *m.* staff; (*fig.*) support; bass-string (*mus.*).
bordar [boor-dar'] *va.* to embroider.
bordejar [boor-dě-zhar'] *vn.* to tack (*naut.*); to stagger.
bordo [bor'doo] *m.* side of ship; tack, course (*naut.*); a —, on board.
boreal [boo-ree-al'] *adj.* northern, north.
borla [bor'lă] *f.* tassel; (*acad.*) doctor's cap; de —, free, for nothing.
borra [boh'ră] *f.* dregs, lees.
borracha [boo-rah'shă] *f.* rubber.
borracho [boo-rah'shoo] *adj.* drunk; *m.* drunkard; young pigeon.
borrador [boo-ră-dohr'] *m.* scribbling pad, rough note-book; bungler, scribbler; day book (*com.*).
borralho [boo-ra'lyoo] *m.* embers; (*fig.*) fireside, hearth.
borrão [boo-rown'] *m.* blot; rough draft, sketch; day book (*com.*).
borrar [boo-rar'] *va.* to smudge; to cross out, erase.
borrasca [boo-rash'kă] *f.* squall, tempest.
borrascoso [boo-răsh-koh'-zoo] *adj.* squally.
borrego [boo-ray'goo] *m.* yearling lamb.
borrifar [boo-ree-far'] *va.* to sprinkle; to spray; to damp (clothes before ironing).
borrifo [boo-ree'foo] *m.* sprinkle, sprinkling; spray; drizzle (rain).
bosque [boshk] *m.* wood, forest.
bosquejar [boosh-kě-zhar'] *va.* to sketch.
bosquejo [boosh-kay'zhoo] *m.* sketch, outline.
bossa [bo'să] *f.* swelling; bump (on head); lump; hump (on

human or camel); ter — para, to have an aptitude for.

bota [bo'tă] *f.* boot.

bota-fora [bo'tă fo'ră] *f.* launching (of ship); send-off (of person).

botânica [boo-tă'nee-kă] *f.* botany.

botânico [boo-tă'nee-koo] *m.* botanist; *adj.* botanical.

botão [boo-tow*n*'] *m.* button; bud; handle, knob (of doors, drawers, etc.); — **de punho**, cuff-link; **casa de —**, button-hole.

botar [boo-tar'] *va.* to put, place; to throw; to blunt.

botaréu [boo-tă-re'oo] *m.* buttress.

bote [bot] *m.* boat; (sword) thrust; **de um —**, at one swoop.

botequim [boo-tĕ-kee*n*'] *m.* bar; café.

botica [boo-tee'kă] *f.* chemist's (shop), dispensary.

botija [boo-tee'zhă] *f.* (stone) bottle, jug.

boto [boh'too] *adj.* blunt, blunted; obtuse; set on edge (teeth).

boxe [boks] *m.* boxing.

braça [brah'să] *f.* fathom.

braçada [bră-sah'dă] *f.* armful.

braço [brah'soo] *m.* arm; *pl.* workmen, hands; **de — dado**, arm-in-arm; **de —s cruzados**, with folded arms; **estar a —s com**, to struggle with; **ser o — direito de**, to be the right hand man of.

braçudo [bră-soo'doo] *adj.* strong, brawny.

bradar [bră-dar'] *vn.* to cry, yell, bawl.

brado [brah'doo] *m.* shout.

braga [brah'gă] *f.* shackle, fetter; *pl.* breeches.

bragal [bră-gal'] *m.* (household) linen.

bramido [bră-mee'doo] *m.* roar, howl, bellow.

bramir [bră-meer'] *vn.* to roar, bellow, howl.

branco [bra*n*'koo] *adj.* white; *m.* white; white man; blank, gap; **em —**, blank; **ficar em —**, to fail to understand.

brancura [bra*n*-koo'ră] *f.* whiteness.

brandir [bra*n*-deer'] *va.* to brandish.

brando [bra*n*'doo] *adj.* soft; gentle, mild.

brandura [bra*n*-doo'ră] *f.* softness, gentleness, mildness.

branquear [bra*n*-kee-ar'] *va.* to whiten; to bleach (cloth).

brasa [brah'ză] *f.* live coal; **estar sobre —s**, to be on tenterhooks.

brasão [bră-zow*n*'] *m.* coat of arms; heraldry.

braseiro [bră-zay'ee-roo] *m.* brazier.

brasileiro [bră-zee-lay'ee-roo] *m/adj.* Brazilian.

bravata [bră-vah'tă] *f.* bravado; boasting.

braveza [bră-vay'ză] *f.* ferocity, savagery, fury.

bravio [bră-vee'oo] *adj.* wild, savage, untamed.

bravo [brah'voo] *adj.* courageous, hardy; fine, splendid; wild, savage; *interj.* hurray!, bravo!

bravura [bră-voo'ră] *f.* courage, bravery.

breca [bre'kă] *f.* cramp; *interj.* **com a —**, damn it!

brecha [bre'shă] *f.* breach.

brejeiro [brĕ-zhay'ee-roo] *m.* scoundrel, rogue; *adj.* naughty, mischievous.

brejo [bre'zhoo] *m.* marsh, swamp.

brenha [brĕ'nyă] *f.* thick (dense) wood.

breu [bray'oo] *m.* tar, pitch.

breve [brev] *adj.* short, brief, concise; **até —**, see you (again)

soon; em —, soon, shortly; *m.* Papal brief.
breviário [brĕ-vee-ah'ree-oo] *m.* breviary.
brevidade [brĕ-vee-dahd'] *f.* brevity, conciseness; speed.
briga [bree'gă] *f.* fight, quarrel.
brigada [bree-gah'dă] *f.* brigade.
brilhante [bree-lya*n*t'] *adj.* brilliant, bright; *m.* diamond.
brilhar [bree-lyar'] *vn.* to shine.
brilho [bree'lyoo] *m.* brightness, brilliance, splendour.
brincadeira [bree*n*-kă-day'-ee-ră] *f.* joke, jest, fun; playing about.
brincar [bree*n*-kar'] *vn.* to play; to joke; to romp, skip.
brinco [bree*n*'koo] *m.* ear-ring; toy; joke; elegant person (or thing).
brindar [bree*n*-dar'] *vn.* to toast, drink a toast to, drink the health of; *va.* to proffer (a gift).
brinde [bree*n*d] *m.* toast; present, gift.
brinquedo [bree*n*-kay'doo] *m.* toy, plaything.
brio [bree'oo] *m.* honour, pride; valour; spirit.
brioso [bree-oh'zoo] *adj.* noble; generous; spirited.
brisa [bree'ză] *f.* breeze.
brita [bree'tă] *f.* crushed stone, road metal.
broa [broh'ă] *f.* maize bread.
broca [bro'kă] *f.* drill.
brocar [broo-kar'] *va.* to drill, bore.
brocha [bro'shă] *f.* tack; axle-pin.
brochado [broo-shah'doo] *adj.* paper-backed (book).
broche [brosh] *m.* brooch; clasp.
brochura [broo-shoo'ră] *f.* brochure, pamphlet; book-binding.
bronco [bro*n*'koo] *adj.* stupid; rough.
bronquite [bro*n*-keet'] *f.* bronchitis.
bronze [bro*n*z] *m.* bronze.
bronzeado [bro*n*-zee-ah'doo] *adj.* bronzed; tanned (by sun).
brossa [bro'să] *f.* hard brush; (printer's) brush; horse brush.
brotar [broo-tar'] *vn.* to bud, sprout; to spring (from); *va.* to produce, put out.
broxa [bro'shă] *f.* (large) brush (for painting, white-washing).
bruços [broo'soosh] *adv.* **de —**, face down(wards), flat on one's face.
bruma [broo'mă] *f.* mist; haze.
brumoso [broo-moh'zoo] *adj.* misty; hazy; foggy.
brunir [broo-neer'] *va.* to polish.
brusco [broosh'koo] *adj.* brusque; rough; sudden.
brutal [broo-tal'] *adj.* brutal.
brutalidade [broo-tă-lee-dahd'] *f.* brutality, savagery.
bruto [broo'too] *m.* brute; ignorant person; *adj.* brutish; unpolished; crude; **peso —**, gross weight; **força —a**, brute force; **em —**, raw; unfinished.
bruxa [broo'shă] *f.* witch; hag.
bruxaria [broo-shă-ree'ă] *f.* witchcraft.
bruxo [broo'shoo] *m.* magician, wizard.
bruxulear [broo-shoo-lee-ar'] *vn.* to flicker.
bubão [boo-bow*n*'] *m.* swollen gland.
bucha [boo'shă] *f.* wad, plug; mouthful.
bucho [boo'shoo] *m.* belly.
buço [boo'soo] *m.* soft hair, down (on upper lip).
bufar [boo-far'] *vn.* to puff, pant; to snort (with anger).
bufete [boo-fayt'] *m.* sideboard; buffet; refreshment room.
bugalho [boo-ga'lyoo] *m.* oak-

apple; misturar alhos com —s, to mix things up.
bugigangas [boo-zhee-*gan*'-găsh] *f.* trinkets, knick-knacks.
bugio [boo-zhee'oo] *m.* howler monkey; ape.
bula [boo'lă] *f.* papal bull.
bule [bool] *m.* tea-pot.
bulha [boo'lyă] *f.* row, noise; quarrel.
bulício [boo-lee'see-oo] *m.* noise; bustle, restlessness.
buliçoso [boo-lee-soh'zoo] *adj.* lively; restless.
bulir [boo-leer'] *vn.* to stir, move; *va.* to touch.
buraco [boo-rah'koo] *m.* hole.
burguês [boor-gaysh'] *adj.* middle-class; bourgeois; *m.* member of the middle class; burgess.
burguesia [boor-gĕ-zee'ă] *f.* middle class.
buril [boo-reel'] *m.* chisel.
burla [boor'lă] *f.* trick, fraud.
burlar [boor-lar'] *va.* to cheat, swindle, hoax.
burlesco [boor-laysh'koo] *adj.* burlesque.
burocracia [boo-ro-kră-see'ă] *f.* bureaucracy.
burocrata [boo-ro-krah'tă] *m.* bureaucrat.
burro [boo'roo] *m.* donkey, ass; blockhead, dolt; crib (translation).
busca [boosh'kă] *f.* search.
buscar [boosh-kar'] *va.* look for, seek, search; ir —, to fetch, go for; mandar —, to send for.
busílis [boo-zee'leesh] *m.* difficulty, knotty point.
bússola [boo'soo-lă] *f.* compass.
busto [boosh'too] *m.* bust.
buzina [boo-zee'nă] *f.* horn (of car); hunting-horn; fog-horn; megaphone.
búzio [boo'zee-oo] *m.* diver; trumpet, horn; conch.

C

cá [kah] *adv.* here.
cabaça [kă-bah'să] *f.* gourd.
cabal [kă-bal'] *adj.* complete, perfect. [intrigue.
cabala [kă-bah'lă] *f.* clique;
cabana [kă-bă'nă] *f.* hut; cottage; hovel.
cabaz [kă-bash'] *m.* basket.
cabeça [kă-bay'să] *f.* head; intelligence, common-sense; top, upper part; *m.* head, chief.
cabeçada [kă-bĕ-sah'dă] *f.* butt with the head; dar uma —, to bang one's head; to make a bad blunder.
cabeçalho [kă-bĕ-sa'lyoo] *m.* headline (in newspaper); title, heading; pole, shaft (of cart).
cabecear [kă-bĕ-see-ar'] *vn.* to nod.
cabeceira [kă-bĕ-say'ee-ră] *f.* head, top (of bed, table); pillow; headstone (on grave); à — de, at the bedside of.
cabeçudo [kă-bĕ-soo'doo] *adj.* obstinate, pig-headed; having a big head.
cabedal [kă-bĕ-dal'] *m.* (shoe) leather; *pl.* resources, wealth.
cabeleira [kă-bĕ-lay'ee-ră] *f.* head of hair; wig; tail (of comet).
cabeleireiro [kă-bĕ-lay-ray'-ee-roo] *m.* hairdresser.
cabelo [kă-bay'loo] *m.* hair; em —, bareheaded.
caber [kă-bayr'] *vn.* to be containable in, have room for, fit in; to be fitting, befit; to fall to one's lot; não — em si de contente, to be overjoyed.
cabide [kă-beed'] *m.* coat-hanger; hatstand, hat-rack.
cabimento [kă-bee-men'too] *m.* acceptance; ter —, to be acceptable; to be opportune.
cabina [kă-bee'na] *f.* cabin.

cabisbaixo [kă-beezh-bȳ'-shoo] *adj.* downcast, crestfallen.
cabo [kah'boo] *m.* cape; end, limit; handle; commander, chief; corporal (*mil.*); cable; rope, line; — **de salvação,** lifeline; **dar — de,** to put an end to; **levar a —,** to finish, complete; **ao — de,** at the end of.
cabotagem [kă-boo-tah'zhen] *f.* coasting trade; coastwise traffic.
cabouco [kă-boh'koo] *m.* ditch, trench; foundation (for building).
cabouqueiro [kă-boh-kay'ee-roo] *m.* navvy, labourer; quarryman.
cabra [ka'bră] *f.* goat; — **cega,** blind-man's-buff.
cabreiro [kă-bray'ee-roo] *m.* goatherd. [*m.* capstan.
cabrestante [kă-brĕsh-tant']
cabriola [kă-bree-o'lă] *f.* caper, leap.
cabrito [kă-bree'too] *m.* kid.
cábula [ka'boo-lă] *m.* idler, slacker, truant (*acad.*); *f.* truancy; dodge (to avoid work); *adj.* wily.
caça [kah'să] *f.* hunting, hunt; game; **partida de —,** hunting party; — **grossa,** big game; — **miúda,** small game.
caçador [kă-să-dohr'] *m.* huntsman; rifleman (*mil.*); *pl.* light infantry.
caça-minas [ka'să mee'năsh] *m.* mine-sweeper.
caçar [kă-sar'] *va.* to hunt, chase, pursue; to catch.
cacarejar [kă-kă-rĕ-zhar'] *vn.* to cackle, cluck.
caçarola [kă-să-ro'lă] *f.* casserole dish; saucepan.
cacatua [kă-kă-too'ă] *f.* cockatoo.
cacau [kă-kow'] *m.* cocoa-bean; cacao-tree.
cacete [kă-sayt'] *m.* club, stick; (*Braz.*) bore, nuisance.
cachaça [kă-sha'să] *f.* rum; (*sl.*) fire-water.
cachaço [kă-sha'soo] *m.* nape of the neck. [pipe.
cachimbo [kă-sheen'boo] *m.*
cacho [ka'shoo] *m.* bunch.
cachoeira [kă-shoo-ay'ee-ră] *f.* waterfall; rapids.
cachopa [kă-sho'pă] *f.* girl, lass. [reef.
cachopo [kă-shoh'poo] *m.* lad;
cachorra [kă-shoh'ră] *f.* (young) bitch.
cachorro [kă-shoh'roo] *m.* pup, puppy; cub (of wolf, etc.); prop.
cacimba [kă-seen'bă] *f.* mist, drizzle; water hole.
cacique [kă-seek'] *m.* political boss; Indian chief.
caco [kah'koo] *m.* bit (of broken pottery, glass, etc.).
caçoar [kă-soo-ar'] *va.* to make fun of, tease.
caçoila [kă-soh'ee-lă] *f.* pan; dish.
cacto [kak'too] *m.* cactus.
cada [kă'dă] *adj.* each; every.
cadafalso [kă-dă-fal'soo] *m.* gallows, scaffold.
cadastro [kă-dash'troo] *m.* register of property; census; criminal record.
cadáver [kă-da'vair] *m.* corpse.
cadeado [kă-dee-ah'doo] *m.* padlock. [prison.
cadeia [kă-day'yă] *f.* chain;
cadeira [kă-day'ee-ră] *f.* chair.
cadela [kă-de'lă] *f.* bitch.
cadência [kă-dayn'see-ă] *f.* cadence, rhythm.
caderneta [kă-dĕr-nay'tă] *f.* register (in school); pass-book (bank).
caderno [kă-dair'noo] *m.* note-book; exercise-book.
cadete [kă-dayt'] *m.* cadet.

cadinho [kă-dee'nyoo] *m.* crucible, melting-pot.
caduco [kă-doo'koo] *adj.* decrepit; broken-down; invalid (*leg.*).
café [kă-fe'] *m.* coffee; café.
cafeeiro [kă-fee-ay'ee-roo] *m.* coffee tree.
cafeteira [kă-fĕ-tay'ee-ră] *f.* coffee-pot.
cafèzal [kă-fe-zal'] *m.* coffee-plantation.
cáfila [ka'fee-lă] *m.* gang; caravan.
cafre [ka'frĕ] *m.* savage; [Kaffir.
cágado [ka'gă-doo] *m.* tortoise, turtle; (*pop.*) 'smartie' (person).
caiar [kă-yar'] *va.* to white- [wash.
cãibra [kȳn'-bră] *f.* cramp.
caídos [kă-ee'doosh] *m.pl.* arrears, dues; leavings, scraps.
caimão [kȳ-mown'] *m.* alligator.
cair [kă-eer'] *vn.* to fall; to happen, befall; — **bem,** to suit, go with; — **na conta,** to comprehend; — **em graça,** to please, find favour with.
cais [kȳsh] *m.* quay, quayside.
caixa [kȳ'shă] *f.* box, case, chest; safe; *m.* cashier; — **económica,** savings bank; **livro —,** cash-book; — **do correio,** post-box, pillar box; **pagar na —,** to pay at the desk.
caixão [kȳ-shown'] *m.* coffin; large box.
caixeiro [kȳ-shay'ee-roo] *m.* shop-assistant; clerk; cashier; — **viajante,** commercial traveller.
caixilho [kȳ-shee'lyoo] *m.* [frame.
caixote [kȳ-shot'] *m.* case, box; — **do lixo,** dust-bin.
cajado [kă-zhah'doo] *m.* (shepherd's) crook, staff.
cal [kal] *f.* lime; whitewash; — **viva,** quicklime; **forno de —,** lime-kiln.
calabouço [kă-lă-boh'soo] *m.* dungeon; jail.
calado [kă-lah'doo] *adj.* silent, quiet; discreet; *m.* draught (*naut.*).
calafetar [kă-lă-fĕ-tar'] *va.* to caulk.
calafrio [kă-lă-free'oo] *m.* chill; shiver, shivering.
calamidade [kă-lă-mee-dahd'] *f.* calamity, disaster.
calamitoso [kă-lă-mee-toh'-zoo] *adj.* calamitous, disastrous.
calandra [kă-lan'dră] *f.* mangle; roller; lark (*orni.*).
calão [kă-lown'] *m.* slang.
calar [kă-lar'] *vn/vr.* to be silent, keep quiet; fall silent; *va.* to silence; to conceal; to cut off (slice of fruit, etc. for sampling).
calçada [kal-sah'dă] *f.* roadway, street; pavement (*Braz.*).
calçadeira [kal-să-day'ee-ră] *f.* shoe-horn.
calçado [kal-sah'doo] *m.* footwear; *adj.* shod; paved.
calcanhar [kal-kă-nyar'] *m.* heel; **dar aos —es,** to take to one's heels.
calcar [kal-kar'] *va.* to tread, trample on; to crush.
calçar [kal-sar'] *va.* to put on (shoes, stockings, gloves, etc.); to pave.
calças [kal'săsh] *f.pl.* trousers; **ver-se em — pardas,** to be in a tight spot.
calcetar [kal-sĕ-tar'] *va.* to pave.
cálcio [kal'see-oo] *m.* calcium.
calço [kal'soo] *m.* or **calce,** *m.* wedge.
calcular [kal-koo-lar'] *va/vn.* to calculate; to make calculations; to estimate, reckon.
cálculo [kal'koo-loo] *m.* estimate; calculation; calculus (*maths.*); stone (*med.*).

calda [kal'dă] *f.* syrup; jelly; *pl.* hot springs.
caldear [kal-dee-ar'] *va.* to weld; to fuse; to smelt.
caldeira [kal-day'ee-ră] *f.* boiler; cauldron.
caldeirada [kal-day-ee-rah'-dă] *f.* fish-stew.
caldeiro [kal-day'ee-roo] *m.* bucket; pan.
caldo [kal'doo] *m.* soup, broth; — verde, cabbage soup.
caleira [kă-lay'ee-ră] *f.* gutter.
calejado [kă-lĕ-zhah'doo] *adj.* hardened, horny.
calendário [kă-le*n*-dah'ree-oo] *m.* calendar.
calha [ka'lyă] *f.* gutter; channel.
calhar [kă-lyar'] *vn.* to happen; to suit; to be fitting; **se —**, probably.
calhau [kă-lyow'] *m.* flint; pebble, stone.
calibrar [kă-lee-brar'] *va.* to gauge; to measure the calibre of.
calibre [kă-lee'brĕ] *m.* calibre; gauge; (*fig.*) quality.
cálice [ka'lees] *m.* chalice; (wine) glass.
caligrafia [kă-lee-gră-fee'ă] *f.* handwriting, calligraphy.
calma [kal'mă] *f.* heat, sultriness; calm; **em —**, becalmed.
calmante [kal-ma*n*t'] *m/adj.* sedative.
calmo [kal'moo] *adj.* calm.
calmoso [kal-moh'zoo] *adj.* sultry, hot.
calo [kah'loo] *m.* corn.
caloiro [kă-loh'ee-roo] *m.* fresher, freshman (*acad.*).
calor [kă-lohr'] *m.* heat; warmth; (*fig.*) ardour, zeal.
caloria [kă-loo-ree'ă] *f.* calorie.
calorífero [kă-loo-ree'fĕ-roo] *m.* heater; stove.
caloroso [kă-loo-roh'zoo] *adj.* warm; fervent, eager.
calotear [kă-loo-tee-ar'] *va.* to swindle, cheat.
caluda [kă-loo'dă] *interj.* quiet!
calúnia [kă-loo'nee-ă] *f.* slander, calumny.
caluniador [kă-loo-nee-ă-dohr'] *m.* slanderer.
calunioso [kă-loo-nee-oh'zoo] *adj.* slanderous.
calva [kal'vă] *f.* bald patch baldness.
calvário [kal-vah'ree-oo] *m.* Calvary; (*fig.*) suffering, trials.
calvície [kal-vee'see-ĕ] *f.* baldness.
calvo [kal'voo] *adj.* bald, bald-headed; hairless; bare.
cama [kă'mă] *f.* bed; **— de casal**, double bed; **estar de —**, to stay in bed (through illness).
camada [kă-mah'dă] *f.* layer, stratum; coat (of paint); **— social**, social group, class.
camaleão [kă-mă-lee-ow*n*'] *m.* chameleon.
câmara [kă'mă-ră] *f.* room; chamber; **— municipal**, town (*or* city) hall; **— de comércio**, chamber of commerce; **— dos Comuns**, House of Commons; **— ardente**, funeral chamber.
camarada [kă-mă-rah'dă] *mf.* companion, comrade, friend.
camaradagem [kă-mă-ră-dah'zhe*n*] *f.* comradeship.
camarão [kă-mă-row*n*'] *m.* shrimp; hook.
camarilha [kă-mă-ree'lyă] *f.* clique, inner circle.
camarim [kă-mă-ree*n*'] *m.* dressing-room (*theat.*).
camarote [kă-mă-rot'] *m.* cabin; box (*theat.*).
cambalear [ka*n*-bă-lee-ar'] *vn.* to totter, reel, stagger.
cambalhota [ka*n*-bă-lyo'tă] *f.* somersault.
cambiante [ka*n*-bee-a*n*t'] *m.* tint, tinge.

cambiar [ka*n*-bee-ar'] *va.* to change, exchange.
câmbio [ka*n*'bee-oo] *m.* exchange; rate of exchange; casa de —, money-changer's; letra de —, bill of exchange.
cambista [ka*n*-beesh'tă] *m.* money-changer.
camelo [kă-may'loo] *m* camel.
camião [kă-mee-ow*n*'] *m.* lorry; (*U.S.A.*) truck.
caminhante [kă-mee-nya*n*t'] *m.* traveller; walker.
caminhar [kă-mee-nyar'] *vn.* to walk; to go, proceed.
caminho [kă-mee'nyoo] *m.* way, path, road; — **de ferro**, railway.
camioneta [kă-mee-oo-ne'tă] *f.* delivery van; bus.
camisa [kă-mee'ză] *f.* shirt; (lady's) chemise; — **de dormir**, night-dress; **meter-se em — de onze varas**, to get into a jam.
camisaria [kă-mee-ză-ree'ă] shirt shop; shirt-maker's.
camisola [kă-mee-zo'lă] *f.* vest.
campa [ka*n*'pă] *f.* grave-stone; bell.
campainha [ka*n*-pă-ee'nyă] *f.* bell.
campal [ka*n*-pal'] *adj.* **batalha** —, pitched battle; **missa** —, open-air Mass.
campanário [ka*n*-pă-nah'ree-oo] *m.* belfry, steeple, church tower; **política de** —, parish-pump politics.
campanha [ka*n*-pă'nyă] *f.* campaign.
campanudo [ka*n*-pă-noo'doo] *adj.* bell-shaped; pompous.
campar [ka*n*-par'] *vn.* to excel, shine; to boast of; to camp.
campeão [ka*n*-pee-ow*n*'] *m.* champion; defender.
campear [ka*n*-pee-ar'] *vn.* to camp; to serve in the field (*mil.*); to scour the country; to show off; to shine.
campeonato [ka*n*-pee-oo-nah'too] *m.* championship; competition (in sport).
campestre [ka*n*-pesh'trĕ] *adj.* country, rustic, rural.
campina [ka*n*-pee'nă] *f.* open country, grassland; meadows.
campino [ka*n*-pee'noo] *m.* countryman; herdsman, cowboy. [camper.
campista [ka*n*-peesh'tă] *m.*
campo [ka*n*'poo] *m.* field; country; range, scope; — **santo**, cemetery; — **de ténis**, tennis court.
camponês [ka*n*-poo-naysh'] *m.* peasant, countryman; *adj.* rural.
campónio [ka*n*-po'nee-oo] *m.* yokel, country bumpkin.
camuflado [kă-moo-flah'doo] *adj.* camouflaged.
camuflagem [kă-moo-flah'-zhe*n*] *f.* camouflage.
camurça [kă-moor'să] *f.* chamois; chamois-leather.
cana [kă'nă] *f.* cane; reed; stalk (of wheat, maize, etc.); — **de pescar**, fishing rod; — **do nariz**, bridge of the nose.
canal [kă-nal'] *m.* channel; canal, waterway; — **da Mancha**, English Channel.
canalha [kă-na'lyă] *f.* mob, rabble, riff-raff; *m.* rotter, scoundrel.
canalização [kă-nă-lee-ză-sow*n*'] *f.* piping system; (water, gas) mains (*or* supply); wiring (*elect.*); canalisation.
canalizar [kă-nă-lee-zar'] *va.* to cut a channel (*e.g.* for irrigation); to lay pipes (for gas, etc.); to channel.
canapé [kă-nă-pe'] *m.* sofa settee, couch.
canário [kă-nah'ree-oo] *m.* canary.

canastra [kă-nash'tră] *f.* basket.
canavial [kă-nă-vee-al'] *m.* cane-brake; cane-plantation.
canção [kan-sown'] *f.* song.
cancela [kan-se'lă] *f.* gate.
cancelamento [kan-sĕ-lă-men'too] *m.* cancellation.
cancelar [kan-sĕ-lar'] *va.* to cancel, annul.
cancioneiro [kan-see-oo-nay'-ee-roo] *m.* collection of lyric poetry; song-book.
cancro [kan'kroo] *m.* cancer.
candeeiro [kan-dee-ay'ee-roo] *m.* lamp. [oil-lamp.
candeia [kan-day'yă] *f.* lamp,
candelabro [kan-dĕ-la'broo] *m.* candelabrum; chandelier.
candente [kan-dent'] *adj.* incandescent; white-hot.
candidato [kan-dee-dah'too] *m.* candidate; applicant.
cândido [kan'dee-doo] *adj.* candid, simple, innocent; white.
candura [kan-doo'ră] *f.* simplicity, innocence; candour; whiteness.
caneca [kă-ne'kă] *f.* large glass; tankard, mug.
canela [kă-ne'lă] *f.* cinnamon; shin (bone). [groove.
canelar [kă-nĕ-lar'] *va.* to
caneta [kă-nay'tă] *f.* fountain pen; penholder. [phor.
cânfora [kan'foo-ră] *f.* cam-
canga [kan'gă] *f.* yoke; pole.
cânhamo [kă'nyă-moo] *m.* hemp.
canhão [kă-nyown'] *m.* gun, cannon; quill (of feather); cuff (of coat).
canhoneira [kă-nyoo-nay'ee-ră] *f.* gunboat.
canhoto [kă-nyoh'too] *adj.* left-handed. [bal.
canibal [ka-nee-bal'] *m.* canni-
caniçada [kă-nee-sah'dă] *f.* trellis.
caniço [kă-nee'soo] *m.* reed.
canicular [kă-nee-koo-lar'] *adj.* very hot.
canil [kă-neel'] *m.* kennel.
canivete [kă-nee-vet'] *m.* penknife.
canja [kan'zhă] *f.* chicken-broth; (*sl.*) cinch.
cano [kă'noo] *m.* tube, pipe; sewer, drain; flue (of chimney); barrel (of gun).
canoa [kă-noh'ă] *f.* boat; canoe.
canonizar [kă-noo-nee-zar'] *va.* to canonize.
canoro [kă-noh'roo] *adj.* melodious; sonorous.
cansaço [kan-sah'soo] *m.* fatigue, weariness.
cansado [kan-sah'doo] *adj.* tired, fatigued, wearied.
cansar [kan-sar'] *va.* to tire, weary; to bore; *vr.* to grow tired, weary; to tire oneself out.
canseira [kan-say'ee-ră] *f.* fatigue; toil, striving.
cantar [kan-tar'] *va.* to sing; to chant; *m.* song.
cântaro [kan'tă-roo] *m.* pitcher, jar, pot; chover a —s, to rain cats and dogs.
cantarolar [kan-tă-roo-lar' *va.* to hum.
canteiro [kan-tay'ee-roo] *m* stonemason; flower-bed.
cântico [kan'tee-koo] *m.* hymn; *pl.* the Song of Solomon (in Bible).
cantiga [kan-tee'gă] *f.* song; lyric; (*pop.*) tale, yarn.
cantilena [kan-tee-lay'nă] *f.* ditty; (*pop.*) yarn, tale.
cantina [kan-tee'nă] *f.* canteen.
canto [kan'too] *m.* corner; corner-stone; song; canto (*poet.*).
canto-chão [kan'too shown] *m.* chant, plainsong.

cantoneiro [ka*n*-too-nay'ee-roo] *m.* road-mender, road-man.
cantor [ka*n*-tohr'] *m.* singer.
canudo [kă-noo'doo] *m.* tube; (*pop.*) swindle, trick.
cão [kow*n*] *m.* dog; hammer (of gun); **pregar um —**, to swindle.
caos [kah'oosh] *m.* chaos.
capa [kah'pă] *f.* cloak, cape; pretence; cover (of book).
capacete [kă-pă-sayt'] *m.* helmet. [(door-)mat.
capacho [kă-pah'shoo] *m.*
capacidade [kă-pă-see-dahd'] *f.* capacity; ability, competence, talent; authority.
capataz [kă-pă-tash'] *m.* overseer; foreman; boss.
capaz [kă-pash'] *adj.* capable; able; suitable, fit.
capela [kă-pe'lă] *f.* (side-) chapel; choir; **— ardente**, funeral chamber.
capelão [kă-pĕ-low*n*'] *m.* chaplain.
capelo [kă-pay'loo] *m.* hood; cowl; cardinal's hat.
capitação [kă-pee-tă-sow*n*'] *f.* poll-tax.
capital [kă-pee-tal'] *adj.* capital, principal; **pena —**, capital punishment, death sentence; *m.* capital, funds, wealth; *f.* capital (city).
capitalista [kă-pee-tă-leesh'-tă] *m.* capitalist.
capitanear [kă-pee-tă-nee-ar'] *va.* to captain, command.
capitânia [kă-pee-tă'nee-ă] *f.* flagship. [captain.
capitão [kă-pee-tow*n*'] *m.*
capitulação [kă-pee-too-lă-sow*n*'] *f.* capitulation; agreement, settlement.
capitular [kă-pee-too-lar'] *vn.* to capitulate; *va.* to classify.
capítulo [kă-pee'too-loo] *m.* chapter (of book, cathedral).
capoeira [kă-poo-ay'ee-ră] *f.* hen-coop; chicken-run.
capota [kă-po'tă] *f.* hood; bonnet.
capotar [kă-poo-tar'] *vn.* to overturn, capsize. [cape.
capote [kă-pot'] *m.* cloak;
capricho [kă-pree'shoo] *m.* caprice, whim.
caprichoso [kă-pree-shoh'-zoo] *adj.* capricious, unreliable.
cápsula [kap'soo-lă] *f.* capsule.
captar [kap-tar'] *va.* to captivate; to collect (water in dam).
captura [kap-too'ră] *f.* capture. [capture.
capturar [kap-too-rar'] *va.* to
capuz [kă-poosh'] *m.* hood.
caquéctico [ka-ke'tee-koo] *adj.* feeble, sickly, debilitated.
cara [kah'ră] *f.* face; look, appearance; head (of coin); **— de Páscoa**, smiling face; **ter boa —**, to look well.
carabina [kă-ră-bee'nă] *f.* rifle; carbine.
caraça [kă-rah'să] *f.* mask.
caracol [kă-ră-kol'] *m.* snail; ringlet, curl; **escada de —**, winding (*or* spiral) staircase.
carácter [kă-rak'tair] *m.* character; disposition; rank, position; letter, type; sign, symbol (*maths.* etc.).
característico [kă-răk-tĕ-reesh'tee-koo] *m.* characteristic, feature, attribute; *adj.* characteristic, typical.
caracterizar [kă-răk-tĕ-ree-zar'] *va.* to characterize; to describe.
caramanchão [kă-ră-ma*n*-show*n*'] *m.* arbour, summer-house.
carambola [kă-ra*n*-bo'lă] *f.* cannon (billiards); red (ball in billiards); trick (*fig.*).
caramelo [kă-ră-me'loo] *m.* caramel.

caramunha [kă-ră-moo'nyă] *f.* tearful face; crying, whimpering (of children).
caranguejo [kă-ran-gay'zhoo] *m.* crab.
carapau [kă-ră-pow'] *m.* horse-mackerel.
carapinha [kă-ră-pee'nyă] *f.* woolly (kinky) hair.
carapuça [kă-ră-poo'să] *f.* cap; se a — serve, if the cap fits; qual —! what nonsense!
caravana [kă-ră-vă'nă] *f.* caravan.
caravela [kă-ră-ve'lă] *f.* caravel, ship.
carbúnculo [kăr-boon'kooloo] *m.* carbuncle (*med.* & precious stone).
carburador [kăr-boo-ră-dohr'] *m.* carburettor.
carcaça [kăr-ka'să] *f.* carcass; skeleton.
cárcere [kar'sĕr] *m.* prison.
carcereiro [kăr-sĕ-ray'ee-roo] *m.* gaoler, jailer, warder.
carcoma [kăr-koh'mă] *f.* woodworm; rot.
carcomido [kăr-koo-mee'doo] *adj.* worm-eaten, rotten.
cardápio [kăr-dah'pee-oo] *m.* menu (*Braz.*).
cardar [kăr-dar'] *va.* to card, comb (wool).
cardeal [kăr-dee-al'] *m/adj.* cardinal.
cardíaco [kăr-dee'ă-koo] *adj.* cardiac, heart; suffering from a weak heart.
cardinal [kăr-dee-nal'] *adj.* cardinal (number); principal.
cardo [kar'doo] *m.* thistle.
cardume [kăr-doom'] *m.* shoal (of fish).
carecer [kă-rĕ-sayr'] *vn.* to be in need of; to lack, not to have.
carência [kă-ren'see-ă] *f.* lack; need, want.
carestia [kă-rĕsh-tee'ă] *f.* scarcity, shortage, dearth; expensiveness, high cost.
careta [kă-ray'tă] *f.* grimace; mask; fazer uma —, to pull a face.
carga [kar'gă] *f.* load, burden; cargo (*naut.*); loading; charge, responsibility; charge (*mil.*); besta de —, beast of burden; — alijada, jetsam.
cargo [kar'goo] *m.* responsibility; dignity, office; tomar — de, to take charge of; a — de, in the charge of.
caricatura [kă-ree-kă-too'ră] *f.* caricature; cartoon.
carícia [kă-ree'see-ă] *f.* caress; stroke, pat.
caridade [kă-ree-dahd'] *f.* charity; alms; benevolence.
cárie [kah'ree-ĕ] *f.* caries; decay, rot.
carimbar [kă-reen-bar'] *va.* to stamp; to seal.
carimbo [kă-reen'boo] *m.* rubber-stamp.
carinho [kă-ree'nyoo] *m.* affection, kindness, tenderness, love.
carinhoso [kă-ree-nyoh'zoo] *adj.* affectionate, kind, tender.
carioca [kă-ree-o'kă] *mf/adj.* native of, pertaining to, Rio de Janeiro; *m.* (*pop.*) strong coffee, with hot water added.
caritativo [kă-ree-tă-tee'voo] *adj.* charitable, benevolent.
cariz [kă-reesh'] *m.* appearance.
carmesim [kăr-mĕ-zeen'] *adj.* crimson.
carnal [kăr-nal'] *adj.* carnal, sensual; related by blood.
carnaval [kăr-nă-val'] *m.* carnival; days immediately before Lent; dia de —, Shrove Tuesday.
carne [karn] *f.* meat; flesh; ser unha e — com, to be hand in glove with.
carneiro [kăr-nay'ee-roo] *m.* sheep; carne de —, mutton.

carnicão [kăr-nee-kow*n*'] *m.* core (of abscess, boil).
carniçaria [kăr-nee-să-ree'ă] *f.* butchery, slaughter.
carniceiro [kăr-nee-say'ee-roo] *m.* butcher; slaughterman; *adj.* voracious, cruel.
carnívoro [kăr-nee'voo-roo] *adj.* carnivorous; *m.* carnivore.
carnudo [kăr-noo'doo] *adj.* fleshy, fat; (*pop.*) beefy.
caro [kah'roo] *adj.* dear; expensive; *adv.* dearly, at a high price.
carocha [kă-ro'shă] *f.* beetle; pointed hat (of victim in auto de fé); dunce's cap (in school); *pl.* witches.
caroço [kă-roh'soo] *m.* stone (of fruit); cash, 'dough' (*sl.*).
carpintaria [kăr-pee*n*-tă-ree'ă] *f.* carpentry; carpenter's shop.
carpinteiro [kăr-pee*n*-tay'ee-roo] *m.* carpenter, joiner.
carpir [kăr-peer'] *vn.* to lament, bewail.
carraça [kă-rah'să] *f.* tick; ser uma —, to stick like a leech.
carranca [kă-ra*n*'kă] *f.* frown, frowning face, scowl, sullen look; — **de proa**, figurehead (*naut.*).
carrancudo [kă-ra*n*-koo'doo] *adj.* sullen, surly, frowning.
carrapicho [kă-ră-pee'shoo] *m.* bun (hair).
carrasco [kă-rash'koo] *m.* hangman, executioner; (*fig.*) tyrant, cruel man.
carregado [kă-rĕ-gah'doo] *adj.* loaded; sombre, sullen; dark, deep (colour).
carregador [kă-rĕ-gă-dohr'] *m.* porter; stevedore.
carregamento [kă-rĕ-gă-me*n*'too] *m.* loading; load.
carregar [kă-rĕ-gar'] *va.* to load; to charge, attack; to increase (prices); *vn.* to weigh, rest on; to press on; to grow worse, more intense (epidemic, storm, etc.).
carreira [kă-ray'ee-ră] *f.* career, profession; race; track, course; slipway (*naut.*); fazer —, to sail (of ships), run (of buses), fly (of planes); avião de —, air-liner; às —s, hurriedly.
carreiro [ka-ray'ee-roo] *m.* track; trail; carter, ox-cart driver.
carreta [kă-ray'tă] *f.* (small) cart; gun-carriage.
carrete [kă-rayt'] *m.* cog-wheel; spool, reel; (small) cart.
carretel [kă-rĕ-tel'] *m.* reel, spool.
carriça [kă-ree'să] *f.* wren.
carril [kă-reel'] *m.* (cart) track; rut; rail.
carrinho [kă-ree'nyoo] *m.* (small) cart; — **de mão**, (wheel-)barrow; — **de linhas**, reel of cotton.
carro [ka'roo] *m.* cart; waggon; (motor-)car; chariot (of Romans, etc.); — **fúnebre**, hearse; — **eléctrico**, tram.
carroça [kă-ro'să] *f.* cart, waggon.
carrocel [kă-roo-sel'] *m.* roundabout, merry-go-round.
carruagem [kă-roo-ah'zhe*n*] *f.* carriage, coach; compartment; — **-cama**, sleeping-car; — **-restaurante**, restaurant-, dining-car.
carta [kar'tă] *f.* letter; (official) despatch; charter; (playing-) card; map, chart; — **branca**, carte blanche; — **de crédito**, letter of credit; — **de saúde**, bill of health.
cartão [kăr-tow*n*'] *m.* card; cardboard; carton; — **de visita**, visiting-card.
cartapácio [kăr-tă-pah'see-oo] *m.* old tome; scrap-book.

cartaz [kăr-tash'] *m.* poster, bill.
cartear-se [kăr-tee-ar'sĕ] *vr.* to correspond (with).
carteira [kăr-tay'ee-ră] *f.* wallet; pocket-book, note-book; writing-desk.
carteirista [kăr-tay-ee-reesh'-tă] *m.* pickpocket.
carteiro [kăr-tay'ee-roo] *m.* postman.
cartilha [kăr-tee'lyă] *f.* primer; spelling-book.
cartógrafo [kăr-to'gră-foo] *m.* cartographer, map-maker.
cartório [kăr-to'ree-oo] *m.* registry; solicitor's office.
cartucheira [kăr-too-shay'ee-ră] *f.* cartridge-belt, -pouch.
cartucho [kăr-too'shoo] *m.* cartridge; paper-bag.
caruncho [kă-roo*n*'shoo] *m.* woodworm; rot.
carvalho [kăr-va'lyoo] *m.* oak-tree.
carvão [kăr-vow*n*'] *m.* coal; [charcoal.
carvoeiro [kăr-voo-ay'ee-roo] *m.* coalman, coal-merchant; charcoal burner.
casa [kah'ză] *f.* house; home; room; firm; square (on chess-board, etc.); buttonhole; **— de malta**, doss-house; **—da moeda**, Mint; **— de penhores**, pawn-shop; **pôr —**, to set up house.
casaca [kă-zah'kă] *f.* dress-coat, (*pop.*) tails; **virar a —**, to turn one's coat (i.e. allegiance).
casaco [kă-zah'koo] *m.* jacket; coat.
casal [kă-zal'] *m.* married couple; farm; hamlet.
casamento [kă-ză-me*n*'too] *m.* marriage; wedding.
casar [kă-zar'] *va.* to marry; *vr.* to get married; to match (colours); to fit in with (temperament, etc.).
casca [kash'kă] *f.* peel, skin, rind (of fruits, vegetables); bark (of tree); shell (of egg, nut, pea, lobster, snail); husk (of maize).
cascalho [kăsh-ka'lyoo] *m.* rubble; gravel.
cascão [kăsh-kow*n*'] *m.* crust; scab (on sore).
cascata [kăsh-kah'tă] *f.* cas-[cade.
cascavel [kăsh-kă-vel'] *m.* rattle; *f.* rattlesnake.
casco [kash'koo] *m.* skull; hoof (of animals); hull (of ship); cask (of wine).
casebre [kă-ze'brĕ] *m.* hovel, [shack.
caseiro [kă-zay'ee-roo] *adj.* home-made (bread, etc.); plain, simple, homespun; home-loving; *m.* tenant.
caserna [kă-zair'nă] *f.* bar-rack-room.
casmurro [kăzh-moo'roo] *adj.* obstinate, stubborn; gloomy; grumpy.
caso [kah'zoo] *m.* case, instance; event, circumstance; position, situation; **em todo o —**, at any rate; **fazer — de**, to notice, pay attention to; **não fazer ao —**, to be irrelevant.
caspa [kash'pă] *f.* scurf, dandruff.
cassar [kă-sar'] *va.* to cancel, [annul.
casta [kash'tă] *f.* caste, lineage, breed; kind, sort.
castanha [kăsh-tă'nyă] *f.* chestnut.
castanheiro [kăsh-tă-nyay'-ee-roo] *m.* chestnut-tree.
castanho [kăsh-tă'nyoo] *adj.* brown, chestnut-coloured; *m.* chestnut-tree.
castanholas [kăsh-tă-nyo'-lăsh] *f.pl.* castanets.
castelhano [kăsh-tĕ-lyă'noo] *m/adj.* Castilian.
castelo [kăsh-te'loo] *m.* castle; **— de popa**, quarter-deck; **— de proa**, forecastle.
castiçal [kăsh-tee-sal'] *m.* candlestick.

castiço [kăsh-tee'soo] *adj.* pure, genuine, untainted; pure-bred, of sound origin (race, stock).
castidade [kăsh-tee-dahd'] *f.* chastity, purity.
castigar [kăsh-tee-gar'] *va.* to punish.
castigo [kăsh-tee'goo] *m.* punishment.
casto [kash'too] *adj.* chaste, pure.
castor [kăsh-tohr'] *m.* beaver.
castrado [kăsh-trah'doo] *m.* eunuch.
castrar [kăsh-trar'] *va.* to castrate.
casual [kă-zoo-al'] *adj.* casual, accidental, fortuitous.
casualidade [kă-zoo-ă-lee-dahd'] *f.* chance, accident; **por —**, by chance, accidentally.
casulo [kă-zoo'loo] *m.* cocoon; pod (of seeds).
cata [kah'tă] *f.* **em** *or* **à — de**, in search of.
cataclismo [kă-tă-kleezh'-moo] *m.* cataclysm.
catacumbas [kă-tă-koon'-băsh] *f.pl.* catacombs.
catadupa [kă-tă-doo'pă] *f.* waterfall, cataract.
catadura [kă-tă-doo'ră] *f.* appearance, look, aspect; frame of mind.
cataléptico [kă-tă-lep'tee-koo] *adj.* subject to fits; cataleptic.
catálogo [kă-ta'loo-goo] *m.* catalogue.
cataplasma [kă-tă-plazh'mă] *f.* poultice.
catar [kă-tar'] *va.* to scrutinize; to search; to pick out (e.g. lice from hair, insects or worms from plants).
catarata [kă-tă-rah'tă] *f.* cataract, waterfall; cataract (*med.*).
catarro [kă-ta'roo] *m.* catarrh; cold.
catástrofe [kă-tash'troof] *f.* catastrophe; dénouement (*theat.*).
cata-vento [ka-tă-ven'too] *m.* weathercock.
catecismo [kă-tĕ-seezh'moo] *m.* catechism.
catedral [kă-tĕ-dral'] *f.* cathedral.
catedrático [kă-tĕ-dra'tee-koo] *m.* (university) professor.
categoria [kă-tĕ-goo-ree'ă] *f.* category; class; **pessoa de —**, person of importance.
categórico [kă-tĕ-go'ree-koo] *adj.* categorical, definite.
caterva [kă-tair'vă] *f.* mob, gang.
catinga [kă-teen'gă] *f.* rank (sweaty) smell; *m.* miser.
catita [kă-tee'tă] *m.* dandy.
cativante [kă-tee-vant'] *adj.* captivating, fascinating.
cativar [kă-tee-var'] *va.* to captivate; to win (sympathy, etc.).
cativeiro [kă-tee-vay'ee-roo] *m.* captivity; bondage.
cativo [kă-tee'voo] *m.* captive, prisoner.
catolicismo [kă-too-lee-seezh'moo] *m.* catholicism.
católico [kă-to'lee-koo] *m/adj.* catholic.
catorze [kă-tohrz'] *adj.* fourteen.
catre [ka'trĕ] *m.* camp-bed.
caturrice [kă-too-rees'] *f.* obstinacy.
caução [kow-sown'] *f.* guarantee; surety; **sob —**, on bail.
caucho [kow'shoo] *m.* rubber-tree; india-rubber.
caucionar [kow-see-oo-nar'] *va.* to stand surety, go bail for; to guarantee.
cauda [kow'dă] *f.* tail; train (of a dress).
caudal [kow-dal'] *adj.* abundant; *m.* torrent.
caudaloso [kow-dă-loh'zoo] *adj.* abundant, copious, ample; deep, full-flowing (river, etc.).

caudilho [kow-dee'lyoo] *m.* leader, chief, head.
caule [kowl] *m.* stalk, stem.
causa [kow'ză] *f.* cause; motive; lawsuit, action; por — de, because of.
causar [kow-zar'] *va.* to cause, give rise to.
cautela [kow-te'lă] *f.* care; caution; wariness; share (of lottery ticket); — de penhores, pawn-ticket.
cauteleiro [kow-tĕ-lay'ee-roo] *m.* lottery-ticket seller.
cauteloso [kow-tĕ-loh'zoo] *adj.* cautious, wary.
cauterizar [kow-tĕ-ree-zar'] *va.* to cauterize.
cauto [kow'too] *adj.* cautious, prudent.
cavaco [kă-vah'koo] *m.* chip (of wood); chat; dar —, to take offence; dar o — por, to be very fond of; não dar —, to say nothing.
cavalaria [kă-vă-lă-ree'ă] *f.* cavalry; knighthood, chivalry; livro de —, tale of chivalry.
cavalariça [kă-vă-lă-ree'să] *f.* stable.
cavaleiro [kă-vă-lay'ee-roo] *m.* horseman; knight; — andante, knight-errant.
cavalete [kă-vă-layt'] *m.* easel (*paint.*); nariz de —, hooked nose.
cavalgar [kă-val-gar'] *vn.* to ride.
cavalheiresco [kă-vă-lyay-resh'koo] *adj.* gentlemanly, noble, chivalrous.
cavalheiro [kă-vă-lyay'ee-roo] *m.* gentleman; — de indústria, swindler; *adj.* gentlemanly, courteous.
cavalo [kă-vah'loo] *m.* horse; horse-power; knight (chess); a —, on horseback.
cavaquear [kă-vă-kee-ar'] *vn.* to chat.
cavar [kă-var'] *va.* to dig.
cave [kahv] *f.* cellar; basement.
caveira [kah-vay'ee-ră] *f.* skull.
caverna [kă-vair'nă] *f.* cave, cavern.
cavidade [kă-vee-dahd'] *f.* cavity.
cavilar [kă-vee-lar'] *vn.* to use false arguments, equivocate, quibble, cavil.
cavilha [kă-vee'lyă] *f.* bolt, peg, pin.
caviloso [kă-vee-loh'zoo] *adj.* captious; tricky.
cavo [kah'voo] *adj.* hollow; concave.
cear [see-ar'] *vn.* to have supper.
cebola [sĕ-boh'lă] *f.* onion; bulb.
cecear [sĕ-see-ar'] *vn.* to lisp.
ceder [sĕ-dayr'] *va.* to yield, cede, give up; *vn.* to give in, give way.
cedilha [sĕ-dee'lyă] *f.* cedilla.
cedo [say'doo] *adv.* early; soon; o mais — possível, as soon as possible.
cedro [sed'roo] *m.* cedar.
cédula [se'doo-lă] *f.* certificate; note; policy.
cegar [sĕ-gar'] *va.* to blind; to deceive; *vn.* to lose one's sight, go blind.
cego [se'goo] *adj.* blind; *m.* blind man; às —as, blindly.
cegonha [sĕ-goh'nyă] *f.* stork.
cegueira [sĕ-gay'ee-ră] *f.* blindness; ignorance, folly.
ceia [say'yă] *f.* supper.
ceifa [say'ee-fă] *f.* harvest.
ceifar [say-ee-far'] *va.* to reap, harvest.
ceifeiro [say-fay'ee-roo] *m.* harvester, reaper.
cela [se'lă] *f.* cell; cubicle.
celebração [sĕ-lĕ-bră-sow*n*'] *f.* celebration, commemoration; acclamation.
celebrante [sĕ-lĕ-bra*n*t'] *m.* celebrant, officiating priest.
celebrar [sĕ-lĕ-brar'] *va.* to

celebrate; to commemorate; to acclaim. [celebrated.
célebre [se'lě-brě] *adj.* famous,
celebridade [sě-lě-bree-dahd'] *f.* fame, renown; celebrity.
celeiro [sě-lay'ee-roo] *m.* granary, barn.
celerado [sě-lě-rah'doo] *m.* criminal, miscreant.
celeridade [sě-lě-ree-dahd'] *f.* celerity, speed.
celeste [sě-lesht'] *adj.* heavenly, celestial; azul —, sky-blue.
celeuma [sě-lay'oo-mă] *f.* uproar, row, hubbub.
celibato [sě-lee-bah'too] *m.* celibacy. [*bot.*, etc.).
célula [se'loo-lă] *f.* cell (*med.*,
celular [sě-loo-lar'] *adj.* cellular, prisão —, solitary confinement.
cem [se*n*] *adj.* a (one) hundred.
cemitério [sě-mee-tair'ee-oo] *m.* cemetery, graveyard.
cena [say'nă] *f.* scene; stage.
cenáculo [sě-na'koo-loo] *m.* Upper Room (scene of Last Supper); coterie, group.
cenário [sě-nah'ree-oo] *m.* scenery (*theat.*).
cenoura [sě-noh'ră] *f.* carrot.
censo [se*n*'soo] *m.* census; annua lrental, payment.
censor [se*n*-sohr'] *m.* censor; critic.
censura [se*n*-soo'ră] *f.* censorship; criticism, reproof censure.
censurar [se*n*-soo-rar'] *va.* to criticize, blame, censure.
censurável [se*n*-soo-rah'vel] *adj.* censurable, blameworthy.
centavo [se*n*-tah'voo] *m.* centavo, cent (i.e. hundredth part of escudo).
centeio [se*n*-tay'yoo] *m.* rye.
centelha [se*n*-tay'lyă] *f.* spark; flash.
centelhar [se*n*-tě-lyar'] *vn.* to flash, glitter.
centena [se*n*-tay'nă] *f.* hundred; às —s, in hundreds.
centenário [se*n*-tě-nah'ree-oo] *m.* centenary; hundredth anniversary *or* birthday; *adj.* centennial.
centésimo [se*n*-te'zee-moo] *adj.* hundredth; *m.* hundredth part. [*m.* centigrade.
centígrado [se*n*-tee'gră-doo]
centímetro [se*n*-tee'mě-troo] *m.* centimetre.
cento [se*n*'too] *m.* one hundred; por —, per cent (*com.*).
centopeia [se*n*-too-pay'yă] *f.* centipede.
central [se*n*-tral'] *adj.* central; *f.* (power, etc.) station; (telephone) exchange.
centralizar [se*n*-tră-lee-zar'] *va.* to centralize.
centro [se*n*'troo] *m.* centre.
cepa [say'pă] *f.* vine-stock, root.
cepilho [sě-pee'lyoo] *m.* plane.
cepo [say'poo] *m.* stump; block, log.
cepticismo [se-tee-seezh'moo] *m.* scepticism.
céptico [se'tee-koo] *m.* sceptic; *adj.* sceptical.
ceptro [se'troo] *m.* sceptre.
cera [say'ră] *f.* wax.
cerâmica [sě-ră'mee-kă] *f.* ceramics.
cerca [sayr'kă] *f.* fence, enclosure; enclosed ground, plot; — de, near; nearly, about.
cercado [sěr-kah'doo] *m.* enclosure.
cercanias [sěr-kă-nee'ăsh] *f. pl.* outskirts, vicinity, suburbs.
cercar [sěr-kar'] *va.* to surround; to enclose; to besiege.
cercear [sěr-see-ar'] *va.* to cut close, clip; to reduce.
cerco [sayr'koo] *m.* siege, encirclement.
cerdas [sayr'dăsh] *f. pl.* bristles.

cereal [sĕ-ree-al'] *m.* cereal.
cérebro [se'rĕ-broo] *m.* brain; intelligence.
cereja [sĕ-ray'zhă] *f.* cherry.
cerejeira [sĕ-rĕ-zhay'ee-ră] *f.* cherry-tree.
cerimónia [sĕ-rĕ-mo'nee-ă] *f.* ceremony; formality; **fazer —**, to stand on ceremony; **traje de —**, formal dress; **visita de —**, formal visit.
cerimonial [sĕ-rĕ-moo-nee-al'] *m.* ceremonial; formalities; *adj.* ceremonial.
cerimonioso [sĕ-rĕ-moo-nee-oh'zoo] *adj.* ceremonious, formal.
ceroulas [sĕ-roh'lăsh] *f.pl.* long pants.
cerração [sĕ-ră-sow*n*'] *f.* fog; gloom; hoarseness (voice).
cerrado [sĕ-rah'doo] *adj.* closed; enclosed; dark, black (sky, etc.); thick (beard, wood, etc.); blurred, mumbled (speech); **filas —as**, serried ranks; *m.* enclosure.
cerrar [sĕ-rar'] *va.* to close, shut, enclose; *vn.* to close in, up (of clouds, warships, etc.); **— com**, to close with (enemy); *vr.* **— a noite**, to be quite dark.
cerro [say'roo] *m.* hillock.
certame [sĕr-tahm'] *m.* *or* **certâmen**, *m.* contest; competition.
certeiro [sĕr-tay'ee-roo] *adj.* well-aimed; sure.
certeza [sĕr-tay'ză] *f.* certainty; assurance, confidence; **ter a —**, to be sure.
certidão [sĕr-tee-dow*n*'] *f.* certificate.
certificado [sĕr-tee-fee-kah'doo] *m.* certificate; licence.
certificar [sĕr-tee-fee-kar'] *va.* to certify; assure; *vr.* to make sure of.
certo [sair'too] *adj.* certain; sure, positive, exact; **ao —**, for certain, exactly; **de, por —**, certainly. [ears).
cerume [sĕ-room'] *m.* wax (in
cerveja [sĕr-vay'zhă] *f.* beer; **fábrica de —**, brewery.
cervejaria [sĕr-vĕ-zhă-ree'ă] *f.* public house, 'pub', bar; brewery.
cerviz [sĕr-veesh'] *f.* neck; nape of neck; **dobrar, curvar a —**, to submit, bow one's head.
cervo [sair'voo] *m.* stag.
cerzidura [sĕr-zee-doo'ră] *f.* darning; darn.
cessação [sĕ-să-sow*n*'] *f.* cessation, discontinuance.
cessão [sĕ-sow*n*'] *f.* cession; transfer (of property, shares).
cessar [sĕ-sar'] *vn.* to cease, stop; **sem —**, continuously.
cessionário [sĕ-see-oo-nah'ree-oo] *m.* grantee, transferee.
cesta [saysh'tă] *f.* basket.
cesto [saysh'too] *m.* basket; **— de vigia**, crow's nest (*naut.*).
cetim [sĕ-tee*n*'] *m.* satin.
céu [se'oo] *m.* sky; heaven.
ceva [se'vă] *f.* fattening of animals; feed (for animals).
cevada [sĕ-vah'dă] *f.* barley.
cevadinha [sĕ-vă-dee'nyă] *f.* pearl-barley.
cevar [sĕ-var'] *va.* to fatten (up) (animals); to satiate (emotion); *vr.* to feed, batten on; to be glutted with.
cevo [say'voo] *m.* feed, fodder; bait.
chá [shah] *m.* tea; tea-party; **não beber — em pequeno**, to lack polish, manners.
chacal [shă-kal'] *m.* jackal.
chacinar [shă-see-nar'] *va.* to slaughter; to cut up into slices.
chacota [shă-ko'tă] *f.* jest.
chafariz [shă-fă-reesh'] *m.* fountain.
chafurda [shă-foor'dă] *f.* pigsty; mire.

chafurdar [shă-foor-dar'] *vn.* to wallow, roll in the mire.
chaga [shah'gă] *f.* wound; sore, ulcer; *pl.* nasturtium (*bot.*).
chalaça [shă-lah'să] *f.* crude joke, jest.
chaleira [shă-lay'ee-ră] *f.* kettle.
chama [shă'mă] *f.* flame.
chamada [shă-mah'dă] *f.* call; roll-call; catchword, sign.
chamamento [shă-mă-men'-too] *m.* call; calling together.
chamar [shă-mar'] *va.* to call; to summon; to name; mandar —, to send for; chamase, his name is.
chamariz [shă-mă-reesh'] *m.* decoy-duck; bird-call; (*fig.*) allurement.
chamejar [shă-mĕ-zhar'] *vn.* to blaze; to glow; to sparkle.
chaminé [shă-mee-ne'] *f.* chimney; funnel (of ship); *m.* limpa- —s, chimney sweep.
chamuscar [shă-moosh-kar'] *va.* to singe.
chancela [shan-se'lă] *f.* seal; rubber-stamp.
chancelaria [shan-sĕ-lă-ree'ă] *f.* chancery; registry; chancellorship.
chantagem [shan-tah'zhen] *f.* blackmail.
chão [shown] *m.* floor; ground; rés-do- —, ground floor; *adj.* flat, level, smooth; plain, straightforward.
chapa [shah'pă] *f.* (metal) plate, sheet; de —, squarely.
chapelaria [shă-pĕ-lă-ree'ă] *f.* hat shop; hat-making.
chapeleira [shă-pĕ-lay'ee-ră] *f.* hat-box.
chapéu [shă-pe'oo] *m.* hat; — de coco, bowler hat; — alto, top hat.
chapinhar [shă-pee-nyar'] *vn.* to splash (about), dabble; to paddle; *va.* to bathe, dab (wound, etc.).
chapuz [shă-poosh'] *m.* (wooden) plug.
charada [shă-rah'dă] *f.* charade.
charanga [shă-ran'gă] *f.* brass-band.
charco [shar'koo] *m.* pool, puddle.
charlatão [shăr-lă-town'] *m.* charlatan, quack.
charneca [shăr-ne'kă] *f.* moor, heath; barren stretch (of country).
charneira [shăr-nay'ee-ră] *f.* hinge.
charrua [shă-roo'ă] *f.* plough.
charuto [shă-roo'too] *m.* cigar.
chasquear [shăsh-kee-ar'] *va.* to chaff, mock.
chato [shah'too] *adj.* flat; dull, tiresome.
chave [shahv] *f.* key; spanner, wrench; — de parafusos, screwdriver; fechar à —, to lock.
chavelho [shă-vay'lyoo] *m.* horn.
chávena [shah'vĕ-nă] *f.* cup.
chefe [shef] *m.* chief, leader, head.
chegada [shĕ-gah'dă] *f.* arrival.
chegar [shĕ-gar'] *vn.* to arrive; to manage to, succeed in; to come near; to suffice; to reach, come to; *va.* to bring (up, near).
cheia [shay'yă] *f.* flood.
cheio [shay'yoo] *adj.* full; em —, completely, full.
cheirar [shay-ee-rar'] *va/vn.* to smell.
cheiro [shay'ee-roo] *m.* smell; scent, perfume.
cheiroso [shay-ee-roh'zoo] *adj.* fragrant, scented.
cheque [shek] *m.* cheque.
cherivia [shĕ-ree-vee'ă] *f.* parsnip.
chiar [shee-ar'] *vn.* to creak; to squeak; to chirp.
chibata [shee-bah'tă] *f.* switch, cane.
chicana [shee-kă'nă] *f.* trick; quibble, chicanery.
chicote [shee-kot'] *m.* whip.

chifre [sheef'rě] *m.* horn.
chilrar [sheel-rar'] *or* **chilrear,** *vn.* to chirp, twitter.
chilro [sheel'roo] *m. or* **chilreio,** chirping, twittering; *adj.* tasteless, flat.
chimpanzé [sheen-pan-ze'] *m.* chimpanzee.
chinela [shee-ne'lă] *f.* slipper.
chinês [shee-naysh'] *m/adj.* Chinese.
chinó [shee-no'] *m.* wig.
chiqueiro [shee-kay'ee-roo] *m.* pigsty.
chispa [sheesh'pă] *f.* spark.
chispar [sheesh-par'] *vn.* to sparkle; to fume (with rage).
chispe [sheesh'pě] *m.* pig's trotter.
chistoso [sheesh-toh'zoo] *adj.* witty, humorous.
chita [shee'tă] *f.* printed cotton, calico.
choça [sho'să] *f.* hut.
chocalhar [shoo-kă-lyar'] *va/vn.* to rattle, jangle.
chocalheiro [shoo-kă-lyay'-ee-roo] *m.* gossip, busybody.
chocalho [shoo-ka'lyoo] *m.* (cow-)bell; rattle.
chocar [shoo-kar'] *va.* to hatch, incubate, sit on (*egg*); to shock; *vn.* to collide with, run against, strike.
chocho [shoh'shoo] *adj.* dry, insipid, empty.
chocolate [shoo-koo-laht'] *m.* chocolate.
chofre [sho'frě] *m.* sudden blow; **de —,** all of a sudden.
choque [shok] *m.* collision; clash; shock.
choramingar [shoo-ră-meen-gar'] *vn.* to whimper, snivel.
chorão [shoo-rown'] *m.* cry-baby; weeping-willow (*bot.*).
chorar [shoo-rar'] *vn.* to cry, weep; *va.* to weep for, (over).
chorudo [shoo-roo'doo] *adj.* substantial; lucrative.
choupal [shoh-pal'] *m.* poplar wood, plantation, grove.
choupana [shoh-pă'nă] *f.* hut; cottage.
choupo [shoh'poo] *m.* poplar.
chouriço [shoh-ree'soo] *m.* sausage.
chover [shoo-vayr'] *vn.* to rain; **— a cântaros,** to teem, (*pop.*) bucket down.
chulo [shoo'loo] *adj.* coarse, common, vulgar.
chumaço [shoo-mah'soo] *m.* padding, stuffing.
chumbar [shoon-bar'] *va.* to seal with lead; to weight with lead (e.g. net); to fail (a candidate).
chumbo [shoon'boo] *m.* lead.
chupar [shoo-par'] *va.* to suck (in, up); to fleece, rob.
chupeta [shoo-pay'tă] *f.* tube (of glass or rubber); straw (for drinking).
chusma [shoozh'mă] *f.* crowd, throng; crew.
chuva [shoo'vă] *f.* rain.
chuveiro [shoo-vay'ee-roo] *m.* shower; shower-bath.
chuviscar [shoo-veesh-kar'] *vn.* to drizzle.
chuvoso [shoo-voh'zoo] *adj.* wet, rainy.
ciar [see-ar'] *vn.* to back water, row backwards.
cicatriz [see-kă-treesh'] *f.* scar.
ciciar [see-see-ar'] *vn.* to rustle (of leaves); to whisper; to lisp.
ciclismo [see-kleezh'moo] *m.* cycling.
ciclo [see'kloo] *m.* cycle.
ciclone [see-klon'] *m.* tornado, hurricane, cyclone.
cidadão [see-dă-down'] *m.* citizen; city dweller, townsman.
cidade [see-dahd'] *f.* city, town.
cidadela [see-dă-de'lă] *f.* citadel, stronghold.

ciência [see-*e*n'see-ă] *f.* science; knowledge.
ciente [see-*e*nt'] *adj.* acquainted with, aware of.
científico [see-*e*n-tee'fee-koo] *adj.* scientific.
cientista [see-*e*n-teesh'tă] *m.* scientist.
cifra [seef'ră] *f.* cipher; zero, [nought.
cifrão [see-frow*n*'] *m.* the sign $.
cifrar [see-frar'] *va.* to put in cipher *or* code; *vr.* to be summed up.
cigano [see-gă'noo] *m/adj.* [gipsy.
cigarra [see-ga'ră] *f.* grasshopper, cicada.
cigarreira [see-gă-ray'ee-ră] *f.* cigarette-case.
cigarro [see-ga'roo] *m.* cigarette; boquilha **de** —, cigarette-holder.
cilada [see-lah'dă] *f.* ambush.
cilindro [see-lee*n*'droo] *m.* cylinder; roller.
cima [see'mă] *f.* top; summit; para —, up(wards); em —, on, above, overhead; por — de, above, over; on; ainda por —, furthermore.
cimentar [see-me*n*-tar'] *va.* to cement; to strengthen.
cimento [see-me*n*'too] *m.* cement; concrete; foundation (*fig.*).
cimo [see'moo] *m.* top; sum- [mit.
cínara [see'nă-ră] *f.* artichoke.
cincho [see*n*'shoo] *m.* cheese-press; olive-press.
cinco [see*n*'koo] *adj.* five.
cinema [see-nay'mă] *f.* cinema; (*pop.*) pictures, (*U.S.A.*) movies.
cingir [see*n*-zheer'] *va.* to gird (on); to encircle; *vr.* to restrict oneself.
cínico [see'nee-koo] *m.* cynic; *adj.* cynical; impudent.
cinismo [see-neezh'moo] *m.* cynicism; shamelessness, impudence.
cinquenta [see*n*-kwe*n*'tă] *adj.* fifty.
cinta [see*n*'tă] *f.* waist-band, sash, girdle; waist; (paper) wrapper.
cintilar [see*n*-tee-lar'] *vn.* to scintillate, sparkle, glitter.
cinto [see*n*'too] *m.* belt; sash; — de salvação, life-belt; — de segurança, safety-belt.
cintura [see*n*-too'ră] *f.* waist.
cinza [see*n*'ză] *f.* ash, cinder; quarta-feira de —s, Ash-Wednesday.
cinzeiro [see*n*-zay'ee-roo] *m.* ash-tray (for cigarettes); ash-pan; ash-heap.
cinzel [see*n*-zel'] *m.* chisel.
cinzelar [see*n*-zĕ-lar'] *va.* to chisel, engrave, carve.
cinzento [see*n*-ze*n*'too] *adj.* grey, ashen.
cioso [see-oh'zoo] *adj.* jealous, envious; zealous.
cipó [see-po'] *m.* (tropical) creeper, liana, climbing plant.
cipreste [see-presht'] *m.* cypress.
circo [seer'koo] *m.* circus.
circuito [seer-koo-ee'too] *m.* circuit; circumference.
circulação [seer-koo-lă-sow*n*'] *f.* circulation; movement (of traffic, pedestrians).
circular [seer-koo-lar'] *va/vn.* to circulate, circle; *f.* circular (document); *adj.* circular.
círculo [seer'koo-loo] *m.* circle; club.
circum-navegação [seer-koo*n*-nă-vĕ-gă-sow*n*'] *f.* circumnavigation.
circum-navegar [seer-koo*n*-nă-vĕ-gar'] *va.* to circumnavigate, sail round.
circundar [seer-koo*n*-dar'] *va.* to surround, encircle.
circunferência [seer-koo*n*-fĕ-re*n*'see-ă] *f.* circumference.

circunflexo [seer-koo*n*-flek'-soo] *m.* circumflex.
circunscrever [seer-koo*n*-shkrĕ-vayr'] *va.* to circumscribe, limit.
circunspecção [seer-koo*n*-shpe-sow*n*'] *f.* circumspection.
circunstância [seer-koo*n*-shta*n*'see-ă] *f.* circumstance; condition.
circunstanciado [seer-koo*n*-shta*n*-see-ah'doo] *adj.* detailed, complete.
circunstante [seer-koo*n*-shtant'] *m.* bystander, onlooker; *m.pl.* audience.
circunvizinho [seer-koo*n*-vi-zee'nyoo] *adj.* neighbouring, adjacent, surrounding.
círio [see'ree-oo] *m.* (long) candle (in church).
cirurgia [see-roor-zhee'ă] *f.* surgery.
cirurgião [see-roor-zhow*n*'] *m.* surgeon.
cisma [seezh'mă] *m.* schism; *f.* preoccupation; misgiving; obsession.
cismar [seezh-mar'] *vn.* to ponder, brood over; to grow obsessed with.
cisne [seezh'nĕ] *m.* swan.
cisterna [seesh-tair'nă] *f.* cistern, tank.
cisto [seesh'too] *m.* cyst.
citação [see-tă-sow*n*'] *f.* quotation; summons (*leg.*).
citar [see-tar'] *va.* to quote; to mention; to summon.
ciúme [see-oom'] *m.* jealousy, envy. [*adj.* jealous.
ciumento [see-oo-me*n*'too]
cívico [see'vee-koo] *adj.* civic.
civil [si-veel'] *adj.* civil (i.e. not *mil.* or *eccl.*); polite; *m.* civilian.
civilidade [see-vĕ-lee-dahd'] *f.* civility, politeness.
civilização [see-vĕ-lee-ză-sow*n*'] *f.* civilization.
civilizado [see-vĕ-lee-zah'doo] *adj.* civilized; well-bred; cultured. [to civilize.
civilizar [see-vĕ-lee-zar'] *va.*
civismo [si-veezh'moo] *m.* good citizenship, public spirit.
cizânia [see-ză'nee-ă] *f.* discord, dissension; tare (*bot.*).
clamar [klă-mar'] *vn.* to shout, cry out. [uproar.
clamor [klă-mohr'] *m.* outcry,
clamoroso [klă-moo-roh'zoo] *adj.* noisy, loud.
clandestino [kla*n*-dĕsh-tee'-noo] *adj.* secret, clandestine.
clara [klah'ră] *f.* white of egg.
clarabóia [klah-ră-boy'ă] *f.* skylight.
clarão [klă-row*n*'] *m.* flash (of lightening); gleam (of hope, etc.).
clarear [klă-ree-ar'] *vn.* to clear up (weather); to grow light; to become clear, intelligible.
clareira [klă-ray'ee-ră] *f.* clearing, glade.
clareza [klă-ray'ză] *f.* clarity, lucidity (of argument, etc.).
claridade [kla-ree-dahd'] *f.* clarity, brightness (of light, etc.).
clarificação [klă-ree-fee-kă-sow*n*'] *f.* clarification; purification (of liquid).
clarificar [klă-ree-fee-kar'] *va.* to clarify; to purify.
clarim [klă-reen'] *m.* bugle, clarion; bugler.
claro [klah'roo] *adj.* clear, bright, light; lucid; *m.* blank (space); clearing; light part; *interj.* of course; naturally; yes; **dia —**, broad daylight; **falar —**, to speak plainly; **passar a noite em —**, to stay awake all night.
classe [klas] *f.* class; group.
clássico [kla'see-koo] *adj.* classic(al).

classificação [klă-see-fee-kă-sown'] *f.* classification.
classificar [klă-see-fee-kar'] *va.* to classify, arrange.
claudicar [klow-dee-kar'] *vn.* to limp; to blunder (*fig.*).
claustro [klowsh'troo] *m.* cloister; monastery.
cláusula [klow'zoo-lă] *f.* clause, condition.
clausura [klow-zoo'ră] *f.* enclosure; seclusion; monastic life.
clava [klah'vă] *f.* club, cudgel.
clave [klahv] *f.* key, clef (*mus.*).
clavícula [klă-vee'koo-lă] *f.* collar-bone.
clemência [klĕ-men'see-ă] *f.* clemency, mercy.
clemente [klĕ-ment'] *adj.* clement, merciful.
clérigo [kle'ree-goo] *m.* priest, cleric, clergyman.
clero [klair'oo] *m.* clergy.
cliché [klee-she'] *m.* negative (*photo.*); printing-plate; cliché (*fig.*).
cliente [klee-ent'] *m.* client (*leg.*); patient (*med.*); customer.
clientela [klee-en-te'lă] *f.* clientele, customers; clients; patients.
clima [klee'mă] *m.* climate.
clínica [klee'nee-kă] *f.* medical practice.
clínico [klee'nee-koo] *adj.* clinical; *m.* doctor.
cloaca [kloo-ah'kă] *f.* sewer.
clube [kloob] *m.* club.
coabitar [koo-ă-bee-tar'] *vn.* to cohabit, live together.
coacção [koo-ah-sown'] *f.* compulsion, constraint.
coadjuvar [koo-ăd-zhoo-var'] *va.* to assist, help.
coador [koo-ă-dohr'] *m.* sieve, strainer, colander.
coagir [koo-ă-zheer'] *va.* to compel, coerce.
coagular [koo-ă-goo-lar'] *va/vn/vr.* to coagulate, congeal, clot.
coágulo [koo-a'goo-loo] *m.* clot.
coalhada [koo-ă-lyah'dă] *f.* curdled milk.
coalizão [koo-ă-lee-zown'] *f.* coalition.
coar [koo-ar'] *va.* to strain, filter; to slip (e.g. money into hand); *vn/vr.* to infiltrate.
coarctar [koo-ăr-tar'] *va.* to restrict, limit.
coaxar [koo-ă-shar'] *vn.* to croak.
cobaia [koo-bȳ'a] *f.* guinea-[pig.
cobarde [koo-bard'] *m.* coward; *adj.* cowardly, faint-hearted; dastardly.
cobardia [koo-băr-dee'ă] *f.* cowardice.
coberta [koo-bair'tă] *f.* deck (*naut.*); quilt; cover, covering.
coberto [koo-bair'too] *adj.* covered; hidden.
cobertor [koo-bĕr-tohr'] *m.* blanket.
cobertura [koo-bĕr-too'ră] *f.* covering, cover.
cobiça [koo-bee'să] *f.* covetousness, greed.
cobiçar [koo-bee-sar'] *va.* to covet, desire eagerly.
cobiçoso [koo-bee-soh'zoo] *adj.* covetous, greedy.
cobra [ko'bră] *f.* snake.
cobrador [koo-bră-dohr'] *m.* collector (of taxes, debts).
cobrança [koo-bran'să] *f.* collection.
cobrar [koo-brar'] *va.* to collect; to regain (courage, etc.].
cobre [ko'brĕ] *m.* copper.
cobrir [koo-breer'] *va.* to cover; to hide; to protect; *vr.* to be covered; to put on one's hat.
coca [ko'kă] *f.* coca (*bot.*); estar à —, to be on the look-out.

coçado [koo-sah'doo] *adj.* threadbare, worn out.
cocaína [koo-kă-ee'nă] *f.* cocaine.
coçar [koo-sar'] *va.* to scratch.
cócegas [ko'sĕ-găsh] *f.* tickles; fazer —, to tickle; estar com — de, to be itching to.
coche [kohsh] *m.* coach.
cocheiro[koo-shay'ee-roo] *m.* coachman.
cochichar [koo-shee-shar'] *vn.* to whisper.
coco [koh'koo] *m.* coconut.
cócoras [ko'koo-răsh], **de —**, squatting.
côdea [koh'dee-ă] *f.* crust (of bread); husk.
código [ko'dee-goo] *m.* code.
codorniz [koo-door-neesh'] *f.* quail.
coelho [koo-ay'lyoo] *m.* rabbit.
coerção [koo-ayr-sow*n*'] *f.* coercion.
coerência [koo-ee-re*n*'see-ă] *f.* coherence.
coerente [koo-ee-re*n*t'] *adj.* coherent.
coesão [koo-ee-zow*n*'] *f.* cohesion.
coetâneo [koo-ay-tă'nee-oo] *adj.* contemporary.
coexistência [koo-ĕ-zeesh-te*n*'see-ă] *f.* coexistence.
cofre [ko'frĕ] *m.* safe, chest.
cogitar [koo-zhee-tar'] *vn.* to cogitate, meditate.
cogumelo [koo-goo-me'loo] *m.* mushroom; — **venenoso**, toadstool.
coibir [koo-ee-beer'] *va.* to restrain, prohibit.
coice [koh'ees] *m.* kick; recoil (of gun); **dar —s**, to kick.
coincidência [koo-ee*n*-sĕ-de*n*'see-ă] *f.* coincidence.
coincidir [koo-ee*n*-si-deer'] *vn.* to coincide; to agree.
coiro [koh'ee-roo] *m.* leather; hide.
coisa [koh'ee-ză] *f.* thing; matter, affair.
coitado [koh-ee-tah'doo] *adj.* pitiful, wretched; *interj.* poor fellow; poor thing.
cola [ko'lă] *f.* glue, paste; track.
colaboração [koo-lă-boo-ră-sow*n*'] *f.* collaboration.
colaborar [koo-lă-boo-rar'] *vn.* to collaborate.
colaço [koo-lah'soo] *m.* foster-brother.
colar [koo-lar'] *va.* to paste, stick, gum; *m.* necklace.
colarinho [koo-lă-ree'nyoo] *m.* collar.
colcha [kol'shă] *f.* bedspread; quilt.
colchão [kohl-show*n*'] *m.* mattress; — **de molas**, spring mattress.
colchete [kohl-shayt'] *m.* hook; clip.
colecção [koo-le-sow*n*'] *f.* collection.
coleccionar [koo-le-see-oo-nar'] *va.* to collect.
colecta [koo-le'tă] *f.* assessment (of taxes); collection; collect (i.e. prayer).
colectar [koo-le-tar'] *va.* to assess (for taxation).
colectividade [koo-le-tee-vee-dahd'] *f.* collective body; community.
colector [koo-le-tohr'] *m.* collector; main (pipe).
colega [koo-le'gă] *mf.* colleague.
colégio [koo-le'zhee-oo] *m.* school; college.
coleira [koo-lay'ee-ră] *f.* collar (for animals).
cólera [ko'lĕ-ră] *f.* anger; cholera (*med.*).
colérico [koo-le'ree-koo] *adj.* bad-tempered, angry.
colete [koo-layt'] *m.* waistcoat; — **de forças**, strait-jacket.
colgaduras [kohl-gă-doo'-răsh] *f.pl.* hangings.
colgar [kohl-gar'] *va.* to hang.
colheita [koo-lyay'ee-tă] *f.* harvest, crop.

colher [koo-lyayr'] *va.* to gather, pick; to catch.
colher [koo-lyair'] *m.* spoon.
colherada [koo-lyĕ-rah'dă] *f.* spoonful. [ladle.
colherão [koo-lyĕ-row*n*'] *m.*
colhimento [koo-lyee-me*n*'-too] *m.* gathering, collecting.
colibri [koo-lee-bree'] *m.* humming-bird.
cólica [ko'lee-kă] *f.* stomach pains, colic.
coligar [koo-lee-gar'] *va.* to unite, bind together.
coligir [koo-lee-zheer'] *va.* to collect, gather.
colina [koo-lee'nă] *f.* hill.
colisão [koo-lee-zow*n*'] *f.* collision.
colmado [kohl-mah'doo] *adj.* thatched; *m.* thatched hut.
colmar [kohl-mar'] *va.* to complete; to pile up; to thatch.
colmeia [kohl-may'yă] *f.* beehive.
colmilho [kohl-mee'lyoo] *m.* canine tooth; tusk (of elephant, etc.), fang.
colmo [kohl'moo] *m.* thatch; straw.
colo [ko'loo] *m.* neck; bosom; lap; ao —, (infant) in one's arms.
colocação [koo-loo-kă-sow*n*'] *f.* placing, arrangement; appointment, job; location, site.
colocar [koo-loo-kar'] *va.* to place; to arrange; to employ; *vr.* to get a job.
colónia [koo-lo'nee-ă] *f.* colony; — infantil, children's camp, home, hostel.
colonização [koo-loo-nee-ză-sow*n*'] *f.* colonization.
colonizar [koo-loo-nee-zar'] *va.* to colonize.
colono [koo-loh'noo] *m.* colonist, settler.
colóquio [koo-lo'kee-oo] *m.* conversation; conference.
colorido [koo-loo-ree'doo] *m.* colouring, colour.
colorir [koo-loo-reer'] *va.* to colour; to gloss over (defects, etc.); to paint in bright colours.
colossal [koo-loo-sal'] *adj.* colossal. [pillar.
coluna [koo-loo'nă] *f.* column;
com [ko*n*] *prep.* with; — **que**, so that; and so.
coma [koh'mă] *f.* coma (*med.*); mane (of lion, horse).
comadre [koo-mah'drĕ] *f.* godmother; gossip, crony.
comandante [koo-ma*n*-da*n*t'] *m.* commander; captain.
comandar [koo-ma*n*-dar'] *va.* to command.
comando [koo-ma*n*'doo] *m.* command; control; **voz de —**, word of command.
comarca [koo-mar'kă] *f.* district.
combalir [ko*n*-bă-leer'] *va.* to weaken, undermine.
combate [ko*n*-bat'] *m.* fight, struggle.
combatente [ko*n*-bă-te*n*t'] *m.* combatant, fighter.
combater [ko*n*-bă-tayr'] *va/vn.* to fight, struggle, combat.
combinação [ko*n*-bee-nă-sow*n*'] *f.* combination; agreement; (woman's) petticoat, slip.
combinar [ko*n*-bee-nar'] *va/vn.* to combine; to agree; to settle, to arrange, fix (a time).
comboiar [ko*n*-boy-yar'] *va.* to convoy, escort.
comboio [ko*n*-boy'yoo] *m.* train; convoy.
combustão [ko*n*-boosh-tow*n*'] *f.* combustion, burning.
começar [koo-mĕ-sar'] *va.* to begin, start.
começo [koo-may'soo] *m.* beginning, commencement.
comédia [koo-me'dee-ă] *f.* play; comedy; pretence, sham

comediante [koo-mĕ-dee-a*n*t'] *m.* comedian, player; impostor.
comedido [koo-mĕ-dee'doo] *adj.* moderate, temperate; respectful.
comedir [koo-mĕ-deer'] *va.* to restrain, moderate; *vr.* to control oneself.
comedouro [koo-mĕ-doh'roo] *m.* feeding place; trough.
comemoração [koo-mĕ-moo-ră-sow*n*'] *f.* commemoration; remembrance.
comemorar [koo-mĕ-moo-rar'] *va.* to commemorate.
comensal [koo-me*n*-sal'] *m.* (fellow-) guest, boarder.
comentar [koo-me*n*-tar'] *va.* to comment (on); to annotate.
comentário [koo-me*n*-tah'-ree-oo] *m.* commentary; comment. [comment.
comento [koo-me*n*'too] *m.*
comer [koo-mayr'] *va.* to eat (up); to consume.
comercial [koo-mĕr-see-al'] *adj.* commercial.
comerciante [koo-mĕr-see-a*n*t'] *m.* merchant, trader.
comércio [koo-mair'see-oo] *m.* trade, business, commerce.
comestível [koo-mĕsh-tee'vel] *adj.* edible, eatable; *m.pl.* food, foodstuffs.
cometa [koo-may'tă] *m.* comet.
cometer [koo-mĕ-tayr'] *va.* to commit; to entrust.
comezinho [koh-mĕ-zee'nyoo] *adj.* plain, simple; good to eat.
comichão [koo-mee-show*n*'] *f.* itch; eager desire.
comício [koo-mee'see-oo] *m.* meeting, assembly, rally.
cómico [ko'mee-koo] *m.* comedian; player; *adj.* comical, ludicrous.
comida [koo-mee'dă] *f.* food; meal.
comigo [koo-mee'go] *pr.* with me.
comilão [koo-mee-low*n*'] *m.* glutton; *adj.* greedy.
comiserar [koo-mee-zĕ-rar'] *va.* to arouse pity in; *vr.* to have pity on.
comissão [koo-mee-sow*n*'] *f.* commission; committee.
comissário [koo-mee-sah'ree-oo] *m.* commissioner, agent; — de bordo, purser; — de polícia, (*approx.*) police-inspector, chief constable.
comisso [koo-mee'soo] *m.* fine; forfeit. [mittee.
comité [ko-mee-te'] *m.* com-
comitiva [koo-mee-tee'vă] *f.* retinue, followers, suite.
como [koh'moo] *adv.* how; in what way; *interrogative*, what (did you say)?; *conj.* like, as; because, since; *interj.* what!; assim —, as well as.
comoção [koo-moo-sow*n*'] *f.* upheaval, commotion; shock.
cómoda [ko'moo-dă] *f.* chest of drawers.
comodidade [koo-moo-dee-dahd'] *f.* convenience; comfort.
cómodo [ko'moo-doo] *adj.* comfortable; convenient, suitable; *m.pl.* accommodation; comforts.
comovedor [koo-moo-vĕ-dohr'] *adj.* moving, touching.
comover [koo-moo-vayr'] *va.* to move, affect.
compacto [ko*n*-pak'too] *adj.* compact; solid.
compadecer [ko*n*-pă-dĕ-sayr'] *va.* to pity, be sorry for; *vr.* sympathize with; to be compatible with.
compadre [ko*n*-pah'drĕ] *m.* godfather; close friend, (*pop.*) pal, crony.
compaixão [ko*n*-pȳ-show*n*'] . compassion, pity.

companheiro [ko*n*-pă-nyay'-ee-roo] *m.* companion, comrade, partner.
companhia [ko*n*-pă-nyee'ă] *f.* company; society.
comparação [ko*n*-pă-ră-sow*n*'] *f.* comparison.
comparar [ko*n*-pă-rar'] *va.* to compare.
comparativo [ko*n*-pă-ră-tee'-voo] *adj.* comparative.
comparecer [ko*n*-pă-rĕ-sayr'] *vn.* to appear.
comparsa [ko*n*-par'să] *mf.* extra (*theat.*); nonentity.
compartilhar [ko*n*-păr-tee-lyar'] *va.* to share (in).
compartimento [ko*n*-păr-tee-me*n*'too] *m.* compartment; section; room.
compassado [ko*n*-pă-sah'-doo] *adj.* unhurried, steady, regular.
compasso [ko*n*-pa'soo] *m.* pair of compasses (*mech.*); callipers (*mech.*); time, measure, beat (*mus.*).
compatibilidade [ko*n*-pă-ti-bee-lee-dahd'] *f.* compatibility. [*adj.* compatible.
compatível [ko*n*-pă-tee'vel]
compatriota [ko*n*-pă-tree-o'-tă] *mf.* compatriot, fellow-countryman *or* -countrywoman.
compêndio [ko*n*-pe*n*'dee-oo] *m.* compendium; handbook, manual.
compenetração [ko*n*-pĕ-nĕ-tră-sow*n*'] *f.* conviction.
compenetrar [ko*n*-pĕ-nĕ-trar'] *va.* to convince; *vr.* to be convinced of; to grasp thoroughly.
compensação [ko*n*-pe*n*-să-sow*n*'] *f.* compensation; balance.
compensar [ko*n*-pe*n*-sar'] *va.* to compensate; to counterbalance, offset.
competência [ko*n*-pĕ-te*n*'-see-ă] *f.* competence; competition.
competente [ko*n*-pĕ-te*n*t'] *adj.* competent; suitable.
competição [ko*n*-pĕ-tee-sow*n*'] *f.* competition.
competir [ko*n*-pĕ-teer'] *vn.* to compete with, rival; to come within the competence of (*leg.*); to be incumbent on.
compilar [ko*n*-pee-lar'] *va.* to compile, collect.
complacência [ko*n*-plă-se*n*'-see-ă] *f.* kindness, civility, benevolence.
compleição [ko*n*-play-ee-sow*n*'] *f.* constitution; temperament.
complemento [ko*n*-plĕ-me*n*'-too] *m.* complement; (*grammatical*) object.
completar [ko*n*-plĕ-tar'] *va.* to complete, finish.
completo [ko*n*-ple'too] *adj.* complete; full up.
complexidade [ko*n*-plek-see-dahd'] *f.* complexity.
complexo [ko*n*-plek'soo] *adj.* complex, complicated; *m.* complex; combination.
complicação [ko*n*-plee-kă-sow*n*'] *f.* complication.
complicar [ko*n*-plee-kar'] *va.* to complicate, make difficult.
componente [ko*n*-poo-ne*n*t'] *m/adj.* component.
compor [ko*n*-pohr'] *va.* to compose; to devise; to reconcile; to put right; to set up (type); *vr.* to be composed of; to be settled; to compose oneself, calm down.
comporta [ko*n*-por'tă] *f.* flood-gate, sluice.
comportamento [ko*n*-poor-tă-me*n*'too] *m.* conduct, behaviour.
comportar [ko*n*-poor-tar'] *va.*

to sustain; to tolerate; *vr.* to behave.

composição [kon-poo-zee-sown'] *f.* composition; arrangement; compromise; typesetting.

compositor [kon-poo-zee-tohr'] *m.* composer; compositor (*print.*).

composto [kon-pohsh'too] *adj.* composite; compound; composed, made up; *m.* compound.

compostura [kon-poosh-too'-ră] *f.* composure, calmness; composition; imposture.

compota [kon-po'tă] *f.* jam; bottled fruit; **— de laranja,** marmalade.

compra [kon'pră] *f.* purchase; **ir às —s, fazer —s,** to go shopping.

comprador [kon-pră-dohr'] *m.* purchaser, buyer.

comprar [kon-prar'] *va.* to buy, purchase.

compreender [kon-pree-en-dayr'] *va.* to understand; to comprise, consist of.

compreensão [kon-pree-en-sown'] *f.* understanding, comprehension.

compreensível [kon-pree-en-see'vel] *adj.* comprehensible.

compreensivo [kon-pree-en-see'voo] *adj.* comprehensive; comprehending.

compressa [kon-pre'să] *f.* compress; **— quente,** hot compress, poultice.

comprido [kon-pree'doo] *adj.* long; **ao —,** lengthways; at full length.

comprimento [kon-pree-men'too] *m.* length.

comprimido [kon-pri-mee'-doo] *m.* pill, tablet; *adj.* compressed.

comprimir [kon-pri-meer'] *va.* to press; to compress, condense; to oppress, repress (*fig.*).

comprometer [kon-proo-mĕ-tayr'] *va.* to compromise, endanger (honour, position, etc.); to pledge; *vr.* to undertake (to); to commit oneself.

compromisso [kon-proo-mee'soo] *m.* obligation, liability; undertaking, pledge; compromise.

comprovar [kon-proo-var'] *va.* to confirm, corroborate.

compunção [kon-poon-sown'] *f.* compunction, contrition.

computador [kon-poo-tă-dohr'] *m.* computer.

comum [koo-moon'] *adj.* common; ordinary, customary; public; frequent; low, vulgar; trivial, commonplace.

comungar [koo-moon-gar'] *va.* to administer Holy Communion; *vn.* to share (opinions); to commune (with); to communicate (*eccl.*).

comunhão [koo-moo-nyown'] *f.* communion.

comunicação [koo-moo-nee-kă-sown'] *f.* communication; message.

comunicado [koo-moo-nee-kah'doo] *m.* communiqué, (official) information, message.

comunicar [koo-moo-nee-kar'] *va.* to communicate; to report, inform.

comunicativo [koo-moo-nee-kă-tee'voo] *adj.* communicative, open, expansive.

comunidade [koo-moo-nee-dahd'] *f.* community.

comunismo [koo-moo-neezh'-moo] *m.* communism.

comunista [koo-moo-neesh'-tă] *mf/adj.* communist.

comutador [koo-moo-tă-dohr'] *m.* switch.

comutar [koo-moo-tar'] *va.* to commute (*leg.*); to exchange.

côncavo [kon'kă-voo] *adj.* concave, hollow; *m.* hollow.
conceber [kon-sĕ-bayr'] *va.* to conceive.
conceder [kon-sĕ-dayr'] *va.* to grant, allow, concede.
conceição [kon-say-ee-sown'] *f.* the Immaculate Conception.
conceito [kon-say'ee-too] *m.* concept, conception, idea; conceit (i.e. far-fetched *or* subtle notion).
conceituado [kon-say-ee-too-ah'doo] *adj.* esteemed, respected.
conselho [kon-say'lyoo] *m.* council; district; paços do —, council offices; town hall.
concentração [kon-sen-tră-sown'] *f.* concentration.
concentrar [kon-sen-trar'] *va.* to concentrate.
concepção [kon-sep-sown'] *f.* conception; creation; imagination.
concertar [kon-sĕr-tar'] *va.* to arrange; to settle; *vn.* to harmonize; to agree.
concerto [kon-sayr'too] *m.* concert; harmony; agreement.
concessão [kon-sĕ-sown'] *f.* concession, grant.
concessionário [kon-sĕ-see-oo-nah'ree-oo] *m.* concessionaire.
concha [kon'shă] *f.* shell; ladle; scale (of balance).
conchego [kon-shay'goo] *m.* comfort.
concidadão [kon-see-dă-down'] *m.* fellow-citizen.
conciliábulo [kon-see-lee-a'-boo-loo] *m.* secret meeting.
conciliação [kon-see-lee-ă-sown'] *f.* conciliation; reconciliation.
conciliador [kon-see-lee-ă-dohr'] *m.* conciliator, arbitrator.
conciliar [kon-see-lee-ar'] *va.* to conciliate; to reconcile; to win (affection, fame, etc.); to induce (sleep).
conciliatório [kon-see-lee-ă-to'ree-oo] *adj.* conciliatory.
concílio [kon-see'lee-oo] *m.* council (*usu. eccl.*).
concisão [kon-see-sown'] *f.* brevity, conciseness.
conciso [kon-see'zoo] *adj.* concise, brief.
concludente [kon-kloo-dent'] *adj.* conclusive, convincing.
concluir [kon-kloo-eer'] *va.* to end, conclude; to deduce, draw the conclusion.
conclusão [kon-kloo-zown'] *f.* conclusion; end.
concomitante [kon-koo-mee-tant'] *adj.* concomitant, accompanying.
concordância [kon-koor-dan'see-ă] *f.* concordance; agreement, conformity.
concordar [kon-koor-dar'] *vn.* to be in agreement, agree.
concórdia [kon-kor'dee-ă] *f.* concord, harmony.
concorrência [kon-koo-ren'-see-ă] *f.* competition; crowd, concourse.
concorrente [kon-koo-rent'] *m.* candidate, competitor; spectator, person present.
concorrer [kon-koo-rayr'] *vn.* to concur; to meet together, attend; to compete.
concretizar [kon-krĕ-tee-zar'] *va.* to render concrete, make real.
concreto [kon-kre'too] *adj.* concrete, real, exact; *m.* concrete.
concupiscência [kon-koo-peesh-sen'see-ă] *f.* lust, greed.
concurso [kon-koor'soo] *m.* competition; crowd, concourse; co-operation; junction, conjunction.
condão [kon-down'] *m.* privi-

lege; magic power; vara de —, magic wand.
conde [ko*n*'dĕ] *m.* count, earl.
condecoração [ko*n*-dĕ-koo-ră-sow*n*'] *f.* decoration, medal.
condecorar [ko*n*-dĕ-koo-rar'] *va.* to decorate, confer (honour, etc.).
condenação [ko*n*-dĕ-nă-sow*n*'] *f.* sentence, condemnation, censure.
condenar [ko*n*-dĕ-nar'] *va.* to sentence, condemn; to reprove.
condensar [ko*n*-de*n*-sar'] *va.* to condense, compress.
condescendência [ko*n*-dĕsh-se*n*-de*n*'see-ă] *f.* readiness to oblige, courtesy.
condescender [ko*n*-dĕsh-se*n*-dayr'] *vn.* to oblige; to agree with, acquiesce in.
condessa [ko*n*-day'să] *f.* countess.
condição [ko*n*-dee-sow*n*'] *f.* condition; proviso, stipulation; state; temperament; situation; rank.
condicionado [ko*n*-dee-see-oo-nah'doo] *adj.* conditioned.
condicional [ko*n*-dee-see-oo-nal'] *adj.* conditional.
condigno [ko*n*-deeg'noo] *adj.* deserved, well-merited.
condimentar [ko*n*-dee-me*n*-tar'] *va.* to season, flavour.
condimento [ko*n*-dee-me*n*'-too] *m.* seasoning, flavouring.
condiscípulo [ko*n*-deesh-see'-poo-loo] *m.* schoolfellow; fellow-student.
condizer [ko*n*-dee-zayr'] *vn.* to fit, suit, match.
condoer [ko*n*-doo-ayr'] *va.* to arouse the pity of; *vr.* to sympathize (with).
condução [ko*n*-doo-sow*n*'] *f.* conduction, transmission; transport.
conduta [ko*n*-doo'tă] *f.* conduct, behaviour, manners; conveyance.
conduto [ko*n*-doo'too] *m.* pipe; conduit.
condutor [ko*n*-doo-tohr'] *m.* conductor; guide; driver (of vehicle).
conduzir [ko*n*-doo-zeer'] *va.* to drive (vehicle); to lead, guide, conduct.
cone [kon] *m.* cone.
cónego [ko'nĕ-goo] *m.* canon.
conexão [koo-nek-sow*n*'] *f.* connexion, connection.
confecção [ko*n*-fek-sow*n*'] *f.* making; completion; ready-made article.
confeccionar [ko*n*-fe-see-oo-nar'] *va.* to make (up).
confederação [ko*n*-fĕ-dĕ-ră-sow*n*'] *f.* confederation.
confederar [ko*n*-fĕ-dĕ-rar'] *va/vr.* to unite.
confeição [ko*n*-fay-ee-sow*n*'] *f.* mixture; concoction.
confeitaria [ko*n*-fay-ee-tă-ree'ă] *f.* sweet-shop, confectioner's.
conferência [ko*n*-fĕ-re*n*'see-ă] *f.* lecture, speech; conference; interview.
conferenciar [ko*n*-fĕ-re*n*-see-ar'] *vn.* to confer, consult together, meet (for discussion).
conferencista [ko*n*-fĕ-re*n*-seesh'tă] *m.* lecturer; speaker.
conferente [ko*n*-fĕ-re*n*t'] *m.* speaker, lecturer; conference member.
conferir [ko*n*-fĕ-reer'] *va.* to compare, collate, check; to confer (on); *vn.* to agree; to confer, discuss.
confessar [ko*n*-fĕ-sar'] *va.* to confess, admit.
confessionário [ko*n*-fĕ-see-oo-nah'ree-oo] *m.* confessional.
confessor [ko*n*-fĕ-sohr'] *m.* confessor.
confiado [ko*n*-fee-ah'doo] *adj.*

confident; cheeky (*pop.*).
confiança [ko*n*-fee-a*n*'sǎ] *f.* confidence, trust, faith; tomar —, to be over-familiar with; digno de —, reliable, trustworthy.
confiar [ko*n*-fee-ar'] *vn.* to trust, have confidence in; *va.* to trust, entrust.
confidência [ko*n*-fee-de*n*'see-ǎ] *f.* secret, confidence; em —, in confidence.
confidencial [ko*n*-fee-de*n*-see-al'] *adj.* confidential.
confidente [ko*n*-fee-de*n*t'] *m.* confidant, trusted friend *or* servant.
configuração [ko*n*-fee-goo-rǎ-sow*n*'] *f.* configuration, shape.
configurar [ko*n*-fee-goo-rar'] *va.* to shape, fashion; to represent.
confinar [ko*n*-fee-nar'] *vn.* to border on; *va.* to confine.
confins [ko*n*-fee*n*sh'] *m.pl.* limits, boundaries.
confirmação [ko*n*-feer-mǎ-sow*n*'] *f.* confirmation.
confirmar [ko*n*-feer-mar'] *va.* to confirm, corroborate, ratify.
confiscação [ko*n*-feesh-kǎ-sow*n*'] *f.* confiscation.
confiscar [ko*n*-feesh-kar'] *va.* to confiscate.
confissão [ko*n*-fee-sow*n*'] *f.* confession; acknowledgment.
conflagração [ko*n*-flǎ-grǎ-sow*n*'] *f.* conflagration.
conflito [ko*n*-flee'too] *m.* conflict, struggle, fight.
confluência [ko*n*-floo-e*n*'see-ǎ] *f.* meeting (of rivers), confluence.
confluir [ko*n*-floo-eer'] *vn.* to join, flow together (rivers).
conformação [ko*n*-foor-mǎ-sow*n*'] *f.* conformation; form; compliance.
conformar [ko*n*-foor-mar'] *va.* to form; to bring into harmony; *vr.* to conform, comply with; to harmonize; *vn.* to be in accord with.
conforme [ko*n*-form'] *adj.* alike, similar; corresponding (to); *adv.* in accordance with; *conj.* as, depending on; é —, it depends.
conformidade [ko*n*-foor-mee-dahd'] *f.* conformity; agreement; submission.
confortar [ko*n*-foor-tar'] *va.* to comfort, console.
confortável [ko*n*-foor-tah'-vel] *adj.* comfortable.
conforto [ko*n*-fohr'too] *m.* comfort.
confrangido [ko*n*-fra*n*-zhee'-doo] *adj.* distressed, grieved.
confraria [ko*n*-frǎ-ree'a] *f.* confraternity, brotherhood.
confrontação [ko*n*-fro*n*-tǎ-sow*n*'] *f.* confrontation; comparison.
confrontar [ko*n*-fro*n*-tar'] *va.* to confront; to compare; *vn.* to face (of house); to adjoin.
confundir [ko*n*-foo*n*-deer'] *va.* to confuse; to confound, defeat; *vr.* to mix, mingle with; to get mixed up.
confusão [ko*n*-foo-zow*n*'] *f.* confusion, disorder; bewilderment.
confuso [ko*n*-foo'zoo] *adj.* confused, jumbled, indistinct; bewildered.
confutar [ko*n*-foo-tar'] *va.* to confute, disprove.
congelar [ko*n*-zhě-lar'] *va.* to freeze; to congeal, solidify.
congénito [ko*n*-zhe'nee-too] *adj.* congenital.
congestão [ko*n*-zhěsh-tow*n*'] *f.* congestion.
congestionar-se [ko*n*-zhěsh-tee-oo-nar'sě] *vr.* to be congested; to flush (with anger, etc.).
conglomerar [ko*n*-gloo-mě-

rar'] *vn.* to conglomerate.
congratular-se [kon-gră-too-lar'sĕ] *vr.* to be pleased at, rejoice at.
congregação [kon-grĕ-gă-sown'] *f.* congregation; society; assembly.
congregar-se [kon-grĕ-gar'-sĕ] *vr.* to congregate, assemble.
congresso [kon-gre'soo] *m.* congress.
congruência [kon-groo-en'-see-ă] *f.* fitness, appropriateness.
congruente [kon-groo-ent'] *adj.* suitable, congruent.
côngruo [kon'groo-oo] *adj.* suitable, appropriate, apt.
conhaque [ko-nyak'] *m.* cognac, brandy.
conhecer [koo-nyĕ-sayr'] *va.* to know; to be acquainted with.
conhecido [koo-nyĕ-see'doo] *adj.* known; *m.* acquaintance.
conhecimento [koo-nyĕ-see-men'too] *m.* knowledge; bill of lading (*com.*); tomar — de, to take cognizance of; to look into.
conimbricense [koo-neen-bree-sens'] *adj.* of Coimbra.
conivência [koo-nee-ven'see-ă] *f.* connivance.
conjectura [kon-zhe-too'ră] *f.* surmise, conjecture.
conjugação [kon-zhoo-gă-sown'] *f.* conjugation.
conjugal [kon-zhoo-gal'] *adj.* conjugal.
conjugar [kon-zhoo-gar'] *va.* to conjugate (a verb); to join together.
cônjuge [kon'zhoozh] *m.* consort, spouse.
conjunção [kon-zhoon-sown'] *f.* conjunction.
conjuntivo [kon-zhoon-tee'-voo] *m.* subjunctive (mood).
conjunto [kon-zhoon'too] *adj.* united; *m.* entirety, whole; entire collection, assembly, group, mass.
conjuntura [kon-zhoon-too'-ră] *f.* (set of) circumstances; situation; occasion.
conjuração [kon-zhoo-ră-sown'] *f.* plot, conspiracy.
conjurado [kon-zhoo-rah'doo] *m.* conspirator.
conjuro [kon-zhoo'roo] *m.* incantation, (magic) spell; exorcism.
conluio [kon-loo'ee-yoo] *m.* collusion; plot.
connosco [kon-nohsh'koo] *pr.* with us.
conquanto [kon-kwan'too] *conj.* although, though.
conquista [kon-keesh'tă] *f.* conquest.
conquistar [kon-keesh-tar'] *va.* to conquer; to win (friendship, respect, etc.).
consagração [kon-să-gră-sown'] *f.* consecration.
consagrar [kon-să-grar'] *va.* to consecrate, hallow; to dedicate; *vr.* to devote oneself; to be sanctioned (e.g. by usage).
consanguíneo [kon-san-gwee'nee-oo] *adj.* related by blood.
consciência [konsh-see-en'-see-ă] *f.* conscience; consciousness, awareness; conscientiousness, devotion to duty; ter a — larga, to be unscrupulous.
consciencioso [konsh-see-en-see-oh'zoo] *adj.* conscientious.
consciente [konsh-see-ent'] *adj.* conscious, aware.
cônscio [konsh-'see-oo] *adj.* conscious, aware.
conscrição [konsh-kree-sown'] *f.* conscription.
consecução [kon-sĕ-koo-sown'] *f.* or **conseguimento** *m.* attainment.
consecutivo [kon-sĕ-koo-tee'-voo] *adj.* consecutive.
conseguinte [kon-sĕ-geent']

adj. consequent; consecutive; por —, consequently, therefore.
conseguir [ko*n*-sĕ-geer'] *va.* to obtain, get; to manage to, succeed in.
conselheiro [ko*n*-sĕ-lyay'ee-roo] *m.* counsellor, adviser; councillor.
conselho [ko*n*-say'lyoo] *m.* advice, counsel; council; court; board; — de ministros, cabinet; — de guerra, court martial; presidente do —, Prime Minister.
consentimento [ko*n*-se*n*-tee-me*n*'too] *m.* consent.
consentir [ko*n*-se*n*-teer'] *va.* to permit; to consent to.
consequência [ko*n*-sĕ-kwe*n*'-see-ă] *f.* consequence, result; importance; por —, consequently; em — de, because of.
consequente [ko*n*-sĕ-kwe*nt*'] *adj.* consequent.
consertar [ko*n*-sĕr-tar'] *va.* to mend, repair.
conserva [ko*n*-sair'vă] *f.* tinned (canned) food; preserve; jam.
conservação [ko*n*-sĕr-vă-sow*n*'] *f.* preservation.
conservador [ko*n*-sĕr-vă-dohr'] *m/adj.* conservative; *m.* curator, keeper.
conservar [ko*n*-sĕr-var'] *va.* to preserve; to maintain, retain; to keep.
consideração [ko*n*-see-dĕ-ră-sow*n*'] *f.* consideration; reflection; respect.
considerado [ko*n*-see-dĕ-rah'doo] *adj.* respected, well thought of.
considerar [ko*n*-see-dĕ-rar'] *va.* to consider, think over.
considerável [ko*n*-see-dĕ-rah'vel] *adj.* considerable.
consignação [ko*n*-seeg-nă-sow*n*'] *f.* consignment.
consignar [ko*n*-seeg-nar'] *va.* to consign; to deposit.
consistência [ko*n*-seesh-te*n*'-see-ă] *f.* consistency; stability.
consistente [ko*n*-seesh-te*nt*'] *adj.* consistent; solid, firm.
consistir [ko*n*-seesh-teer'] *vn.* to lie in; to consist of.
consoada [ko*n*-soo-ah'dă] *f.* Christmas Eve dinner; Christmas present.
consoante [ko*n*-soo-a*nt*'] *f/adj.* consonant; *prep.* in accordance with.
consolação [ko*n*-soo-lă-sow*n*'] *f.* consolation, comfort.
consolar [ko*n*-soo-lar'] *va.* to console, comfort, soothe.
consolidação [ko*n*-soo-lee-dă-sow*n*'] *f.* consolidation.
consolidar [ko*n*-soo-lee-dar'] *va.* to consolidate.
consonância [ko*n*-soo-na*n*'-see-ă] *f.* consonance; harmony.
consórcio [ko*n*-sor'see-oo] *m.* marriage; partnership.
consorte [ko*n*-sort'] *mf.* consort; associate; partner.
conspícuo [ko*n*sh-pee'koo-oo] *adj.* prominent.
conspiração [ko*n*sh-pee-ră-sow*n*'] *f.* conspiracy, plot.
conspirador [ko*n*sh-pee-ră-dohr'] *m.* conspirator.
conspirar [ko*n*sh-pee-rar'] *vn.* to conspire, plot; to combine.
constância [ko*n*sh-ta*n*'see-ă] *f.* steadiness, perseverance, constancy.
constante [ko*n*sh-ta*nt*'] *adj.* constant; steady; steadfast; — de, consisting of.
constar [ko*n*sh-tar'] *vn.* to consist of; to be reported; to be evident.
constelação [ko*n*sh-tĕ-lă-sow*n*'] *f.* constellation.
constelado [ko*n*sh-tĕ-lah'doo] *adj.* starry; star-studded.
consternação [ko*n*sh-tĕr-nă-

sown'] *f.* consternation, dismay; dejection.
consternado [konsh-tĕr-nah'doo] *adj.* astounded, aghast; dismayed, depressed.
constipação [konsh-tee-pă-sown'] *f.* cold.
constipar-se [konsh-tee-par'sĕ] *vr.* to catch a cold.
constitucional [konsh-tee-too-see-oo-nal'] *adj.* constitutional.
constituição [konsh-tee-too-ee-sown'] *f.* constitution.
constituir [konsh-tee-too-eer'] *va.* to constitute, establish.
constranger [konsh-tran-zhayr'] *va.* to constrain, compel.
constrangimento [konsh-tran-zhee-men'too] *m.* constraint; force.
constrição [konsh-tree-sown'] *f.* constriction.
constringir [konsh-treen-zheer'] *va.* to constrict, squeeze.
constritor [konsh-tree-tohr'] *adj.* constricting; *m.* constrictor (*anat.*); boa-constrictor (*zool.*).
construção [konsh-troo-sown'] *f.* construction; building.
construir [konsh-troo-eer'] *va.* to construct, build; to construe.
construtor [konsh-troo-tohr'] *m.* builder, constructor.
consuetudinário [kon-soo-ĕ-too-dee-nah'ree-oo] *adj.* customary; **direito —**, common law.
cônsul [kon'sool] *m.* consul.
consulado [kon-soo-lah'doo] *m.* consulate.
consulta [kon-sool'tă] *f.* consultation; conference; **livro de —**, reference book; **horas de —**, (doctor's) surgery, *or* (consulting) hours.
consultar [kon-sool-tar'] *va.* to consult; to consider.
consultivo [kon-sool-tee'voo] *adj.* advisory. [adviser.
consultor [kon-sool-tohr'] *m.*
consultório [kon-sool-to'ree-oo] *m.* (doctor's) surgery, consulting-room.
consumação [kon-soo-mă-sown'] *f.* consummation, completion.
consumado [kon-soo-mah'-doo] *adj.* consummate, perfect.
consumar [kon-soo-mar'] *va.* to consummate, complete, perfect.
consumidor [kon-soo-mee-dohr'] *m.* consumer.
consumir [kon-soo-meer'] *va.* to consume, eat (up), devour; to destroy, waste; *vr.* to waste away, pine away.
consumo [kon-soo'moo] *m.* consumption (of food, etc.); waste; **artigos de —**, consumer goods.
consumpção [kon-soon-sown'] *f.* (*med.*) consumption, tuberculosis, (*abbrev.*) T.B.
conta [kon'tă] *f.* account; bill; reckoning; *pl.* beads; **à, por, —**, on account; **— corrente**, current account; **afinal de —s**, after all; **por — própria**, on one's own account; **ser da — de**, to be the responsibility of; **ter em —**, to bear in mind; **tomar — de**, to take charge of.
contabilidade [kon-tă-bee-lee-dahd'] *f.* book-keeping, accountancy; accounts department.
contabilista [kon-tă-bee-leesh'tă] *m.* accountant.
contacto [kon-tak'too] *m.* contact, touch.
contado [kon-tah'doo] *adj.* counted; told, narrated; **din-**

heiro de —, cash payment.
contador [kon-tă-dohr'] *m.* accountant; (gas, etc.) meter.
contadoria [kon-tă-doo-ree'ă] *f.* accounts department.
contagiar [kon-tă-zhee-ar'] *va.* to infect; to contaminate.
contágio [kon-tah'zhee-oo] *m.* infection, contagion.
contagioso [kon-tă-zhee-oh'-zoo] *adj.* contagious.
contaminar [kon-tă-mee-nar'] *va.* to contaminate, infect; to corrupt.
contanto que [kon-tan'too kĕ] *conj.* provided that.
conta-quilómetros [kon-tă-kee-lo'mĕ-troosh] *m.* speedometer.
contar [kon-tar'] *va.* to count; to tell, relate, narrate; to intend; — **com,** to count on, rely on.
contemplação [kon-ten-plă-sown'] *f.* contemplation.
contemplar [kon-ten-plar'] *va.* to contemplate, gaze on.
contemporâneo [kon-ten-poo-ră'nee-oo] *m.* contemporary; *adj.* contemporary; contemporaneous.
contemporizar [kon-ten-poo-ree-zar'] *vn.* to temporize.
contenção [kon-ten-sown'] *m.* contention, strife.
contencioso [kon-ten-see-oh'-zoo] *adj.* contentious.
contenda [kon-ten'dă] *f.* dispute; struggle.
contentar [kon-ten-tar'] *va.* to satisfy, please; *vr.* to be content with.
contente [kon-tent'] *adj.* satisfied, pleased, contented.
contento [kon-ten'too] *m.* contentment, satisfaction.
conter [kon-tayr'] *va.* to contain, hold; to comprise; to restrain; *vr.* to restrain oneself.
conterrâneo [kon-tĕ-ră'nee-oo] *m.* fellow-countryman.
contestação [kon-tĕsh-tă-sown'] *f.* contention, controversy, dispute; reply.
contestar [kon-tĕsh-tar'] *va.* to contest, dispute.
conteúdo [kon-tee-oo'doo] *m.* contents. [context.
contexto [kon-taysh'too] *m.*
contido [kon-tee'doo] *adj.* contained; curbed, restrained.
contigo [kon-tee'goo] *pr.* with you, thee.
contiguidade [kon-tee-gwee-dahd'] *f.* proximity.
contíguo [kon-tee'gwoo] *adj.* adjacent, adjoining; nearby.
continência [kon-tee-nen'see-ă] *f.* continence; salute (*mil.*).
continente [kon-tee-nent'] *m.* continent; mainland; *adj.* chaste; continent.
contingência [kon-teen-zhen'see-ă] *f.* contingency; circumstance.
contingente [kon-teen-zhent'] *adj.* contingent; *m.* quota, share; contingent (*mil.*).
continuação [kon-tee-noo-ă-sown'] *f.* continuation.
continuar [kon-tee-noo-ar'] *va/vn.* to continue, go on; to extend, prolong.
continuidade [kon-tee-noo-ee-dahd'] *f.* continuity.
contínuo [kon-tee'noo-oo] *adj.* continual; continuous, incessant; *m.* office boy; porter.
contista [kon-teesh'tă] *mf.* (short)story writer.
conto [kon'too] *m.* (short) story, tale; yarn; 1,000 escudos *or* (*Braz.*) cruzeiros; **sem** —, countless.
contorcer [kon-toor-sayr'] *va.* to twist; *vr.* to writhe.
contorno [kon-tohr'noo] *m.* contour, outline.
contra [kon'tră] *prep.* against,

facing, over against; os prós e os —s, the pros and cons.
contra-almirante [kon-tral-mee-rant'] *m.* rear-admiral.
contrabalançar [kon-tră-bă-lan-sar'] *va.* to counterbalance.
contrabandista [kon-tră-ban-deesh'tă] *m.* smuggler.
contrabando [kon-tră-ban'-doo] *m.* smuggling; contraband, smuggled goods.
contracção [kon-trah-sown'] *f.* contraction.
contracifra [kon-tră-see'-fră] *f.* key (to cipher, code).
contradição [kon-tră-dee-sown'] *f.* contradiction.
contraditório [kon-tră-dee-to'ree-oo] *adj.* contradictory.
contradizer [kon-tră-dee-zayr'] *va.* to contradict; to deny.
contrafazer [kon-tră-fă-zayr'] *va.* to forge, counterfeit; to disguise.
contrafé [kon-tră-fe'] *f.* writ, subpoena.
contrafeito [kon-tră-fay'ee-too] *adj.* counterfeit, false; ill at ease.
contraforte [kon-tră-fort'] *m.* buttress.
contrair [kon-tră-eer'] *va.* to contract; to acquire (habits); — matrimónio, to marry; *vr.* to shrink.
contramandar [kon-tră-man-dar'] *va.* to countermand.
contramestre [kon-tră-mesh'trĕ] *m.* overseer, foreman; boatswain (*naut.*).
contrapeso [kon-tră-pay'zoo] *m.* counterpoise.
contrapor [kon-tră-pohr'] *va.* to oppose, set against.
contraproducente [kon-tră-proo-doo-sent'] *adj.* self-defeating; which defeats its own purpose.
contra-revolução [kon-tră-rĕ-voo-loo-sown'] *f.* counter-revolution.
contrariar [kon-tră-ree-ar'] *va.* to contradict; to frustrate; to annoy; to disappoint.
contrariedade [kon-tră-ree-ĕ-dahd'] *f.* opposition; annoyance; obstacle.
contrário [kon-trah'ree-oo] *adj.* contrary; adverse, unfavourable; *m.* contrary; adversary; ao, pelo, —, on the contrary.
contra-senha [kon-tră-sĕ'-nyă] *f.* password; counter-sign.
contra-senso [kon-tră-sen'-soo] *m.* absurdity, nonsense.
contrastar [kon-trăsh-tar'] *va.* to oppose ; to assay (gold, etc.); *vn.* to contrast with.
contraste [kon-trasht'] *m.* contrast; opposition.
contratante [kon-tră-tant'] *adj.* contracting; *m.pl.* contracting parties.
contratar [kon-tră-tar'] *va.* to contract for, undertake; *vr.* to make a contract, bind oneself.
contratempo [kon-tră-ten'-poo] *m.* drawback; setback, disappointment.
contrato [kon-trah'too] *m.* contract, pact, agreement.
contravenção [kon-tră-ven-sown'] *f.* contravention, violation.
contravir [kon-tră-veer'] *va.* to contravene, infringe; *vn.* to retort.
contribuição [kon-tree-boo-ee-sown'] *f.* contribution; tax.
contribuinte [kon-tree-boo-eent'] *m.* tax-payer; ratepayer.
contribuir [kon-tree-boo-eer'] *va.* to contribute; to pay taxes.
contrição [kon-tree-sown'] *f.* contrition, repentance.

contristar [kon-treesh-tar'] *va.* to grieve, sadden.
contrito [kon-tree'too] *adj.* contrite, penitent.
controvérsia [kon-troo-vair'-see-ă] *f.* controversy, dispute.
controverter [kon-troo-vĕr-tayr'] *va.* to dispute, deny.
contudo [kon-too'doo] *conj.* nevertheless, however.
contumácia [kon-too-mah'-see-ă] *f.* obstinacy; contempt of court (*leg.*).
contumaz [kon-too-mash'] *adj.* obstinate, contumacious.
contumélia [kon-too-me'lee-ă] *f.* contumely, abuse.
contundente [kon-toon-dent'] *adj.* bruising; **instrumento —**, blunt instrument.
contundir [kon-toon-deer'] *va.* to bruise, batter.
conturbar [kon-toor-bar'] *va.* to disturb, stir up.
contusão [kon-too-zown'] *f.* bruise, contusion.
convalescença [kon-vă-lĕsh-sen'să] *f.* convalescence.
convalescer [kon-vă-lĕsh-sayr'] *vn.* to convalesce.
convenção [kon-ven-sown'] *f.* convention; agreement; pact.
convencer [kon-ven-sayr'] *va.* to convince; *vr.* to be convinced.
convencional [kon-ven-see-oo-nal'] *adj.* conventional.
conveniência [kon-vĕ-nee-en'see-ă] *f.* convenience; propriety; *pl.* social conventions.
conveniente [kon-vĕ-nee-ent'] *adj.* suitable, convenient; fitting, appropriate.
convénio [kon-ve'nee-oo] *m.* agreement, convention.
convento [kon-ven'too] *m.* convent (for nuns); monastery (for monks).
convergir [kon-vĕr-zheer'] *vn.* to converge, come together.
conversa [kon-vair'să] *f.* conversation, talk, chat; chatter, idle talk.
conversação [kon-vĕr-să-sown'] *f.* conversation.
conversão [kon-vĕr-sown'] *f.* conversion.
conversar [kon-vĕr-sar'] *vn.* to talk, converse.
conversibilidade [kon-vĕr-see-bee-lee-dahd'] *f.* convertibility.
conversível [kon-vĕr-see'vell] *adj.* convertible.
converter [kon-vĕr-tayr'] *va.* to convert, transform, change; *vr.* to be converted.
convertido [kon-vĕr-tee'doo] *m.* convert.
convés [kon-vesh'] *m.* (top-) deck.
convicção [kon-veek-sown'] *f.* conviction; certainty.
convicto [kon-veek'too] *adj.* convinced; convicted (criminal).
convidado [kon-vee-dah'doo] *m.* guest, person invited.
convidar [kon-vee-dar'] *va.* to invite; to attract.
convincente [kon-veen-sent' *adj.* convincing.
convir [kon-veer'] *vn.* to agree; to suit; to befit.
convite [kon-veet'] *m.* invitation.
convivência [kon-vee-ven'-see-ă] *f.* living together; companionship; close association.
convívio [kon-vee'vee-oo] *m.* conviviality; banquet, feast.
convocar [kon-voo-kar'] *va.* to convene, call together, summon.
convulsão [kon-vool-sown'] *f.* convulsion; upheaval (*polit.*).
convulsionar [kon-vool-see-oo-nar'] *va.* to convulse, cause a convulsion in, plunge into turmoil.
convulso [kon-vool'soo] *adj.* convulsed; shaking.

cooperação [koo-oo-pĕ-ra-sown'] *f.* co-operation.
cooperar [koo-oo-pĕ-răr'] *vn.* to co-operate.
cooperativa [koo-oo-pĕră-tee'vă] *f.* co-operative society.
coordenar [koo-oor-dĕ-nar'] *va.* to co-ordinate.
copa [ko'pă] *f.* pantry; top (of tree); crown (of hat); *pl.* hearts (cards). [butler.
copeiro [koo-pay'ee-roo] *m.*
cópia [ko'pee-ă] *f.* copy; imitation; abundance.
copiador [koo-pee-ă-dohr'] *m.* copier, copyist; copy-book; duplicating machine.
copiar [koo-pee-ar'] *va.* to copy; to imitate.
copioso [koo-pee-oh'zoo] *adj.* copious, abundant.
copista [koo-peesh'tă] *mf.* copyist; plagiarist (*fig.*).
copla [kop'lă] *f.* ballad; verse; couplet.
copo [ko'poo] *m.* glass.
coque [kok] *m.* coke; rap on the head.
coqueiro [koo-kay'ee-roo] *m.* coconut-tree; palm tree.
coqueluche [ko-kĕ-loosh'] *f.* whooping-cough.
cor [kohr] *f.* colour; hue; complexion; pretence (*fig.*).
cor [kor] de —, by heart.
coração [koo-ră-sown'] *m.* heart.
coragem [koh-rah'zhen] *f.* courage, bravery.
corajoso [koo-ră-zhoh'zoo] *adj.* brave, courageous.
corar [ko-rar'] *vn.* to blush; to flush; *va.* to dye; to bleach (in sun); to gloss over.
corbelha [koor-bay'lyă] *f.* basket (of fruit, flowers).
corça [kohr'să] *f.* deer.
corcel [koor-sel'] *m.* steed, charger.
corço [kohr'soo] *m.* roebuck.
corcova [koor-ko'vă] *f.* hump.
corcovado [koor-koo-vah'-doo] *adj.* hunchbacked.
corcovar [koor-koo-var'] *vn.* to stoop. [hunchback.
corcunda [koor-koon'dă] *mf.*
corda [kor'dă] *f.* rope; string; chord (*mus.*, vocal); dar — a, to wind (watch, clock).
cordão [koor-down'] *m.* twine; cord; cordon (*mil.*)
cordeiro [koor-day'ee-roo] *m.* lamb.
cordel [koor-del'] *m.* string; literatura de —, cheap literature.
cordial [koor-dee-al'] *adj.* cordial, warm; *m.* cordial.
cordialidade [koor-dee-ă-lee-dahd'] *f.* cordiality, friendliness, warmth.
cordura [koor-doo'ră] *f.* good sense; prudence.
coreia [koo-re'yă] *f.* St. Vitus' dance (*med.*). [stand.
coreto [koo-ray'too] *m.* band-
co–reu [koo-re'oo] *m.* accomplice, co-defendant.
corifeu [koo-ree-fay'oo] *m.* leader, head.
corisco [koo-reesh'koo] *m.* flash, flicker.
corista [koo-reesh'tă] *mf.* member of a chorus; *f.* chorus girl (*theat.*).
corja [kor'zhă] *f.* mob, rabble.
corneta [koor-nay'tă] *f.* bugle; cornet; — acústica, ear-trumpet.
coro [koh'roo] *m.* chorus, choir; menino de—, choir boy.
coroa [koo-roh'ă] *f.* crown; 5 escudos; garland; tonsure.
coroação [koo-roo-ă-sown'] *f.* coronation.
coroar [koo-roo-ar'] *va.* to crown; to honour, reward; to complete.
coroça [koo-ro'să] *f.* straw cape.

coronel [koo-roo-nel'] *m.* colonel.
coronha [koo-roh'nyă] *f.* butt (of rifle); handle (of revolver).
corpo [kohr'poo] *m.* body; mass, substance; society, association; corps (*mil.*, diplomatic); — **a** —, hand-to-hand (fighting).
corporação [koor-poo-ră-sow*n*'] *f.* corporation; society.
corpulento [koor-poo-le*n*'too] *adj.* corpulent, stout.
correcção [koo-re-sow*n*'] *f.* correction; improvement; correctness; **casa de** —, reformatory.
correcto [koo-re'too] *adj.* correct; right.
corredor [koo-rĕ-dohr'] *m.* corridor; race-horse; runner.
correia [koo-ray'yă] *f.* leather belt, strap; (dog)leash.
correio [koo-ray'yoo] *m.* post-office; post, mail; courier.
corrente [koo-re*n*t'] *m.* current; flow; chain; — **de ar**, draught; *adj.* current; usual; fluent.
correr [koo-rayr'] *vn.* to run, race; to flow; to proceed, go on; *va.* to run over, examine; to draw (curtains); to chase (out, off, away).
correspondência [koo-rĕsh-pon-de*n*'see-ă] *f.* correspondence; letters.
correspondente [koo-rĕsh-po*n*-de*n*t'] *m.* correspondent; *adj.* corresponding; appropriate.
corresponder [koo-rĕsh-po*n*-dayr'] *vn.* to correspond; to answer to, tally with.
corretor [koo-rĕ-tohr'] *m.* broker; commission agent.
corrida [koo-ree'dă] *f.* race; — **de touros**, bullfight.
corrido [koo-ree'doo] *adj.* ashamed; repelled.
corrigir [koo-ree-zheer'] *va.* to correct; to amend; to admonish.
corrilho [koo-ree'lyoo] *m.* secret meeting.
corrimão [koo-ree-mow*n*'] *m.* handrail.
corriqueiro [koo-ree-kay'ee-roo] *adj.* commonplace, hackneyed.
corroborar [koo-roo-boo-rar'] *va.* to corroborate, confirm.
corroer [koo-roo-ayr'] *va.* to corrode.
corromper [koo-ro*n*-payr'] *va.* to corrupt; to taint; to deprave.
corrupção [koo-roo-sow*n*'] *f.* corruption; deterioration.
corrupto [koo-roo'too] *adj.* corrupt; rotten, depraved.
corsário [koor-sah'ree-oo] *m.* privateer; pirate.
cortadura [koor-tă-doo'ră] *f.* cut, incision; ditch; gap (between hills).
cortar [koor-tar'] *va.* to cut (off, out, up, etc.).
corte [kort] *m.* cut, gash; cutting edge; style.
corte [kohrt] *f.* (royal) court; **fazer a** — **a**, to court; *pl.* parliament.
cortejo [koor-tay'zhoo] *m.* greetings; retinue, suite; procession.
cortês [koor-taysh'] *adj.* polite, courteous.
cortesão [koor-tĕ-zow*n*'] *m.* courtier; *adj.* courtly.
cortesia [koor-tĕ-zee'ă] *f.* courtesy, politeness.
cortiça [koor-tee'să] *f.* cork.
cortiço [koor-tee'soo] *m.* beehive.
cortina [koor-tee'nă] *f.* curtain; screen.
coruchéu [koo-roo-she'oo] *m.* spire.
coruja [koo-roo'zhă] *f.* owl.

coruscar [koo-roosh-kar'] *vn.* to sparkle, shine.
corvo [kohr'voo] *m.* crow; raven.
cós [kosh] *m.* waistband.
coser [koo-zayr'] *va.* to sew, stitch. [*m.* cosmetic.
cosmético [koozh-me'tee-koo]
cosmopolita [koozh-moo-poo-lee'tă] *m/adj.* cosmopolitan. [*pl.* back.
costa [kosh'tă] *f.* coast, shore;
costado [koosh-tah'doo] *m.* back; **dos quatro —s,** thoroughgoing, thoroughbred.
costear [koosh-tee-ar'] *vn.* to coast (along), follow the coast.
costela [koosh-te'lă] *f.* rib.
costeleta [koosh-tĕ-lay'tă] *f.* cutlet, chop.
costumado [koosh-too-mah'-doo] *adj.* usual, customary; accustomed (to).
costumar [koosh-too-mar'] *vn.* to be in the habit (of); *va.* to accustom; *vr.* to get used to.
costume [koosh-toom'] *m.* custom, habit, practice; **de —,** usual, customary.
costura [koosh-too'ră] *f.* sewing, needlework; stitch, seam.
costureira [koosh-too-ray'ee-ră] *f.* needlewoman; dressmaker.
cota [ko'tă] *f.* classification, catalogue number (e.g. of book); quota.
cotação [koo-tă-sown'] *f.* quotation (*com.*); price-list; assessment; **— bancária,** bank rate.
cotão [koo-town'] *m.* fluff.
cotar [koo-tar'] *va.* to quote (*com.*); to assess; to register.
cote [kot] *m.* whetstone; **de —,** daily.
cotejar [koo-tĕ-zhar'] *va.* to compare; to collate.
cotejo [koo-tay'zhoo] *m.* collation comparison.
coto [koh'too] *m.* stump.
cotovelo [koo-too-vay'loo] *m.* elbow; bend (of river, road, etc.); **falar pelos —s,** to talk non-stop. [lark.
cotovia [koo-too-vee'ă] *f.* (sky-)
couraça [koh-rah'să] *f.* breastplate, cuirass; armour-plate.
couraçado [koh-ră-sah'doo] *m.* battleship. [preserve.
coutada [koh-tah'dă] *f.* game
couve [kohv] *f.* cabbage; **—-flor,** cauliflower.
cova [ko'vă] *f.* pit; cave; hole, cavity; grave.
coveiro [koo-vay'ee-roo] *m.* grave-digger.
covil [koo-veel'] *m.* den, lair.
covinha [koo-vee'nyă] *f.* dimple.
coxa [koh'shă] *f.* thigh.
coxear [koo-shee-ar'] *vn.* to limp, hobble.
coxia [koo-shee'ă] *f.* passage, aisle, gangway.
coxim [koo-sheen'] *m.* cushion.
coxo [koh'shoo] *adj.* lame.
cozer [koo-zayr'] *va.* to cook, boil; to bake (bread); **— a bebedeira,** to sleep it off (i.e. intoxication).
cozinha [koo-zee'nyă] *f.* kitchen; cooking, cuisine.
cozinhar [koo-zee-nyar'] *va.* to cook.
cozinheiro [koo-zee-nyay'ee-roo] *m.* cook chef.
craca [krah'kă] *f.* barnacle.
crânio [kră'nee-oo] *m.* skull.
crapuloso [kră-poo-loh'zoo] *adj.* dissolute; drunken.
crasso [kra'soo] *adj.* thick, dense; (*fig.*) crass, gross.
cratera [kră-tair'ă] *f.* crater.
cravar [kră-var'] *va.* to drive in (nail, etc.); to set (jewels); to rivet, fix.
craveiro [kră-vay'ee-roo] *m.* carnation plant; flower-pot.
cravelha [kră-vay'lyă] *f.* tuning peg (*mus.*).

cravo [krah'voo] *m.* carnation; — da India, clove.
cré [kre] *f.* chalk.
creche [kresh] *f.* day-nursery; crèche.
crédito [kre'dee-too] *m.* credit; honour; belief; a —, on credit.
credo [kre'doo] *m.* creed; *interj.* good heavens!, God forbid!
credor [kre-dohr'] *m.* creditor.
credulidade [krĕ-doo-lee-dahd'] *f.* credulity.
crédulo [kre'doo-loo] *adj.* credulous, gullible.
cremalheira [krĕ-mă-lyay'ee-ră] *f.* cog-rail; hook and chain (for cooking-pot).
cremar [krĕ-mar'] *va.* to cremate. [custard.
creme [krem'] *m.* cream;
crença [kre*n*'să] *f.* belief.
crendice [kre*n*-dees'] *f.* foolish belief.
crente [kre*n*t] *mf.* believer; *adj.* believing; estar — em, to believe in.
crepitação [krĕ-pee-tă-sow*n*'] *f.* crackling. [crackle.
crepitar [krĕ-pee-tar'] *vn.* to
crepuscular [krĕ-poosh-koo-lar'] *adj.* twilight; dim.
crepúsculo [krĕ-poosh'koo-loo] *m.* twilight, dusk.
crer [krayr] *vn.* to believe; to think.
crescente [krĕsh-se*n*t'] *m.* crescent (*moon*); *f.* high tide; *adj.* increasing, growing.
crescer [krĕsh-sayr'] *vn.* to grow, increase; to rise (up).
crescido [krĕsh-see'doo] *adj.* grown up; big; enlarged.
crescimento [krĕsh-see-me*n*'-too] *m.* growth; increase.
crespo [kraysh'poo] *adj.* curly (hair); rough; bristling.
crestar [krĕsh-tar'] *va.* to singe. [cretin, idiot.
cretino [krĕ-tee'noo] *m.*
cria [kree'ă] *f.* young (of animals), cub.
criação [kree-ă-sow*n*'] *f.* creation; rearing, breeding.
criada [kree-ah'dă] *f.* maid, servant.
criado [kree-ah'doo] *m.* servant; waiter (in café).
criador [kree-ă-dohr'] *m.* creator; breeder (of cattle).
criança [kree-a*n*'să] *f.* child.
criar [kree-ar'] *va.* to create; to bring up, rear (children); to breed, raise (animals); — raizes, to take root.
criatura [kree-ă-too'ră] *f.* creature; person.
crime [kreem] *m.* crime; offence.
criminoso [kri-mee-noh'zoo] *m/adj.* criminal.
crina [kree'nă] *f.* (horse's) mane; horsehair.
crioulo [kree-oh'loo] *m.* creole, colonial (in America); (*Braz. usu.*) negro.
cripta [kreep'tă] *f.* crypt.
crise [kreez] *f.* crisis.
crisma [kreezh'mă] *f.* holy oil; Confirmation.
crismar [kreezh-mar'] *va.* to confirm; to name, call.
crisol [kree-zol'] *m.* crucible; test.
crista [kreesh'tă] *f.* cock's comb; ridge, crest.
cristal [kreesh-tal'] *m.* crystal.
cristandade [kreesh-ta*n*-dahd'] *f.* Christendom; Christianity.
cristão [kreesh-tow*n*'] *m/adj.* Christian; — novo, converted Jew.
cristianismo [kreesh-tee-ă-neezh'moo] *m.* Christianity.
Cristo [kreesh'too] *m.* Christ; crucifix.
critério [kree-tair'ee-oo] *m.* criterion; judgment.

crítica [kree'tee-kă] *f.* criticism; critical article.
criticar [kree-tee-kar'] *va.* to criticize, find fault with; to judge. [*adj.* critical.
crítico [kree'tee-koo] *m.* critic;
crivar [kree-var'] *va.* to pierce, riddle (e.g. with bullets).
crível [kree'vel] *adj.* credible.
crivo [kree'voo] *m.* sieve.
crocitar [kroo-see-tar'] *vn.* to croak, caw (of crows).
crocodilo [kroo-koo-dee'loo] *m.* crocodile.
crónica [kro'nee-kă] *f.* chronicle; (literary, etc.) column (in newspaper). [chronic.
crónico [kro'nee-koo] *adj.*
cronista [kroh-neesh'tă] *m.* chronicler; columnist (in newspaper).
cronológico [kroh-noo-lo'-zhee-koo] *adj.* chronological.
croque [krok] *m.* boat-hook.
crosta [krohsh'tă] *f.* crust.
cru [kroo] *adj.* raw; crude; coarse; cruel.
crucificação [kroo-see-fee-kă-sow*n*'] *f.* crucifixion.
crucificar [kroo-see-fee-kar'] *va.* to crucify; to torture.
crucifixo [kroo-see-feek'soo] *m.* crucifix.
cruel [kroo-el'] *adj.* cruel.
crueldade [kroo-ĕl-dahd'] *f.* cruelty.
cruento [kroo-e*n*'too] *adj.* bloody (battle, etc.); bloodthirsty, cruel.
crueza [kroo-ay'ză] *f.* rawness; crudeness; coarseness; cruelty.
crupe [kroop] *m.* croup.
cruz [kroosh] *f.* cross; —gamada, swastika; —es e cunhos, heads and tails (of coins). [sade.
cruzada [kroo-zah'dă] *f.* cru-
cruzado [kroo-zah'doo] *m.* crusader; *adj.* crossed; braços —s, folded arms; palavras —as, crossword puzzle.
cruzamento [kroo-ză-me*n*'-too] *m.* crossing.
cruzar [kroo-zar'] *va/vn.* to cross; to lay across; to cruise (*naut.*).
cruzeiro [kroo-zay'ee-roo] *m.* cruiser (*naut.*); (large) cross; transept (in church); Brazilian monetary unit; (sea-) cruise.
cruzeta [kroo-zay'tă] *f.* coat-hanger.
cuba [koo'bă] *f.* wine vat, barrel, cask. [bucket.
cubo [koo'boo] *m.* cube;
cuco [koo'koo] *m.* cuckoo.
cuecas [koo-e'kăsh] *f.pl.* pants, underpants.
cueiro [koo-ay'ee-roo] *m.* (baby's) napkin.
cuidado [kwee-dah'doo] *m.* care; attention; anxiety; *interj.* be careful!, look out!
cuidadoso [kwee-dă-doh'zoo] *adj.* careful, painstaking.
cuidar [kwee-dar'] *va.* to take care of, attend to; to think.
cujo [koo'zhoo] *pr.* whose; of which. [(of gun).
culatra [koo-la'tră] *f.* breech
culminação [kool-mee-nă-sow*n*'] *f.* culmination, zenith.
culpa [kool'pă] *f.* fault; guilt; blame.
culpabilidade [kool-pă-bee-lee-dahd'] *f.* guilt.
culpado [kool-pah'doo] *adj.* guilty; (person *or* thing) to blame.
culpar [kool-par'] *va.* to blame; *vr.* to take the blame; to incriminate oneself.
culpável [kool-pah'vel] *adj.* culpable, blameworthy.
cultivar [kool-tee-var'] *va.* to cultivate; to grow; to till.
culto [kool'too] *adj.* educated; well-bred; civilized; *m.* worship; religion, cult.

cultura [kool-too'ră] *f.* culture; cultivation; cultivated land; refinement.
cultural [kool-too-ral'] *adj.* cultural.
cume [koom] *m.* top, summit.
cumeada [koo-mee-ah'dă] *f.* (mountain) ridge.
cumeeira [koo-mee-ay'ee-ră] *f.* ridge, crest.
cúmplice [koo*n*'plees] *mf.* accomplice, accessory.
cumplicidade [koo*n*-plee-see-dahd'] *f.* complicity.
cumprimentar [koo*n*-pree-me*n*-tar'] *va.* to greet; to congratulate.
cumprimento [koo*n*-pree-me*n*'too] *m.* greeting; fulfilment, completion, execution (of a task, order, etc).; *pl.* kind regards; greetings; best wishes.
cumprir [koo*n*-preer'] *va.* to fulfil, carry out, accomplish; to be a duty to; — **a palavra**, to keep one's word.
cúmulo [koo'moo-loo] *m.* heap, pile; summit, top; **é o —**, that's the limit.
cunha [koo'nyă] *f.* wedge.
cunhada [koo-nyah'dă] *f.* sister-in-law.
cunhado, [koo-nyah'-doo] *m.* brother-in-law,
cunhar [koo-nyar'] *va.* to mint, coin.
cunho [koo'nyoo] *m.* stamp.
cupão [koo-pow*n*'] *m.* coupon.
cupidez [koo-pee-daysh'] *f.* cupidity, avarice.
cupim [koo-pee*n*'] *m.* white ant, termite. [cup (*bot.*).
cúpula [koo'poo-lă] *f.* dome;
cura [koo'ră] *f.* cure, remedy; *m.* parish priest, rector, vicar.
curador [koo-ră-dohr'] *m.* guardian; trustee; curator.
curandeiro [koo-ra*n*-day'ee-roo] *m.* quack; witch doctor.
curar [koo-rar'] *va.* to cure, heal; to preserve, cure (meat, etc.).
curativo [koo-ră-tee'voo] *adj.* curative; *m.* treatment, dressing (*med.*).
curiosidade [koo-ree-oo-zee-dahd'] *f.* curiosity; inquisitiveness; rare object, curio.
curioso [koo-ree-oh'zoo] *adj.* curious; inquisitive; odd, strange.
curral [koo-ral'] *m.* pen, enclosure (for cattle).
curro [koo'roo] *m.* bull pen.
cursar [koor-sar'] *va.* to attend, follow a course (of study); to travel.
curso [koor'soo] *m.* course (of study, river, etc.); direction; **ter —**, to be current; **em —**, in progress.
curtir [koor-teer'] *va.* to tan (hides); to toughen; to endure, suffer (hardship).
curto [koor'too] *adj.* short; brief; dull, backward; — **de vista**, short-sighted.
curva [koor'vă] *f.* curve, bend.
curvar [koor-var'] *va.* to bend; *vr.* to bow (down).
curvatura [koor-vă-too'ră] *f.* curvature, bend.
cúspide [koosh'peed] *f.* tip, sharp point.
cuspideira [koosh-pĕ-day'ee-ră] *f.* spittoon. [spit.
cuspir [koosh-peer'] *vn.* to
custa [koosh'tă] *f.* expense, cost; *pl.* costs (*leg.*).
custar [koosh-tar'] *vn.* to cost; to be difficult, painful.
custear [koosh-tee-ar'] *va.* to defray the expenses, bear the cost of.
custo [koosh'too] *m.* cost, expense; **a —**, with difficulty.
custódia [koosh-to'dee-ă] *f.* custody; guardianship; monstrance (*eccl.*).

custódio [koosh-to'dee-oo] *adj.* anjo —, guardian angel.
custoso [koosh-toh'zoo] *adj.* costly; arduous.
cutelaria [koo-tĕ-lă-ree'ă] *f.* cutlery.
cutelo [koo-te'loo] *m.* chopper, cleaver; cutlass.
cutilada [koo-tee-lah'dă] *f.* slash, cut (with sword, etc.).
cútis [koo'teesh] *f.* (human) skin.

D

da [dă] of the, from the.
dactilógrafa [dak-tee-lo'gră-fă] *f.* typist.
dactilografar [dak-tee-loo-gră-far'] *va.* to type.
dactilografia [dak-tee-loo-gră-fee'ă] *f.* typing.
dádiva [da'dee-vă] *f.* gift.
dadivoso [dă-dee-voh'zoo] *adj.* generous, bountiful.
dado [dah'doo] *m.* datum, basic fact; dice (in games); **o — está lançado,** the die is cast.
daí [dă-ee'] from there; from that; for that reason; **— em (por) diante,** from then on, thereafter.
dama [dă'mă] *f.* lady; **— de honor,** maid of honour; **primeira —,** leading lady (*theat.*); queen (in chess, cards); *pl.* draughts.
damasco [dă-mash'koo] *m.* apricot; damask (fabric).
damasqueiro [dă-măsh-kay'-ee-roo] *m.* apricot-tree.
danação [dă-nă-sow*n*'] *f.* rabies; fury, rage.
danado [dă-nah'doo] *adj.* rabid, raging; damned; **cão —,** mad dog.
dança [da*n*'să] *f.* dance.
dançar [da*n*-sar'] *vn.* to dance.
dançarina [da*n*-să-ree'nă] *f.*; **dançarino** [da*n*-să-ree'-noo] *m.* (professional) dancer.
daninho [dă-nee'nyoo] *adj.* harmful, injurious, noxious.
dano [dă'noo] *m.* injury, hurt; damage.
danoso [dă-noh'zoo] *adj.* harmful, detrimental.
dantes [da*n*tsh] *adv.* formerly.
daqui [dă-kee'] *prep/adv.* from here; from now; **— em diante,** from now on.
dar [dar] *va.* to give; to bestow, present, grant; **— gritos,** to shout, yell; **— à luz,** to give birth; **— horas,** to strike the hour; **— em,** to hit; **— para,** to look on to; **— com,** to meet, come across; **— -se bem com,** to get on well with; **— de si,** to give way; **— um passeio,** to take a walk.
dardejar [dăr-dĕ-zhar'] *va.* to throw (out), dart, hurl.
dardo [dar'doo] *m.* dart.
data [da'tă] *f.* date; time, epoch; **de longa —,** of long standing.
de [dĕ] *prep.* of; from; with; by.
deão [dee-own'] *m.* dean (*eccl.*).
debaixo [dĕ-bȳ'shoo] *adv.* below, underneath; *prep.* **— de,** under, beneath.
debalde [dĕ-bald'] *adv.* in vain.
debandada [dĕ-ba*n*-dah'dă] *f.* rout, stampede.
debate [dĕ-bat'] *m.* debate; argument.
debater [dĕ-bă-tayr'] *va.* to debate, discuss; *vr.* to struggle.
debelar [dĕ-bĕ-lar'] *va.* to put down, suppress.
debicar [dĕ-bee-kar'] *vn.* to peck.
débil [de'beel] *adj.* weak, [feeble.
debilidade [dĕ-bee-lee-dahd'] *f.* weakness, debility.
debilitar [dĕ-bee-lee-tar'] *va.* to weaken; *vr.* to get weak.

debitar [dĕ-bee-tar'] *va.* to debit.
débito [de'bee-too] *m.* debit.
debruçar-se [dĕ-broo-sar'sĕ] *vr.* to bend over, lean over, lean out of.
debrum [dĕ-broo*n*'] *m.* hem.
debulha [dĕ-boo'lyă] *f.* threshing (of corn).
debulhar [dĕ-boo-lyar'] *va.* to thresh; — **-se em lágrimas,** to dissolve into tears.
debuxo [dĕ-boo'shoo] *m.* sketch, rough draft.
década [de'kă-dă] *f.* decade.
decadência [dĕ-kă-de*n*'see-ă] *f.* decadence, decline, decay.
decadente [dĕ-kă-de*n*t'] *adj.* decadent, decaying.
decair [dĕ-kă-eer'] *vn.* to decay, fall away; to go down in the world.
decano [dĕ-kă'noo] *m.* oldest member (of a society, etc.); doyen (of diplomatic corps, etc.).
decantar [dĕ-ka*n*-tar'] *va.* to decant (liquids); to praise (in verse, song).
decapitar [dĕ-kă-pee-tar'] *va.* to behead, decapitate.
decência [dĕ-se*n*'see-ă] *f.* decency; respectability; tidiness, neatness (e.g. in dress).
decénio [dĕ-se'nee-oo] *m.* ten-year period, decade.
decente [dĕ-se*n*t'] *adj.* decent; respectable; clean, tidy.
decepar [dĕ-sĕ-par'] *va.* to cut off, chop off.
decepção [dĕ-sep-sow*n*'] *f.* disappointment; disillusion.
decepcionar [dĕ-sep-see-oo-nar'] *va.* to disappoint.
decerto [dĕ-sair'too] *adv.* certainly.
decidido [dĕ-see-dee'doo] *adj.* determined, resolute; decided.
decidir [dĕ-see-deer'] *va.* to decide; to determine.
decifrar [dĕ-see-frar'] *va.* to decipher, decode; to unravel (a mystery); to guess.
decisão [dĕ-see-zow*n*'] *f.* decision.
decisivo [dĕ-see-zee'voo] *adj.* decisive, conclusive.
declamação [dĕ-klă-măsow*n*'] *f.* declamation, pompous speech.
declamar [dĕ-klă-mar'] *va/vn* to declaim; to rant.
declaração [dĕ-klă-ră-sow*n*'] *f.* declaration, statement; — **jurada,** affidavit.
declarar [dĕ-klă-rar'] *va.* to declare; to state; to explain.
declinação [dĕ-klee-nă-sow*n*'] *f.* decline; fading away; (*grammatical*) declension.
declinar [dĕ-klee-nar'] *vn.* to decline, diminish; *va.* to decline (an offer, etc.).
declive [dĕ-kleev'] *m.* slope, incline, declivity.
decomposição [dĕ-ko*n*-poo-zee-sow*n*'] *f.* decomposition; disintegration.
decoração [dĕ-koo-ră-sow*n*'] *f.* decoration; — **teatral,** stage setting, scenery.
decorar [dĕ-koo-rar'] *va.* to decorate; to learn by heart.
decorativo [dĕ-koo-ră-tee'voo] *adj.* decorative.
decoro [de-ko'roo] *m.* decorum, decency, seemliness.
decoroso [dĕ-koo-roh'zoo] *adj.* proper, seemly, decorous.
decorrer [dĕ-koo-rayr'] *vn.* to pass, elapse (of time); to occur.
decote [dĕ-kot'] *m.* low neckline (of dress).
decrépito [dĕ-kre'pee-too] *adj.* decrepit, infirm; ramshackle.
decrescente [dĕ-krĕsh-se*n*t'] *adj.* diminishing, decreasing.
decrescer [dĕ-krĕsh-sayr'] *vn.* to go down, diminish, grow less.

decrescimento [dĕ-krĕsh-see-men'too] *m.* decrease.
decretar [dĕ-krĕ-tar'] *va.* to decree, order.
decreto [dĕ-kre'too] *m.* decree, order, ordinance.
decuplar [dĕ-koo-plar'] *va.* to multiply by ten; to increase tenfold.
decurso [dĕ-koor'soo] *m.* course (of time); *adj.* elapsed, passed.
dedada [dĕ-dah'dă] *f.* finger-mark.
dedal [dĕ-dal'] *m.* thimble; thimbleful, very small amount.
dédalo [de'dă-loo] *m.* maze, labyrinth.
dedeira [dĕ-day'ee-ră] *f.* covering on the finger, finger-stall.
dedicação [dĕ-dee-kă-sown'] *f.* dedication, devotion.
dedicar [dĕ-dee-kar'] *va.* to dedicate, devote.
dedicatória [dĕ-dee-kă-to'-ree-ă] *f.* dedication (of book, etc.).
dedo [day'doo] *m.* finger; — polegar, thumb; — indicador, forefinger; — médio, middle finger; — mínimo, little finger *or* toe; — anular, third, *or* ring, finger; —s dos pés, toes; — grande, big toe.
dedução [dĕ-doo-sown'] *f.* deduction; inference.
deduzir [dĕ-doo-zeer'] *va.* to deduct, subtract; *vn.* to infer, deduce.
defecção [dĕ-fek-sown'] *f.* defection, desertion.
defeito [dĕ-fay'ee-too] *m.* defect, fault, flaw.
defeituoso [dĕ-fay-ee-too-oh'-zoo] *adj.* defective, faulty.
defender [dĕ-fen-dayr'] *va.* to defend, protect; to forbid.
defensiva [dĕ-fen-see'vă] *f.* defensive.
defensor [dĕ-fen-sohr'] *m.* defender; counsel for the defence, defending counsel (*leg.*).
deferência [dĕ-fĕ-ren'see-ă] *f.* respect, deference.
deferimento [dĕ-fĕ-ree-men'-too] *m.* approval, granting (of request).
deferir [dĕ-fĕ-reer'] *va.* to grant, approve (request, application); *vn.* to defer, give way to.
defesa [dĕ-fay'ză] *f.* defence; counsel for the defence; full-back (in football).
defeso [dĕ-fay'zoo] *adj.* forbidden, prohibited.
deficiência [dĕ-fee-see-en'-see-ă] *f.* deficiency, lack, shortcoming.
deficiente [dĕ-fee-see-ent'] *adj.* deficient, defective.
definhar [dĕ-fee-nyar'] *vn.* to waste away; to droop, languish; to grow thin.
definição [dĕ-fee-nee-sown'] *f.* definition.
definido [dĕ-fee-nee'doo] *adj.* clear, defined, definite.
definir [dĕ-fee-neer'] *va.* to define; to determine.
definitivo [dĕ-fi-nee-tee'voo] *adj.* definite; definitive, final.
deformação [dĕ-foor-mă-sown'] *f.* deformation, disfigurement, distortion.
deformar [dĕ-foor-mar'] *va.* to deform, distort.
deforme [dĕ-form'] *adj.* deformed, disfigured, ugly.
deformidade [dĕ-foor-mee-dahd'] *f.* deformity; (*fig.*) depravity.
defraudar [dĕ-frow-dar'] *va.* to defraud, swindle.
defrontar [dĕ-fron-tar'] *va.* to face.
defronte [dĕ-front'] *adv.* opposite, facing; — de, in front of.
defumar [dĕ-foo-mar'] *va.* to

smoke, cure (meat, fish, etc.).
defunto [dě-foo*n*'too] *adj.* deceased, dead; the late; *m.* corpse.
degelar [dě-zhě-lar'] *va.* to [thaw (out).
degelo [dě-zhay'loo] *m.* thaw.
degeneração [dě-zhě-ně-ră-sow*n*'] *f.* degeneration; depravity.
degenerar [dě-zhě-ně-rar'] *vn.* to degenerate.
deglutir [dě-gloo-teer'] *va.* to swallow.
degolar [dě-goo-lar'] *va.* to behead; to cut the throat of.
degradação [dě-gră-dă-sow*n*'] *f.* degradation; debasement, corruption.
degradar [dě-gră-dar'] *va.* to degrade; to debase.
degrau [dě-grow'] *m.* step; rung (of ladder); stage (e.g. in hierarchy).
degredar [dě-grě-dar'] *va.* to banish, exile.
degredo [dě-gray'doo] *m.* exile, banishment.
degustar [dě-goosh-tar'] *va.* to taste, sip.
deificar [day-ee-fee-kar'] *va.* [to deify.
deitado [day-ee-tah'doo] *adj.* in bed; lying down.
deitar [day-ee-tar'] *va.* to lay (flat), spread (out); to place, put; to throw (out, off, up); — **a correr**, to start running; — **uma carta**, to post a letter; — **abaixo**, to knock down; — **sangue**, to bleed; — **o chá**, to pour out the tea; *vr.* to go to bed; to lie down.
deixa [day'ee-shă] *f.* cue (*theat.*).
deixar [day-ee-shar'] *va.* to leave; to abandon; to allow, permit, let; — **de**, to cease to, stop; — **cair**, to drop.
delatar [dě-lă-tar'] *va.* to denounce, inform against, report.
delator [dě-lă-tohr'] *m.* informer; accuser.
delegação [dě-lě-gă-sow*n*'] *f.* delegation.
delegado [dě-lě-gah'doo] *m.* delegate; deputy; commissioner.
delegar [dě-lě-gar'] *va.* to delegate; to commission.
deleitar [dě-lay-ee-tar'] *va.* to delight; *vr.* to delight in.
deleite [dě-lay'eet] *m.* delight, pleasure, joy.
deleitoso [dě-lay-ee-toh'zoo] *adj.* delightful, charming.
deletério [dě-lě-tair'ee-oo] *adj.* noxious, harmful.
delgadeza [del-gă-day'ză] *f.* slenderness; thinness.
delgado [del-gah'doo] *adj.* slim, slender; thin; delicate.
deliberação [dě-lee-bě-ră-sow*n*'] *f.* deliberation; decision.
deliberar [dě-lee-bě-rar'] *va.* to decide; *vn.* to deliberate (on), discuss.
delicadeza [dě-lee-kă-day'ză] *f.* kindness, courtesy; delicacy; gentleness.
delicado [dě-lee-kah'doo] *adj.* delicate; soft; slender; gentle; refined.
delícia [dě-lee'see-ă] *f.* delight, [pleasure, joy.
delicioso [dě-lee-see-oh'zoo] *adj.* delightful; delicious.
delimitação [dě-lee-mee-tă-sow*n*'] *f.* delimitation, demarcation.
delimitar [dě-lee-mee-tar'] *va.* to delimit, fix the boundaries of.
delinear [dě-lee-nee-ar'] *va.* to sketch; to plan (out).
delinquência [dě-lee*n*-kwe*n*'-see-ă] *f.* delinquency; offence.
delinquente [dě-lee*n*-kwe*n*t'] *m.* delinquent; criminal.
delirante [dě-lee-ra*n*t'] *adj.* delirious; insane.

delirar [dĕ-lee-rar'] *vn.* to rave, be delirious; to talk wildly, rant; to be wild, mad (with excitement, passion, etc.)
delírio [dĕ-lee'ree-oo] *m.* delirium, madness, frenzy.
delito [dĕ-lee'too] *m.* crime, offence.
delongar [dĕ-lo*n*-gar'] *va.* to delay, defer, postpone.
demagogo [dĕ-mă-go'goo] *m.* demagogue, agitator.
demais [dĕ-mȳzh'] *adv.* besides, in addition; too; too much; — **a mais,** furthermore; in addition; *m.* the rest.
demanda [dĕ-ma*n*'dă] *f.* lawsuit; plea; claim; **em — de,** in search of.
demandar [dĕ-ma*n*-dar'] *va.* to sue (*leg.*); to seek; to require.
demão [dĕ-mow*n*'] *f.* coat (of paint, etc.).
demarcar [dĕ-măr-kar'] *va.* to demarcate.
demasia [dĕ-mă-zee'ă] *f.* excess, surplus.
demasiado [dĕ-mă-zee-ah'doo] *adj.* excessive; *adv.* too.
demência [dĕ-me*n*'see-ă] *f.* insanity, madness.
demente [dĕ-me*n*t'] *adj.* insane, demented.
demissão [dĕ-mee-sow*n*'] *f.* resignation; dismissal.
demitir [dĕ-mee-teer'] *va.* to dismiss; *vr.* to resign.
demo [de'moo] *m.* devil, demon.
democracia [dĕ-moo-krăsee'ă] *f.* democracy.
democrata [dĕ-moo-krah'tă] *m.* democrat.
democrático [dĕ-moo-kra'tee-koo] *adj.* democratic.
demolição [dĕ-moo-lee-sow*n*'] *f.* demolition; destruction.
demolir [dĕ-moo-leer'] *va.* to demolish, knock down.
demónio [dĕ-mo'nee-oo] *m.* demon, devil; *interj.* damn!, dash (it)!
demonstração [dĕ-mo*n*sh-tră-sow*n*'] *f.* demonstration; proof.
demonstrar [dĕ-mo*n*sh-trar'] *va.* to demonstrate, show; to prove.
demonstrativo [dĕ-mo*n*sh-tră-tee'voo] *adj.* demonstrative; conclusive (reasons).
demora [dĕ-mo'ră] *f.* delay; (temporary) stop.
demorar [dĕ-moo-rar'] *va.* to delay, hold up; *vn.* to stay, remain, linger; *vr.* to stop, stay; to linger; to be long, take a long time (doing something, etc.).
denguice [de*n*-gees'] *f.* affectation.
denodado [dĕ-noo-dah'doo] *adj.* bold, daring.
denominação [dĕ-noo-meenă-sow*n*'] *f.* denomination, title.
denotar [dĕ-noo-tar'] *va.* to denote, indicate.
densidade [de*n*-see-dahd'] *f.* density; compactness.
denso [den'soo] *adj.* dense, thick; compact.
dentado [de*n*-tah'doo] *adj.* serrated, notched.
dentadura [de*n*-tă-doo'ră] *f.* teeth, set of teeth.
dente [de*n*t] *m.* tooth; fang; tusk; **—s postiços,** false teeth; **— abalado,** loose tooth; **falar por entre os —s,** to mutter.
dentista [de*n*-teesh'tă] *m.* dentist.
dentro [de*n*'troo] *adv.* inside; **— em breve,** soon, shortly; **— de,** in, within.
denudar [dĕ-noo-dar'] *va.* to denude, make bare.
denúncia [dĕ-noo*n*'see-ă] *f.* denunciation; accusation; publication of banns of marriage.
denunciar [dĕ-noo*n*-see-ar']

va. to denounce; to reveal.
deparar [dĕ-pă-rar′] *va.* to reveal; *vn.* — **com**, to come across, encounter; *vr.* to present itself.
departamento [dĕ-păr-tă-men′too] *m.* department.
depenar [dĕ-pĕ-nar′] *va.* to pluck.
dependência [dĕ-pen-den′see-ă] *f.* dependence; subordination; dependency (e.g. colony).
depender [dĕ-pen-dayr′] *vn.* to depend.
deplorar [dĕ-ploo-rar′] *va.* to lament, deplore.
deplorável [dĕ-ploo-rah′vel] *adj.* lamentable, deplorable.
depoimento [dĕ-poo-ee-men′too] *m.* evidence, testimony; deposition.
depois [dĕ-poh′eesh] *adv.* afterwards, then; — **de**, *prep.* after.
depor [dĕ-pohr′] *va.* to lay aside, down; to depose (king, etc.); to testify (*leg.*).
deportar [dĕ-poor-tar′] *va.* to deport, banish.
deposição [dĕ-poo-zee-sown′] *f.* deposition, removal (from power); evidence.
depositante [dĕ-poo-zee-tant′] *m.* depositor.
depositar [dĕ-poo-zee-tar′] *va.* to deposit; — **confiança em**, to place confidence in.
depositário [dĕ-poo-zee-tah′ree-oo] *m.* trustee; repository; confidant.
depósito [dĕ-po′zee-too] *m.* deposit; thing deposited; act of depositing; storehouse; sediment (in liquid); — **de água**, tank, reservoir.
depravação [dĕ-pră-vă-sown′] *f.* depravity, corruption.
depravar [dĕ-pră-var′] *va.* to deprave, corrupt.
deprecar [dĕ-prĕ-kar′] *va.* to pray, entreat.
depreciação [dĕ-prĕ-see-ă-sown′] *f.* depreciation.
depreciar [dĕ-prĕ-see-ar′] *va.* to depreciate, undervalue; to debase (coinage).
depredação [dĕ-prĕ-dă-sown′] *f.* depredation.
depredar [dĕ-prĕ-dar′] *va.* to pillage, rob.
depressa [dĕ-pre′să] *adv.* fast, quickly.
depressão [dĕ-prĕ-sown′] *f.* depression.
deprimir [dĕ-pri-meer′] *va.* to depress; to lower; to humble.
depuração [dĕ-poo-ră-sown′] [*f.* purification.
depurar [dĕ-poo-rar′] *va.* to purify, refine.
deputação [dĕ-poo-tă-sown′] *f.* deputation.
deputado [dĕ-poo-tah′doo] *m.* deputy; member of parliament. [delegate.
deputar [dĕ-poo-tar′] *va.* to
derivação [dĕ-ree-vă-sown′] *f.* derivation.
derivar [dĕ-ree-var′] *va.* to derive; to deflect.
derradeiro [dĕ-ră-day′ee-roo] *adj.* last. [tax.
derrama [dĕ-ră′mă] *f.* (local)
derramamento [dĕ-ră-mă-men′too] *m.* pouring; spilling; shedding (of blood).
derramar [dĕ-ră-mar′] *va.* to shed (blood, tears); to pour (out); to scatter.
derredor [dĕ-rĕ-dohr′] *adv/prep.* **em** —, around.
derreter [dĕ-rĕ-tayr′] *va.* to melt; to smelt (metal); to dissolve.
derribar [dĕ-ree-bar′] *va.* to knock down, demolish; to overthrow.
derrocar [dĕ-roo-kar′] *va.* to demolish, knock down, raze.

derrota [dĕ-ro'tă] *f.* defeat, rout; course, route.
derrotar [dĕ-roo-tar'] *va.* to defeat, rout; to destroy.
derrubar [dĕ-roo-bar'] *va.* to knock down; to destroy.
desabafar [dĕ-ză-bă-far'] *va.* to clear, disentangle; to give vent to (one's feelings).
desabar [dĕ-ză-bar'] *vn.* to collapse, fall, tumble down.
desabitado [dĕ-ză-bee-tah'-doo] *adj.* uninhabited.
desabrido [dĕ-ză-bree'doo] *adj.* insolent, rude, brusque; rough (weather).
desabrochar [dĕ-ză-broo-shar'] *vn.* to bloom, blossom.
desacato [dĕ-ză-kah'too] *m.* disrespect, contempt.
desacerto [dĕ-ză-sair'too] *m.* mistake, blunder.
desacordo [dĕ-ză-kohr'doo] *m.* disagreement; disharmony.
desacostumado [dĕ-ză-koosh-too-mah'doo] *adj.* unaccustomed, unusual.
desacreditar [dĕ-ză-krĕ-dee-tar'] *va.* to discredit, disparage.
desafiar [dĕ-ză-fee-ar'] *va.* to defy, challenge.
desafio [dĕ-ză-fee'oo] *m.* challenge; match (sport).
desafogado [dĕ-ză-foo-gah'-doo] *adj.* clear, unencumbered; spacious; free from care, untroubled; comfortably off (financially).
desafogo [dĕ-ză-foh'goo] *m.* ease, relief; easy circumstances.
desaforado [dĕ-ză-foo-rah'-doo] *adj.* impudent, insolent.
desafortunado [dĕ-ză-foor-too-nah'doo] *adj.* unfortunate.
desagradar [dĕ-ză-gră-dar'] *va.* to displease.
desagradável [dĕ-ză-gră-dah'vel] *adj.* disagreeable, unpleasant.
desagrado [dĕ-ză-grah'doo] *m.* displeasure.
desagravo [dĕ-ză-grah'voo] *m.* reparation, redress, amends.
desagregação [dĕ-ză-grĕ-gă-sow*n*'] *f.* separation, disintegration.
desagregar [dĕ-ză-grĕ-gar'] *va.* to break up, disintegrate.
desaguar [dĕ-za-gwar'] *va.* to drain (off); *vn.* to flow (into).
desairoso [dĕ-zȳ-roh'zoo] *adj.* awkward, clumsy; unseemly.
desajeitado [dĕ-ză-zhay-ee-tah'doo] *adj.* clumsy, awkward, ungainly.
desalentado [dĕ-ză-le*n*-tah'-doo] *adj.* disheartened.
desalento [dĕ-ză-le*n*'too] *m.* despondency, low spirits.
desalinhado [dĕ-ză-lee-nyah'-doo] *adj.* untidy, unkempt; out of line.
desalinho [dĕ-ză-lee'nyoo] *m.* untidiness, slovenliness; disarray, disarrangement.
desalmado [dĕ-zal-mah'doo] *adj.* cruel, merciless.
desamor [dĕ-ză-mohr'] *m.* aversion, dislike.
desamortização [dĕ-ză-moor-tee-ză-sow*n*'] *f.* redemption (of property) from entail.
desamparado [dĕ-za*n*-pă-rah'doo] *adj.* forsaken, abandoned.
desamparar [dĕ-za*n*-pă-rar'] *va.* to abandon, forsake.
desandar [dĕ-za*n*-dar'] *va.* to turn back; to unscrew; *vn.* to go back.
desanimado [dĕ-ză-nee-mah'-doo] *adj.* discouraged, downhearted, depressed.
desanimar [dĕ-ză-nee-mar'] *va.* to discourage, depress; *vr.* to lose heart, become discouraged.
desânimo [dĕ-ză'nee-moo] *m.*

depression, despondency, discouragement.
desanuviar [dĕ-ză-noo-vee-ar'] *va.* to clear; *vr.* to clear up.
desapaixonado [dĕ-ză-pȳ-shoo-nah'doo] *adj.* dispassionate.
desaparecer [dĕ-ză-pă-rĕ-sayr'] *vn.* to disappear, vanish, fade away.
desaparição [dĕ-ză-pă-ree-sow*n*'] *f.* disappearance.
desapego [dĕ-ză-pay'goo] *m.* indifference, detachment; lack of affection.
desapercebido [dĕ-ză-pĕr-sĕ-bee'doo] *adj.* unprepared; unprovided with.
desapiedado [dĕ-ză-pee-ĕ-dah'doo] *adj.* unmerciful, ruthless.
desapontado [dĕ-ză-po*n*-tah'-doo] *adj.* disappointed.
desapontamento [dĕ-ză-po*n*-tă-me*n*'too] *m.* disappointment.
desapossar [dĕ-ză-poo-sar'] *va.* to dispossess; to take away.
desaprovar [dĕ-ză-proo-var'] *va.* to disapprove of.
desaproveitamento [dĕ-ză-proo-vay-ee-tă-me*n*'too] *m.* waste, squandering; lack of application, negligence.
desarmamento [dĕ-zar-mă-me*n*'too] *m.* disarmament.
desarmar [dĕ-zar-mar'] *va.* to disarm; to dismantle (gun, clock, etc.).
desarraigar [dĕ-ză-rȳ-gar'] *va.* to uproot, root out.
desarranjar [dĕ-ză-ra*n*-zhar'] *va.* to disarrange, disturb.
desarranjo [dĕ-ză-ra*n*'zhoo] *m.* disarrangement, confusion, disturbance.
desarrumar [dĕ-ză-roo-mar'] *va.* to disarrange; to unpack (cases).
desarticulado [dĕ-zăr-tee-koo-lah'doo] *adj.* out of joint, dislocated.
desassossego [dĕ-ză-soo-say'goo] *m.* disquiet; restlessness.
desastrado [dĕ-zăsh-trah'-doo] *adj.* disastrous; clumsy, awkward.
desastre [dĕ-zash'trĕ] *m.* disaster; accident.
desastroso [dĕ-zăsh-troh'zoo] *adj.* disastrous.
desatar [dĕ-ză-tar'] *va.* to untie, undo, unfasten; — a chorar, to burst into tears.
desatenção [dĕ-ză-te*n*-sow*n*'] *f.* lack of attention; discourtesy.
desatender [dĕ-ză-te*n*-dayr'] *va.* to neglect, pay no attention to; to be discourteous, inconsiderate (to).
desatinado [dĕ-ză-tee-nah'-doo] *adj.* crazy, wild; foolish.
desatino [dĕ-ză-tee'noo] *m.* folly, madness; tactlessness.
desavença [dĕ-ză-ve*n*'să] *f.* disagreement, quarrel.
desavergonhado [dĕ-ză-vĕr-goo-nyah'doo] *adj.* shameless, impudent.
desbaratar [dĕzh-bă-ră-tar'] *va.* to destroy, defeat; to squander (money, etc.).
desbastar [dĕzh-băsh-tar'] *va.* to thin out; to pare down.
desbotar [dĕzh-boo-tar'] *va.* to cause to fade; *vn.* to fade.
descair [dĕsh-kă-eer'] *vn.* to sink, fall, drop.
descalço [dĕsh-kal'soo] *adj.* barefoot(ed).
descamisado [dĕsh-kă-mee-zah'doo] *adj.* shirtless, ragged; *m.* ragamuffin.
descampado [dĕsh-ka*n*-pah'-doo] *m.* open country.
descansado [dĕsh-ka*n*-sah'-doo] *adj.* rested; restful, quiet; ficar —, to rest assured.

descansar [dĕsh-ka*n*-sar'] *vn.* to rest; to take (have) a rest; to trust, rely on.
descanso [dĕsh-ka*n*'soo] *m.* rest; repose, relaxation.
descarado [dĕsh-kă-rah'doo] *adj.* impudent, cheeky, brazen.
descarga [dĕsh-kar'gă] *f.* unloading (of cargo); volley (*mil.*); broadside (*naut.*); discharge (of electricity, firearms, etc.).
descargo [dĕsh-kar'goo] *m.* discharge (of an obligation); exoneration; relief (of conscience).
descarregadoiro [dĕsh-kă-rĕ-gă-doh'ee-roo] *m.* wharf, unloading place.
descarregar [dĕsh-kă-rĕ-gar'] *va.* to unload (cargo); to discharge (firearms); to relieve (of cares); to give vent (to anger).
descarrilar [dĕsh-kă-ree-lar'] *va.* to derail; *vn.* to leave the rails.
descascar [dĕsh-kăsh-kar'] *va.* to shell (peas), peel (fruit), strip (bark).
descendência [dĕsh-se*n*-de*n*'see-ă] *f.* offspring, descendants; ancestry.
descendente [dĕsh-se*n*-de*n*t'] *mf.* descendant; *adj.* descending.
descender [dĕsh-se*n*-dayr'] *vn.* to descend from.
descentralizar [dĕsh-se*n*-tră-lee-zar'] *va.* to decentralize.
descer [dĕsh-sayr'] *vn.* to go, come, get down; to descend.
descerrar [dĕsh-sĕ-rar'] *va.* to open; to disclose, reveal.
descida [dĕsh-see'dă] *f.* descent; fall, drop.
desclassificar [dĕsh-klă-see-fee-kar'] *va.* to degrade; to discredit; to disqualify.
descoberta [dĕsh-koo-bair'tă] *f.* discovery.
descoberto [dĕsh-koo-bair'-too] *adj.* uncovered, exposed; discovered; a —, in the open; openly.
descobridor [dĕsh-koo-bree-dohr'] *m.* discoverer.
descobrimento [dĕsh-koo-bree-me*n*'too] *m.* discovery.
descobrir [dĕsh-koo-breer'] *va.* to discover, find; to uncover, reveal; to discern.
descolar [dĕsh-koo-lar'] *va.* to unstick; *vn.* to take off (aeroplane).
descomedido [dĕsh-koo-mĕ-dee'doo] *adj.* unmannerly, rude.
descompor [dĕsh-ko*n*-pohr'] *va.* to disarrange; to abuse.
descompostura [dĕsh-ko*n*-poosh-too'ră] *f.* disarrangement; immodesty; dar uma —, to rebuke, give a dressing down to.
descomunal [dĕsh-koo-moo-nal'] *adj.* enormous, monstrous, huge.
desconceituar [dĕsh-ko*n*-say-ee-too-ar'] *va.* to discredit.
desconcertar [dĕsh-ko*n*-sĕr-tar'] *va.* to disconcert, upset, disturb.
desconexo [dĕsh-koo-nek'soo] *adj.* disconnected, unrelated, rambling.
desconfiado [dĕsh-ko*n*-fee-ah'doo] *adj.* distrustful, suspicious; *m.* suspicious person.
desconfiança [dĕsh-ko*n*-fee-a*n*'să] *f.* distrust, suspicion.
desconfiar [dĕsh-ko*n*-fee-ar'] *vn.* to distrust.
desconforto [dĕsh-ko*n*-fohr'-too] *m.* discomfort; depression.
desconhecer [dĕsh-koo-nyĕ-sayr'] *va.* to fail to recognize; to ignore; not to know.
desconhecido [dĕsh-koo-nyĕ-

see'doo] *adj.* unknown; unrecognized.
desconjuntar [dĕsh-ko*n*-zhoo*n*-tar'] *va.* to dislocate (limb); to separate, take to pieces.
desconsolado [dĕsh-ko*n*-soo-lah'doo] *adj.* disconsolate; dull; low-spirited.
descontar [dĕsh-ko*n*-tar'] *va.* to discount; to deduct.
descontentadiço [dĕsh-ko*n*-te*n*-tă-dee'soo] *adj.* discontented; hard to please.
descontentamento [dĕsh-ko*n*-te*n*-tă-me*n*'too] *m.* discontent; dissatisfaction.
descontente [dĕsh-ko*n*-te*n*t'] *adj.* dissatisfied, discontented.
desconto [dĕsh-ko*n*'too] *m.* discount, allowance, rebate.
descorar [dĕsh-ko-rar'] *va.* to discolour.
descortês [dĕsh-koor-taysh'] *adj.* discourteous, ill-mannered.
descortiçar [dĕsh-koor-tee-sar'] *va.* to strip off the bark.
descortinar [dĕsh-koor-tee-nar'] *va.* to reveal, unveil.
descoser [dĕsh-koo-zayr'] *va.* to unstitch; to rip apart.
descrédito [dĕsh-kre'dee-too] *m.* discredit, disrepute.
descrença [dĕsh-kre*n*'să] *f.* unbelief; disbelief.
descrever [dĕsh-krĕ-vayr'] *va.* to describe.
descrido [dĕsh-kree'doo] *m.* unbeliever, infidel.
descrição [dĕsh-kree-sow*n*'] *f.* description, account.
descuidado [dĕsh-kwee -dah'-doo] *adj.* careless, thoughtless, negligent.
descuidar [dĕsh-kwee-dar'] *va.* to neglect, disregard.
descuido [dĕsh-kwee'doo] *m.* carelessness, neglect; oversight.
desculpa [dĕsh-kool'pă] *f.* excuse; pedir —, to apologize.
desculpar [dĕsh-kool-par'] *va.* to excuse; to pardon; *interj.* desculpe, excuse me, (I'm) sorry!
descurar [dĕsh-koo-rar'] *va.* [to neglect.
desde [dayzh'dĕ] *prep.* since, from; — já, immediately, here and now.
desdém [dĕzh-de*n*'] *m.* disdain, [scorn.
desdenhar [dĕzh-dĕ-nyar'] *va.* to scorn, disdain.
desdentado [dĕzh-de*n*-tah'-doo] *adj.* toothless.
desdizer [dĕzh-dee-zayr'] *va.* to contradict; *vr.* to retract; to go back on one's word.
desdobrar [dĕzh-doo-brar'] *va.* to unfold; to unfurl (flag); to deploy (*mil.*).
desejar [dĕ-zĕ-zhar'] *va.* to desire, wish, want, like.
desejo [dĕ-zay'zhoo] *m.* wish, desire, longing.
desejoso [dĕ-zĕ-zhoh'zoo] *adj.* desirous; eager.
desembainhar [dĕ-ze*n*-bȳ-nyar'] *va.* to unsheathe.
desembaraçado [dĕ-ze*n*-bă-ră-sah'doo] *adj.* unhampered; active, handy; unconstrained.
desembaraçar [dĕ-ze*n*-bă-ră-sar'] *va.* to rid, clear; to disentangle.
desembaraço [dĕ-ze*n*-bă-rah'soo] *m.* ease, readiness, promptness.
desembarcar [dĕ-ze*n*-băr-kar'] *vn.* to disembark, land; *va.* to unload; to land (passengers).
desembarque [dĕ-ze*n*-bark'] *m.* disembarkation, landing.
desembocadura [dĕ-ze*n*-boo-kă-doo'ră] *f.* mouth (of river).
desembocar [dĕ-ze*n*-boo-kar'] *vn.* to flow (out), run into.
desembolso [dĕ-ze*n*-bohl'soo]

m. expenditure, disbursement.
desembraiar [dě-zen-brȳ-ar'] *va.* to declutch.
desembrulhar [dě-zen-broo-lyar'] *va.* to unpack, unwrap; to unravel, clear up (mystery, problem).
desempatar [dě-zen-pă-tar'] *va.* to decide; to break a deadlock.
desempenhar [dě-zen-pě-nyar'] *va.* to get out of pawn, redeem; to fulfil, carry out; — um papel, to play a part.
desempenho [dě-zen-pě'-nyoo] *m.* fulfilment (of promise); discharge (of duty); acting, performance (*theat.*).
desemperrar [dě-zen-pě-rar'] *va.* to loosen; *vr.* (*fig.*) to stop being sulky, obstinate.
desempregado [dě-zen-prě-gah'doo] *adj.* unemployed.
desemprego [dě-zen-pray'-goo] *m.* unemployment.
desencadear [dě-zen-kă-dee-ar'] *va.* to unchain, unleash; *vr.* to burst (storm).
desencalhar [dě-zen-kă-lyar'] *va.* to refloat (*naut.*).
desencaminhar [dě-zen-kă-mee-nyar'] *va.* to mislead; to misappropriate, embezzle (money); *vr.* to go astray.
desenfado [dě-zen-fah'doo] *m.* amusement; relaxation; calmness, composure.
desenfreado [dě-zen-free-ah'-doo] *adj.* unruly, unbridled, wild.
desenganar [dě-zen-gă-nar'] *va.* to disillusion; *vr.* to lose one's illusions.
desengano [dě-zen-gă'noo] *m.* disillusion(ment).
desengonçado [dě-zen-gon-sah'doo] *adj.* unhinged; ungainly (in movements).
desenhar [dě-zě-nyar'] *va.* to draw; to bring out, reveal (features, form, etc.).
desenho [dě-zě'nyoo] *m.* drawing; design; sketch.
desenlace [dě-zen-las'] *m.* end, outcome, conclusion; dénouement.
desenredar [dě-zen-rě-dar'] *va.* to unravel; to clear up (mystery).
desenrolar [dě-zen-roo-lar'] *va.* to unfold; to develop (theme, etc.).
desentendido [dě-zen-ten-dee'doo] *adj.* ignorant; **fazer-se —**, to feign ignorance; to pretend not to notice.
desenterrar [dě-zen-tě-rar'] *va.* to dig up, unearth, disinter.
desentoado [dě-zen-too-ah'-doo] *adj.* discordant.
desentranhar [dě-zen-tră-nyar'] *va.* to disembowel; (*fig.*) to fathom, get to the bottom of.
desenvolto [dě-zen-vohl'too] *adj.* self-assured, confident; restless; uninhibited.
desenvoltura [dě-zen-vohl-too'ră] *f.* self-confidence; liveliness; forwardness.
desenvolver [dě-zen-vohl-vayr'] *va.* to develop.
desenvolvimento [dě-zen-vohl-vee-men'too] *m.* development, expansion, growth.
desequilibrado [dě-zě-kee-lee-brah'doo] *adj.* unbalanced.
desequilibrar [dě-zě-kee-lee-brar'] *va.* to upset the balance of.
deserção [dě-zěr-sown'] *f.* desertion.
desertar [dě-zěr-tar'] *va.* to abandon; *vn.* to desert.
deserto [dě-zair'too] *m.* desert; wilderness; *adj.* deserted; lonely.
desesperação [dě-zěsh-pě-ră-sown'] *f.* despair; desperation; fury.

desesperado [dĕ-zĕsh-pĕ-rah'doo] *adj.* desperate.
desesperança [dĕ-zĕsh-pĕ-ran'sā] *f.* despair.
desesperar [dĕ-zĕsh-pĕ-rar] *vn.* to despair, lose hope.
desfaçado [dĕsh-fă-sah'doo] *adj.* impertinent, insolent.
desfalcar [dĕsh-fal-kar'] *va.* to embezzle.
desfalecer [dĕsh-fă-lĕ-sayr'] *vn.* to weaken; to faint; to pine away.
desfalque [dĕsh-falk'] *m.* embezzlement, misappropriation.
desfavorável [dĕsh-fă-voo-rah'vel] *adj.* unfavourable.
desfazer [dĕsh-fă-zayr'] *va.* to undo; to break, smash, destroy; to dissolve; to dissipate; to unravel, solve; *vr.* to get rid of; to be profuse (in compliments, etc.).
desfechar [dĕsh-fĕ-shar'] *va.* to fire (gun); to let fly, hurl; to dart (a glance); *vn.* to burst (clouds); to end (in).
desfecho [dĕsh-fay'shoo] *m.* end(ing); outcome.
desfeito [dĕsh-fay'ee-too] *adj.* destroyed; dissolved; violent (storm).
desferir [dĕsh-fĕ-reer'] *va.* to unfurl (sails, flag); to strike notes (*mus.*).
desfigurar [dĕsh-fee-goo-rar'] *va.* to disfigure, distort.
desfilar [dĕsh-fee-lar'] *vn.* to file past, march past.
desfile [dĕsh-feel'] *m.* march-past, parade.
desfolhar [dĕsh-foo-lyar'] *va.* to strip off (leaves, petals).
desforra [dĕsh-fo'ră] *f.* revenge, retaliation; tirar a —, to recoup (losses).
desfraldar [dĕsh-fral-dar'] *va.* to unfurl (sails, flag).
desfrutar [dĕsh-froo-tar'] *va.* to enjoy (benefits of); to make fun of.
desgalgar [dĕzh-gal-gar'] *vn.* to fall over the side, hurtle down.
desgalhar [dĕzh-gă-lyar'] *va.* to prune.
desgarrar [dĕzh-gă-rar'] *vn.* to go astray.
desgastar [dĕzh-găsh-tar'] *va.* to wear away, erode.
desgasto [dĕzh-gash'too] *m.* *or* **desgaste,** *m.* wear and tear, wear.
desgostar [dĕzh-goosh-tar'] *va.* to displease, irritate; *vn.* to dislike; *vr.* to lose one's liking for.
desgosto [dĕzh-gohsh'too] *m.* sorrow, trouble; annoyance; disappointment.
desgraça [dĕzh-grah'să] *f.* misfortune; trouble.
desgraçado [dĕzh-gră-sah'doo] *adj.* unfortunate, wretched, unlucky.
desgrenhado [dĕzh-grĕ-nyah'doo] *adj.* dishevelled, tousled (hair).
desidratar [dĕ-zee-dră-tar'] *va.* to dehydrate.
designar [dĕ-zeeg-nar'] *va.* to designate; to denote.
desígnio [dĕ-zeeg'nee-oo] *m.* design, purpose, intention.
desigual [dĕ-zee-gwal'] *adj.* unequal; uneven (ground); changeable (character).
desilusão [dĕ-zee-loo-zow*n*'] *f.* disillusion(ment).
desimpedir [dĕ-zee*n*-pĕ-deer'] *va.* to clear (obstacles) away.
desinchar [dĕ-zee*n*-shar'] *va.* to deflate; to reduce a swelling.
desinência [dĕ-zee-ne*n*'see-ă] *f.* ending, termination (of word).
desinfectante [dĕ-seen-fek-ta*n*t'] *m/adj.* disinfectant.

desinfectar [dĕ-zeen-fek-tar′] *va.* to disinfect; to decontaminate.
desintegração [dĕ-zeen-tĕ-gră-sown′] *f.* disintegration, break-up.
desinteligência [dĕ-zeen-tĕ-lee-zhen′see-ă] *f.* misunderstanding; disagreement.
desinteressado [dĕ-zeen-tĕ-rĕ-sah′doo] *adj.* disinterested, unbiassed.
desinteresse [dĕ-zeen-tĕ-rays′] *m.* impartiality, disinterestedness.
desistência [dĕ-zeesh-ten′see-ă] *f.* discontinuance, cessation.
desistir [dĕ-zeesh-teer′] *vn.* to desist, cease, give up.
desleal [dĕzh-lee-al′] *adj.* treacherous, disloyal.
deslealdade [dĕzh-lee-al-dahd′] *f.* disloyalty, treachery.
desleixo [dĕzh-lay′ee-shoo] *m.* carelessness, negligence, slackness.
desligar [dĕzh-lee-gar′] *va.* to disconnect; to unfasten, undo; to release; (*Braz.*) to switch off (light, etc.); to ring off (telephone).
deslindar [dĕzh-leen-dar′] *va.* to unravel, clear up (mystery, etc.); to demarcate, delimit.
deslizar [dĕzh-lee-zar′] *vn.* to glide, slide, slip.
deslize [dĕzh-leez′] *m.* lapse; slip; false step.
deslocar [dĕzh-loo-kar′] *va.* to dislocate; to move.
deslumbramento [dĕzh-loon-bră-men′too] *m.* glare, dazzle; fascination.
deslumbrar [dĕzh-loon-brar′] *va.* to dazzle, blind; to overwhelm, amaze; to fascinate.
deslustrar [dĕzh-loosh-trar′] *va.* to tarnish; to sully (honour, fame).
desluzir [dĕzh-loo-zeer′] *va.* to tarnish; to darken; to discredit.
desmaiado [dĕzh-mȳ-yah′-doo] *adj.* in a faint, unconscious; faint, pale.
desmaiar [dĕzh-mȳ-yar′] *vn.* to faint; to turn pale; to falter (in a resolution).
desmaio [dĕzh-mȳ′oo] *m.* faint; pallor.
desmamar [dĕzh-mă-mar′] *va.* to wean.
desmanchar [dĕzh-man-shar′] *va.* to disarrange; to spoil; to undo; to break (contract); to dislocate; to take to pieces.
desmandar-se [dĕzh-man-dar′sĕ] *vr.* to go to extremes; to transgress orders.
desmando [dĕzh-man′doo] *m.* disobedience, insubordination.
desmantelar [dĕzh-man-tĕ-lar′] *va.* to dismantle.
desmascarar [dĕzh-măsh-kă-rar′] *va.* to unmask.
desmazelado [dĕzh-mă-zĕ-lah′doo] *adj.* slovenly, untidy.
desmedido [dĕzh-mĕ-dee′doo] *adj.* excessive; enormous.
desmentir [dĕzh-men-teer′] *va.* to deny, contradict; to give the lie (to somebody).
desmerecer [dĕzh-mĕ-rĕ-sayr′] *vn.* to be unworthy of; to fall in the esteem of; to fade.
desmesurado [dĕzh-mĕ-zoo-rah′doo] *adj.* immense, enormous.
desmobilizar [dĕzh-moo-bee-lee-zar′] *va.* to demobilize.
desmontar [dĕzh-mon-tar′] *va.* to take to pieces, dismantle; *vn/vr.* to dismount (from horse).
desmoralizar [dĕzh-moo-ră-lee-zar′] *va.* to demoralize.
desmoronar [dĕzh-moo-roo-nar′] *va.* to demolish; *vn.* to collapse, fall down.

desnecessário [dĕzh-nĕ-sĕ-sah'ree-oo] *adj.* unnecessary.
desnível [dĕzh-nee'vel] *m.* difference in levels.
desnorteado [dĕzh-nor-tee-ah'doo] *adj.* bewildered, muddled; off course, astray.
desnudar [dĕzh-noo-dar'] *va.* to strip; to denude.
desobedecer [dĕ-zoh-bĕ-dĕ-sayr'] *va.* to disobey.
desobediência [dĕ-zoh-bĕ-dee-en'see-ă] *f.* disobedience.
desocupado [dĕ-zoh-koo-pah'doo] *adj.* vacant, unoccupied (house, seat); unemployed.
desocupar [dĕ-zoh-koo-par'] *va.* to leave, vacate.
desolação [dĕ-zoh-lă-sown'] *f.* desolation; ruin; grief.
desolado [dĕ-zoh-lah'doo] *adj.* desolate, ravaged; deeply grieved.
desolar [dĕ-zoh-lar'] *va.* to ravage, devastate; to distress.
desonesto [dĕ-zoo-nesh'too] *adj.* indecent, unseemly.
desonra [dĕ-zon'ră] *f.* dishonour, disgrace.
desonrar [dĕ-zon-rar'] *va.* to dishonour, disgrace; to seduce.
desoras [dĕ-zo'răsh] *adv.* **a —**, at a late hour; in the small hours.
desordem [dĕ-zor'den] *f.* disorder; confusion; tumult.
desorganizar [dĕ-zohr-gă-nee-zar'] *va.* to disorganize, break up.
desorientação [dĕ-zoh-ree-en-tă-sown'] *f.* confusion; bewilderment.
desorientar [dĕ-zoh-ree-en-tar'] *va.* to lead astray, mislead, confuse.
despachante [dĕsh-pă-shant'] *m.* forwarding agent; shipping clerk.
despachar [dĕsh-pă-shar'] *va.* to despatch, send off; to deal with (quickly); to appoint.
despacho [dĕsh-pa'shoo] *m.* despatch; official communication; **— dum navio**, clearance (of ship).
despedaçar [dĕsh-pĕ-dă-sar'] *va.* to shatter, break, smash to pieces; to tear apart.
despedida [dĕsh-pĕ-dee'dă] *f.* farewell, leave-taking.
despedir [dĕsh-pĕ-deer'] *va.* to dismiss; to emit; *vr.* to say good-bye, take leave.
despegar [dĕsh-pĕ-gar'] *va.* to detach; *vr.* to abandon.
despego [dĕsh-pay'goo] *m.* detachment, indifference.
despeitado [dĕsh-pay-ee-tah'-doo] *adj.* spiteful; resentful.
despeito [dĕsh-pay'ee-too] *m.* spite; **a — de**, in spite of, despite.
despejar [dĕsh-pĕ-zhar'] *va.* to clear away (obstacles); to empty; to pour out; to order to leave (house).
despejo [dĕsh-pay'zhoo] *m.* clearance, clearing away (of obstacles); emptying; boldness; slops, garbage; **mandado (ordem) de —**, notice to quit, leave.
despenhadeiro [dĕsh-pĕ-nyă-day'ee-roo] *m.* precipice, cliff.
despenhar [dĕsh-pĕ-nyar'] *va.* to hurl down; *vr.* to crash down.
despensa [dĕsh-pen'să] *f.* pantry, larder.
desperdiçar [dĕsh-pĕr-dee-sar'] *va.* to waste, squander.
desperdício [dĕsh-pĕr-dee'-see-oo] *m.* waste, squandering.
despertador [dĕsh-pĕr-tă-dohr'] *m.* alarm-clock.
despertar [dĕsh-pĕr-tar'] *va.* to wake, awaken; *vn.* to awake, wake up.

despesa [dĕsh-pay'ză] *f.* expense, expenditure, payment.
despique [dĕsh-peek'] *m.* spite, revenge; redress.
despir [dĕsh-peer'] *va/vr.* to undress; to strip; to take off; to divest.
despistar [dĕsh-peesh-tar'] *va.* to mislead, throw off the scent.
despojar [dĕsh-poo-zhar'] *va.* to rob, deprive, despoil.
despojo [dĕsh-poh'zhoo] *m.* booty, loot; **—s mortais,** mortal remains.
despontar [dĕsh-po*n*-tar'] *vn.* to emerge; to sprout, bud; *va.* to trim; to blunt; **ao — do dia,** at daybreak.
desporto [dĕsh-pohr'too] *m.* sport, games.
desposar [dĕsh-poo-zar'] *va.* to marry; *vr.* to be betrothed to; to get married.
déspota [desh'poo-tă] *m.* despot, tyrant.
despotismo [dĕsh-poo-teezh'-moo] *m.* despotism.
despovoar [dĕsh-poo-voo-ar'] *va.* to depopulate; to empty, clear.
despregar [dĕsh-prĕ-gar'] *va.* to detach, take off; to unfold; to unfurl (flag, etc.); **— os olhos de,** to take one's eyes off.
desprender [dĕsh-pre*n*-dayr'] *va.* to detach, remove; to loosen, unfasten.
despreocupado [dĕsh-pree-oh-koo-pah'doo] *adj.* carefree, unconcerned.
despretensioso [dĕsh-prĕ-te*n*-see-oh'zoo] *adj.* unpretentious; modest.
desprevenido [dĕsh-prĕ-vĕ-nee'doo] *adj.* unwary; unprepared; unbiased.
desprezar [dĕsh-prĕ-zar'] *va.* to despise; to disregard.
desprezo [dĕsh-pray'zoo] *m.* contempt, disdain.
desproporção [dĕsh-proo-poor-sow*n*'] *f.* disproportion.
despropósito [dĕsh-proo-po'-zee-too] *m.* absurdity, nonsense, folly.
desprovido [dĕsh-proo-vee'-doo] *adj.* lacking in, destitute of.
desquite [dĕsh-keet'] *m.* separation.
desregrado [dĕzh-rĕ-grah'-doo] *adj.* uncontrolled, disorderly.
dessecar [dĕ-sĕ-kar'] *va.* to desiccate, dry up.
destacado [dĕsh-tă-kah'doo] *adj.* outstanding.
destacamento [dĕsh-tă-kă-me*n*'too] *m.* detachment (*mil.*).
destapar [dĕsh-tă-par'] *va.* to uncover, take the top (lid, etc.) off.
destemido [dĕsh-tĕ-mee'doo] *adj.* bold, fearless.
destemperado [dĕsh-te*n*-pĕ-rah'doo] *adj.* uncontrolled, intemperate; tasteless.
destemperar [dĕsh-te*n*-pĕ-rar'] *va.* to dilute, weaken; to upset; to soften (steel); *vn.* to lose one's head.
desterrar [dĕsh-tĕ-rar'] *va.* to banish, exile.
desterro [dĕsh-tay'roo] *m.* exile, banishment.
destilar [dĕsh-tee-lar'] *va.* to distil; *vn.* to drip, trickle.
destinar [dĕsh-tee-nar'] *va.* to destine; to determine.
destinatário [dĕsh-tee-nă-tah'ree-oo] *m.* addressee.
destino [dĕsh-tee'noo] *m.* destiny, fortune, fate; destination; **com — a,** bound for.
destituição [dĕsh-tee-too-ee-sow*n*'] *f.* dismissal (from office).
destituir [dĕsh-tee-too-eer'] *va.* to dismiss; to deprive of.

destoar [dĕsh-too-ar′] *vn.* to jar, be out of harmony.
destrancar [dĕsh-tra*n*-kar′] *va.* to unbolt, unbar.
destreza [dĕsh-tray′ză] *f.* skill, dexterity.
destrinçar [dĕsh-tree*n*-sar′] *va.* to treat (state) in detail.
destro [desh′troo] *adj.* skilful, agile.
destroçar [dĕsh-troo-sar′] *va.* to wreck, destroy, shatter.
destroço [dĕsh-troh′soo] *m.* destruction, havoc; *pl.* wreckage, ruins.
destronar [dĕsh-troo-nar′] *va.* to dethrone.
destruição [dĕsh-troo-ee-sow*n*′] *f.* destruction, ruin.
destruir [dĕsh-troo-eer′] *va.* to destroy.
desumano [dĕ-zoo-mă′noo] *adj.* inhuman, savage.
desunião [dĕ-zoo-nee-ow*n*′] *f.* disunion, disunity.
desunir [dĕ-zoo-neer′] *va.* to separate, disunite.
desusado [dĕ-zoo-zah′doo] *adj.* not used, obsolete; unusual, unaccustomed.
desuso [dĕ-zoo′zoo] *m.* disuse.
desvairado [dĕzh-vȳ-rah′-doo] *adj.* wild, frantic, crazy.
desvairar [dĕzh-vȳ-rar′] *va.* to delude, bewilder; *vn/vr.* to lose one's head; to act strangely.
desvalido [dĕzh-vă-lee′doo] *adj.* helpless, unprotected; destitute.
desvanecer [dĕzh-vă-nĕ-sayr′] *va.* to dispel, dissipate; to fill with pride; *vr.* to fade (away), vanish.
desvanecido [dĕzh-vă-nĕ-see′doo] *adj.* proud, vain; faded, dispelled.
desvantagem [dĕzh-va*n*-tah′zhe*n*] *f.* disadvantage.
desvão [dĕzh-vow*n*′] *m.* nook; attic.
desvario [dĕzh-vă-ree′oo] *m.* folly, extravagance.
desvelar [dĕzh-vĕ-lar′] *va.* to unveil, reveal; to keep awake; *vr.* to be zealous; to be watchful.
desvelo [dĕzh-ve′loo] *m.* vigilance; zeal.
desvendar [dĕzh-ve*n*-dar′] *va.* to unveil, disclose.
desventura [dĕzh-ve*n*-too′-ră] *f.* misfortune, unhappiness.
desvergonha [dĕzh-vĕr-goh′-nyă] *f.* shamelessness, impudence.
desviar [dĕzh-vee-ar′] *va.* to divert, turn aside; to shift, move; to embezzle (money); to dissuade; *vr.* to turn away from, avoid; to turn aside.
desvio [dĕzh-vee′oo] *m.* diversion, detour, change of direction; evasion, subterfuge; embezzlement.
desvirtuar [dĕzh-veer-too-ar′] *va.* to disparage; to misrepresent (facts, etc.).
detalhar [dĕ-tă-lyar′] *va.* to give (describe, relate) in detail; to detail (*mil.*).
detalhe [dĕ-ta′lyĕ] *m.* detail.
detenção [dĕ-te*n*-sow*n*′] *f.* detention.
deter [dĕ-tayr′] *va.* to detain; to stop.
detergente [dĕ-tĕr-zhe*n*t′] *m.* detergent.
deterioração [dĕ-tĕ-ree-oo-ră-sow*n*′] *f.* deterioration, wear; decay.
deteriorar [dĕ-tĕ-ree-oo-rar′] *va.* to spoil, damage; *vr.* to deteriorate.
determinação [dĕ-tĕr-mee-nă-sow*n*′] *f.* decision, determination.
determinar [dĕ-tĕr-mee-nar′] *va.* to determine, decide.
detestar [dĕ-tĕsh-tar′] *va.* to hate, detest.

detestável [dĕ-tĕsh-tah'vel] *adj.* horrible, abominable.
detidamente [dĕ-tee-dă-me*n*t'] *adv.* minutely, carefully, at length.
detonar [dĕ-too-nar'] *va.* to detonate. [disparage.
detrair [dĕ-tră-eer'] *va.* to
detrás [dĕ-trash'] *adv.* behind; — **de,** behind, at the back of.
detrito [dĕ-tree'too] *m.* remains, debris.
deturpar [dĕ-toor-par'] *va.* to disfigure; to defile.
deus [day'oosh] *m.* God.
deusa [day'oo-ză] *f.* goddess.
deus-dará [day'oozh dă-ra'] *adv.* **ao —,** at random, heedless of the future.
devagar [dĕ-vă-gar'] *adv.* slowly.
devanear [dĕ-vă-nee-ar'] *vn.* to wander (mentally); to daydream.
devaneio [dĕ-vă-nay'yoo] *m.* fancy, daydream.
devassa [dĕ-va'să] *f.* official inquiry.
devassidão [dĕ-vă-see-dow*n*'] *f.* licentiousness, debauchery.
devasso [dĕ-va'soo] *adj.* licentious, immoral; *m.* rake, lecher. [devastate.
devastar [dĕ-văsh-tar'] *va.* to
devedor [dĕ-vĕ-dohr'] *m.* debtor; *adj.* indebted (to).
dever [dĕ-vayr'] *m.* duty, obligation.
dever [dĕ-vayr'] *va.* to owe; must, ought; to have to.
deveras [dĕ-vair'ăsh] *adv.* truly, really.
devidamente [dĕ-vee-dă-me*n*t'] *adv.* duly, properly.
devido [dĕ-vee'doo] *m.* what is due, owing; *adj.* due; proper; — **a,** owing to.
devoção [dĕ-voo-sow*n*'] *f.* devotion.
devolução [dĕ-voo-loo-sow*n*'] *f.* restitution; devolution.
devolver [dĕ-vohl-vayr'] *va.* to give back, return.
devorar [dĕ-voo-rar'] *va.* to devour.
devoto [dĕ-vo'too] *adj.* devout; *m.* devotee.
dez [desh] *adj.* ten.
dezembro [dĕ-ze*n*'broo] *m.* December.
dezena [dĕ-zay'nă] *f.* ten, half a score.
dia [dee'ă] *m.* day; daylight; — **feriado,** holiday; — **útil,** week-day; working-day; — **de anos,** birthday; **de —,** in the day-time, by day; **estar (andar) em —,** to be up-to-date; **hoje em —,** nowadays; **mais — menos —,** sooner or later; **no outro —,** on the next day.
diabo [dee-ah'boo] *m.* devil; **dos —s,** fiendish, horrible; **onde —?** where the deuce?; **que —?** what the deuce?
diabrete [dee-ă-brayt'] *m.* imp.
diabrura [dee-ă-broo'ră] *f.* mischief; trick; devilry.
diagnóstico [dee-ăg-nosh'-tee-koo] *m.* diagnosis.
dialecto [dee-ă-le'too] *m.* dialect. [dialogue.
diálogo [dee-a'loo-goo] *m.*
diamante [dee-ă-ma*n*t'] *m.* diamond; — **bruto,** rough (uncut) diamond.
diâmetro [dee-ă'mĕ-troo] *m.* diameter.
diante [dee-a*n*t'] *adv.* before; in front; — **de,** before, in front of; **ir por —,** to go on; **daqui em (por) —,** from this time, (now), on; **e assim por —,** and so on; **para —,** forward.
dianteira [dee-a*n*-tay'ee-ră] *f.* front; vanguard; **tomar a —,** to get ahead.

diário [dee-ah'ree-oo] *m.* diary; accounts book; newspaper; register; — de bordo, ship's log; *adj.* daily.
diarreia [dee-ă-re'yă] *f.* diarrhoea.
dicção [deek-sow*n*'] *f.* diction.
dicionário [dee-see-oo-nah'ree-oo] *m.* dictionary.
dieta [dee-e'tă] *f.* diet.
difamação [dee-fă-mă-sow*n*'] *f.* libel, defamation.
difamar [dee-fă-mar'] *va.* to defame, slander, libel.
diferença [dee-fĕ-re*n*'să] *f.* difference.
diferençar [dee-fĕ-re*n*-sar'] *va.* to differentiate, distinguish.
diferente [dee-fĕ-re*n*t'] *adj.* different.
diferir [dee-fĕ-reer'] *va.* to postpone, defer; *vn.* to differ, be different.
difícil [di-fee'seel] *adj.* difficult, hard.
dificuldade [dee-fee-kool-dahd'] *f.* difficulty; obstacle; trouble.
dificultar [dee-fee-kool-tar'] *va.* to make difficult, impede, obstruct.
difteria [deef-tĕ-ree'ă] *f.* [diphtheria.
difundir [dee-foo*n*-deer'] *va.* to spread; to diffuse.
difusão [dee-foo-zow*n*'] *f.* spread(ing), diffusion.
digerir [dee-zhĕ-reer'] *va.* to digest.
digestão [dee-zhĕsh-tow*n*'] *f.* [digestion.
dignar-se [deeg-nar'sĕ] *vr.* to deign, condescend.
dignidade [deeg-nee-dahd'] *f.* dignity; dignified manner; high office.
digno [deeg'noo] *adj.* worthy; [dignified.
digressão [dee-grĕ-sow*n*'] *f.* digression; excursion.
dilação [dee-lă-sow*n*'] *f.* delay, postponement.
dilacerar [dee-lă-sĕ-rar'] *va.* to lacerate, tear to pieces.
dilapidação [dee-lă-pee-dă-sow*n*'] *f.* dilapidation.
dilatar [dee-lă-tar'] *va.* to dilate; to spread (out); to delay.
dilecto [dee-le'too] *adj.* favourite, dearly loved.
dilema [dee-lay'mă] *m.* dilemma.
diligência [dee-lee-zhe*n*'see-ă] *f.* diligence, industry, perseverance; investigation; stagecoach.
diligente [dee-lee-zhe*n*t'] *adj.* assiduous, diligent.
diluir [dee-loo-eer'] *va.* to dilute; *vr.* to dissolve.
dilúvio [dee-loo'vee-oo] *m.* deluge, flood.
dimensão [dee-me*n*-sow*n*'] *f.* dimension.
diminuição [di-mee-noo-ee-sow*n*'] *f.* diminution.
diminuir [di-mee-noo-eer'] *va.* to reduce, diminish; *vn.* to grow less, diminish.
diminuto [di-mee-noo'too] *adj.* very small, tiny, minute.
dinamarquês [dee-nă-măr-kaysh'] *m.* Dane; Danish (language); *adj.* Danish.
dinamismo [dee-nă-meezh'-moo] *m.* energy, drive; rush, bustle; dynamism.
dinamite [dee-nă-meet'] *f.* dynamite.
dínamo [dee'nă-moo] *m.* dynamo.
dinastia [dee-năsh-tee'ă] *f.* dynasty.
dinheiro [dee-nyay'ee-roo] *m.* money; cash; currency.
dintel [dee*n*-tel'] *m.* lintel.
diocese [dee-oo-sez'] *f.* diocese.
diploma [dee-ploh'mă] *m.* diploma, certificate.
diplomacia [dee-ploo-mă-see'ă] *f.* diplomacy.

diplomata [dee-ploo-mah'tă] *m.* diplomat.
diplomático [dee-ploo-ma'-tee-koo] *adj.* diplomatic; tactful. [lock (in canal).
dique [deek] *m.* dike; dam;
direcção [dee-re-sown'] *f.* direction, way; management; board of directors; address; steering, control (*mech.*).
directo [dee-re'too] *adj.* direct; straight; **comboio —**, through train.
director [dee-re-tohr'] *m.* director; manager; principal; headmaster (of school); conductor (*mus.*).; dean (of faculty).
direita [dee-ray'ee-tă] *f.* right hand; right-hand side; *pl.* right wing (*polit.*); **às —s**, upright, honest; proper.
direito [dee-ray'ee-too] *adj.* straight, direct; right; just; *m.* right; law; *pl.* taxes, duties, dues; rights; **de —**, by right(s), lawfully.
dirigir [di-ree-zheer'] *va.* to direct; to manage; to conduct (*mus.*); to address (letters, remarks, etc.); *vr.* **— a**, to speak to; **— para**, to make for (place). [annul, cancel.
dirimir [di-ree-meer'] *va.* to
discernimento [dish-sĕr-nee-men'too] *m.* discernment, insight.
discernir [dish-sĕr-neer'] *va.* to perceive, discern.
disciplina [dish-see-plee'nă] *f.* discipline; training; subject (*acad.*); *pl.* scourge (*eccl.*).
disciplinar [dish-see-plee-nar'] *va.* to discipline; to train; *adj.* disciplinary.
discípulo [dish-see'poo-loo] *m.* disciple; pupil.
disco [deesh'koo] *m.* disc; (gramophone) record; discus (in athletics); **— voador**, flying saucer; **— de telefone** (*Braz.*), telephone dial.
discordância [dish-koor-dan'see-ă] *f.* disagreement; discordance, disharmony.
discordar [dish-koor-dar'] *vn.* to disagree; to be out of harmony.
discórdia [dish-kor'dee-ă] *f.* discord; strife.
discorrer [dish-koo-rayr'] *vn.* to consider, think about; to talk about.
discrepância [dish-krĕ-pan'-see-ă] *f.* discrepancy, difference; disagreement.
discrepar [dish-krĕ-par'] *vn.* to differ, disagree.
discreto [dish-kre'too] *adj.* discreet, prudent; wise.
discrição [dish-kree-sown'] *f.* discretion, prudence; good sense; **à —**, as much as one wishes; in abundance; at one's own choice.
discriminar [dish-kree-mee-nar'] *va.* to discriminate, differentiate.
discursar [dish-koor-sar'] *vn.* to discourse, expatiate (on).
discurso [dish-koor'soo] *m.* speech, address, oration.
discussão [dish-koo-sown'] *f.* discussion, debate; argument.
discutir [dish-koo-teer'] *va.* to discuss, debate.
disenteria [dee-zen-tĕ-ree'ă] *f.* dysentery.
disfarçar [dish-făr-sar'] *va.* to disguise, conceal, mask.
disfarce [dish-fars'] *m.* disguise, mask.
disforme [dish-form'] *adj.* deformed, hideous.
disparar [dish-pă-rar'] *va.* to discharge, fire (gun, etc.); to let fly.
disparatado [dish-pă-ră-tah'doo] *adj.* ridiculous, absurd, crazy.

disparate [dish-pă-rat'] *m.* nonsense, absurdity, rubbish.
dispêndio [dish-pe*n*'dee-oo] *m.* expenditure, outlay.
dispensa [dish-pe*n*'să] *f.* dispensation (*eccl.*), exemption.
dispensar [dish-pe*n*-sar'] *va.* to exempt; to dispense with, do without; to grant.
dispensário [dish-pe*n*-sah'-ree-oo] *m.* dispensary.
dispersar [dish-pĕr-sar'] *va.* to disperse, scatter.
displicência [dish-plee-se*n*'-see-ă] *f.* displeasure; discontent; boredom.
disponível [dish-poo-nee'vel] *adj.* available, ready.
dispor [dish-pohr'] *va.* to arrange, set in order; to prepare; to predispose; *vn.* — **de,** to have available, at one's disposal; to count on (aid of friends, etc.); to make use of; *vr.* to get ready (to); to decide to; **ao (seu) —,** at your service.
disposição [dish-poo-zee-sow*n*'] *f.* arrangement; disposition; inclination; regulation (*leg.*).
disposto [dish-pohsh'too] *adj.* disposed (to), ready, willing; **estar bem —,** to be in good form, feeling fine.
disputa [dish-poo'tă] *f.* dispute, argument.
disputar [dish-poo-tar'] *va.* to dispute, contest; to compete in, for (games, etc.).
dissecar [dee-sĕ-kar'] *va.* to dissect.
dissemelhança [dee-sĕ-mĕ-lya*n*'să] *f.* dissimilarity, difference.
disseminar [dee-sĕ-mee-nar'] *va.* to disseminate, spread.
dissensão [dee-se*n*-sow*n*'] *f.* dissension.
dissertação [dee-sĕr-tă-sow*n*'] *f.* thesis, dissertation; discourse, lecture.
dissertar [dee-sĕr-tar'] *vn.* to speak (write) on; to discuss.
dissidente [dee-see-de*n*t'] *m/adj.* dissident, dissentient.
dissimulação [dee-see-moo-lă-sow*n*'] *f.* dissimulation.
dissimular [dee-see-moo-lar'] *va.* to conceal; to disguise.
dissipação [dee-see-pă-sow*n*'] *f.* dissipation; dispersion.
dissipar [dee-see-par'] *va.* to dissipate, waste; to dispel, disperse; *vr.* to vanish.
dissociar [dee-soo-see-ar'] *va.* to dissociate; to separate.
dissolução [dee-soo-loo-sow*n*'] *f.* dissolution.
dissoluto [dee-soo-loo'too] *adj.* dissolute.
dissolver [dee-sohl-vayr'] *va.* to dissolve.
dissuadir [dee-swă-deer'] *va.* to dissuade; to deter.
distância [dish-ta*n*'see-ă] *f.* distance.
distanciar [dish-ta*n*-see-ar'] *va.* to space out; to place at a distance; *vr.* to move away.
distante [dish-ta*n*t'] *adj.* distant, far (-off).
distar [dish-tar'] *vn.* to be far, distant (from); to differ.
distinção [dish-tee*n*-sow*n*'] *f.* distinction; honour; difference; discrimination.
distinguir [dish-tee*n*-geer'] *va.* to distinguish; to differentiate; to honour; *vr.* to distinguish oneself, excel.
distintivo [dish-tee*n*-tee'voo] *adj.* distinctive, characteristic; *m.* badge, emblem.
distinto [dish-tee*n*'too] *adj.* distinct, different; clear; distinguished, notable; refined.
distracção [dish-trah-sow*n*'] *f.* distraction; absent-mindedness, forgetfulness.

distraído [dish-tră-ee'doo] *adj.* absent-minded, forgetful.
distrair [dish-tră-eer'] *va.* to distract, divert; to amuse, entertain.
distribuição [dish-tree-boo-ee-sow*n*'] *f.* distribution; arrangement; — **postal**, delivery (of letters).
distribuir [dish-tree-boo-eer'] *va.* to distribute, share out, divide; to classify.
distrito [dish-tree'too] *m.* district, area; county.
distúrbio [dish-toor'bee-oo] *m.* disturbance, disorder.
dita [dee'tă] *f.* good fortune.
ditado [dee-tah'doo] *m.* dictation; saying, proverb.
ditador [dee-tă-dohr'] *m.* dictator. [dictatorship.
ditadura [dee-tă-doo'ră] *f.*
ditame [dee-tahm'] *m.* dictate (of conscience, reason); rule, precept.
ditar [dee-tar'] *va.* to dictate.
dito [dee'too] *m.* saying, remark; *adj.* said; — **e feito**, no sooner said than done.
ditongo [dee-to*n*'goo] *m.* diphthong.
ditoso [dee-toh'zoo] *adj.* happy; lucky; fortunate, blessed.
divagar [dee-vă-gar'] *vn.* to wander, stray; to digress.
divergência [dee-vĕr-zhe*n*'-see-ă] *f.* divergence.
diversão [dee-vĕr-sow*n*'] *f.* amusement, entertainment, pastime; diversion, feint (*mil.*).
diversidade [dee-vĕr-see-dahd'] *f.* diversity; difference.
diversificar [dee-vĕr-see-fee-kar'] *va.* to diversify; *vn.* to vary.
diverso [dee-vair'soo] *adj.* different; varied; *pl.* various.
divertido [dee-vĕr-tee'doo] *adj.* amusing, funny.
divertimento [dee-vĕr-tee-me*n*'too] *m.* amusement, entertainment.
divertir [dee-vĕr-teer'] *va.* to amuse, entertain; to divert (attention); *vr.* to enjoy oneself, have a good time.
dívida [dee'vee-dă] *f.* debt; indebtedness.
dividir [di-vee-deer'] *va.* to divide. [vine, heavenly.
divino [di-vee'noo] *adj.* di-
divisa [di-vee'ză] *f.* emblem, device; motto, slogan; stripe (*mil.*); *pl.* foreign exchange credits.
divisão [di-vee-zow*n*'] *f.* division; section.
divisar [di-vee-zar'] *va.* to discern, observe.
divisório [di-vee-zo'ree-oo] *adj.* dividing.
divorciar [dee-voor-see-ar'] *va.* to divorce; *vr.* to get (be) divorced. [divorce.
divórcio [dee-vor'see-oo] *m.*
divulgar [dee-vool-gar'] *va.* to spread (news, etc.); to divulge (secret).
dizer [dee-zayr'] *va.* to say; to tell; to speak, express, state; — **bem com**, to go well with; **por assim** —, so to speak; **querer**, — to mean; **quer** —, that is to say; *m.* saying; opinion; mode of speech.
dízimo [dee'zee-moo] *m.* tithe (*eccl.*).
dó [do] *m.* pity; mourning.
doação [doo-ă-sow*n*'] *f.* grant, bequest, endowment.
doar [doo-ar'] *va.* to grant.
dobadoira [doo-bă-doh'ee-ră] *f.* reel. [reel.
dobar [doo-bar'] *va.* to wind,
dobra [dob'ră] *f.* pleat, fold, turn-up (of trousers).
dobradiça [doo-bră-dee'să] *f.* hinge.
dobradiço [doo-bră-dee'soo]

adj. flexible, pliable, supple.
dobrar [doo-brar'] *va.* to double; to fold; to bend; to round (corner, cape); to toll (bell).
dobre [do'brĕ] *adj.* double; double-dealing, two-faced; *m.* knell.
dobro [doh'broo] *m.* double.
doca [do'kă] *f.* dock.
doce [dohs] *adj.* sweet; gentle, soft; *m.* sweet; pudding; tart.
docente [doo-se*n*t] *adj.* teaching; corpo —, teaching staff.
dócil [do'seel] *adj.* docile.
documentação [doo-koo-me*n*-tă-sow*n*'] *f.* documentation; documents.
documento [doo-koo-me*n*'-too] *m.* document; title-deed; proof.
doçura [doo-soo'ră] *f.* sweetness; gentleness.
doença [doo-e*n*'să] *f.* illness; disease; complaint, ailment.
doente [doo-e*n*t'] *adj.* ill, sick; *m.* patient; sick person.
doentio [doo-e*n*-tee'oo] *adj.* sickly, ailing; unhealthy (climate); morbid (curiosity, etc.).
doer [doo-ayr'] *va/vn.* to hurt; to ache; *vr.* to grieve.
doestar [doo-esh-tar'] *va.* to insult.
dogmático [dog-ma'tee-koo] *adj.* dogmatic.
dogue [dog] *m.* bulldog.
doidice [doh-ee-dees'] *f.* madness, craziness, foolishness.
doido [doh'ee-doo] *adj.* mad, insane, crazy.
dois [doh'eesh] *adj.* two.
doloroso [doo-loo-roh'zoo] *adj.* painful, grievous.
doloso [doo-loh'zoo] *adj.* fraudulent.
dom [do*n*] *m.* gift; title before Christian name (in royal family, aristocracy, higher clergy).
domar [doo-mar'] *va.* to tame; to subdue.
doméstico [doo-mesh'tee-koo] *adj.* domestic.
domicílio [doo-mi-see'lee-oo] *m.* domicile, residence.
dominação [doo-mee-nă-sow*n*'] *f.* domination, ascendancy.
dominante [doo-mee-na*n*t'] *adj.* dominant, predominant, prevailing.
dominar [doo-mee-nar'] *va.* to rule over, dominate; to predominate; to overlook.
domingo [doo-mee*n*'goo] *m.* Sunday.
domínio [doo-mee'nee-oo] *m.* domain, dominion; control; rule.
dona [doh'nă] *f.* lady; landlady; title before Christian name.
donaire [doo-nȳr'] *m.* elegance; adornment; witticism.
donde [do*n*d] *adv.* from where, whence.
dono [doh'noo] *m.* owner; master; landlord.
dor [dohr] *f.* pain; ache; sorrow, grief; suffering.
dorido [doo-ree'doo] *adj.* painful, sore; aching; sorrowful; *m.* mourner, bereaved person.
dormir [door-meer'] *vn.* to sleep; — a sono solto, — como uma pedra, to sleep soundly (like a log, a top).
dormitar [door-mee-tar'] *vn.* to doze.
dormitório [door-mee-to'ree-oo] *m.* dormitory.
dorna [dor'nă] *f.* vat.
dorso [dohr'soo] *m.* back.
dosagem [doo-zah'zhe*n*] *m.* dosing; dosage.
dose [doz] *f.* dose.
dossel [doo-sel'] *m.* canopy.
dotação [doo-tă-sow*n*'] *f.* endowment, provision.

dotar [doo-tar'] *va.* to endow; to give as a dowry.
dote [dot] *m.* dowry; *pl.* (natural) gifts.
dourar [doh-rar'] *va.* to gild.
douto [doh'too] *adj.* learned, erudite.
doutor [doh-tohr'] *m.* doctor (title for all university graduates in Portugal); — de capelo, doctor (i.e. Ph.D., D.Phil, etc.).
doutorado [doh-too-rah'doo] *m.* doctorate.
doutrina [doh-tree'nă] *f.* doctrine; principle.
doutrinação [doh-tree-nă-sow*n*'] *f.* indoctrination.
doze [dohz] *adj.* twelve.
draga [drah'gă] *f.* dredger.
dragão [dră-gow*n*'] *m.* dragon; dragoon (*mil.*).
drama (dră'mă] *m.* play, drama.
dramaturgo [dră-mă-toor'-goo] *m.* dramatist, playwright.
drenar [drĕ-nar'] *va.* to drain.
droga [dro'gă] *f.* drug; ingredient (*med.*).
drogaria [droo-gă-ree'ă] *f.* chemist's (shop).
duas [doo-ăsh] *adj.* two.
dúbio [doo'bee-oo] *adj.* doubtful; vague, ambiguous.
ducado [doo-kah'doo] *m.* duchy; ducat (money).
ducha [doo'shă] *f.* shower (-bath).
duelo [doo-e'loo] *m.* duel.
dueto [doo-ay'too] *m.* duet.
duna [doo'nă] *f.* sand dune.
duplicador [doo-plee-kă-dohr'] *m.* duplicator.
duplicar [doo-plee-kar'] *va.* to duplicate.
duplicidade [doo-plee-see-dahd'] *f.* duplicity.
duque [dook] *m.* duke.
duração [doo-ră-sow*n*'] *f.* duration; durability.
duradouro [doo-ră-doh'roo] *adj.* lasting, enduring.
durante [doo-ra*n*t'] *prep.* during.
durar [doo-rar'] *vn.* to last; to continue; to wear well.
dureza [doo-ray'ză] *f.* hardness; toughness; harshness, severity.
duro [doo'roo] *adj.* hard; [tough; harsh.
dúvida [doo'vee-dă] *f.* doubt; hesitation; uncertainty.
duvidar [doo-vee-dar'] *va.* to doubt.
duvidoso [doo-vee-doh'zoo] *adj.* doubtful, uncertain; suspicious, dubious.
duzentos [doo-ze*n*'toosh] *adj.* two hundred.
dúzia [doo'zee-ă] *f.* dozen; — de frade, baker's dozen; **às —s**, abundantly.

E

e [ee] *conj.* and.
ébano [e'bă-noo] *m.* ebony.
ébrio [eb'ree-oo] *adj.* drunk, intoxicated.
ebulição [ee-boo-lee-sow*n*'] *f.* ebullience; boiling.
eclipse [ĕ-kleeps'] *m.* eclipse.
eclosão [ĕ-kloo-zow*n*'] *f.* emergence; hatching.
eclusa [ĕ-kloo'ză] *f.* lock (of canal).
eco [e'koo] *m.* echo.
economia [ee-ko-noo-mee'ă] *f.* economy; thrift; **fazer —s**, to save.
económico [ee-koo-no'mee-koo] *adj.* economic(al); thrifty; **caixa —a**, savings bank.
ecuménico [ee-koo-me'nee-koo] *adj.* ecumenical, universal.
edição [ee-dee-sow*n*'] *f.* publication; edition.
edicto [ee-deek'too] *m.* edict, decree.

edificação [ee-di-fee-kă-sow*n*'] *f.* building, construction; edification (moral).
edificar [ee-di-fee-kar'] *va.* to build; to edify.
edifício [ee-di-fee'see-oo] *m.* building, edifice.
edital [ee-dee-tal'] *m.* (official) notice, order. [publish.
editar [ee-dee-tar'] *va.* to
édito [e'dee-too] *m.* order, ordinance, legal notice.
editor [ee-dee-tohr'] *m.* publisher.
editorial [ee-dee-too-ree-al'] *m.* (newspaper) editorial; casa —, publishing house.
educação [ee-doo-kă-sow*n*'] *f.* education; upbringing; good manners.
educar [ee-doo-kar'] *va.* to educate; to bring up.
efectivamente [ee-fe-tee-vă-me*nt*'] *adv.* in fact; really.
efectivo [ee-fe-tee'voo] *adj.* actual, real; *m.* effective (*mil.*).
efectuar [ee-fe-too-ar'] *va.* to bring about, put into effect; *vr.* to take place.
efeito [ee-fay'ee-too] *m.* effect, result; fulfilment; purpose; com —, in fact, indeed.
efémero [ee-fe'mĕ-roo] *adj.* ephemeral, short-lived.
efervescente [ee-fĕr-vĕsh-se*nt*'] *adj.* effervescent; irascible; turbulent.
eficácia [ee-fee-kah'see-ă] *f.* effectiveness, efficacy.
eficaz [ee-fee-kash'] *adj.* effective; powerful.
eficiência [ee-fee-see-e*n*'see-ă] *f.* efficiency. [efficient.
eficiente [ee-fee-see-e*nt*'] *adj.*
efusão [ee-foo-zow*n*'] *f.* effusion; shedding (of blood).
efusivo [ee-foo-zee'voo] *adj.* effusive.
égide [e'zheed] *f.* protection; sponsorship, patronage.
egípcio [ee-zheep'see-oo] *m/adj.* Egyptian.
egoísmo [ee-goo-eezh'moo] *m.* selfishness; egoism, egotism.
egoísta [ee-goo-eesh'tă] *mf.* egoist; *adj.* selfish; egoistic.
egrégio [ee-gre'zhee-oo] *adj.* distinguished, outstanding.
egresso [ee-gre'soo] *m.* egress, way out; former monk.
égua [e'gwă] *f.* mare.
eira [ay'ee-ră] *f.* threshing-floor. [race.
eirado [ay-ee-rah'doo] *m.* ter-
eis [ay'eesh] *interj.* here is, are.
eiva [ay'ee-vă] *f.* crack, flaw.
eivado [ay-ee-vah'doo] *adj.* contaminated, full (of flaws); marred; stained.
eixo [ay'ee-shoo] *m.* axle; axis.
elaboração [ee-lă-boo-ră-sow*n*'] *f.* working out; development.
elaborar [ee-lă-boo-rar'] *va.* to work out, develop.
elasticidade [ee-lăsh-tee-see-dahd'] *f.* elasticity; resilience.
elástico [ee-lash'tee-koo] *m/adj.* elastic.
electricidade [ee-le-tree-see-dahd'] *f.* electricity.
eléctrico [ee-le'tree-koo] *adj.* electric(al); (*Port.*) tram.
electrizar [ee-le-tree-zar'] *va.* to electrify.
elefante [ee-lĕ-fa*nt*'] *m.* elephant. [elegance.
elegância [ee-lĕ-ga*n*'see-ă] *f.*
elegante [ee-lĕ-ga*nt*'] *adj.* elegant, graceful; polished; fashionable, smart.
eleger [ee-lĕ-zhayr'] *va.* to choose, select; to elect.
elegia [ee-lĕ-zhee'ă] *f.* elegy.
elegível [ee-lĕ-zhee-vel] *adj.* eligible.
eleição [ee-lay-ee-sow*n*'] *f.* election; choice.
eleito [ee-lay'ee-too] *adj.* elected; chosen.

eleitorado [ee-lay-too-rah'-doo] *m.* electorate.
elementar [ee-lĕ-me*n*-tar'] *adj.* elementary.
elemento [ee-lĕ-me*n*'too] *m.* element; component, constituent, ingredient.
elenco [ee-le*n*'koo] *m.* list; index; cast (*theat.*).
elevação [ee-lĕ-vă-sow*n*'] *f.* elevation; height; rise.
elevador [ee-lĕ-vă-dohr'] *m.* lift, elevator.
elevar [ee-lĕ-var'] *va.* to raise, lift; to exalt, praise; *vr.* to rise.
eliminar [ee-li-mee-nar'] *va.* to eliminate, remove.
elo [e'loo] *m.* link.
elocução [ee-loo-koo-sow*n*'] *f.* elocution; manner of speaking.
elogiar [ee-loo-zhee-ar'] *va.* to praise, extol.
elogio [ee-loo-zhee'oo] *m.* eulogy, praise.
eloquência [ee-loo-kwe*n*'see-ă] *f.* eloquence; oratory.
elucidar [ee-loo-see-dar'] *va.* to elucidate, explain.
em [e*n*] *prep.* in, into, at, on.
emaciado [ee-mă-see-ah'doo] *adj.* emaciated, gaunt.
emagrecer [ee-mă-grĕ-sayr'] *vn.* to grow thin; *va.* to make thin.
emanar [ee-mă-nar'] *vn.* to emanate, proceed from.
emancipar [ee-ma*n*-see-par'] *va.* to emancipate, free.
emaranhar [ee-mă-ră-nyar'] *va.* to entangle; to complicate.
embair [e*n*-bă-eer'] *va.* to trick.
embaixada [en-bȳ-shah'dă] *f.* embassy; message.
embaixador [e*n*-bȳ-shă-dohr'] *m.* ambassador; envoy.
embalagem [e*n*-bă-lah'zhen] *f.* packing.
embalar [e*n*-bă-lar'] *va.* to pack, wrap; to rock, lull to sleep.
embalsamar [e*n*-bal-să-mar'] *va.* to embalm.
embaraçar [e*n*-bă-ră-sar'] *va.* to embarrass, obstruct.
embaraço [e*n*-bă-rah'soo] *m.* embarrassment, hindrance, encumbrance.
embarcação [e*n*-băr-kă-sow*n*'] *f.* boat.
embarcadiço [e*n*-băr-kă-dee'soo] *adj.* sea-faring, -going; *m.* seafarer.
embarcar [e*n*-băr-kar'] *va.* to ship; *vn.* to embark, go on board.
embargo [e*n*-bar'goo] *m.* embargo; impediment; attachment (*leg.*); **sem —**, nevertheless.
embarque [e*n*-bark'] *m.* embarkation; shipment (of goods).
embasbacado [e*n*-băzh-bă-kah'doo] *adj.* gaping, open-mouthed.
embate [e*n*-bat'] *m* collision, clash; *pl.* blows (of fate).
embeber [e*n*-bĕ-bayr'] *va.* to soak (up); *vr.* to be absorbed in.
embeleco [e*n*-bĕ-lay'koo] *m.* [deceit; lure, bait.
embelezar [e*n*-bĕ-lĕ-zar'] *va.* to embellish, adorn.
embicar [e*n*-bee-kar'] *vn.* to stumble; **— com**, to have an argument with.
embirrar [e*n*-bee-rar'] *vn.* to persist; **— com**, to dislike.
emblema [e*n*-blay'mă] *m.* emblem, badge.
embocadura [e*n*-boo-kă-doo'ră] *f.* bit (of bridle); mouthpiece (*mus.*); mouth (of river). [(*mech.*).
êmbolo [e*n*'boo-loo] *m.* piston
embora [e*n*-bo'ră] *conj.* though, although; **ir-se —**, to go away, off.

emboscada [*en*-boosh-kah'-dă] *f.* ambush.
embotar [*en*-boo-tar'] *va.* to blunt; to deaden, dull.
embravecer [*en*-bră-vĕ-sayr'] *vn.* to rage, become enraged; *va.* to enrage.
embreagem [*en*-bree-ah'-zhe*n*] *f.* clutch (*mech.*).
embrenhar-se [*en*-brĕ-nyar'-sĕ] *vr.* to plunge into (woods, thickets).
embriagar [*en*-bree-ă-gar'] *va.* to intoxicate.
embriaguez [en-bree-ă-gaysh'] *f.* intoxication.
embrião [*en*-bree-ow*n*'] *m.* embryo; germ.
embrulhada [*en*-broo-lyah'-dă] *f.* mix-up, muddle, mess.
embrulhar [*en*-broo-lyar'] *va.* to wrap, pack (up); to complicate; to confuse; — o estômago, to upset the stomach.
embrulho [*en*-broo'lyoo] *m.* parcel, package; jumble, mix-up; intrigue; papel de —, wrapping-, brown-paper.
embrutecer [*en*-broo-tĕ-sayr'] *va.* to brutalize; to stupefy. [veil.
embuço [*en*-boo'soo] *m.* hood;
embuste [*en*-boosht'] *m.* trick, hoax, deceit.
embusteiro [*en*-boosh-tay'ee-roo] *m.* liar, trickster, rogue.
embutido [*en*-boo-tee'doo] *m.* inlay work, mosaic.
emenda [ee-me*n*'dă] *f.* correction; amendment.
emendar [ee-me*n*-dar'] *va.* to correct; to amend; *vr.* to mend one's ways, reform.
ementa [ee-me*n*'tă] *f.* menu.
emergência [ee-mĕr-zhe*n*'-see-ă] *f.* emergency, crisis; emergence, appearance.
emergir [ee-mĕr-zheer'] *vn.* to emerge, appear.
emigração [ee-mee-gră-sow*n*'] *f.* emigration; (voluntary) exile; migration (*zool.*).
emigrado [ee-mee-grah'doo] *m.* or **emigrante**, *m.* emigrant; (voluntary) exile.
emigrar [ee-mee-grar'] *vn.* to emigrate; to migrate (*zool.*).
eminência [ee-mi-ne*n*'see-ă] *f.* eminence; height.
eminente [ee-mee-ne*n*t'] *adj.* eminent; distinguished.
emissão [ee-mee-sow*n*'] *f.* issue (of bank-notes, shares, etc.); emission; (radio)broadcast.
emissário [ee-mee-sah'ree-oo] *m.* envoy, emissary; secret agent.
emissor [ee-mee-sohr'] *m* transmitter.
emissora [ee-mee-soh'ră] *f.* radio (broadcasting)station.
emitir [ee-mee-teer'] *va.* to issue (shares, etc.); to emit, send out.
emoção [ee-moo-sow*n*'] *f.* emotion; excitement.
emocionante [ee-moo-see-oo-na*n*t'] *adj.* moving; thrilling.
emolumento [ee-moo-loo-me*n*'too] *m.* emolument, fee; *pl.* profits; perquisites.
emotividade [ee-moo-tee-vee-dahd'] *f.* excitability, emotionalism.
empa [*en*'pă] *f.* propping, staking (of vines).
empacotar [*en*-pă-koo-tar'] *va.* to pack.
empada [*en*-pah'dă] *f.* (meat-, fish-)pie.
empalhar [*en*-pă-lyar'] *va.* to pack (cover) with straw; to stuff (animals, birds, etc.); to stow hay.
empalidecer [*en*-pă-lee-dĕ-sayr'] *vn.* to turn pale.
empalmar [*en*-pal-mar'] *va.* to hide in the hand; to pilfer.

empanar [*en*-pă-nar'] *va.* to dull, dim; to tarnish.
empapar [*en*-pă-par'] *va.* to soak, steep.
emparelhar [*en*-pă-rĕ-lyar'] *va.* to join together.
empatar [*en*-pă-tar'] *va.* to tie up (money); to hinder, check; to draw (match, game).
empate [*en*-pat'] *m.* draw (in games); tie (in voting); deadlock (in negotiations).
empecer [*en*-pĕ-sayr'] *va.* to obstruct, impede.
empecilho [*en*-pĕ-see'lyoo] *m.* obstacle, 'snag'.
empedernido [*en*-pĕ-dĕr-nee'doo] *adj.* hardened, hard-hearted, heartless.
empedrar [*en*-pĕ-drar'] *va.* to pave; to cover with stones.
empenar [*en*-pĕ-nar'] *va.* to warp.
empenhar [*en*-pĕ-nyar'] *va.* to pawn; to pledge (one's word); to devote (energy, etc.); to lay under an obligation; *vr.* to strive, persist.
empenho [*en*-pay'nyoo] *m.* pledge; promise; keen interest; earnestness, determination; influence, backing.
emperrar [*en*-pĕ-rar'] *vn.* to be stuck.
empinado [*en*-pee-nah'doo] *adj.* steep; pompous; rearing up. [plaster (*med.*).
emplastro [*en*-plash'troo] *m.*
empobrecer [*en*-poo-brĕ-sayr'] *va.* to impoverish; *vn.* to become poor.
empobrecimento [*en*-poo-brĕ-see-me*n*'too] *m.* impoverishment.
empola [*en*-poh'lă] *f.* blister.
empolgante [*en*-pohl-gant'] *adj.* exciting, thrilling.
empolgar [*en*-pohl-gar'] *va.* to seize, grasp; to grip (attention, interest).
emprazar [*en*-pră-zar'] *va.* to summon; *vr.* to arrange to meet.
empreendedor [*en*-pree-*en*-dĕ-dohr'] *adj.* enterprising.
empreendimento [*en*-pree-*en*-dee-me*n*'too] *m.* undertaking, enterprise.
empregado [*en*-prĕ-gah'doo] *m.* employee; clerk; shop assistant.
empregar [*en*-prĕ-gar'] *va.* to employ; to use, spend.
emprego [*en*-pray'goo] *m.* employment; use; job, occupation.
empreitada [*en*-pray-ee-tah'-dă] *f.* contract work; piece-work.
empreiteiro [*en*-pray-tay'ee-roo] *m.* contractor.
empresa [*en*-pray'ză] *f.* enterprise, undertaking; firm, company (*com.*).
emprestado [*en*-prĕsh-tah'-doo] *adj.* lent, loaned; borrowed; pedir —, to borrow.
emprestar [*en*-prĕsh-tar'] *va.* to lend, loan.
empréstimo [*en*-presh'tee-moo] *m.* loan; lending; borrowing.
empunhar [*en*-poo-nyar'] *va.* to seize, grasp; — **o ceptro**, to wield the sceptre.
empurrão [*en*-poo-row*n*'] *m.* shove, push; aos —ões, jostling, pushing.
empurrar [*en*-poo-rar'] *va.* to push; to shove; to thrust.
emudecer [ee-moo-dĕ-sayr'] *vn.* to be silent.
emulação [ee-moo-lă-sow*n*'] *f.* emulation; rivalry.
emular [ee-moo-lar'] *va.* to emulate, rival.
émulo [e'moo-loo] *m.* rival.
enaltecer [ĕ-nal-tĕ-sayr'] *va.* to exalt.
enamorado [ee-nă-moo-rah'-

doo] *adj.* in love; enamoured.
enamorar [ee-nă-moo-rar'] *va.* to win the love of; *vr.* to fall in love with.
encadeamento [*en*-kă-dee-ă-me*n*'too] *m.* link(ing), connexion, concatenation.
encadear [*en*-kă-dee-ar'] *va.* to chain, link, together.
encadernação [*en*-kă-dĕr-nă-sow*n*'] *f.* binding.
encadernar [*en*-kă-dĕr-nar'] *va.* to bind (books).
encaixar [*en*-kȳ-shar'] *va.* to pack (in a box), encase; to fit in; *vn.* to fit easily into place.
encaixe [*en*-kȳsh'] *m.* fitting; notch, groove, socket.
encalço [*en*-kal'soo] *m.* close pursuit; **ir no —**, to chase, pursue.
encalhar [*en*-kă-lyar'] *vn.* to run aground, be stranded.
encaminhar [*en*-kă-mee-nyar'] *va.* to direct, set on the right road; to guide; *vr.* to make for, go towards.
encantado [*en*-ka*n*-tah'doo] *adj.* delighted; enchanted, charmed.
encantador [*en*-ka*n*-tă-dohr'] *adj.* delightful; charming; ravishing; *m.* enchanter, sorcerer.
encantar [*en*-ka*n*-tar'] *va.* to enchant, charm, fascinate; to delight, please.
encanto [*en*-ka*n*'too] *m.* enchantment, charm, fascination; delight.
encapelar-se [*en*-kă-pĕ-lar'-sĕ] *vr.* to get rough (sea).
encapotar [*en*-kă-poo-tar'] *va.* to cloak, conceal.
encarar [*en*-kă-rar'] *va.* to face; to look at.
encarcerar [*en*-kăr-sĕ-rar'] *va.* to imprison, incarcerate.
encarecer [*en*-kă-rĕ-sayr'] *va.* to extol, praise to the skies; to raise the price; to exaggerate.
encarecimento [*en*-kă-rĕ-see-me*n*'too] *m.* praise; earnestness; raising of prices; exaggeration.
encargo [*en*-kar'goo] *m.* duty, responsibility; office, position.
encarnação [*en*-kăr-nă-sow*n*'] *f.* incarnation.
encarnado [*en*-kăr-nah'doo] *adj.* incarnate; red, scarlet; flesh-coloured.
encarniçado [*en*-kăr-nee-sah'doo] *adj.* fierce, bloodthirsty.
encarregado [*en*-kă-rĕ-gah'-doo] *adj.* charged (entrusted) with; *m.* foreman; person in charge; agent; chargé d'affaires.
encarregar [*en*-kă-rĕ-gar'] *va.* to charge, entrust; to burden; *vr.* to take charge of, undertake.
encarrilhar [*en*-kă-ree-lyar'] *va.* to put on the right track; to put back on the rails.
encerado [*en*-sĕ-rah'doo] *m.* oilskin; tarpaulin; oil-cloth.
encerramento [*en*-sĕ-ră-me*n*'too] *m.* closing; end.
encerrar [*en*-sĕ-rar'] *va.* to close; to enclose; to contain; *vr.* to stay indoors, in seclusion; to be contained in.
encetar [*en*-sĕ-tar'] *va.* to begin, start.
enchente [*en*-shent'] *f.* flood; [big crowd.
encher [*en*-shayr'] *va.* to fill.
enchimento [*en*-shee-me*n*'-too] *m.* filling (up); stuffing (in couch, etc.).
encíclica [*en*-see'klee-kă] *f.* (papal) encyclical.
enciclopédia [*en*-see-kloo-pe'dee-ă] *f.* encyclopaedia.
encoberta [*en*-koo-bair'tă] *f.* hiding-place; pretext.
encoberto [*en*-koo-bair'too]

adj. concealed; dull, overcast (sky).
encobridor [*en*-koo-bree-dohr'] *m.* receiver of stolen goods, "fence" (*sl.*).
encobrir [*en*-koo-breer'] *va.* to conceal, hide.
encolerizar [*en*-koo-lĕ-ree-zar'] *va.* to exasperate, irritate, make angry; *vr.* to get angry.
encolher [*en*-koo-lyayr'] *vn.* to shrink; *va.* to shrug (one's shoulders); to cramp, restrict; *vr.* to cringe.
encomenda [*en*-koo-men'dă] *f.* order; article ordered.
encomendar [*en*-koo-men-dar'] *va.* to order; to entrust.
encontrar [*en*-kon-trar'] *va.* to meet, encounter; to find.
encontro [*en*-kon'troo] *m.* meeting, encounter; find; collision, clash.
encorajar [*en*-koo-ră-zhar'] *va.* to encourage.
encosta [*en*-kosh'tă] *f.* slope; hillside.
encostar [*en*-koosh-tar'] *va.* to lean (against, on); to prop; *vr.* to lie down, rest.
encosto [*en*-kohsh'too] *m.* support; back (of chair).
encrespar [*en*-krĕsh-par'] *va.* to curl; to ruffle; *vr.* to bristle; to get choppy (sea).
encruzilhada [*en*-kroo-zee-lyah'dă] *f.* crossroads.
encurralar [*en*-koo-ră-lar'] *va.* to shut (pen) in; to corral.
encurtar [*en*-koor-tar'] *va.* to shorten, curtail.
endecha [*en*-day'shă] *f.* dirge.
endémico [*en*-de'mee-koo] *adj.* endemic.
endereçar [*en*-dĕ-rĕ-sar'] *va.* to address (letter); to direct.
endereço [*en*-dĕ-ray'soo] *m.* address.
endiabrado [*en*-dee-ă-brah'-doo] *adj.* devilish; mischievous.
endireitar [*en*-dee-ray-tar'] *va.* to straighten; to rectify; to right; *vn.* to make straight for; *vr.* to stand straight.
endividar-se [*en*-dee-vee-dar'sĕ] *vr.* to run into debt.
endoidecer-se [*en*-doh-ee-dĕ-sayr'sĕ] *vr.* to go mad.
endossar [*en*-doo-sar'] *va.* to endorse.
endosso [*en*-doh'soo] *m.* endorsement.
endurecer [*en*-doo-rĕ-sayr'] *va.* to harden.
endurecido [*en*-doo-rĕ-see'-doo] *adj.* hardened; hard (-hearted); inured.
energia [ee-nĕr-zhee'ă] *f.* energy, vigour, drive.
enérgico [ee-nair'zhee-koo] *adj.* energetic, active, vigorous.
energúmeno [ee-nĕr-goo'mĕ-noo] *m.* fanatic.
enervação [ee-nĕr-vă-sow*n*'] *f.* enervation.
enevoar [ee-nĕ-voo-ar'] *va.* to cloud (over), blur, dim.
enfadar [*en*-fă-dar'] *va.* to weary, irritate, bore; *vr.* to get tired of, bored with.
enfado [*en*-fah'doo] *m.* irritation, annoyance; fatigue, weariness.
enfadonho [*en*-fă-doh'nyoo] *adj.* tiresome, tedious, boring.
ênfase [*en*'fahz] *f.* emphasis.
enfastiar [*en*-făsh-tee-ar'] *va.* to weary, bore; to sicken; *vr.* to grow tired, weary, of.
enfático [*en*-fa'tee-koo] *adj.* emphatic.
enfeitar [*en*-fay-ee-tar'] *va.* to adorn, decorate.
enfeite [*en*-fay'eet] *m.* adornment, ornament, decoration.
enfeitiçar [*en*-fay-tee-sar'] *va.* to bewitch.
enfermar [*en*-fĕr-mar'] *vn.* to be taken ill, fall ill.
enfermaria [*en*-fĕr-mă-ree'ă]

f. (hospital) ward; sick-bay (*naut.*).
enfermeira [*en*-fĕr-may'ee-ră] *f.* nurse.
enfermidade [*en*-fĕr-mee-dahd'] *f.* illness; (chronic) infirmity.
enfermo [*en*-fayr'moo] *adj.* infirm; ill; *m.* sick person, patient.
enferrujar [*en*-fĕ-roo-zhar'] *va/vn.* to rust.
enfezar [*en*-fe-zar'] *va.* to stunt (growth); (*fig.*) to annoy.
enfiada [*en*-fee-ah'dă] *f.* string, row (of pearls, etc.); series (of events); **de —**, without pause.
enfiar [*en*-fee-ar'] *va.* to thread (needle); to string (beads) together; to slip on (clothes, shoes); to resume the thread (of story, argument); to enfilade (*mil.*).
enfileirar [*en*-fee-lay-ee-rar'] *va.* to line up.
enfim [*en*-fee*n*'] *adv.* at last, finally; in short; after all.
enforcar [*en*-foor-kar'] *va.* to hang.
enfraquecer [*en*-fră-kĕ-sayr'] *va.* to weaken; *vn.* to grow weak.
enfrear [*en*-free-ar'] *va.* to bridle, curb.
enfrentar [*en*-fre*n*-tar'] *va.* to confront, face.
enfurecer [*en*-foo-rĕ-sayr'] *va.* to infuriate; *vr.* to get furious; to rage.
enganado [*en*-gă-nah'doo] *adj.* **estar —**, to be mistaken, in error, wrong; **ser —**, to be deceived.
enganar [*en*-gă-nar'] *va.* to deceive, mislead; *vr.* to be mistaken, make a mistake; to deceive oneself.
engano [*en*-gă'noo] *m.* mistake, error; deception, trick; delusion.
enganoso [*en*-gă-noh'zoo] *adj.* deceitful, false.
engarrafar [*en*-gă-ră-far'] *va.* to bottle.
engasgar [*en*-găzh-gar'] *va/vn.* to choke, stifle; to gag.
engastar [*en*-găsh-tar'] *va.* to set, mount (precious stones).
engaste [*en*-gasht'] *m.* setting, mounting.
engatar [*en*-gă-tar'] *va.* to couple (railway coaches); to clamp, hitch together.
engelhar [*en*-zhĕ-lyar'] *va/vn.* to wrinkle; to shrivel (of plants).
engendrar [*en*-zhe*n*-drar'] *va.* to beget; to devise, produce.
engenharia [*en*-zhĕ-nyă-ree'ă] *f.* engineering.
engenheiro [*en*-zhĕ-nyay'ee-roo] *m.* engineer.
engenho [*en*-zhĕ'nyoo] *m.* talent, ability; ingenuity; inventiveness; skill; wit; mill.
engenhoso [*en*-zhĕ-nyoh'zoo] *adj.* ingenious, clever; resourceful.
englobar [*en*-gloo-bar'] *va.* to comprise, bring together.
engodo [*en*-goh'doo] *m.* bait; decoy; enticement.
engolfar [*en*-gohl-far'] *va.* to engulf; *vr.* to plunge into.
engolir [*en*-goo-leer'] *va.* to swallow (up, down).
engomar [*en*-goo-mar'] *va.* to starch and iron.
engonço [*en*-go*n*'soo] *m.* hinge; joint.
engordar [*en*-goor-dar'] *va.* to fatten; *vn.* to grow fat.
engraçado [*en*-gră-sah'doo] *adj.* pretty, attractive, pleasing; amusing, funny.
engrandecer [*en*-gra*n*-dĕ-sayr'] *va.* to aggrandize; to honour, exalt; *vn.* to become

greater (or richer, etc.).
engraxador [*en*-grǎ-shǎ-dohr'] *m.* bootblack, shoeblack.
engraxar [*en*-grǎ-shar'] *va.* to clean, polish (shoes).
engrenagem [*en*-grě-nah'-zhe*n*] *f.* gear, gearing.
engrenar [*en*-grě-nar'] *va.* to put into gear; to engage.
engrossar [*en*-groo-sar'] *va.* to swell, augment, thicken.
enguia [*en*-gee'ǎ] *f.* eel.
enguiço [*en*-gee'soo] *m.* bad luck; bad omen; foreboding.
enigma [ee-neeg'mǎ] *m.* enigma, puzzle.
enjeitado [*en*-zhay-ee-tah'-doo] *m.* foundling, waif; *adj.* rejected.
enjeitar [*en*-zhay-ee-tar'] *va.* to reject, repudiate; to abandon (child).
enjoado [en-zhoo-ah'doo] *adj.* (sea-)sick.
enjoar [*en*-zhoo-ar'] *vn.* to be sick; *va.* to sicken.
enjoo [*en*-zhoh'oo] *m.* (sea-) sickness.
enlaçar [*en*-lǎ-sar'] *va.* to bind, link, tie; to entwine.
enlace [*en*-las'] *m.* wedding, marriage; union.
enlamear [*en*-lǎ-mee-ar'] *va.* to spatter (splash) with mud; to besmirch (reputation).
enlatar [*en*-lǎ-tar'] *va.* to can (fruits, etc.); to train (vines) on a trellis.
enlear [*en*-lee-ar'] *va.* to perplex, puzzle; to bind.
enleio [*en*-lay'yoo] *m.* perplexity; entanglement.
enlevo [*en*-lay'voo] *m.* rapture, delight.
enlouquecer [*en*-loh-kě-sayr'] *vn.* to become insane, go mad; *va.* to madden.
enlutar [*en*-loo-tar'] *va.* to plunge into mourning.
enobrecer [e-noo-brě-sayr'] *va.* to ennoble.
enojar [ee-noo-zhar'] *va.* to disgust, sicken.
enojo [ee-noh'zhoo] *m.* disgust, loathing.
enorme [ee-norm'] *adj.* enormous.
enormidade [ee-nor-mee-dahd'] *f.* enormity.
enovelar [ee-noo-vě-lar'] *va.* to wind (thread) in a ball; to coil.
enquadrar [*en*-kwǎ-drar'] *va.* to frame.
enquanto [*en*-kwa*n*'too] *conj.* while; as long as; **por —**, for the time being, for the present.
enraivecer [*en*-rȳ-vě-sayr'] *va.* to infuriate.
enraizar [*en*-rȳ-zar'] *vn.* to take root.
enredar [*en*-rě-dar'] *va.* to catch in a net; to entangle; to embroil (in plot); to tangle up.
enredo [*en*-ray'doo] *m.* plot (of play, etc.); intrigue; trickery.
enrijar [*en*-ree-zhar'] *va.* to harden, toughen.
enriquecer [*en*-ree-kě-sayr'] *va.* to enrich; *vn/vr.* to grow rich.
enrolar [*en*-roo-lar'] *va.* to roll up, wind, twist round.
enroscar [*en*-roosh-kar'] *va.* to twist, wind, coil round.
enrouquecer [*en*-roh-kě-sayr'] *vn.* to get hoarse.
enrugar [*en*-roo-gar'] *va.* to wrinkle, crease.
ensaboar [*en*-sǎ-boo-ar'] *va.* to lather, soap.
ensaiar [*en*-sǎ-yar'] *va.* to test; to practise; to rehearse (play, etc.).
ensaio [*en*-sȳ'oo] *m.* essay; test, trial; attempt; practice; rehearsal.
ensaísta [*en*-sǎ-eesh'tǎ] *mf.* essayist, essay-writer.
ensalmo [*en*-sal'moo] *m.* spell, charm, magic.

ensamblador [*en*-san-blă-dohr'] *m.* joiner.
ensanguentar [*en*-san-gwen-tar'] *va.* to stain with blood.
enseada [*en*-see-ah'dă] *f.* (small) bay, inlet, cove.
ensejo [*en*-say'zhoo] *m.* opportunity.
ensinar [*en*-see-nar'] *va.* to teach, instruct; to show.
ensino [*en*-see'noo] *m.* teaching, instruction, education.
ensoberbecer-se [*en*-soo-bĕr-bĕ-sayr'sĕ] *vr.* to become proud, haughty.
ensopar [*en*-soo-par'] *va.* to soak, drench.
ensurdecer [*en*-soor-dĕ-sayr'] *va.* to deafen; *vn.* to grow deaf.
entabular [*en*-tă-boo-lar'] *va.* to open, start (negotiations, etc.).
entalar [*en*-tă-lar'] *va.* to put in a difficult situation; to trap, squeeze.
entalhador [*en*-tă-lyă-dohr'] *m.* wood carver.
entalho [*en*-ta'lyoo] *m.* carving; groove, notch.
entanto [*en*-tan'too] *adv.* meanwhile; no —, nevertheless, however; in the meantime.
então [*en*-town'] *adv.* then, at that time; *interj.* what!; well then!; now then!
ente [ent] *m.* being; creature.
enteado; -da [*en*-tee-ah'doo; 'dă] *m.* stepson; *f.* stepdaughter.
entender [*en*-ten-dayr'] *va.* to understand; to perceive, realize; to know; **dar a —**, to imply; **no meu —**, in my opinion.
entendido [*en*-ten-dee'doo] *adj.* expert, skilful; **dar-se por —**, to take a hint.
entendimento [*en*-ten-dee-men'too] *m.* understanding; comprehension; intellect, intelligence.
enterite [*en*-tĕ-reet'] *f.* enteritis.
enternecer [*en*-tĕr-nĕ-sayr'] *va.* to move, touch (the affections); *vr.* to be moved.
enterrar [*en*-tĕ-rar'] *va.* to bury.
enterro [*en*-tay'roo] *m.* burial; funeral.
entesar [*en*-tĕ-zar'] *va.* to stiffen, stretch tight.
entidade [*en*-tee-dahd'] *f.* entity, being; body, group; person of importance.
entoação [*en*-too-ă-sown'] *f.* intonation.
entoar [*en*-too-ar'] *va.* to intone, chant.
entontecer [*en*-ton-tĕ-sayr'] *va.* to stupefy, stun, bewilder.
entornar [*en*-toor-nar'] *va.* to spill; to upset.
entorpecer [*en*-toor-pĕ-sayr'] *va.* to numb, paralyse, deaden.
entorpecimento [*en*-toor-pĕ-see-men'too] *m.* torpor, sluggishness.
entortar [*en*-toor-tar'] *va.* to twist, bend; **— os olhos**, to squint.
entrada [*en*-trah'dă] *f.* entrance, way in; entry, arrival; admission; entrance fee; beginning; **direitos de —**, import duties.
entrado [*en*-trah'doo] *adj.* **— em anos**, elderly.
entrançar [*en*-tran-sar'] *va.* to braid, interweave.
entranhar [*en*-tră-nyar'] *va.* to drive into; *vr.* to penetrate, go deep into.
entranhas [*en*-tră-nyăsh] *f.pl.* bowels, entrails; innermost parts; (*fig.*) affections, heart, love.
entrar [*en*-trar'] *vn.* to go in, get into, come in, enter; to begin; **— em vigor**, to come

into force, become effective.
entravar [*en*-tră-var'] *va.* to obstruct, impede.
entre [*en*'trĕ] *prep.* among, amongst; between; — mãos, (work) in hand.
entreabrir [*en*'tree-ă-breer'] *va.* to half-open; *vn.* to open (flowers).
entrecho [*en*-tray'shoo] *m.* plot (of play, etc.).
entrecortar [*en*-trĕ-koor-tar'] *va.* to interrupt; *vr.* to intersect.
entrecosto [*en*-trĕ-kohsh'too] *m.* rib (of beef, etc.).
entrega [*en*-tre'gă] *f.* delivery, handing over; **pagamento na** —, C.O.D. (cash on delivery).
entregar [*en*-trĕ-gar'] *va.* to deliver, hand over; to yield, surrender; *vr.* to be given over to, dedicated to.
entregue [*en*-treg'] *adj.* given over to; delivered, handed over.
entrelaçar [*en*-trĕ-lă-sar'] *va.* to entwine, interlace.
entreluzir [*en*-trĕ-loo-zeer'] *vn.* to glimmer, shine faintly.
entremeter-se [*en*-trĕ-mĕ-tayr'sĕ] *vr.* to concern oneself with, meddle in.
entremetido [*en*-trĕ-mĕ-tee'-doo] *adj.* meddlesome.
entreolhar-se [*en*-tree-oo-lyar'sĕ] *vr.* to eye (look at) each other.
entretanto [*en*-trĕ-ta*n*'too] *adv.* meanwhile, in the meantime.
entretecer [*en*-trĕ-tĕ-sayr'] *va.* to interweave.
entreter [*en*-trĕ-tayr'] *va.* to delay, put off (with empty promises, etc.); to entertain.
entrevar [*en*-trĕ-var'] *va.* to paralyse, cripple.
entrever [*en*-trĕ-vayr'] *vn.* to catch a glimpse of; to discern.
entrevista [*en*-trĕ-veesh'tă] *f.* interview; meeting.
entrevistar [*en*-trĕ-veesh-tar'] *va.* to interview; *vr.* to have an interview with.
entrincheirar-se [*en*-tree*n*-shay-ee-rar'sĕ] *vr.* to entrench oneself, dig in.
entristecer [*en*-treesh-tĕ-sayr'] *va.* to sadden, grieve; *vr.* to become sad.
entroncamento [*en*-tro*n*-kă-me*n*'too] *m.* junction.
entroncar [*en*-tro*n*-kar'] *vn.* to join, connect; to fill out (of body).
entronizar [*en*-troo-nee-zar'] *va.* to enthrone; to exalt.
entrudo [*en*-troo'doo] *m.* carnival, Shrovetide.
entulho [*en*-too'lyoo] *m.* rubble, debris, rubbish.
entupir [*en*-too-peer'] *va.* to stop up, clog, choke.
entusiasmar [*en*-too-zee-ăzh-mar'] *va.* to fill with enthusiasm, captivate; *vr.* to be enthusiastic, excited about.
entusiasmo [*en*-too-zee-azh'-moo] *m.* enthusiasm, eagerness, keenness.
entusiasta [*en*-too-zee-ash'-tă] *mf.* enthusiast; *adj.* enthusiastic.
enumerar [ee-noo-mĕ-rar'] *va.* to enumerate, count.
enunciar [ee-noo*n*-see-ar'] *va.* to express, state.
envaidar [*en*-vȳ-dar] *va.* to puff up; *vr.* to grow vain, conceited.
envelhecer [*en*-vĕ-lyĕ-sayr'] *vn.* to age, grow old.
envelope [*en*-vĕ-lop'] *m.* envelope.
envenenar [*en*-vĕ-nĕ-nar'] *va.* to poison.
enverdecer [*en*-vĕr-dĕ-sayr'] *va.* to make green; *vn.* to grow green; (*fig.*) to revive.
envergadura [*en*-vĕr-gă-doo'-

ră] *f.* spread (of sails, wings); wing-span (of aeroplane); competence; scope, extent.
envergonhado [*en*-věr-goo-nyah'doo] *adj.* ashamed; shy.
envergonhar [*en*-věr-goo-nyar'] *va.* to shame; *vr.* to be ashamed.
envessar [*en*-vě-sar'] *va.* to turn inside out.
enviado [*en*-vee-ah'doo] *m.* envoy, representative.
enviar [*en*-vee-ar'] *va.* to send, despatch.
envio [*en*-vee'oo] *m.* sending, despatch, remittance.
enviuvar [*en*-vee-oo-var'] *vn.* to become a widow *or* widower.
envolto [*en*-vohl'too] *adj.* wrapped.
envoltório [*en*-vohl-to'ree-oo] *m.* wrapper, cover.
envolver [*en*-vohl-vayr'] *va.* to wrap up; to involve; to include; to embrace; to cover.
enxada [*en*-shah'dă] *f.* mattock.
enxaguar [*en*-sha-gwar'] *va.* to rinse (out).
enxame [*en*-shahm'] *m.* swarm.
enxergão [*en*-shěr-gow*n*'] *m.* straw-mattress.
enxergar [*en*-shěr-gar'] *va.* to catch sight of, perceive, see.
enxertar [*en*-shěr-tar'] *va.* to graft (on).
enxó [*en*-sho'] *m.* adze.
enxofre [*en*-shoh'frě] *m.* sulphur.
enxota-moscas [*en*-sho'tă mohsh'kăsh] *m.* fly-whisk, -swat(ter).
enxotar [*en*-shoo-tar'] *va.* to drive out, off.
enxoval [*en*-shoo-val'] *m.* trousseau (of bride); layette (of infant).
enxovalhar [*en*-shoo-vă-lyar'] *va.* to crumple; to soil, stain; to insult.
enxugar [*en*-shoo-gar'] *va.* to dry (up, off, out).
enxurrada [*en*-shoo-rah'dă] *f.* torrent, spate.
enxuto [*en*-shoo'too] *adj.* dry.
épico [e'pee-koo] *adj.* epic, heroic; *m.* epic poet.
epidemia [ě-pee-dě-mee'ă] *f.* epidemic.
epígrafe [ě-pee'grăf] *f.* inscription, epigraph; title.
epilepsia [ě-pee-lep-see'ă] *f.* epilepsy.
epílogo [ě-pee'loo-goo] *m.* epilogue, conclusion.
episcopado [ě-peesh-koo-pah'doo] *m.* episcopate; bishopric.
episódio [ě-pee-zo'dee-oo] *m.* episode; incident.
epístola [ě-peesh'too-lă] *f.* epistle, letter.
epitáfio [ě-pee-tah'fee-oo] *m.* epitaph, inscription.
epíteto [ě-pee'tě-too] *m.* epithet.
epítome [ě-pee'toom] *m.* summary; epitome.
época [e'poo-kă] *f.* period, time, epoch.
epopeia [ee-poo-pe'yă] *f.* epic.
equador [ee-kwă-dohr'] *m.* equator.
equanimidade [ee-kwă-nee-mee-dahd'] *f.* equanimity.
equidade [ee-kee-dahd'] *f.* equity; justice.
equilibrar [ee-kee-lee-brar'] *va.* to balance.
equilíbrio [ee-kee-lee'bree-oo] *m.* balance, equilibrium.
equinócio [ee-kee-no'see-oo] *m.* equinox.
equipa [ee-kee'pă] *f.* team (in sports); group, section.
equipagem [ee-kee-pah'zhe*n*] *f.* crew (*naut.*); equipment, supplies.
equipamento [ee-kee-pă-men'too] *m.* equipment, outfit.

escaldar [ish-kal-dar'] *va.* to scald, burn.
escaler [ish-kă-layr'] *m.* (small) boat, cutter.
escalfar [ish-kal-far'] *va.* to poach (eggs).
escalpelo [ish-kal-pe'loo] *m.* scalpel, surgeon's knife.
escama [ish-kă'mă] *f.* scale (of fish, snakes).
escamoteação [ish-kă-moo-tee-ă-sown'] *f.* conjuring, sleight of hand; pilfering.
escandalizar [ish-kan-dă-lee-zar'] *va.* to scandalize, shock; *vr.* to take offence.
escândalo [ish-kan'-dă-loo] *m.* scandal; row.
escandaloso [ish-kan-dă-loh'zoo] *adj.* scandalous.
escandinavo [ish-kan-dee-nah'voo] *m/adj.* Scandinavian.
escangalhar [ish-kan-gă-lyar'] *va.* to break (smash) up.
escaninho [ish-kă-nee'nyoo] *m.* hiding-place, recess; pigeon-hole (in desk).
escapar [ish-kă-par'] *vn.* to escape.
escaramuça [ish-kă-ră-moo'-să] *f.* skirmish.
escaravelho [ish-kă-ră-vay'-lyoo] *m.* beetle. [scarlet.
escarlate [ish-kăr-lat'] *m.*
escarlatina [ish-kăr-lă-tee'-nă] *f.* scarlet-fever.
escarmentar [ish-kăr-men-tar'] *va.* to punish, reprimand (severely); *vr.* to learn from (bitter) experience.
escarmento [ish-kăr-men'-too] *m.* warning; punishment.
escarnecer [ish-kăr-nĕ-sayr'] *vr.* to make fun of, jeer, scoff at.
escárnio [ish-kar'nee-oo] *vn.* mockery, ridicule.
escarpado [ish-kăr-pah'doo] *adj.* steep.
escarranchar [ish-kă-ran-shar'] *va/vr.* to straddle.
escarrar [ish-kă-rar'] *va/vn.* to spit (up, out).
escarro [ish-ka'roo] *m.* phlegm, mucus.
escassear [ish-kă-see-ar'] *vn.* to become scarce, diminish; *va.* to curtail, withhold.
escassez [ish-kă-saysh'] *f.* scarcity, lack, want.
escasso [ish-ka'soo] *adj.* scarce, rare; scanty, meagre.
escavação [ish-kă-vă-sown'] *f.* digging; hole; excavation.
esclarecer [ish-klă-rĕ-sayr'] *va.* to explain, clarify.
esclarecimento [ish-klă-rĕ-see-men'too] *m.* explanation, elucidation; information.
esclusa [ish-kloo'ză] *f.* (canal) lock.
escoadouro [ish-koo-ă-doh'-roo] *m.* drain; gutter; drain pipe.
escoar [ish-koo-ar'] *va.* to drain (off, away); *vr.* to drip; to trickle (away).
escocês [ish-koo-saysh'] *adj.* Scottish; *m.* Scotsman, Scot.
escol [ish-kol'] *m.* the finest, best; o — da sociedade, the cream of society.
escola [ish-ko'lă] *f.* school; college.
escolar [ish-koo-lar'] *adj.* school; *m.* student, pupil.
escolha [ish-koh'lyă] *f.* choice.
escolher [ish-koo-lyayr'] *va.* to choose, select, pick out.
escolho [ish-koh'lyoo] *m.* reef; (*fig.*) dangerous obstacle.
escolta [ish-kol'tă] *f.* escort, (body)guard.
escoltar [ish-kohl-tar'] *va.* to escort; to convoy (*naut.*).
escombros [ish-kon'broosh] *m.pl.* rubbish, débris, ruins.
esconder [ish-kon-dayr'] *va.* to hide, conceal.

esconderijo [ish-ko*n*-dĕ-ree'-zhoo] *m.* hiding-place, hideout.
escondidas [ish-ko*n*-dee'-dăsh] *f.pl.* hide-and-seek (game); às —, secretly, furtively, on the sly.
esconjurar [ish-ko*n*-zhoo-rar'] *va.* to adjure; to exorcize.
escopo [ish-koh'poo] *m.* aim.
escopro [ish-koh'proo] *m.* chisel.
escora [ish-ko'ră] *f.* prop, support. [slag.
escória [ish-ko'ree-ă] *f.* dross;
escoriar [ish-koo-ree-ar'] *va.* to graze, chafe (skin).
escorpião [ish-koor-pee-ow*n*'] *m.* scorpion.
escorregadela [ish-koo-rĕ-gă-de'lă] *f.* slip; mistake.
escorregadiço [ish-koo-rĕ-gă-dee'soo] *adj.* slippery.
escorregar [ish-koo-rĕ-gar'] *vn.* to slip, slide.
escorrer [ish-koo-rayr'] *va.* to drain off; *vn.* to drip; to trickle.
escotilha [ish-koo-tee'lyă] *f.* hatch(way) (*naut.*).
escova [ish-koh'vă] *f.* brush.
escovar [ish-koo-var'] *va.* to brush.
escravatura [ish-kră-vă-too'-ră] *f.* slave trade; slavery.
escravidão [ish-kră-vee-dow*n*'] *f.* slavery, bondage.
escravizar [ish-kră-vee-zar'] *va.* to enslave.
escravo [ish-krah'voo] *m.* slave.
escrever [ish-krĕ-vayr'] *va/vn.* to write; — à màquina, to type.
escrevinhar [ish-krĕ-vee-nyar'] *va.* to scribble, scrawl.
escrita [ish-kree'tă] *f.* handwriting.
escrito [ish-kree'too] *m.* piece of writing; note; **pôr por** —, to put in writing.
escritor [ish-kree-tohr'] *m.* writer, author.
escritório [ish-kree-to'ree-oo] *m.* office; study.
escritura [ish-kree-too'ră] *f.* deed, document, covenant (*leg.*); — Sagrada, the Scriptures, Holy Writ.
escrituração [ish-kree-too-ră-sow*n*'] *f.* book-keeping.
escriturar [ish-kree-too-rar'] *va.* to keep (write up, enter up) accounts, *or* books (*com.*).
escrivaninha [ish-kri-vă-nee'nyă] *f.* (writing)desk; — de tampo corrediço, roll-top desk.
escrivão [ish-kree-vow*n*'] *m.* registrar; clerk; — da puridade (*archaic*), (royal) secretary.
escrúpulo [ish-kroo'poo-loo] *m.* hesitation, doubt, scruple; qualm of conscience; careful attention.
escrupuloso [ish-kroo-poo-loh'zoo] *adj.* scrupulous; careful.
escrutar [ish-kroo-tar'] *va.* to scrutinize, examine, search.
escrutinar [ish-kroo-tee-nar'] *va.* to count votes.
escrutínio [ish-kroo-tee'nee-oo] *m.* (voting by) ballot; counting of votes.
escudeiro [ish-koo-day'ee-roo] *m.* squire (*archaic*).
escudela [ish-koo-de'lă] *f.* wooden bowl.
escudo [ish-koo'doo] *m.* shield; Portuguese monetary unit.
esculpir [ish-kool-peer'] *va.* to carve. [sculptor.
escultor [ish-kool-tohr'] *m.*
escultura [ish-kool-too'ră] *f.* sculpture, carving.
escuma [ish-koo'mă] *f.* froth; foam; scum. [schooner.
escuna [ish-koo'nă] *f.*
escurecer [ish-koo-rĕ-sayr']

vn/vr. to get (grow) dark; *va.* to darken, obscure.
escuridão [ish-koo-ree-down'] *f.* darkness; ignorance.
escuro [ish-koo'roo] *adj.* dark; obscure; dim; às —as, in the dark.
escusado [ish-koo-zah'doo] *adj.* needless, unnecessary.
escusar [ish-koo-zar'] *va.* to excuse, forgive; to have no need of; to exempt from; *vr.* to avoid (doing something); to apologize.
escutar [ish-koo-tar'] *va.* to listen (to); to hear.
escuteiro [ish-koo-tay'ee-roo] *m. or* **escoteiro,** Boy Scout.
esfacelar [ish-fă-sĕ-lar'] *va.* to ruin, destroy, cut up.
esfaimar [ish-fȳ-mar'] *va.* to starve.
esfalfar [ish-fal-far'] *va.* to tire out, overwork.
esfaquear [ish-fă-kee-ar'] *va.* to knife, stab.
esfarrapado [ish-fă-ră-pah'-doo] *adj.* ragged, tattered.
esfera [ish-fair'ă] *f.* sphere; globe; scope, field, range.
esférico [ish-fair'ee-koo] *adj.* spherical, globular.
esfinge [ish-feenzh'] *f.* sphinx.
esfolar [ish-foo-lar'] *va.* to flay; to fleece, rob.
esfolhar [ish-foo-lyar'] *va.* to strip off (husks of maize, leaves).
esfomeado [ish-foo-mee-ah'-doo] *adj.* starving, famished.
esforçado [ish-foor-sah'doo] *adj.* valiant, courageous; strong.
esforçar [ish-foor-sar'] *va.* to encourage, stimulate; *vr.* to strive, endeavour, try hard.
esforço [ish-fohr'soo] *m.* effort; endeavour, exertion.
esfregar [ish-frĕ-gar'] *va.* to rub; to scrub.
esfriar [ish-free-ar'] *va.* to cool, chill; *vr/vn.* to get cold; to lose one's zest, enthusiasm.
esfumar [ish-foo-mar'] *va.* to tone down, soften; *vr.* to fade away, vanish.
esganar [izh-gă-nar'] *va.* to strangle, choke.
esgaravatar [izh-gă-ră-vă-tar'] *va.* to scratch, scrape, pick; to delve, probe into.
esgotado [izh-goo-tah'doo] *adj.* exhausted, worn out; out of print (books).
esgotamento [izh-goo-tă-men'too] *m.* exhaustion.
esgotar [izh-goo-tar'] *va.* to exhaust; to drain, empty; *vr.* to become exhausted.
esgoto [izh-goh' too] *m.* drain.
esgrimir [izh-gree-meer'] *vn.* to fence; *va.* to brandish, wield.
esgueirar-se [izh-gay-ee-rar'sĕ] *vr.* to slip away.
esguelha [izh-gay'lyă] *f.* slant; de —, slanting; olhar de —, to look out of the corner of one's eye, look slyly.
esguichar [izh-gee-shar'] *va/vn.* to squirt (out).
esguio [izh-gee'oo] *m.* tall and slender, slim; lanky.
eslavo [izh-lah'voo] *m/adj.* Slav.
esmagar [izh-mă-gar'] *va.* to crush, smash; to overwhelm.
esmalte [izh-malt'] *m.* enamel.
esmerado [izh-mĕ-rah'doo] *adj.* refined, polished, faultless, perfect.
esmeralda [izh-mĕ-ral'dă] *f.* emerald.
esmerar-se [izh-mĕ-rar'sĕ] *vr.* to take great care, pains.
esmero [izh-mair'oo] *m.* care, attention; refinement, delicacy.
esmiuçar [izh-mee-oo-sar'] *va.* to examine (relate) in detail; to crumble (bread, etc.).

esmo [ayzh'moo] *m.* (rough) estimate; a —, at random.
esmoer [izh-moo-ayr'] *va.* to munch, chew.
esmola [izh-mo'lă] *f.* alms, charity; (*pop.*) beating.
esmorecer [izh-moo-rĕ-sayr'] *va.* to discourage; *vn.* to lose heart; to become faint-hearted; to grow faint (light, sound, etc.).
espaço [ish-pah'soo] *m.* space; room; period (of time); a —s, from time to time.
espaçoso [ish-pă-soh'zoo] *adj.* spacious, roomy, extensive.
espada [ish-pah'dă] *f.* sword; *pl.* spades (cards).
espádua [ish-pa'doo-ă] *f.* shoulder-blade.
espaldar [ish-pal-dar'] *m.* back (of chair).
espalhafato [ish-pa-lyă-fah'too] *m.* fuss, noise, commotion.
espalhar [ish-pă-lyar'] *va.* to scatter, spread (around).
espanador [ish-pă-nă-dohr'] *m.* duster (cloth); soft brush (for dusting).
espanar [ish-pă-nar'] *va.* to dust.
espancar [ish-pa*n*-kar'] *va.* to beat (up), thrash; to drive off.
espanhol [ish-pă-nyol'] *m.* Spaniard; Spanish (language); *adj.* Spanish.
espantadiço [ish-pa*n*-tă-dee'-soo] *adj.* timid, nervous.
espantalho [ish-pa*n*-ta'lyoo] *m.* scarecrow.
espantar [ish-pa*n*-tar'] *va.* to frighten; to amaze, astonish.
espanto [ish-pa*n*'too] *m.* fright, fear; amazement.
espantoso [ish-pa*n*-toh'zoo] *adj.* frightful, fearful; frightening; astonishing, astounding.
espargir [ish-păr-zheer'] *va.* to sprinkle; to scatter, spread.
espargo [ish-par'goo] *m.* asparagus.
espasmo [ish-pazh'moo] *m.* convulsion, spasm.
espavorir [ish-pă-voo-reer'] *va.* to terrify, frighten.
especial [ish-pĕ-see-al'] *adj.* special.
especialidade [ish-pĕ-see-ă-lee-dahd'] *f.* speciality; special line, subject; specialisation.
especialista [ish-pĕ-see-ă-leesh'tă] *mf.* specialist.
especializar [ish-pĕ-see-ă-lee-zar'] *va.* to specify; *vr.* to specialize (in).
especiaria [ish-pĕ-see-ă-ree'ă] *f.* spice.
espécie [ish-pe'see-ĕ] *f.* kind, sort; species; specie, coin; causar —, to take aback; de toda a —, of all kinds; pagar em —, to pay in kind (i.e. with foodstuffs).
especificar [ish-pĕ-see-fee-kar'] *va.* to specify.
espécime [ish-pe'seem] *m. or* **espécimen**, *m.* specimen.
especioso [ish-pĕ-see-oh'zoo] *adj.* specious.
espectáculo [ish-pe-ta'koo-loo] *m.* spectacle, sight; performance, show (*theat.*, etc.).
espectador [ish-pe-tă-dohr'] *m.* spectator, onlooker.
espectro [ish-pe'troo] *m.* ghost, spectre, phantom; spectrum (in physics, etc.).
especular [ish-pe-koo-lar'] *vn.* to speculate (*com.*); *va.* to ponder over, consider.
espelho [ish-pay'lyoo] *m.* mirror, looking-glass; (*fig.*) model, example.
espelunca [ish-pĕ-loo*n*'kă] *f.* cavern, den; hovel; gambling den.
espera [ish-pair'ă] *f.* expectation; wait; delay; à — de,

waiting for; sala de —, waiting room. [hope.
esperança [ish-pĕ-ran'să] *f.*
esperar [ish-pĕ-rar'] *va.* to hope (for); to wait for, await; to expect.
espertalhão [ish-pĕr-tă-lyown'] *m.* (*sl.*) smart Aleck; clever, cunning, crafty fellow.
esperteza [ish-pĕr-tay'ză] *f.* sharpness, cleverness; cunning.
esperto [ish-pair'too] *adj.* clever, sharp, smart.
espesso [ish-pay'soo] *adj.* thick; dense.
espessura [ish-pĕ-soo'ră] *f.* thickness; density; thicket, wood.
espetar [ish-pĕ-tar'] *va.* to stick on a spit; to stab, pierce.
espia [ish-pee'ă]. *f.* spy; rope, hawser (*naut.*).
espião [ish-pee-own'] *m.* spy.
espiar [ish-pee-ar'] *va.* to spy on, watch.
espichar [ish-pee-shar'] *va.* to string (fish) together; to tap (barrel); to stretch, peg out (hides); *vn.* (*sl.*) to peg out, kick the bucket, die.
espiga [ish-pee'gă] *f.* ear of corn; (*sl.*) nuisance, bore; difficulty.
espigueiro [ish-pee-gay'ee-roo] *m.* granary.
espinafre [ish-pee-na'frĕ] *m.* spinach; (*pop.*) lanky, gawky person.
espingarda [ish-peen-gar'dă] *f.* gun, rifle.
espinha [ish-pee'nyă] *f.* spine; fish-bone.
espinheiro [ish-pee-nyay'ee-roo] *m.* briar; thorn-bush; — alvar, hawthorn.
espinho [ish-pee'nyoo] *m.* thorn; prickle.
espionagem [ish-pee-oo-nah'-zhen] *f.* espionage, spying.
espionar [ish-pee-oo-nar'] *vn.* to spy.
espiritismo [ish-pee-ree-teezh'moo] *m.* spiritualism.
espírito [ish-pee'ree-too] *m.* spirit; soul; genius; vigour, liveliness; character; ghost; alcohol, spirits; — Santo, Holy Ghost, Holy Spirit.
espirituoso [ish-pee-ree-too-oh'zoo] *adj.* witty, lively; strong, very alcoholic (wines, etc.).
espirrar [ish-pee-rar'] *vn.* to sneeze; to burst out; (*pop.*) to take offence.
esplêndido [ish-plen'dee-doo] *adj.* splendid, excellent, magnificent.
esplendor [ish-plen-dohr'] *m.* splendour, brilliance, radiance.
espoleta [ish-poo-lay'tă] *f.* fuse.
espoliação [ish-poo-lee-ă-sown'] *f.* plunder, spoliation.
espoliar [ish-poo-lee-ar'] *va.* to rob, plunder, despoil.
espólio [ish-po'lee-oo] *m.* estate, property, goods (of dead person); loot, spoils, booty.
esponja [ish-pon'zhă] *f.* sponge; (*fig.*) sponger, parasite.
esponsais [ish-pon-sȳsh'] *m. pl.* engagement, betrothal; wedding.
espontâneo [ish-pon-tă'nee-oo] *adj.* spontaneous.
espontar [ish-pon-tar'] *va.* to trim.
espora [ish-po'ră] *f.* spur; stimulus.
esporádico [ish-poo-ra'dee-koo] *adj.* sporadic.
esporão [ish-poo-rown'] *m.* (cock's) spur; buttress (*archit.*).
esporear [ish-poo-ree-ar'] *va.* to spur on; to incite.

esposa [ish-poh'ză] *f.* wife; bride.
esposo [ish-poh'zoo] *m.* husband; spouse, consort; *pl.* husband and wife.
espraiar [ish-prȳ-yar'] *vn/vr.* to spread (out), expand.
espreguiçar-se [ish-prĕ-gee-sar'sĕ] *vr.* to stretch.
espreitar [ish-pray-ee-tar'] *va.* to spy out; to observe; to peep.
espremer [ish-prĕ-mayr'] *va.* to squeeze.
espuma [ish-poo'mă] *f.* foam, froth.
espumante [ish-poo-m*a*nt'] *adj.* foaming, frothy; **vinhos —s**, sparkling wines.
espúrio [ish-poo'ree-oo] *adj.* spurious, fake; bastard.
esquadra [ish-kwad'ră] *f.* naval squadron; (army) squad; police station.
esquadrão [ish-kwă-drow*n*'] *m.* (cavalry) squadron.
esquadrilha [ish-kwă-dree'-lyă] *f.* (air-force) squadron; flotilla (*naut.*).
esquadrinhar [ish-kwă-dree-nyar'] *va.* to scrutinize, scan.
esquadro [ish-kwa'droo] *m.* set-square (*mech.*, etc.).
esquecer [ish-ke-sayr'] *va/vr.* to forget.
esquecimento [ish-ke-see-me*n*'too] *m.* forgetfulness; oblivion; omission.
esqueleto [ish-kĕ-lay'too] *m.* skeleton; framework; outline.
esquema [ish-kay'mă] *m.* scheme, plan; sketch.
esquerda [ish-kayr'dă] *f.* left (side, hand).
esquerdo [ish-kayr'doo] *adj.* left.
esquilo [ish-kee'loo] *m.* squirrel.
esquina [ish-kee'nă] *f.* (exterior) corner.
esquisito [ish-ki-zee'too] *adj.* odd, strange, peculiar, queer; finicky, faddy; exquisite.
esquivar [ish-kee-var'] *va/vr.* to avoid, escape (from).
esquivo [ish-kee'voo] *adj.* elusive; unsociable.
essência [ee-say*n*'see-ă] *f.* essence; perfume.
essencial [ee-se*n*-see-al'] *adj.* essential, indispensable.
estabelecer [ish-tă-blĕ-sayr'] *va.* to establish, found, set up.
estabelecimento [ish-tă-blĕ-see-me*n*'too] *m.* establishment; institution; business; shop.
estabilidade [ish-tă-bi-lee-dahd'] *f.* stability, steadiness.
estábulo [ish-ta'boo-loo] *m.* cow-, cattle-shed.
estaca [ish-tah'kă] *f.* stake, post; peg.
estacada [ish-tă-kah'dă] *f.* fencing; stockade.
estação [ish-tă-sow*n*'] *f.* station (railway, etc.); season (of year).
estacar [ish-tă-kar'] *va/vn.* to stop suddenly; *va.* to prop up (with stakes).
estacionamento [ish-tă-see-oo-nă-me*n*'too] *m.* parking (cars).
estacionar [ish-tă-see-oo-nar'] *vn.* to stop; to remain stationary; to park (of cars).
estadia [ish-tă-dee'ă] *f.* stay.
estádio [ish-tah'dee-oo] *m.* stadium.
estadista [ish-tă-deesh'tă] *m.* statesman.
estado [ish-tah'doo] *m.* state; condition; status, position; **— maior**, general staff (*mil.*).
estafar [ish-tă-far'] *va.* to tire out.
estafermo [ish-tă-fayr'moo] *m.* scarecrow; ninny; good-for-nothing.
estafeta [ish-tă-fay'tă] *m.* dispatch-rider, courier.
estagiário [ish-tă-zhee-ah'-

ree-oo] *m.* probationer, trainee; student-teacher.
estágio [ish-tah'zhee-oo] *m.* training (probationary) period; apprenticeship.
estagnação [ish-tăg-nă-sown'] *f.* stagnation.
estagnar [ish-tăg-nar'] *vn.* to stagnate.
estalagem [ish-tă-lah'zhen] *f.* [inn.
estalar [ish-tă-lar'] *vn.* to break, snap, crack; to explode, burst; to break out (war, etc.).
estaleiro [ish-tă-lay'ee-roo] *m.* shipyard.
estalido [ish-tă-lee'doo] *m.* snap; crash; crack (of whip).
estampa [ish-tan'pă] *f.* (printed) picture; dar à —, to publish, print, send to press.
estampar [ish-tan-par'] *va.* to (im)print, stamp.
estampido [ish-tan-pee'doo] *m.* crash, explosion.
estampilha [ish-tan-pee'lyă] *f.* stamp.
estancar [ish-tan-kar'] *va.* to staunch, stop (flow of blood, tears, etc.); *vn.* to run dry.
estância [ish-tan'see-ă] *f.* place to stay, stop; — **balnear**, seaside resort; — **de madeiras**, timber yard; — **de carvão**, coal yard.
estandarte [ish-tan-dart'] *m.* standard, banner.
estanho [ish-tă'nyoo] *m.* tin.
estanque [ish-tank'] *adj.* tight, water-tight.
estante [ish-tant'] *f.* book-case; book-shelf; book-rest; — **de música**, music stand.
estar [ish-tar'] *vn.* to be.
estatística [ish-tă-teesh'tee-kă] *f.* statistics.
estátua [ish-ta'too-ă] *f.* statue.
estatura [ish-tă-too'ră] *f.* statue, height.
estatuto [ish-tă-too'too] *m.* statute, ordinance.
estável [ish-tah'vel] *adj.* stable, firm, steady.
este [esht] *m.* east.
este [aysht] *adj.* this; *pr.* this one; the latter.
esteio [ish-tay'yoo] *m.* support, stay, prop.
esteira [ish-tay'ee-ră] *f.* mat; wake (of ship); path, track.
estender [ish-ten-dayr'] *va.* to extend, stretch, spread (out).
esteno-dactilógrafa [ish-tay'no dak-tee-lo'gră-fă] *f.* shorthand-typist.
estenografia [ish-tĕ-noo-gră-fee'ă] *f.* shorthand, stenography.
esterco [ish-tayr'koo] *m.* dung, excrement, manure.
estéril [ish-te'reel] *adj.* sterile, barren; fruitless.
esterlina [ish-tĕr-lee'nă] *adj.* libra —, pound sterling.
estética [ish-te'tee-kă] *f.* aesthetics.
estiar [ish-tee-ar'] *vn.* to clear up, become dry, fine (weather).
estibordo [ish-tee-bor'doo] *m.* starboard.
esticar [ish-tee-kar'] *va.* to stretch; *vn.* (*pop.*) to die.
estigma [ish-teeg'mă] *m.* stigma; mark, scar.
estigmatizar [ish-teeg-mă-tee-zar'] *va.* to stigmatize.
estilha [ish-tee'lyă] *f.* splinter, fragment.
estilo [ish-tee'loo] *m.* style; manner, fashion.
estima [ish-tee'mă] *f.* esteem, respect, regard, appreciation; reckoning (*naut.*).
estimação [ish-tee-mă-sown'] *f.* appreciation, esteem, estimation; estimate, calculation.
estimar [ish-tee-mar'] *va.* to esteem, have a high regard for; to appreciate; to estimate.
estimulante [ish-tee-moo-

la*n*t'] *adj.* stimulating; *m.* stimulant.
estimular [ish-tee-moo-lar'] *va.* to encourage, stimulate.
estímulo [ish-tee'moo-loo] *m.* encouragement, stimulus, incentive.
estio [ish-tee'oo] *m.* summer.
estiolar [ish-tee-oo-lar'] *vn/vr.* to wither, fade.
estipêndio [ish-tee-pe*n*'dee-oo] *m.* stipend, pay.
estipulação [ish-tee-poo-lă-sow*n*'] *f.* stipulation, condition; contract.
estipular [ish-tee-poo-lar'] *va.* to stipulate; to agree.
estirar [ish-tee-rar'] *va.* to stretch (out).
estirpe [ish-teerp'] *f.* stock, family, descent.
estocada [ish-too-kah'dă] *f.* stab, jab, thrust.
estofa [ish-toh'fă] *f.* material, stuff; condition.
estofar [ish-too-far'] *va.* to pad; to upholster.
estofo [ish-toh'foo] *m.* padding; material.
estóico [ish-toy'koo] *adj.* stoic(al).
estoirar [ish-toh-ee-rar'] *vn.* to burst, explode; — de fome, to be starving.
estojo [ish-toh'zhoo] *m.* set (of tools, etc.), case.
estólido [ish-to'lee-doo] *adj.* stupid, obtuse.
estômago [ish-toh'mă-goo] *m.* stomach.
estontear [ish-to*n*-tee-ar'] *va.* to stun, bewilder.
estopa [ish-toh'pă] *f.* tow.
estore [ish-tor'] *m.* blind; window shade.
estorninho [ish-toor-nee'-nyoo] *m.* starling.
estorvar [ish-toor-var'] *va.* to obstruct, hamper, hinder.
estorvo [ish-tohr'voo] *m.* hindrance, obstacle, obstruction.
estouvado [ish-toh-vah'doo] *adj.* stupid, scatter-brained.
estrabismo [ish-tră-beezh'-moo] *m.* squint.
estrada [ish-trah'dă] *f.* road.
estrado [ish-trah'doo] *m.* platform; dais.
estragar [ish-tră-gar'] *va.* to spoil, damage; to corrupt; to ruin.
estrago [ish-trah'goo] *m.* damage, havoc, ravage; waste; corruption.
estrangeiro [ish-tra*n*-zhay'-ee-roo] *adj.* foreign; *m.* foreigner, alien; foreign lands; no —, abroad.
estrangular [ish-tra*n*-goo-lar'] *va.* to strangle, choke.
estranhar [ish-tră-nyar'] *va.* to find strange, odd, unpleasant.
estranho [ish-tră-nyoo] *adj.* strange, odd, queer, outlandish; *m.* stranger.
estratagema [ish-tră-tă-zhay'mă] *m.* stratagem, trick.
estrear [ish-tree-ar'] *va.* to use, wear, try out (for the first time); to inaugurate; *vr.* to make one's début (*theat.*, etc.).
estrebaria [ish-trĕ-bă-ree'ă] [*f.* stable.
estrebuchar [ish-trĕ-boo-shar'] *vn.* to struggle, toss about.
estreia [ish-tray'yă] *f.* first performance, first night (of play, etc.); début (of actor, etc.); opening, beginning; inauguration.
estreitar [ish-tray-ee-tar'] *va.* to narrow; to tighten (up); to clasp, embrace.
estreiteza [ish-tray-ee-tay'ză] *f.* narrowness; poverty; rigour.
estreito [ish-tray'ee-too] *adj.* narrow, tight; close (relationship, etc.); *m.* strait(s).

estrela [ish-tray'lă] *f.* star; fate, destiny.
estrelado [ish-trĕ-lah'doo] *adj.* starry, star-spangled; ovos —s, fried eggs.
estremecer [ish-trĕ-mĕ-sayr'] *va.* to shake; to love dearly; *vn.* to shudder, tremble.
estremenho [ish-trĕ-may'-nyoo] *m.* (native of) Estremadura.
estrépito [ish-tre'pee-too] *m.* noise, din, row.
estrepitoso [ish-trĕ-pee-toh'-zoo] *adj.* noisy, loud, rowdy.
estria [ish-tree'ă] *f.* groove.
estribar [ish-tree-bar'] *va.* to base, (rest) on.
estribilho [ish-trĕ-bee'lyoo] *m.* refrain (*poet.*, *mus.*).
estribo [ish-tree'boo] *m.* stirrup; running board (of train, etc.).
estridente [ish-tree-de*n*t'] *adj.* shrill, strident.
estrofe [ish-trof'] *f.* stanza, verse.
estroinice [ish-troh-ee-nees'] *f.* wildness; extravagance.
estrôncio [ish-troh*n*'see-oo] *m.* strontium.
estrondo [ish-tro*n*'doo] *m.* (loud) noise, thunder, roar; pomp, brilliance.
estropalho [ish-troo-pa'lyoo] *m.* dish-cloth.
estropiar [ish-troo-pee-ar'] *va.* to maim, cripple; to mangle.
estrume [ish-troom'] *m.* manure.
estrutura [ish-troo-too'ră] *f.* structure.
estucar [ish-too-kar'] *va.* to [plaster.
estudante [ish-too-da*n*t'] *mf.* student; undergraduate; pupil.
estudar [ish-too-dar'] *va.* to study.
estudo [ish-too'doo] *m.* study.
estufa [ish-too'fă] *f.* hot house; — fria, greenhouse.
estufado [ish-too-fah'doo] *m.* stew.
estulto [ish-tool'too] *adj.* stupid, foolish.
estupefacto [ish-too-pĕ-fak'-too] *adj.* amazed, astounded.
estupendo [ish-too-pe*n*'doo] *adj.* wonderful, stupendous, amazing.
estupidez [ish-too-pee-daysh'] *f.* stupidity; stupid thing, action.
estúpido [ish-too'pee-doo] *adj.* stupid, slow, dull.
estupro [ish-too'proo] *m.* rape.
estuque [ish-took'] *m.* plaster, stucco.
estúrdia [ish-toor'dee-ă] *f.* foolishness, silly prank.
esturrar [ish-too-rar'] *va.* to scorch, burn; *vn.* to get furious.
esvaecer-se [izh-vă-ee-sayr'-sĕ] *vr.* to vanish, fade away.
esvaimento [izh-vă-ee-me*n*'-too] *m.* fainting, swooning.
esvair-se [izh-vă-eer'sĕ] *vr.* to faint; to fade away, vanish.
esvaziar [izh-vă-zee-ar'] *va.* to empty. [to flutter.
esvoaçar [izh-voo-ă-sar'] *vn.*
eternidade [ee-tĕr-nee-dahd'] *f.* eternity.
eterno [ee-tair'noo] *adj.* eternal, everlasting.
ética [e'tee-kă] *f.* ethics.
etimologia [ee-tee-moo-loo-zhee'ă] *f.* etymology.
etiqueta [ee-tee-kay'tă] *f.* etiquette; label.
eucaristia [ay-oo-kă-reesh-tee'ă] *f.* Eucharist, Holy Communion.
eufemismo [ay-oo-fĕ-meezh'-moo] *m.* euphemism.
europeu [ay-oo-roo-pay'oo] *m/adj.* European.
evacuar [ee-vă-koo-ar'] *va.* to evacuate, leave.
evadir [ee-vă-deer'] *va.* to evade, avoid; *vr.* to escape.

evangelho [ee-va*n*-zhe'lyoo] *m.* Gospel.
evangélico [ee-va*n*-zhe'lee-koo] *adj.* evangelical; Protestant.
evaporação [ee-vă-poo-ră-sow*n*'] *f.* evaporation.
evaporar [ee-vă-poo-rar'] *va.* to evaporate.
evasão [ee-vă-zow*n*'] *f.* escape; evasion, subterfuge.
evasivo [ee-vă-zee'voo] *adj.* evasive, elusive.
eventual [ee-ve*n*-too-al'] *adj.* fortuitous, accidental.
evidência [ee-vee-de*n*'see-ă] *f.* evidence.
evidenciar[ee-vee-de*n*-see-ar'] *va.* to make clear, show.
evidente [ee-vee-de*n*t'] *adj.* evident, clear, obvious.
evitar [ee-vee-tar'] *va.* to avoid, shun, elude.
evocar [ee-voo-kar'] *va.* to evoke.
evolução [ee-voo-loo-sow*n*'] *f.* evolution, development; manoeuvre (*mil.*).
exacerbar [ee-ză-sĕr-bar'] *va.* to irritate, exacerbate.
exactidão [ee-za-tee-dow*n*'] *f.* exactness, accuracy.
exacto [ee-zah'too] *adj.* exact, accurate, precise.
exageração [ee-ză-zhĕ-ră-sow*n*'] *f.* exaggeration.
exagerar [ee-ză-zhĕ-rar'] *va.* to exaggerate, overstate.
exagero [ee-ză-zhay'roo] *m.* exaggeration.
exalação [ee-ză-lă-sow*n*'] *f.* exhalation, emanation.
exalar [ee-ză-lar'] *va.* to exhale, emit, give off (smell); to breathe out.
exaltar [ee-zal-tar'] *va.* to exalt, extol, praise; *vr.* to get excited, angry.
exame [ee-zahm'] *m.* examination.
examinar [ee-ză-mee-nar'] *va.* to examine, inspect, look into.
exangue [ee-za*n*g'] *adj.* exhausted; bloodless.
exarar [ee-ză-rar'] *va.* to put down in writing; to engrave.
exasperar [ee-zăsh-pĕ-rar'] *va.* to exasperate.
exaurir [ee-zow-reer'] *va.* to exhaust.
exausto [ee-zowsh'too] *adj.* exhausted, worn out.
exceder [ish-sĕ-dayr'] *va.* to exceed, surpass.
excelência [ish-sĕ-le*n*'see-ă] *f.* excellence; vossa —, you; your excellency.
excelente [ish-sĕ-le*n*t'] *adj.* excellent.
excentricidade [ish-se*n*-tree-see-dahd'] *f.* eccentricity.
excêntrico [ish-se*n*'tree-koo] *adj.* eccentric.
excepção [ish-se-sow*n*'] *f.* exception.
excepcional [ish-se-see-oo-nal'] *adj.* exceptional, unusual.
excepto [ish-se'too] *prep.* except(ing), save.
exceptuar [ish-se-too-ar'] *va.* to except.
excessivo [ish-sĕ-see'voo] *adj.* excessive, too much.
excesso [ish-se'soo] *m.* excess, surplus; immoderation; violence.
excitação [ish-see-tă-sow*n*'] *f.* excitement, agitation.
excitado [ish-see-tah'doo] *adj.* excited, worked-up; agitated.
excitar [ish-see-tar'] *va.* to excite, stimulate, incite; to irritate.
exclamação [ish-klă-mă-sow*n*'] *f.* exclamation.
exclamar [ish-klă-mar'] *vn.* to exclaim, cry out, shout.
excluir [ish-kloo-eer'] *va.* to exclude, shut out, debar.
exclusivo [ish-kloo-zee'voo] *adj.* exclusive.

excomungar [ish-koo-moon-gar'] *va.* to excommunicate.
excursão [ish-koor-sown'] *f.* excursion, trip, tour.
execrar [ee-zĕ-krar'] *va.* to execrate, curse, detest.
execução [ee-zĕ-koo-sown'] *f.* execution; performance, fulfilment, carrying out.
executante [ee-zĕ-koo-tant'] *mf.* performer, player (*mus.*, *theat.*, etc.).
executar [ee-zĕ-koo-tar'] *va.* to execute; to carry out, perform, fulfil.
executivo [ee-zĕ-koo-tee'voo] *m/adj.* executive.
exemplar [ee-zen-plar'] *adj.* exemplary; *m.* example, model; copy (*print.*).
exemplo [ee-zen'ploo] *m.* example; instance; **dar o —**, to set the example.
exéquias [ee-ze'kee-ăsh] *f.pl.* funeral rites, obsequies.
exercer [ee-zĕr-sayr'] *va.* to exercise; to practise (profession, etc.).
exercício [ee-zĕr-see'see-oo] *m.* exercise; training; practice.
exercitar [ee-zĕr-see-tar'] *va.* to exercise; to practise.
exército [ee-zair'see-too] *m.* army. [exhibit, display.
exibir [ee-zee-beer'] *va.* to
exigente [ee-zee-zhent'] *adj.* exacting, hard to please.
exigir [ee-zee-zheer'] *va.* to demand, require, insist on.
exíguo [ee-zee'gwoo-oo] *adj.* scanty, small, exiguous.
exilado [ee-zee-lah'doo] *m.* exile; *adj.* exiled, banished.
exilar [ee-zee-lar'] *va.* to exile, banish.
exílio [ee-zee'lee-oo] *m.* exile.
exímio [ee-zee'mee-oo] *adj.* eminent, famous.
eximir [ee-zee-meer'] *va.* to exempt; *vr.* to avoid, shirk.
existência [ee-zeesh-ten'see-ă] *f.* existence.
existir [ee-zeesh-teer'] *vn.* to exist; to be.
êxito [ay'zee-too] *m.* success; result, outcome.
exonerar [ee-zoo-nĕ-rar'] *va.* to discharge, dismiss.
exorbitante [ee-zoor-bee-tant'] *adj.* exorbitant.
exortação [ee-zoor-tă-sown'] *f.* exhortation, admonition.
exortar [ee-zoor-tar'] *va.* to exhort, warn; to urge.
exótico [ee-zo'tee-koo] *adj.* exotic.
expansão [ish-pan-sown'] *f.* expansion, spread.
expectativa [ish-pek-tă-tee'vă] *f.* expectation, hope.
expedição [ish-pĕ-dee-sown'] *f.* expedition (*mil.*, *naut.*, etc.); despatch (of goods); rapidity, speed.
expediente [ish-pĕ-dee-ent'] *m.* expedient, device; official papers; office correspondence; office hours.
expedir [ish-pĕ-deer'] *va.* to forward, dispatch, send.
experiência [ish-pĕ-ree-en'see-ă] *f.* experience; experiment, test.
experimentado [ish-pĕ-ree-men-tah'doo] *adj.* experienced.
experimentar [ish-pĕ-ree-men-tar'] *va.* to test, try out; to experience.
expiar [ish-pee-ar'] *va.* to expiate, atone for.
expirar [ish-pee-rar'] *vn.* to expire, end; to die.
explicação [ish-plee-kă-sown'] *f.* explanation.
explicar [ish-plee-kar'] *va.* to explain, elucidate; to give (course of lectures).
explícito [ish-plee'see-too] *adj.* explicit. [to explode.
explodir [ish-ploo-deer'] *vn.*

exploração [ish-ploo-ră-sow*n*'] *f.* exploration; exploitation (*com.*).
explorar [ish-ploo-rar'] *va.* to explore; to exploit.
explosão [ish-ploo-zow*n*'] *f.* explosion, blast.
explosivo [ish-ploo-zee'voo] *m/adj.* explosive.
expor [ish-pohr'] *va.* to state, expound, explain; to expose, exhibit; to abandon (child); *vr.* to take risks; to face (danger, etc.).
exportação [ish-poor-tă-sow*n*'] *f.* export(ation).
exportar [ish-poor-tar'] *va.* to export.
exposição [ish-poo-zee-sow*n*'] *f.* exhibition, show; statement, exposition.
exposto [ish-pohsh'too] *m.* foundling, abandoned child.
expressão [ish-prĕ-sow*n*'] *f.* expression.
expressar [ish-prĕ-sar'] *va.* to express.
expresso [ish-pre'soo] *adj.* express, definite; *m.* special messenger; express (train).
exprimir [ish-prĕ-meer'] *va.* to express.
expropriar [ish-proo-pree-ar'] *va.* to expropriate.
expulsão [ish-pool-sow*n*'] *f.* expulsion, ejection.
expulsar [ish-pool-sar'] *va.* to expel, eject.
expurgar [ish-poor-gar'] *va.* to expurgate; to cleanse, purify.
êxtase [aysh'tă-zĕ] *m.* ecstasy, rapture, delight.
extensão [ish-te*n*-sow*n*'] *f.* extent, area, expanse; extension, expansion.
extenso [ish-te*n*'soo] *adj.* extensive, vast; long; **por —**, in full.
extenuar [ish-tĕ-noo-ar'] *va.* to exhaust, wear out, weaken.
exterior [ish-tĕ-ree-ohr'] *adj.* exterior, outer, external; *m.* the outside, exterior; outward appearance, demeanour.
exteriorizar [ish-tĕ-ree-oo-ree-zar'] *va.* to express.
exterminar [ish-tĕr-mee-nar'] *va.* to exterminate, wipe out.
extermínio [ish-tĕr-mee'nee-oo] *m.* extermination.
externato [ish-tĕr-nah'too] *m.* day school.
externo [ish-tair'noo] *adj.* external, outward; (**aluno**) **—**, day boy (at school).
extinguir [ish-tee*n*-geer'] *va.* to extinguish; to suppress, abolish.
extinto [ish-tee*n*'too] *adj.* extinct; dead; extinguished.
extirpar [ish-teer-par'] *va.* to root out, extirpate.
extorquir [ish-toor-keer'] *va.* to extort.
extracção [ish-trah-sow*n*'] *f.* extraction, taking out; draw (in lottery).
extracto [ish-trah'too] *m.* extract; summary.
extrair [ish-tră-eer'] *va.* to extract, take out.
extraordinário [ish-tră-ohr-dee-nah'ree-oo] *adj.* extraordinary, unusual, rare; special (meeting, etc.); extra, supplementary (expenses, etc.).
extravagância [ish-tră-vă-ga*n*'see-ă] *f.* strange antic, odd behaviour; extravagance.
extravagante [ish-tră-vă-ga*n*t] *adj.* odd, queer, strange, wild; extravagant; *m.* wastrel; madcap, wild (odd) person.
extraviado [ish-tră-vee-ah'-doo] *adj.* missing, mislaid, lost; odd, peculiar (person).
extraviar [ish-tră-vee-ar'] *va.* to mislead, lead astray; to embezzle (money); *vr.* to go astray.

extravio [ish-tră-vee'oo] *m.* loss, misplacement; embezzlement; going astray.
extremado [ish-trĕ-mah'doo] *adj.* distinguished, outstanding.
extremar [ish-trĕ-mar'] *va.* to mark out, distinguish between; to select; *vr.* to distinguish oneself.
extremidade [ish-trĕ-mee-dahd'] *f.* extremity; edge; end; tip.
extremo [ish-tray'moo] *adj.* extreme, farthest, utmost; *m.* extreme; end, border.
extremoso [ish-trĕ-moh'zoo] *adj.* affectionate, loving.
extrínseco [ish-treen'zĕ-koo] *adj.* extraneous, external, extrinsic.
exuberância [ee-zoo-bĕ-ran'-see-ă] *f.* (super)abundance, profusion; exuberance.
exuberante [ee-zoo-bĕ-rant'] *adj.* abundant, luxuriant, lush; exuberant.
exultar [ee-zool-tar'] *vn.* to rejoice, exult.
exumar [ee-zoo-mar'] *va.* to exhume.
ex-voto [ayzh-vo'too] *m.* votive offering.

F

fábrica [fa'bree-kă] *f.* factory, works, mill; structure.
fabricação [fă-bree-kă-sown'] *f.* manufacture, making, production; fabrication.
fabricante [fă-bree-kant'] *m.* manufacturer, maker.
fabricar [fă-bree-kar'] *va.* to make, manufacture, produce; to fabricate.
fábula [fa'boo-lă] *f.* fable; tale, story.
faca [fah'kă] *f.* knife.
façanha [fă-să'nyă] *f.* exploit, feat, heroic deed.
facção [fak-sown'] *f.* faction.
faccioso [fak-see-oh'zoo] *adj.* seditious, factious.
face [fas] *f.* face; countenance; cheek; surface; **fazer — a**, to face; **em — de**, in view of.
facécia [fă-se'see-ă] *f.* jest, quip.
fachada [fă-shah'dă] *f.* front, façade; frontispiece (of book).
facho [fah'shoo] *m.* torch.
fácil [fah'seel] *adj.* easy, simple; compliant.
facilidade [fă-see-lee-dahd'] *f.* ease; facility; compliance.
facilitar [fă-see-lee-tar'] *va.* to facilitate, make easy.
facínora [fă-see'noo-ră] *m.* criminal.
facinoroso [fă-see-noo-roh'-zoo] *adj.* wicked, vicious.
facto [fak'too] *m.* fact; act; event; **estar ao — de**, to be aware of, acquainted with; **de —**, in fact.
factor [fak-tohr'] *m.* factor.
factura [fak-too'ră] *f.* invoice.
faculdade [fă-kool-dahd'] *f.* faculty; capacity, ability; power, authority.
facultativo [fă-kool-tă-tee'-voo] *adj.* optional; *m.* doctor.
fada [fah'dă] *f.* fairy.
fadado [fă-dah'doo] *adj.* fated, destined; **bem —**, fortunate, lucky.
fadário [fă-dah'ree-oo] *m.* fate; hard life.
fadiga [fă-dee'gă] *f.* fatigue, tiredness; hardship, drudgery.
fadista [fă-deesh'tă] *mf.* singer of 'fados'; *m.* ruffian; idler; *f.* prostitute.
fado [fah'doo] *m.* fate, destiny; a type of Portuguese song.
fagueiro [fa-gay'ee-roo] *adj.* caressing, blandishing.
faia [fȳ'yă] *f.* beech (-tree).
faina [fȳ'nă] *f.* toil, task; work.

faisão [fȳ-zow*n*'] *m.* pheasant.
faisca [fă-eesh'kă] *f.* spark; flash.
faiscar [fă-eesh-kar'] *vn.* to flash; to spark; to sparkle, glitter.
faixa [fȳ'shă] *f.* belt; waistband; zone, area.
fala [fah'lă] *f.* (mode of) speech; voice; conversation; remark.
falador [fă-lă-dohr'] *m.* talker; chatterbox; *adj.* talkative.
falar [fă-lar'] *va/vn.* to speak, talk; — **pelos cotovelos**, to talk one's head off; **está a —**, (number) engaged (telephone); **ouvir — de**, to hear of, about.
falaz [fă-lash'] *adj.* false, misleading, fallacious.
falecer [fă-lĕ-sayr'] *vn.* to die, pass away; to be lacking, insufficient.
falência [fă-le*n*'see-ă] *f.* bankruptcy, insolvency.
falha [fah'lyă] *f.* flaw, defect.
falhar [fă-lyar'] *vn.* to fail; to miss; to fall short.
falho [fah'lyoo] *adj.* defective, imperfect, flawed; lacking.
falido [fă-lee'doo] *m.* bankrupt.
falir [fă-leer'] *vn.* to fail in business; to go bankrupt.
falível [fă-lee'vel] *adj.* fallible.
falsário [fal-sah'ree-oo] *m.* forger; perjurer.
falsificar [fal-see-fee-kar'] *va.* to forge, falsify.
falso [fal'soo] *adj.* false; dishonest; inaccurate, wrong.
falta [fal'tă] *f.* lack, need, shortage; fault, defect; misdemeanour; **sentir — de**, to miss; **sem —**, without fail; **fazer —**, to be needed.
faltar [fal-tar'] *vn.* to be lacking; to be needed; to miss; to fail; **falta-me**, I need; I haven't (got); — **à palavra**, to break one's word; — **pouco para**, to be almost, nearly.
fama [fă'mă] *f.* fame, reputation, renown.
famélico [fă-me'lee-koo] *adj.* famished, starving.
famigerado [fă-mee-zhĕ-rah'-doo] *adj.* famous, renowned.
familia [fă-mee'lee-ă] *f.* family.
familiar [fă-mee-lee-ar'] *adj.* familiar; domestic; homely, simple; **ares —es**, family likeness.
familiarizar-se [fă-mee-lee-ă-ree-zar'sĕ] *vr.* to familiarize oneself with; to become closely acquainted with.
faminto [fă-mee*n*'too] *adj.* starving, hungry.
famoso [fă-moh'zoo] *adj.* famous, noted.
fâmulo [fă'moo-loo] *m.* attendant, servant.
fanal [fă-nal'] *m.* lighthouse; (guiding)light; ship's lantern.
fanático [fă-na'tee-koo] *m.* fanatic; *adj.* fanatical, rabid.
fanatismo [fă-nă-teezh'moo] *m.* fanaticism; bigotry.
fanfarrão [fa*n*-fă-row*n*'] *m.* boaster, bragger; bully.
fanqueiro [fa*n*-kay'ee-roo] *m.* draper.
fantasia [fa*n*-tă-zee'ă] *f.* fancy, imagination; caprice, whim; fantasy; fancy dress.
fantasma [fa*n*-tazh'mă] *m.* ghost, phantom, spectre.
fantástico [fa*n*-tash'tee-koo] *adj.* fantastic, fanciful; imaginary; weird, strange.
fantoche [fa*n*-tosh'] *m.* puppet.
farda [far'dă] *f.* uniform; livery (of attendants).
fardo [far'doo] *m.* bale, bundle; burden, load.
farejar [fă-rĕ-zhar'] *va.* to smell out, sniff out.

farfalhar [fă̆r-fă-*lyar'*] *vn.* to jabber, gabble; to talk big.
farinha [fă-ree'nyă] *f.* flour; meal.
fariseu [fă-ree-zay'oo] *m.* Pharisee; hypocrite.
farmácia [fă̆r-mah'see-ă] *f.* chemist's (shop); pharmacy.
farol [fă-rol'] *m.* lighthouse; light; beacon; headlamp, light (of car).
farpa [far'pă] *f.* dart, barb; tear (in clothes); splinter.
farrapo [fă-rah'poo] *m.* rag.
farsa [far'să] *f.* farce; trick, imposture.
farsante [fă̆r-sa*n*t'] *m.* impostor, humbug.
fartar [fă̆r-tar'] *va.* to satiate, satisfy, fill up.
farto [far'too] *adj.* full, satiated, glutted; (*fig.*) fed up with, sick of.
fartura [fă̆r-too'ră] *f.* plenty, abundance.
fascículo [fă̆sh-see'koo-loo] *m.* part, instalment, fascicule.
fascinação [fă̆sh-see-nă-sow*n*'] *f.* fascination, charm.
fascinar [fă̆sh-see-nar'] *va.* to fascinate, charm, bewitch.
fase [fahz] *f.* phase, stage, period. [wooden strip.
fasquia [fă̆sh-kee'ă] *f.* lath,
fastidioso [fă̆sh-tee-dee-oh'zoo] *adj.* wearisome, boring, annoying; disgusting.
fastiento [fă̆sh-tee-e*n*'too] *adj.* cross, grumpy; over-fastidious, hard to please.
fastio [fă̆sh-tee'oo] *m.* disgust, repugnance; lack of appetite.
fasto [fash'too] *adj.* happy, fortunate; *m.* pomp; *m.pl.* annals.
fatal [fă-tal'] *adj.* fatal, deadly; fateful, destined, fated.
fatalidade [fă-tă-lee-dahd'] *f.* disaster, calamity; fate.
fatia [fă-tee'ă] *f.* slice, piece.
fatigante [fă-tee-ga*n*t'] *adj.* tiring, fatiguing; boring, tiresome. [(out), exhaust.
fatigar [fă-tee-gar'] *va.* to tire
fato [fah'too] *m.* (*Port.*) suit; — feito, ready-made suit; (*Braz.*) fact.
fátuo [fa'too-oo] *adj.* fatuous, inane, silly; fogo —, will-o'-the-wisp. [mouth, jaws.
fauce [fows] *f.* gullet, throat;
fausto [fowsh'too] *m.* pomp, show, splendour; *adj.* happy, fortunate.
fautor [fow-tohr'] *m.* promoter, patron; abettor.
fava [fah'vă] *f.* broad bean.
favo [fah'voo] *m.* honeycomb.
favor [fă-vohr'] *m.* favour, kindness; assistance, (*pop.*) good turn; faça (faz) — (de), please; em — de, on behalf of.
favorável [fă-voo-rah'vel] *adj.* favourable; suitable.
favorecer [fă-voo-rĕ-sayr'] *va.* to favour; to assist; to facilitate. [favourite.
favorito [fă-voo-ree'too] *m.*
faxina [fă-shee'nă] *f.* fatigues, fatigue duty (in army).
fazenda [fă-ze*n*'dă] *f.* estate, property; farm; plantation; ranch; fabric, material; *pl.* goods; — nacional, treasury, exchequer.
fazendeiro [fă-ze*n*-day'eeroo] *m.* farmer; planter; ranchowner.
fazer [fă-zayr'] *va.* to do; to make, produce, create; — água, to leak; — das suas, to be up to his tricks; — frio, to be cold; — a barba, to shave; — as vezes de, to take the place of; — caso de, to take notice of; — fazer, to have made; — com que, to see to it that; — por, to try to; não faz mal, never mind; it doesn't matter; *vr.* to become.

fé [fe] *f.* faith, belief; **dar — de,** to take notice of.
fealdade [fee-al-dahd'] *f.* ugliness.
febre [fe'brĕ] *f.* fever.
febril [fĕ-breel'] *adj.* feverish.
fechadura [fĕ-shă-doo'ră] *f.* lock.
fechar [fĕ-shar'] *va.* to close, shut; to turn off (light, tap); — **à chave,** to lock.
fecho [fay'shoo] *m.* bolt; latch; fastener; conclusion.
fecundar [fĕ-koo*n*-dar'] *va.* to fertilize.
feder [fĕ-dayr'] *vn.* to stink.
federação [fĕ-dĕ-ră-sow*n*'] *f.* federation. [stench.
fedor [fĕ-dohr'] *m.* stink,
feição [fay-ee-sow*n*'] *f.* form, shape; aspect; *pl.* features.
feijão [fay-ee-zhow*n*'] *m.* kidney bean.
feio [fay'yoo] *adj.* ugly, plain; disreputable, repulsive.
feira [fay'ee-ră] *f.* fair.
feitiçaria [fay-ee-tee-să-ree'ă] *f.* witchcraft, magic.
feiticeiro [fay-ee-tee-say'ee-roo] *m.* wizard, sorcerer, magician; *adj.* enchanting, alluring, bewitching.
feitiço [fay-ee-tee'soo] *m.* magic spell, charm; enchantment.
feitio [fay-ee-tee'oo] *m.* shape, form; manner, temperament; workmanship.
feito [fay'ee-too] *m.* deed, exploit, action; *adj.* done; made; grown-up.
feitor [fay-ee-tohr'] *m.* manager; administrator; foreman.
feixe [fay'eesh] *m.* bundle; sheaf (of corn).
fel [fel] *m.* bile, gall; (*fig.*) bitterness, spite.
felicidade [fĕ-lee-see-dahd'] *f.* happiness; joy, bliss; good fortune.
felicitações [fĕ-lee-see-tă-soy*n*sh'] *f.pl.* congratulations.
felicitar [fĕ-lee-see-tar'] *va.* to congratulate.
feliz [fĕ-leesh'] *adj.* happy; fortunate; successful.
felpudo [fel-poo'doo] *adj.* rough, hairy, shaggy.
feltro [fel'troo] *m.* felt.
fêmea [fay'mee-ă] *f.* female.
fementido [fĕ-me*n*-tee'doo] *adj.* false, treacherous.
feminino [fĕ-mi-nee'noo] *adj.* feminine, female.
fenda [fe*n*'dă] *f.* slit, crack, opening.
fender [fe*n*-dayr'] *va.* to split; to crack, break open.
fenecer [fĕ-nĕ-sayr'] *vn.* to die; to come to an end.
feno [fay'noo] *m.* hay.
fenómeno [fĕ-no'mĕ-noo] *m.* phenomenon; wonder, prodigy.
fera [fair'ă] *f.* wild animal.
feracidade [fĕ-ră-see-dahd'] *f.* fertility. [coffin.
féretro [fe'rĕ-troo] *m.* bier;
férias [fair'ee-ăsh] *f.pl.* holidays, vacation. [holiday.
feriado [fĕ-ree-ah'doo] *m.*
ferida [fĕ-ree'dă] *f.* wound; cut; sore.
ferir [fĕ-reer'] *va.* to wound, hurt, cut, strike.
fermentação [fĕr-me*n*-tă-sow*n*'] *f.* fermentation; (*fig.*) turmoil, excitement.
fermentar [fĕr-me*n*-tar'] *vn.* to ferment; *va.* to stir up.
fero [fair'oo] *adj.* fierce, savage.
ferocidade [fĕ-roo-see-dahd'] *f.* ferocity, fierceness.
feroz [fĕ-rosh'] *adj.* savage, fierce, cruel.
ferradura [fĕ-ră-doo'ră] *f.* horseshoe.
ferragem [fĕ-rah'zhe*n*] *f.* ironwork; *pl.* hardware.

ferramenta [fĕ-ră-men'tă] *f.* tool(s), implement(s).
ferrão [fĕ-rown'] *m.* goad; sting (of insects).
ferrar [fĕ-rar'] *va.* to shoe (horse); to brand (cattle); to bite.
ferreiro [fĕ-ray'ee-roo] *m.* blacksmith.
ferrenho [fĕ-rĕ'nyoo] *adj.* stubborn, inflexible, relentless.
férreo [fe'ree-oo] *adj.* (made of) iron; hard, relentless.
ferrete [fĕ-rayt'] *m.* branding iron; (*fig.*) stigma, brand.
ferro [fe'roo] *m.* iron; anchor (*naut.*); — **fundido**, cast iron; — **batido**, wrought iron; **passar a** —, to iron; to press; — **-velho**, junk man, rag and bone man.
ferrolho [fĕ-roh'lyoo] *m.* bolt.
ferrugem [fĕ-roo'zhen] *f.* rust; blight (on plants).
fértil [fair'teel] *adj.* fertile, fruitful.
fertilidade [fĕr-tee-lee-dahd'] *f.* fertility, fruitfulness, copiousness.
fertilizar [fĕr-tee-lee-zar'] *va.* to fertilize.
férula [fe'roo-lă] *f.* rod, cane.
fervente [fĕr-vent'] *adj.* boiling; tempestuous; (*fig.*) fervent.
ferver [fĕr-vayr'] *va/vn.* to boil.
férvido [fair'vee-doo] *adj.* ardent, fervid.
fervor [fĕr-vohr'] *m.* fervour, ardour, eagerness.
festa [fesh'tă] *f.* festival; celebration; party; fête; *pl.* caresses; **boas** —, Merry Christmas; Happy New Year; Easter greetings.
festejar [fĕsh-tĕ-zhar'] *va.* to celebrate; to greet, welcome.
festejo [fĕsh-tay'zhoo] *m.* festivity, celebration; caresses; wooing.
festim [fĕsh-teen'] *m.* banquet; entertainment.
festividade [fĕsh-tee-vee-dahd'] *f.* festivity, celebration.
festivo [fĕsh-tee'voo] *adj.* festive, joyous; merry, jovial.
festoar [fĕsh-too-ar'] *va.* to festoon.
fetiche [fe-teesh'] *m.* fetish.
fétido [fe'tee-doo] *adj.* fetid, stinking, rank.
feto [fe'too] *m.* fern (*bot.*); foetus (*anat.*).
feudo [fay'oo-doo] *m.* fief, manor, domain.
fêvera [fay'vră] *f.* fibre, filament; slice (of meat).
fevereiro [fĕ-vray'ee-roo] *m.* February.
fezes [fe'zĕsh] *f.* dregs.
fiado [fee-ah'doo] *adj.* trusting; on trust; **comprar** —, to buy on credit.
fiador [fee-ă-dohr'] *m.* guarantor, surety.
fiambre [fee-an'brĕ] *m.* ham.
fiança [fee-an'să] *f.* surety, guarantee, security; bail.
fiar [fee-ar'] *va.* to trust, rely on; to spin (wool, etc.).
fiasco [fee-ash'koo] *m.* fiasco, failure, flop.
fibra [fee'bră] *f.* fibre; thread, filament; nerve.
ficar [fee-kar'] *vn.* to stay, remain; to be left; to be; — **com**, to keep; — **bem**, to suit (well).
ficção [feek-sown'] *f.* fabrication, invention; imagination; fiction.
ficha [fee-shă] *f.* index-card, slip; (*elect.*) plug.
ficheiro [fee-shay'ee-roo] *m.* filing-cabinet.
fictício [feek-tee'see-oo] *adj.* fictitious, imaginary; false.
fidalgo [fee-dal'goo] *m.* nobleman, gentleman.
fidedigno [fee-de-deeg'noo]

adj. trustworthy, reliable.
fidelidade [fee-dĕ-lee-dahd′] *f.* fidelity, loyalty; faithfulness.
fiel [fee-el′] *adj.* faithful, true, loyal; accurate.
fígado [fee′gă-doo] *m.* liver.
figo [fee′goo] *m.* fig.
figueira [fee-gay′ee-ră] *f.* fig-tree.
figura [fee-goo′ră] *f.* figure, form, shape; aspect.
figurar [fee-goo-rar′] *vn.* to figure; to appear; *va.* to depict.
figurino [fee-goo-ree′noo] *m.* fashion plate.
fila [fee′lă] *f.* row; rank, file.
filantropia [fee-la*n*-troo-pee′-ă] *f.* philanthropy.
filar [fee-lar′] *va.* to seize, catch, hold on to.
filarmónica [fee-lar-mo′nee-kă] *f.* band; music society.
filatelia [fee-lă-tĕ-lee′ă] *f.* philately, stamp-collecting.
fileira [fee-lay′ee-ră] *f.* rank, file; row, line.
filete [fee-layt′] *m.* thread; narrow border; fillet (of fish).
filha [fee′lyă] *f.* daughter.
filho [fee′lyoo] *m.* son; child; — **adoptivo**, adopted child.
filigrana [fee-lee-gră′nă] *f.* filigree.
filmar [feel-mar′] *va.* to film.
filme [feelm] *m.* film.
filologia [fee-loo-loo-zhee′ă] *f.* philology.
filosofia [fee-loo-zoo-fee′ă] *f.* philosophy.
filósofo [fee-lo′zoo-foo] *m.* philosopher.
filtrar [feel-trar′] *va.* to filter, strain.
filtro [feel′troo] *m.* filter.
fim [fee*n*] *m.* end; aim, object; **por —**, at last; **por — de contas**, after all.
fimbria [fee*n*′bree-ă] *f.* fringe, hem.
finado [fee-nah′doo] *adj.* dead; *m.* deceased, dead person; **dia de —s**, All Souls' Day.
final [fee-nal′] *adj.* final, last; ultimate.
finalizar [fee-nă-lee-zar′] *va.* to finish, conclude.
finanças [fee-na*n*′săsh] *f.pl.* finances; the (Government) Treasury.
financeiro [fee-na*n*-say′ee-roo] *adj.* financial; *m.* financier.
fincar [fee*n*-kar′] *va.* to fix, drive in.
findar [fee*n*-dar′] *va/vn.* to end, finish.
fineza [fee-nay′ză] *f.* fineness, delicacy; kindness.
fingimento [fee*n*-zhee-me*n*′-too] *m.* pretence; deceit.
fingir [fee*n*-zheer′] *va.* to pretend, feign.
fino [fee′noo] *adj.* fine; slender; elegant.
finório [fee-no′ree-oo] *adj.* sly, cunning, shrewd, foxy.
fio [fee′oo] *m.* thread; wire; string; — **de água**, trickle of water.
firma [feer′mă] *f.* signature; (business) firm.
firmar [feer-mar′] *va.* to sign; to make firm.
firme [feerm] *adj.* firm, steady.
firmeza [feer-may′ză] *f.* firmness, steadiness.
fiscal [feesh-kal′] *m.* inspector; controller; supervisor.
fiscalizar [feesh-kă-lee-zar′] *va.* to inspect, check, control, supervise.
fisco [feesh′koo] *m.* exchequer, treasury.
fisga [feezh′gă] *f.* chink, narrow opening; harpoon, spear (for catching fish).
física [fee′zee-kă] *f.* physics.
físico [fee′zee-koo] *adj.* physical; bodily; *m.* physique; physicist.
fisionomia [fee-zee-oo-noo-mee′ă] *f.* physiognomy, visage.
fita [fee′tă] *f.* ribbon; tape; film.

fitar [fee-tar'] *va.* to stare at, fix one's eyes on.
fito [fee'too] *m.* aim, purpose; *adj.* fixed.
fivela [fee-ve'lă] *f.* buckle.
fixar [feek-sar'] *va.* to fix; to stick (poster, etc.); to establish.
fixo [feek'soo] *adj.* fixed, steady; fast (colour).
flagelar [flă-zhĕ-lar'] *va.* to scourge.
flagrante [flă-grant'] *adj.* flagrant, glaring; **apanhado em —**, caught red-handed, in the act.
flamante [flă-mant'] *adj.* brilliant, gleaming; brand new.
flamejar [flă-mĕ-zhar'] *vn.* to blaze, glow.
flanco [flan'koo] *m.* flank, side.
flanela [flă-ne'lă] *f.* flannel.
flauta [flow'tă] *f.* flute.
flexível [flek-see'vel] *adj.* flexible.
floco [flo'koo] *m.* (snow)flake; tuft (of wool, etc.).
flor [flohr] *f.* flower; blossom; (*fig.*) the choicest, the finest, the cream; **em —**, in bloom; **à — de**, on the surface of, level with.
florescer [floo-rĕsh-sayr'] *vn.* to prosper, flourish; to blossom, bloom.
floresta [floo-resh'tă] *f.* forest, wood.
florido [floo-ree'doo] *adj.* [flowery.
fluência [floo-en'see-ă] *f.* fluency, ease (of speech, writing).
fluido [floo'ee-doo] *m.* fluid.
fluir [floo-eer'] *vn.* to flow.
fluminense [floo-mee-nen'sĕ] *adj.* fluvial; *m/adj.* pertaining to, *or* native of, State of Rio de Janeiro.
flutuar [floo-too-ar'] *vn.* to float; (*fig.*) to waver.
fluxo [flook'soo] *m.* flow; flux.
foca [fo'kă] *f.* seal.
focar [foo-kar'] *va.* to focus, bring into focus; to dwell on, deal with, draw attention to (problem, subject, etc.).
focinho [foo-see'nyoo] *m.* snout, muzzle.
foco [fo'koo] *m.* focus.
fofo [foh'foo] *adj.* soft; (*fig.*) vain.
fogão [foo-gown'] *m.* stove.
fogo [foh'goo] *m.* fire; ardour, passion; **— de artifício**, fireworks; **deitar — a**, to set fire to; **— fátuo**, will-o'-the-wisp; **fazer —**, to fire.
fogoso [foo-goh'zoo] *adj.* fiery, ardent, passionate.
fogueira [foo-gay'ee-ră] *f.* bonfire; **morrer na —**, to die at the stake.
foguete [foo-gayt'] *m.* rocket.
fojo [foh'zhoo] *m.* pitfall, trap; bog, slough; cave.
fole [fol] *m.* bellows.
fôlego [foh'lĕ-goo] *m.* breath; wind; breathing-spell, interval (for recuperation); **obra de largo —**, long, extensive work.
folga [fol'gă] *f.* rest, respite, breathing-spell; room, space (for movement); **dia de —**, free day.
folgado [fohl-gah'doo] *adj.* easy-going, idle; rested; slack, loose (clothes).
folgar [fohl-gar'] *vn.* to relax; to take pleasure in, rejoice; to make merry; *va.* to loosen slacken.
folha [foh'lyă] *f.* leaf; sheet (of paper, etc.); blade (of knife, etc.); **— de estanho**, tin foil.
folhagem [foo-lyah'zhen] *f.* foliage.
folhear [foo-lyee-ar'] *va.* to look through, skim through.
folhetim [foo-lyĕ-teen'] *m.* part, serial.
folheto [foo-lyay'too] *m.* booklet, pamphlet.

folia [foo-lee'ă] *f.* fun, jollification.
fome [fom] *f.* hunger; famine; (*fig.*) passionate desire.
fomentar [foo-me*n*-tar'] *va.* to promote, stimulate, foment.
fomento [foo-me*n*'too] *m.* stimulation, promotion; progress.
fonética [foo-ne'tee-kă] *f.* phonetics.
fonte [fo*n*t] *f.* fountain; spring (of water); source; temple (*anat.*).
fora [fo'ră] *adv.* out; outside; *prep.* except; **lá** —, abroad; outside; — **de si**, beside oneself.
foragido [foo-ră-zhee'doo] *m.* fugitive; refugee.
foral [foo-ral'] *m.* charter.
forasteiro [foo-răsh-tay'ee-roo] *m.* foreigner; stranger.
forca [fohr'kă] *f.* gallows.
força [fohr'să] *f.* strength; force; energy, vigour; **à — de**, by dint of. [pitchfork.
forcado [foor-kah'doo] *m.*
forçado [foor-sah'doo] *m.* convict; galley-slave; *adj.* forced; **trabalhos —s**, hard labour.
forçar [foor-sar'] *va.* to force, compel; to strain (voice, eyes, etc.).
forçoso [foor-soh'zoo] *adj.* imperative, necessary; powerful. [lessee.
foreiro [foo-ray'ee-roo] *m.*
forja [for'zhă] *f.* forge; foundry, smithy.
forjar [foor-zhar'] *va.* to forge; to shape, create.
forma [for'mă] *f.* form, shape; manner, way; **de — que**, so that. [(for shoes).
forma [fohr'mă] *f.* mould; last
formação [foor-mă-sow*n*'] *f.* formation.
formal [foor-mal'] *adj.* formal, explicit.
formalidade [foor-mă-lee-dahd'] *f.* formality; ceremony.
formão [foor-mow*n*'] *m.* chisel.
formar [foor-mar'] *va.* to form; shape; *vr.* to graduate, take one's degree.
formidável [foor-mee-dah'-vel] *adj.* formidable; impressive; considerable; amazing.
formiga [foor-mee'gă] *f.* ant.
formigar [foor-mee-gar'] *vn.* to swarm; to itch.
formigueiro [foor-mee-gay'-ee-roo] *m.* ant-hill; swarm of people.
formoso [foor-moh'zoo] *adj.* beautiful, lovely, handsome.
formosura [foor-moo-zoo'ră] *f.* beauty, loveliness.
fórmula [for'moo-lă] *f.* formula; prescription.
formular [foor-moo-lar'] *va.* to formulate; to prescribe (*med.*). [nace.
fornalha [foor-na'lyă] *f.* fur-
fornecer [foor-nĕ-sayr'] *va.* to provide, supply.
fornecimento [foor-nĕ-see-me*n*'too] *m.* supply(ing).
forno [fohr'noo] *m.* oven; furnace, kiln.
foro [foh'roo] *m.* quit-rent; privilege, right; power, jurisdiction; law courts; forum; — **de cidadão**, citizenship.
forrado [foo-rah'doo] *adj.* lined; covered.
forragem [foo-rah'zhe*n*] *f.* fodder.
forrar [foo-rar'] *va.* to line; to cover; to save (money); — **com (de) papel**, to paper (wall).
forro [foh'roo] *m.* lining; covering; padding; loft (of house); *adj.* free, freed.
fortalecer [foor-tă-lĕ-sayr'] *va.* to strengthen; to encourage.
fortaleza [foor-tă-lay'ză] *f.* fortress; fortitude, courage.
forte [fort] *adj.* strong, sturdy, robust; *m.* fort, fortress; strong

point (of a person, argument, etc.). [*va.* to fortify.
fortificar [foor-tee-fee-kar']
fortuito [foor-twee'-too] *adj.* fortuitous, accidental.
fortuna [foor-too'nă] *f.* fortune, wealth, riches; good luck; destiny, fate. [tarnished.
fosco [fohsh'koo] *adj.* dull,
fósforo [fosh'foo-roo] *m.* phosphorus; match.
fossa [fo'să] *f.* pit; ditch; cesspool; dimple (on cheek); **—s nasais**, nostrils.
fóssil [fo'seel] *m/adj.* fossil.
fosso [foh'soo] *m.* trench, ditch; moat; gutter.
fotografar [foo-too-gră-far'] *va.* to photograph.
fotografia [foo-too-gră-fee'ă] *f.* photograph; photography.
fotógrafo [foo-to'gră-foo] *m.* photographer.
fouce [fohs] *f.* scythe.
foucinha [foh-see'nyă] *f.* sickle. [estuary.
foz [fosh] *f.* mouth (of river),
fracassar [fră-kă-sar'] *vn.* to fail, collapse.
fracasso [fră-ka'soo] *m.* failure, (*sl.*) flop, washout.
fracção [frah-sow*n*'] *f.* fraction.
fraccionar [fra-see-oo-nar'] *va.* to divide into fractions; to break into pieces.
fraco [frah'koo] *adj.* weak, feeble; insipid.
fractura [frak-too'ră] *f.* fracture, break; (geological) fault.
frade [frahd] *m.* monk, friar; **— leigo**, lay brother.
fradesco [fră-daysh'koo] *adj.* of monks, monastic; monkish.
fraga [frah'gă] *f.* crag, rock.
fragata [fră-gah'tă] *f.* frigate (warship); lighter.
fragateiro [fră-gă-tay'ee- roo] *m.* lighterman.
frágil [frah'zheel] *adj.* fragile; breakable, brittle.
fragilidade [fră-zhee-lee-dahd'] *f.* fragility; frailty.
fragmento [frag-me*n*'too] *m.* fragment, piece, bit.
fragor [fră-gohr'] *m.* crash, roar, din.
fragoso [fră-goh'zoo] *adj.* rugged; inaccessible.
fragrância [fră-gra*n*'see-ă] *f.* fragrance, scent.
frágua [fra'gwă] *f.* forge, furnace; intense heat; sorrow.
fralda [fral'dă] *f.* shirt-tail; napkin (for babies), 'nappy'; foot (of mountain); **— do mar**, seashore.
framboesa [fra*n*-boo-ay'ză] *f.* raspberry.
francês [fra*n*-saysh'] *adj.* French; *m.* Frenchman; French (language).
franco [fra*n*'koo] *adj.* frank, sincere; outspoken; **porto —**, free port; **— de porte**, post paid; *m.* franc.
frangalho [fra*n*-ga'lyoo] *m.* rag, tatter.
frango [fra*n*'goo] *m.* chicken, young cockerel.
franja [fra*n*'zhă] *f.* fringe.
franquear [fra*n*-kee-ar'] *va.* to frank (letters); to grant free access *or* passage; to open up; to clear away (obstacles).
franqueza [fra*n*-kay'ză] *f.* frankness, sincerity.
franquia [fra*n*-kee'ă] *f.* postage; exemption; free entry *or* passage.
franzino [fra*n*-zee'noo] *adj.* weakly, thin, delicate.
franzir [fra*n*-zeer'] *va.* to wrinkle; to fold; **— as sobrancelhas**, to frown.
fraque [frak] *m.* morning-coat; tail-coat.
fraqueza [fră-kay'ză] *f.* weakness, feebleness, frailty.

frasco [frash'koo] *m.* flask; small bottle.
frase [frahz] *f.* sentence; phrase; — feita, stock phrase.
fraseologia [fră-see-oo-loo-zhee'ă] *f.* wording, phraseology.
frasqueira [frăsh-kay'ee-ră] *f.* case (for bottles).
fraternidade [fră-tĕr-nee-dahd'] *f.* brotherhood.
fraterno [fră-tair'noo] *adj.* brotherly, fraternal.
fraude [frowd] *f.* fraud, deception.
fraudulento [frow-doo-le*n*'-too] *adj.* fraudulent.
freguês [fre-gaysh'] *m.* customer, client; parishioner (*eccl.*).
freguesia [fre-gĕ-zee'ă] *f.* parish; customers.
frei [fray'ee] *m.* Brother (*eccl.*).
freio [fray'yoo] *m.* brake; bit (of bridle); (*fig.*) restriction, check.
freira [fray'ee-ră] *f.* nun.
freire [fray'ee-rĕ] *m.* monk; member of Christian military order.
freixo [fray'ee-shoo] *m.* ash-tree.
frementé [frĕ-me*n*t'] *adj.* violent, frenzied; quivering, trembling.
fremir [frĕ-meer'] *vn.* to roar; to tremble, quiver.
frémito [fre'mee-too] *m.* din, roaring; murmur; thrill.
frenesi [frĕ-nĕ-zee'] *m.* frenzy.
frenético [frĕ-ne'tee-koo] *adj.* frantic, furious, frenzied.
frente [fre*n*t] *f.* front; face; **em** —, opposite; **à — de**, at the head of.
frequência [frĕ-kwe*n*'see-ă] *f.* frequency; attendance (at school, etc.).
frequentar [frĕ-kwe*n*-tar'] *va.* to frequent, attend, visit regularly.
frequente [frĕ-kwe*n*t'] *adj.* frequent.
fresco [fraysh'koo] *adj.* fresh; cool; (*pop.*) indecent; *m.* freshness; fresh air, breeze; **de** —, recently, freshly, newly; **ao** —, in the open air; **pôr-se ao** —, to take to one's heels.
frescura [frĕsh-koo'ră] *f.* freshness, coolness.
fresta [fresh'tă] *f.* narrow window, opening; loophole, slit.
fretar [frĕ-tar'] *va.* to charter, hire.
frete [fret] *m.* freight, cargo.
frialdade [free-al-dahd'] *f.* coldness, chilliness.
friável [free-ah'vel] *adj.* brittle, crumbly.
fricção [freek-sow*n*'] *f.* friction, rubbing; massage.
frieira [free-ay'ee-ră] *f.* chilblain.
frieza [free-ay'ză] *f.* coldness, chilliness, coolness.
frigideira [free-zhee-day'ee-ră] *f.* frying-pan.
frigorífico [free-goo-ree'fee-koo] *m.* refrigerator; cold storage plant.
frincha [free*n*'shă] *f.* chink, (narrow)gap.
frio [free'oo] *m/adj.* cold; **faz** —, it is cold (weather); **tenho** —, I am cold.
frioleira [free-oo-lay'ee-ră] *f.* (useless)trifle; *pl.* trimmings.
frisante [free-za*n*t'] *adj.* significant, striking (example, etc.).
frisar [free-zar'] *va.* to curl; *vn.* (*fig.*) to touch on (problems, etc.).
friso [free'zoo] *m.* frieze; wainscot.
frito [free'too] *adj.* fried.
frívolo [free'voo-loo] *adj.* frivolous, silly; trivial.
frondoso [fro*n*-doh'zoo] *adj.* leafy.
fronha [froh'nyă] *f.* pillow(-case).
fronte [fro*n*t] *f.* forehead.

brow; front; curvar a —, to bow, bend; de —, opposite, facing.
fronteira [fro*n*-tay'ee-ră] *f.* frontier, border.
frontispício [fro*n*-tĕsh-pee'-see-oo] *m.* title-page (of book); façade, front (*archit.*).
frota [fro'tă] *f.* fleet.
frouxo [froh'shoo] *adj.* slack, lax, weak.
frugal [froo-gal'] *adj.* frugal; thrifty.
fruição [froo-ee-sow*n*'] *f.* enjoyment.
frumento [froo-me*n*'too] *m.* wheat (of good quality); grain, corn.
frustrar [froosh-trar'] *va.* to frustrate, thwart; *vr.* to fail, miscarry.
fruta [froo'tă] *f.* (edible) fruit.
frutífero [froo-tee'fĕ-roo] *adj.* fruit-bearing; fruitful; (*fig.*) profitable.
fruto [froo'too] *m.* product, result; fruit; — **proibido**, forbidden fruit; **dar** —, to bear fruit.
fuga [foo'gă] *f.* flight, escape; leak (gas, water, etc.).
fugaz [foo-gash'] *adj.* fleeting; swift.
fugir [foo-zheer'] *vn.* to run away, flee, escape, fly from.
fugitivo [foo-zhee-tee'voo] *adj.* fugitive; fleeting (glimpse, interval, etc.).
fulano [foo-lă'noo] *m.* (Mr.) So-and-so.
fulcro [fool'kroo] *m.* fulcrum; support, prop.
fulgor [fool-gohr'] *m.* splendour, brilliance.
fuligem [foo-lee'zhe*n*] *f.* soot.
fulminado [fool-mee-nah'doo] *adj.* struck (down).
fulminante [fool-mee-na*n*t'] *adj.* devastating, crushing.
fulminar [fool-mee-nar'] *va.* to blast, destroy; to fulminate, hurl threats.
fumada [foo-mah'dă] *f.* smoke signal; puff of smoke.
fumador [foo-mă-dohr'] *m.* smoker.
fumar [foo-mar'] *va*/*vn.* to smoke; (*fig.*) to fume.
fumigar [foo-mee-gar'] *va.* to fumigate.
fumo [foo'moo] *m.* smoke; vapour; (*fig.*) vanity.
função [foo*n*-sow*n*'] *f.* function, action; (religious, etc.) ceremony; task, duty, office.
funcionalismo [foo*n*-see-oo-nă-leezh'moo] *m.* civil service; public officials, civil servants.
funcionamento [foo*n*-see-oo-nă-me*n*'too] *m.* working, functioning.
funcionar [foo*n*-see-oo-nar'] *vn.* to work, function.
funcionário [foo*n*-see-oo-nah'ree-oo] *m.* civil servant, public official.
funda [foo*n*'dă] *f.* sling; truss, belt (*med.*).
fundação [foo*n*-dă-sow*n*'] *f.* foundation; establishment; endowed institution.
fundamental [foo*n*-dă-me*n*-tal'] *adj.* fundamental.
fundamentar [foo*n*-dă-me*n*-tar'] *va.* to establish, base.
fundamento [foo*n*-dă-me*n*'-too] *m.* foundation; basis; motive.
fundar [foo*n*-dar'] *va.* to [found, establish.
fundear [foo*n*-dee-ar'] *vn.* to anchor.
fundição [foo*n*-dee-sow*n*'] *f.* smelting (of metals); foundry.
fundir [foo*n*-deer'] *va.* to smelt (metals); to cast (statue); *vr.* to fuse; to liquefy.
fundo [foo*n*'doo] *m.* bottom; depth(s); inmost part(s); background; fund (of goodwill, etc.); eye (of needle); **artigo de**

—, leading article; dar —, to cast anchor; ir ao —, to sink, go to the bottom; a —, thoroughly; no —, at bottom, in essence; *pl.* funds; *adj.* deep; profound.
fúnebre [foo'nĕ-brĕ] *adj.* funereal; mournful; cortejo—, funeral procession, cortège.
funesto [foo-nesh'too] *adj.* fatal, disastrous, lamentable.
fungar [foo*n*-gar'] *va/vn.* to sniff.
funil [foo-neel'] *m.* funnel.
furacão [foo-ră-kow*n*'] *m.* hurricane.
furão [foo-row*n*'] *m.* ferret.
furar [foo-rar'] *va.* to bore, pierce.
fura-vidas [foo'ră vee'dăsh] *m.* (*pop.*) live-wire, go-getter.
furgão [foor-gow*n*'] *m.* luggage-van, guard's van.
furgoneta [foor-goo-nay'tă] *f.* (delivery)van.
fúria [foo'ree-ă] *f.* fury, rage; fierceness; passion, zeal.
furibundo [foo-ree-boo*n*'doo] *adj.* furious, wild.
furioso [foo-ree-oh'zoo] *adj.* furious, wild, raving; fierce.
furo [foo'roo] *m.* hole, perforation; loophole, way out (of a difficulty).
furor [foo-rohr'] *m.* fury, rage; passion; enthusiasm; fazer —, to be all the rage.
furtar [foor-tar'] *va.* to steal; *vr.* to evade, escape (from).
furtivo [foor-tee'voo] *adj.* furtive, stealthy.
furto [foor'too] *m.* theft, robbery; thieving.
furúnculo [foo-roo*n*'koo-loo] *m.* boil.
fusão [foo-zow*n*'] *f.* fusion, union; melting.
fusco [foosh'koo] *adj.* dark, dusky; *m.* lusco- —, dusk, twilight.
fusível [foo-zee'vel] *m.* fuse.
fuso [foo'zoo] *m.* spindle.
fuste [foosht] *m.* shaft.
fustigar [foosh-tee-gar'] *va.* to thrash, beat; to whip on.
futebolista [foot-boo-leesh'tă] *m.* footballer, soccer-player.
fútil [foo'teel] *adj.* futile.
futilidade [foo-tee-lee-dahd'] *f.* futility, uselessness; futile thing, affair, etc.
futuro [foo-too'roo] *m/adj.* future.
fuzilar [foo-zee-lar'] *va.* to shoot, execute (by shooting); *vn.* to flash.
fuzilaria [foo-zee-lă-ree'ă] *f.* fusillade, steady fire; volley.

G

gabão [gă-bow*n*'] *m.* (large) cloak (with sleeves and hood).
gabar [gă-bar'] *va.* to praise; *vr.* to boast of, brag about.
gabardina [gă-băr-dee'nă] *f.* raincoat.
gabinete [gă-bee-nayt'] *m.* private room, office; study; cabinet (*polit.*); — **de leitura**, reading room.
gadanha [gă-dă'nyă] *f.* scythe; soup ladle.
gadanho [gă-dă'nyoo] *m.* [talon, claw.
gado [gah'doo] *m.* livestock; cattle; — **lanígero**, sheep; — **grosso**, cows, bulls, horses and mules; — **miúdo**, sheep, goats and pigs.
gafanhoto [gă-fă-nyoh'too] *m.* locust; grasshopper.
gaguejar [gă-gĕ-zhar'] *vn.* to stammer, stutter.
gaio [gȳ'yoo] *m.* jay (*orni.*).
gaiola [gă-yo'lă] *f.* cage; jail.
gaita [gȳ'tă] *f.* pipe, flute, fife; — **de foles** *or* **galega**, bagpipe.
gaivota [gȳ-vo'tă] *f.* seagull.

gajo [gah'zhoo] *m.* (*sl.*) guy, type.
gala [ga'lă] *f.* gala; pomp, ostentation; traje de —, gala dress; fazer — de, to display, show off.
galã [gă-lan'] *m.* leading man (*theat.*); lover, beau.
galantaria [gă-lan-tă-ree'ă] *f.* politeness, courtliness.
galante [gă-lant'] *adj.* polite, elegant, polished; *m.* gallant.
galantear [gă-lan-tee-ar'] *va.* to pay court to; to flirt with.
galão [gă-lown'] *m.* braid, trimming; stripe (*mil.*); gallon (measure).
galardão [gă-lăr-down'] *m.* reward, prize.
galé [gă-le'] *f.* galley.
galego [gă-lay'goo] *m/adj.* Galician.
galeria [gă-lĕ-ree'ă] *f.* gallery; [corridor.
galês [gă-laysh'] *adj.* Welsh; *m.* Welshman; Welsh language.
galgar [gal-gar'] *va.* to leap over; to clear at a bound; to stride over; to spring up to.
galgo [gal'goo] *m.* greyhound.
galhardia [gă-lyăr-dee'ă] *f.* elegance, grace; gallantry, bravery.
galheta [gă-lyay'tă] *f.* cruet; (*sl.*) slap, smack.
galho [ga'lyoo] *m.* branch (of tree); antler.
galhofeiro [gă-lyoo-fay'ee-roo] *adj.* jolly, jovial, full of fun; *m.* comical fellow, 'comic.'
galinha [gă-lee'nyă] *f.* hen.
galo [ga'loo] *m.* cock, rooster; missa do —, Midnight Mass (at Christmas).
galochas [gă-lo'shăsh] *f.pl.* (rubber)overshoes, galoshes.
galopar [gă-loo-par'] *vn.* to gallop.
galvanizar [gal-vă-nee-zar'] *va.* to galvanize; to electrify.
gama [gă'mă] *f.* doe (*zool.*); gamut, range.
gamela [gă-me'lă] *f.* bowl; pail. [buck.
gamo [gă'moo] *m.* fallow-deer,
gana [gă'nă] *f.* craving; ill-will, hate. [hairpin.
gancho [gan'shoo] *m.* hook;
gandaia [gan-dȳ'yă] *f.* rag-picking; (*pop.*) scrounging; loafing.
gangrena [gan-gray'nă] *f.* gangrene; (*fig.*) corruption.
ganhão [gă-nyown'] *m.* day labourer; wage earner.
ganha-pão [gă'nyă pown] *m.* living, livelihood.
ganhar [gă-nyar'] *va.* to gain; to earn; to win.
ganho [gă'nyoo] *m.* profit, gain; earnings.
ganir [gă-neer'] *vn.* to yelp.
ganso [gan'soo] *m.* gander, goose. [garage.
garagem [gă-rah'zhen] *f.*
garantia [gă-ran-tee'ă] *f.* guarantee.
garantir [gă-ran-teer'] *va.* to guarantee; to vouch for.
garatujar [gă-ră-too-zhar'] *va.* to scribble, scrawl.
garbo [gar'boo] *m.* elegance, gracefulness; smart (distinguished) bearing.
garboso [găr-boh'zoo] *adj.* elegant, dashing, smart.
garça [gar'să] *f.* heron.
garço [gar'soo] *adj.* (greenish-) blue.
garfo [gar'foo] *m.* fork.
gargalhada [găr-gă-lyah'dă] *f.* burst (roar)of laughter; rir às —s, to roar with laughter.
garganta [găr-gan'tă] *f.* throat; ravine, gorge, defile.
gargarejar [găr-gă-rĕ-zhar'] *vn.* to gargle.
gárgula [gar'goo-lă] *f.* gargoyle.
garoto [gă-roh'too] *m.* young-

ster, 'kid'; street-arab, urchin; (*sl.*) coffee with milk.
garrafa [gă-rah'fă] *f.* bottle.
garrafão [gă-ră-fown'] *m.* large bottle.
garras [ga'răsh] *f.pl.* claws; talons (of eagle, etc.); (*fig.*) clutches (of poverty, etc.).
garrido [gă-ree'doo] *adj.* lively, bright (colours, etc.); smart, elegant.
garrotilho [gă-roo-tee'lyoo] *m.* croup (*med.*).
gárrulo [ga'roo-loo] *adj.* garrulous, chattering.
garupa [gă-roo'pă] *f.* croup, crupper, hindquarters (of horse); saddle pack.
gás [gash] *m.* gas; **— lacrimogénio,** tear gas.
gasganete [găzh-gă-nayt'] *m.* (*pop.*) throat; neck.
gasolina [gă-zoo-lee'nă] *f.* petrol; gasoline, 'gas' (in U.S.A.).
gasosa [gă-zo'ză] *f.* mineral water, 'pop', 'fizzy drink'.
gastar [găsh-tar'] *va.* to spend; to waste, squander; to wear out.
gasto [gash'too] *m.* expenditure; waste; *pl.* charges; expenses; *adj.* worn out.
gata [gah'tă]*f.* cat; **— borralheira,** Cinderella; stay-at-home; **andar de —s,** to crawl on all-fours.
gatafunhos [gă-tă-foo'-nyoosh] *m.pl.* scribbles, scrawls.
gatilho [gă-tee'lyoo] *m.* trigger.
gato [gah'too] *m.* (tom-)cat; clamp (*mech.*); hook; **— montês,** wildcat; **comprar — por lebre,** to buy a pig in a poke; **fazer — sapato,** to make game of.
gatuno [gă-too'noo] *m.* thief, pickpocket.
gávea [ga'vee-ă] *f.* topsail.
gaveta [gă-vay'tă] *f.* drawer.
gaza [gah'ză] *or* **gaze,** *f.* gauze.
gazeta [gă-zay'tă] *f.* gazette; **fazer —,** to play truant.
geada [zhee-ah'dă] *f.* frost.
gelado [zhĕ-lah'doo] *m.* ice-cream; *adj.* frozen.
gelar [zhĕ-lar'] *va/vn.* to freeze.
geléia [zhĕ-le'yă] *f.* jelly.
geleira [zhĕ-lay'ee-ră] *f.* glacier; ice-box.
gélido [zhe'lee-doo] *adj.* frigid, icy, frozen.
gelo [zhay'loo] *m.* ice; (*fig.*) frigidity, indifference.
gelosia [zhĕ-loo-zee'ă] *f.* (Venetian) blind.
gema [zhay'mă] *f.* yolk (of egg); gem, jewel; bud, shoot (of plant, etc.); **ser da —,** to be genuine, the genuine article.
gémeo [zhe'mee-oo] *m.* twin.
gemer [zhĕ-mayr'] *vn.* to groan, moan.
gemido [zhĕ-mee'doo] *m.* groan, moan; lamentation.
genealogia [zhe-nee-ă-loo-zhee'ă] *f.* genealogy, lineage.
genebra [zhĕ-ne'bră] *f.* gin.
general [zhĕ-nĕ-ral'] *m.* general.
generalidade [zhĕ-nĕ-ră-lee-dahd'] *f.* generality; greater part, general run (of mankind, etc.); **na —,** in general; in most cases.
generalização [zhĕ-nĕ-ră-lee-ză-sown'] *f.* generalization.
generalizar [zhĕ-nĕ-ră-lee-zar'] *vn.* to generalize; *vr.* to spread, become general.
género [zhe'nĕ-roo] *m.* kind, sort; species, class; (literary) genre; gender (grammar); *pl.* goods, products, commodities.
generosidade [zhĕ-nĕ-roo-zee-dahd'] *f.* generosity.
generoso [zhĕ-nĕ-roh'zoo] *adj.*

generous; noble; vinho —, full-bodied, (strong) wine.
génese [zhe'něz] *f.* origin, beginning. [ginger.
gengibre [zhen-zhee'brě] *m.*
gengiva [zhen-zhee'vă] *f.* gum.
genial [zhě-nee-al'] *adj.* inspired, brilliant, marked by genius; cheerful.
génio [zhe'nee-oo] *m.* genius; temperament, character; **mau** —, bad temper. [law.
genro [zhen'roo] *m.* son-in-
gente [zhent] *f.* people, folk; (*pop.*) we, I; **ser** —, to be grown-up; to be important.
gentil [zhen-teel'] *adj.* lovely, comely; handsome; courteous.
gentileza [zhen-tee-lay'ză] *f.* kindness, courtesy; elegance.
gentio [zhen-tee'oo] *m/adj.* heathen, pagan; *m.* mob, crowd.
genuflexão [zhě-noo-flesown'] *f.* genuflexion, bending the knee.
genuíno [zhě-noo-ee'noo] *adj.* genuine; pure.
geógrafo [zhee-o'gră-foo] *m.* geographer. [geologist.
geólogo [zhee-o'loo-goo] *m.*
geração [zhe-ră-sown'] *f.* generation; creation.
gerador [zhe-ră-dohr'] *m.* generator (*mech.*); originator (of plan, etc.); (parent) begetter; *adj.* productive of; generative.
geral [zhě-ral'] *adj.* general; **em** —, in general, generally; *m.* the majority, the general run; the general (in opposition to the particular); general (head of Jesuits).
gerar [zhě-rar'] *va.* to generate (electricity, etc.); to beget, procreate (children); to produce, originate (new idea, etc.).
gerência [zhě-ren'see-ă] *f.* management. [ager.
gerente [zhě-rent'] *m.* man-
geringonça [zhě-reen-gon'să] *f.* jargon; slang; jerry-built, rickety thing.
germe [zhair'mě] *m.* *or* **gérmen** [zhair'men] *m.* germ; (*fig.*) origin, source.
germinar [zhěr-mee-nar'] *vn.* to sprout, bud.
gesso [zhay'soo] *m.* gypsum; plaster of Paris; plaster model.
gesticulação [zhěsh-tee-koo-lă-sown'] *f.* gesticulation.
gesto [zhesh'too] *m.* gesture.
giba [zhee'bă] *f.* hump.
giesta [zhee-esh'tă] *f.* broom (*bot.*).
gigante [zhee-gant'] *m.* giant; *adj.* gigantic, giant.
ginásio [zhee-nah'zee-oo] *m.* gymnasium.
ginástica [zhee-nash'tee-kă] *f.* gymnastics, physical exercises, P.T. (i.e. physical training). [cherry.
ginja [zheen'zhă] *f.* morello
ginjinha [zheen-zhee'nyă] *f.* cherry brandy.
gira-discos [zhee'ră deesh'-koosh] *m.* record-player.
girafa [zhee-rah'fă] *f.* giraffe.
girar [zhee-rar'] *va/vn.* to revolve, turn round, rotate, spin. [flower.
girassol [zhee-ră-sol'] *m.* sun-
gíria [zhee'ree-ă] *f.* slang; jargon (of newspapers, etc.).
giro [zhee'roo] *m.* rotation; movement, circulation; turn (in game, at work, etc.); **dar um** —, to take a stroll.
giz [zheesh] *m.* chalk.
glacial [glă-see-al'] *adj.* icy.
glândula [glan'doo-lă] *f.* gland.
glicerina [glee-sě-ree'nă] *f.* glycerine. [*f.* glucose.
glicose [glee-koz'] *or* **glucose**
globo [gloh'boo] *m.* globe, sphere; Earth; — **do olho**, eye ball; **em** —, as a whole, *in toto*.

glóbulo [glo'boo-loo] *m.* globule; blood corpuscle.
glória [glo'ree-ă] *f.* glory; fame; splendour, radiance.
gloriar-se [gloo-ree-ar'sĕ] *vr.* to boast of; to glory in.
glorificar [gloo-ree-fee-kar'] *va.* to glorify, exalt.
glorioso [gloo-ree-oh'zoo] *adj.* glorious sublime, splendid.
glosa [glo'ză] *f.* commentary.
glosar [gloo-zar'] *va.* to comment on; to annotate.
glossário [gloo-sah'ree-oo] *m.* glossary.
glutão [gloo-town'] *m.* glutton; *adj.* gluttonous.
glutinoso [gloo-tee-noh'zoo] *adj.* sticky, glutinous.
goiaba [goy-ah'bă] *f.* guava (fruit).
goivo [goh'ee-voo] *m.* wallflower, gillyflower. [band.
gola [go'lă] *f.* collar neck-
gole [gol] *m.* mouthful gulp, draught; **de um só —**, at one gulp. [spurt out.
golfar [gohl-far'] *vn.* to gush,
golfinho [gol-fee'nyoo] *m.* dolphin.
golfo [gohl'foo] *m.* gulf.
golo [goh'loo] *m.* goal.
golpe [golp] *m.* blow, stroke, knock; **— de estado**, coup d'état; **de um só —**, at one stroke. [strike, hit.
golpear [gool-pee-ar'] *va.* to
goma [goh'mă] *f.* gum; starch; (*Braz.*) tapioca; **— laca**, lacqueur, shellac.
gomo [goh'moo] *m.* bud, sprout; **— de laranja**, slice of orange.
gonzo [gon'zoo] *m.* hinge.
gorar [goo-rar'] *va.* to frustrate, thwart; *vn.* to miscarry, fail; to be addled (egg).
gordo [gohr'doo] *adj.* fat, stout, plump; **terça-feira —a**, Shrove Tuesday.
gordura [goor-doo'ră] *f.* fat; lard; grease; corpulence
gordurento [goor-doo-ren'too] *adj.* greasy.
gorgolejar [goor-goo-lĕ-zhar'] *vn.* to gurgle.
gorila [goo-ree'lă] *m.* gorilla.
gorjear [goor-zhee-ar'] *vn.* to warble. [gratuity.
gorjeta [goor-zhay'tă] *f.* tip,
gorro [goh'roo] *m.* beret; cap.
gostar [goosh-tar'] *vn.* to like, be fond of.
gosto [gohsh'too] *m.* taste; flavour; pleasure.
gostoso [goosh-toh'zoo] *adj.* delicious, tasty, savoury.
gota [goh'tă] *f.* drop; (*med.*) gout.
goteira [goo-tay'ee-ră] *f.* gutter (on roof); downspout; leak (in roof).
gotejar [goo-tĕ-zhar'] *vn.* to drip, trickle.
gótico [go'tee-koo] *adj.* Gothic.
governador [goo-vĕr-nă-dohr'] *m.* governor.
governar [goo-vĕr-nar'] *va.* to govern; to control; to steer (*naut.*); *vr.* to manage one's affairs.
governo [goo-vayr'noo] *m.* government; control; management; steering (*naut.*).
gozar [goo-zar'] *va.* to enjoy; *vr.* to rejoice in.
gozo [goh'zoo] *m.* enjoyment; delight.
graça [grah'să] grace; elegance, charm; pardon; joke, witticism; **de —**, free, gratis; **ter —**, to be funny, amusing; **—s a**, thanks to; **—s a Deus**, thank God; **acção de —s**, act of) thanksgiving; **não ser para —s**, not to be trifled with
gracejar [gră-sĕ-zhar'] *vn.* to joke, jest. [joke.
gracejo [gră-say'zhoo] *m.*
grade [grahd] *f.* railing, grat-

ing; harrow (agricultural); crate (box).
grado [grah'doo] *adj.* mature, ripe (grain); important (people); **de bom —**, willingly, readily; **de mau —**, unwillingly, grudgingly.
graduação [grǎ-doo-ǎ-sow*n*'] *f.* division (of scale); rank (*mil.*); social position.
gradual [grǎ-doo-al'] *adj.* gradual.
graduar [grǎ-doo-ar'] *va.* to grade; to classify; *vr.* to graduate (*acad.*).
gráfico [gra'fee-koo] *m.* diagram; chart, graph; *adj.* diagrammatic; **artes —as**, graphic arts.
gralha [gra'lyǎ] *f.* jackdaw; rook; (*Braz.*) jay; misprint (*print.*). [(*bot.*) grass.
grama [grǎ'mǎ] *f.* gramme;
gramática [grǎ-ma'tee-kǎ] *f.* grammar.
gramático [grǎ-ma'tee-koo] *m.* grammarian.
gramofone [grǎ-moo-fon'] *m.* gramophone.
grampo [gra*n*'poo] *m.* clamp, brace; staple.
granada [grǎ-nah'dǎ] *f.* hand-grenade; bomb, shell.
grande [gra*n*d] *adj.* big, large; great; *m.* grandee; **viver à —**, to live in style.
grandeza [gra*n*-day'zǎ] *f.* greatness; size; grandeur, splendour.
grandioso [gra*n*-dee-oh'zoo] *adj.* grand, magnificent.
granel [grǎ-nell]' *m.* barn, granary; galley-proof (*print.*); **a —**, in bulk; loose, unpacked.
granito [grǎ-nee'too] *m.* granite.
granizo [grǎ-nee'zoo] *m.* hail.
granja [gra*n*'zhǎ] *f.* farm, farm-house, grange.
granjear [gra*n*-zhee-ar'] *va.* to cultivate; to attract, win (sympathy, etc.).
grão [grow*n*] *m.* grain, corn; grain (of sand, etc.); **— de bico**, chick-pea.
grão-mestre [grow*n* mesh'-trě] *m.* grand master.
grasnar [grǎzh-nar'] *vn.* to croak, caw (crow, raven); to quack (duck).
gratidão [grǎ-tee-dow*n*'] *f.* gratitude.
gratificação [grǎ-tee-fee-kǎ-sow*n*'] *f.* gratuity; tip; bonus.
gratificar [grǎ-tee-fee-kar'] *va.* to tip; to reward.
grátis [grah'teesh] *adv.* free, gratis.
grato [grah'too] *adj.* grateful; pleasing, gratifying.
gratuito [grǎ-twee'too] *adj.* free; voluntary; baseless, pointless, gratuitous.
grau [grow] *m.* degree; grade, class.
gravame [grǎ-vǎm'] *m.* gravamen, (serious part of) charge, complaint; burden; hardship; grievance.
gravar [grǎ-var'] *va.* to engrave; to carve; to stamp, imprint; to register.
gravata [grǎ-vah'tǎ] *f.* tie.
grave [grahv] *adj.* serious, grave; important; grave (accent).
gravidade [grǎ-vee-dahd'] *f.* gravity; seriousness, importance.
gravidez [grǎ-vee-daysh'] *f.* pregnancy.
grávida [gra'vee-dǎ] *adj.* pregnant.
gravitação [grǎ-vee-tǎ-sow*n*'] *f.* gravitation.
gravura [grǎ-voo'rǎ] *f.* engraving; illustration, picture.
graxa [grah'shǎ] *f.* (shoe) polish.
greda [gray'dǎ] *f.* chalk.

grego [gray'goo] *m/adj.* Greek. [people.
grei [gray'ee] *f.* flock; nation,
grelar [grĕ-lar'] *vn.* to sprout.
grelha [gre'lyă] *f.* grill; bar, grate (in fireplace).
grelhar [grĕ-lyar'] *va.* to grill.
grelo [gray'loo] *m.* sprout, bud.
grémio [gre'mee-oo] *m.* guild, syndicate, corporation; community; club.
grenha [grĕ'nyă] *f.* tangled (matted) hair; mop (of hair).
grés [gresh] *m.* sandstone.
greta [gray'tă] *f.* crack.
greve [grev] *f.* strike; **fazer —**, to strike. [striker.
grevista [grĕ-veesh'tă] *mf.*
grifado [gree-fah'doo] *adj.* italicized, in italics (*print.*).
grifar [gree-far'] *va.* to italicize.
grilhão [gree-lyow*n*'] *m.* chain.
grilo [gree'loo] *m.* cricket.
grimpa [gree*n*'pă] *f.* weather-vane, -cock; top; **levantar a —**, to get on one's high horse.
grinalda [gree-nal'dă] *f.* garland.
gripe [greep] *f.* influenza, flu.
grisalho [gree-za'lyoo] *adj.* grey (hair).
gritar [gree-tar'] *vn.* to shout; to call out; to cry; to yell; to shriek.
gritaria [gree-tă-ree'ă] *f.* shouting, din, row.
grito [gree'too] *m.* shout, cry; yell; scream.
grosa [gro'ză] *f.* rasp, file (*mech.*); gross (*com.*).
groselha [groo-ze'lyă] *f.* (red-, black-, white-)currant; gooseberry.
grosseiro [groo-say'ee-roo] *adj.* coarse, crude, boorish.
grosso [groh'soo] *adj.* thick; large; *m.* main body (of army, etc.); **erro —**, gross error; **por —**, wholesale (*com.*); **fazer vista —a**, to close one's eyes.
grossura [groo-soo'ră] *f.* thickness; bulk.
grotesco [groo-taysh'koo] *adj.* ridiculous, grotesque.
grou [groh] *m.* crane (*zool.*).
grua [groo'ă] *f.* crane (*mech.*, *zool.*).
grude [grood] *f.* glue.
grumete [groo-met'] *m.* cabin-boy.
grunhir [groo-nyeer'] *vn.* to grunt; to growl, grumble.
grupo [groo'poo] *m.* group; collection; team (sport).
gruta [groo'tă] *f.* cave; grotto.
guarda [gwar'dă] *f.* protection; defence; guard (*mil.*); *m.* guard; warden; **— florestal**, forester.
guarda-chuva [gwar'dă shoo'vă] *m.* umbrella.
guarda-fogo [gwar'dă foh'goo] *m.* fireguard; fire-screen.
guarda-freio [gwar'dă fray'yoo] *m.* tram-driver.
guarda-livros [gwar'dă-leev'roosh] *m.* book-keeper, accountant.
guardanapo [gwăr-dă-na'poo] *m.* napkin.
guardar [gwăr-dar'] *va.* to guard, protect, defend; to keep (a secret, etc.).
guarda-redes [gwar'dă-raydsh] *m.* goalkeeper.
guarda-roupa [gwar'dă roh'pă] *m.* wardrobe.
guarda-sol [gwar'dă sol] *m.* sunshade, parasol.
guarida [gwă-ree'dă] *f.* lair, den (of animals); refuge, shelter.
guarita [gwă-ree'tă] *f.* sentry box.
guarnecer [gwăr-nĕ-sayr'] *va.* to furnish, provide with; to adorn; to garrison, man (*mil.*).
guarnição [gwăr-nee-sow*n*'] *f.* garrison (*mil.*); crew (*naut.*); trimming (of dress).

guedelha [gĕ-day'lyă] *f.* mop, lock (of hair).
guelra [gel'ră] *f.* gill (of fish).
guerra [ge'ră] *f.* war; warfare; — de morte, war to the death; em pé de —, on a war footing; após —, post-war.
guerrear [gĕ-ree-ar'] *vn.* to wage war.
guerreiro [gĕ-ray'ee-roo] *m.* warrior, soldier; *adj.* warlike.
guerrilha [gĕ-ree'lyă] *f.* guerilla war(fare).
guerrilheiro [gĕ-ree-lyay'ee-roo] *m.* guerilla.
guia [gee'ă] *mf.* guide-book; (telephone) directory; handbook, manual; delivery note (*com.*); (customs) permit; *mf.* guide; leader.
guiar [gee-ar'] *va.* to guide, lead, direct. [guillotine.
guilhotina [gee-lyoo-tee'nă] *f.*
guinada [gee-nah'dă] *f.* shift of course, lurch, swerve; sudden (sharp) pain.
guincho [gee*n*'shoo] *m.* yell, squeal, shriek; winch (*mech.*).
guindar [gee*n*-dar'] *va.* to hoist, lift.
guindaste [gee*n*-dasht'] *m.* crane, hoist, derrick.
guisado [gee-zah'doo] *m.* stew.
guita [gee'tă] *f.* twine, string.
guitarra [gee-ta'ră] *f.* guitar.
guitarrada [gee-tă-rah'dă] *f.* guitar piece, solo; guitar concert. [round) bell.
guizo [gee'zoo] *m.* (small
gula [goo'lă] *f.* greed; gluttony.
gulodice [goo-loo-dees'] *f.* titbit, delicacy; greediness.
guloseima [goo-loo-zay'ee-mă] *f.* delicacy, sweet (dish); sweet tooth; greediness.
guloso [goo-loh'zoo] *adj.* greedy
gume [goom] *m.* edge (of sword, etc.;) sharpness, perspicacity.
gusano [goo-ză'noo] *m.* wood worm; grub; horsefly.

H

hábil [ah'beel] *adj.* clever, skilful, capable.
habilidade [ă-bee-lee-dahd'] *f.* ability, skill, talent; *pl.* tricks; skilful exercises.
habilidoso [ă-bee-lee-doh'-zoo] *adj.* handy, skilful, clever (with one's hands).
habilitação [ă-bee-lee-tă-sow*n*'] *f.* qualification; competence; eligibility; *pl.* (certificates of) competence, qualifications.
habilitar [ă-bee-lee-tar'] *va.* to qualify, entitle; to enable; to prepare, equip.
habitação [ă-bee-tă-sow*n*'] *f.* dwelling, residence.
habitante [ă-bee-ta*nt*'] *mf.* inhabitant; resident.
habitar [ă-bee-tar'] *va/vn.* to inhabit; to live in.
hábito [a'bee-too] *m.* habit, custom; (monk's) robes, habit.
habitual [ă-bee-too-al'] *adj.* usual, customary, habitual.
habituar [ă-bee-too-ar'] *va.* to accustom; *vr.* to get accustomed to.
hálito [a'lee-too] *m.* breath; vapour.
harmonia [ăr-moo-nee'ă] *f.* harmony; agreement, friendship, concord.
harmónica [ăr-mo'nee-kă] *f.* mouth-organ.
harmónio *m.* [ăr-mo'nee-oo] accordeon.
harpa [ăr-pă] *f.* harp.
hasta [ash-tă] *f.* spear, lance; auction. [flagpole.
haste [asht] *f.* rod, shaft, staff;
hastear [ăsh-tee-ar'] *va.* to hoist (flag, etc.).
haurir [ow-reer'] *va.* to drain.

suck up; to draw out, off; to exhaust.
haver [ă-vayr'] *impersonal verb*, (1) there + to be, e.g. **há muita gente lá**, there are many people there; **haverá**, there will be; **houve**, there was, were; **deve haver**, there must be; (2) *auxiliary verb*, to have; — **de**, to be bound to, have to; will, shall; (3) ago, e.g. **há poucos dias**, a few days ago; (4) *va.* to possess; — **por**, to consider, judge; — **mister**, to need.
haveres [ă-vay'rĕsh] *m.pl.* possessions, assets, wealth.
hebdomadário [eb-doo-mă-dah'ree-oo] *m/adj.* weekly.
hediondo [ĕ-dee-*on*'doo] *adj.* hideous, repulsive, revolting.
hélice [e'lees] *f.* propeller (*mech.*).
helicóptero [e-lee-kop'tĕ-roo] *m.* helicopter.
hemisfério [ĕ-meesh-fair'ee-oo] *m.* hemisphere.
hemorragia [ĕ-moo-ră-zhee'-ă] *f.* haemorrhage.
hera [air'ă] *f.* ivy.
herança [ĕ-ran'să] *f.* inheritance, heritage.
herdade [ĕr-dahd'] *f.* farm.
herdar [ĕr-dar'] *va/vn.* to inherit.
herdeiro [ĕr-day'ee-roo] *m.* [heir.
hereditário [ĕ-rĕ-dee-tah'-ree-oo] *adj.* hereditary; inherited.
herege [ee-rezh'] *mf.* heretic.
heresia [ee-rĕ-zee'ă] *f.* heresy.
herético [ee-re'tee-koo] *adj.* heretical; *m.* heretic.
herói [ee-roy'] *m.* hero.
heróico [ee-roy'koo] *adj.* heroic, valiant.
heroismo [ee-roo-eezh'moo] *m.* heroism, courage, gallantry.
hesitação [ee-zee-tă-sow*n*'] *f.* hesitation.
hesitar [ee-zee-tar'] *vn.* to hesitate.
heterogéneo [ee-tĕ-ro-zhe'-nee-oo] *adj.* heterogeneous, different.
hiato [ee-ah'too] *m.* hiatus; gap, interval.
híbrido [ee'bree-doo] *m/adj.* hybrid, mongrel.
hidráulico [ee-drow'lee-koo] *adj.* hydraulic.
hidroavião [ee-dro-ă-vee-ow*n*'] *m.* flying-boat, seaplane.
hidrofobia [ee-dro-foo-bee'ă] [*f.* rabies.
hidropisia [ee-dro-pĕ-zee'ă] *f.* dropsy.
hiena [ee-ay'nă] *f.* hyena.
hierarquia [ee-e-rar-kee'ă] *f.* hierarchy.
hifen [ee'fen] *m.* hyphen.
higiene [ee-zhee-en'] *f.* hygiene, sanitation; cleanliness.
higiénico [ee-zhee-e'nee-koo] *adj.* hygienic, sanitary.
hino [ee'noo] *m.* hymn; — nacional, national anthem.
hípico [ee'pee-koo] *adj.* of horses, equine; **concurso** —, horse-race.
hipnotismo [eep-noo-teezh'-moo] *m.* hypnotism.
hipocrisia [ee-poo-krĕ-zee'ă] *f.* hypocrisy, pretence.
hipócrita [ee-po'kree-tă] *mf.* hypocrite; *adj.* hypocritical, false.
hipódromo [ee-po'droo-moo] *m.* race-course.
hipoteca [ee-poo-te'kă] *f.* mortgage.
hipotecar [ee-poo-tĕ-kar'] *va.* to mortgage.
hipótese [ee-po'tĕz] *f.* hypothesis, theory, assumption.
hipotético [ee-poo-te'tee-koo] *adj.* hypothetical, imaginary.
hirsuto [eer-soo'too] *adj.* hairy, shaggy, bristly.
hirto [eer'too] *adj.* rigid, stiff.

hispânico [eesh-pă'nee-koo] *adj.* Hispanic.
histeria [eesh-tĕ-ree'ă] *f.* hysteria.
história [eesh-to'ree-ă] *f.* history; story, tale; fable, legend; fabrication, cock-and-bull story; **— da carochinha,** nursery story.
historiador [eesh-too-ree-ă-dohr'] *m.* historian.
histórico [eesh-to'ree-koo] *adj.* historical; historic, famous.
historieta [eesh-too-ree-ay'-tă] *f.* tale, yarn.
hodierno [oo-dee-air'noo] *adj.* present-day, modern.
hoje [ohzh] *adv.* today; **— em dia,** nowadays; **de — em diante,** from now (today) on; **de — para amanhã,** at any moment (i.e. when least expected).
holandês [oo-la*n*-daysh'] *adj.* Dutch; *m.* Dutchman; Dutch language.
holocausto [oo-loo-kowsh'-too] *m.* holocaust; sacrifice.
homem [o'me*n*] *m.* man; mankind; **— de bem,** honest, reliable man; **— de negócios,** businessman; **— de estado,** statesman.
homenagem [oh-mĕ-nah'-zhe*n*] *f.* honour, homage, respect.
homicídio [oo-mĕ-see'dee-oo] *m.* homicide, murder; manslaughter.
homiziado [oo-mee-zee-ah'-doo] *m.* fugitive (from justice); *adj.* in hiding.
homiziar [oo-mee-zee-ar'] *va.* to shelter, hide (fugitive); *vr.* to abscond, run off; to hide.
homogéneo [oh-moo-zhe'nee-oo] *adj.* homogeneous, similar, identical.
honestidade [oo-nĕsh-tee-dahd'] *f.* chastity, purity, virtue; decency; honesty.
honesto [oo-nesh'too] *adj.* decent, honourable; trustworthy, honest; virtuous, pure.
honorário [oo-noo-rah'ree-oo] *adj.* honorary, unpaid; *m.pl.* fee(s).
honra [o*n*'ră] *f.* honour; reputation; virtue.
honradez [o*n*-ră-daysh'] *f.* honesty, integrity.
honrado [o*n*-rah'doo] *adj.* honest, reliable, conscientious; honourable.
honrar [o*n*-rar'] *va.* to honour, esteem; to do honour to.
honroso [o*n*-roh'zoo] *adj.* honourable, distinguished, creditable.
hóquei [o'kay] *m.* hockey; **— em patins,** roller-hockey.
hora [o'ră] *f.* hour; time; **— de jantar,** dinner time; **mais — menos—,** sooner or later; **última —,** stop-press (news); **que —s são?** what time is it?; **—s extraordinárias,** overtime; **a altas —s,** late at night, in the small hours; **chegar a —s,** to arrive on time.
horário [oo-rah'ree-oo] *m.* time-table.
horda [or'dă] *f.* horde, gang, mob.
horizonte [oo-ree-zo*n*t'] *m.* horizon.
horoscópio [oh-rohsh-ko'pee-oo] *m.* horoscope.
horrendo [oo-re*n*'doo] *adj.* horrible, horrifying, dreadful.
hórrido [o'ree-doo] *adj.* horrid, horrible.
horripilante [oo-ree-pee-la*n*t'] *adj.* ghastly, terrifying.
horripilar [oo-ree-pee-lar'] *va.* to terrify, horrify.
horríssono [oo-ree'soo-noo'] *adj.* horrid-, (dreadful-) sounding.

horrível [oo-ree'vel] *adj.* horrible, dreadful, horrid.
horror [oo-rohr'] *m.* horror, terror; loathing, abhorrence; que —! how awful, dreadful!
horrorizar [oo-roo-ree-zar'] *va.* to horrify, terrify, shock.
horroroso [oo-roo-roh'zoo] *adj.* horrible, frightful, awful.
horta [or'tă] *f.* garden (for vegetables, fruit).
hortaliças [ohr-tă-lee'săsh] *f. pl.* vegetables.
hortelã [ohr-tĕ-la*n*'] *f.* mint (*bot.*); — pimenta, peppermint. [gardener.
hortelão [ohr-tĕ-low*n*'] *m.*
hospedagem [ohsh-pĕ-dah'zhe*n*] *f.* accommodation; hospitality.
hospedar [ohsh-pĕ-dar'] *va.* to give accommodation to, put up, lodge; *vr.* to stay, stop at.
hospedaria [ohsh-pĕ-dă-ree'ă] *f.* lodging-house; boarding-house.
hóspede [osh'pĕd] *m.* guest; boarder, lodger.
hospedeiro [ohsh-pĕ-day'ee-roo] *m.* host; landlord; *adj.* hospitable.
hospício [ohsh-pee'see-oo] *m.* home (for poor, sick, and for animals).
hospital [ohsh-pee-tal'] *m.* hospital, infirmary.
hospitaleiro [ohsh-pee-tă-lay'ee-roo] *adj.* hospitable.
hospitalidade [ohsh-pee-tă-lee-dahd'] *f.* hospitality.
hospitalizar [ohsh-pee-tă-lee-zar'] *va.* to admit to hospital.
hoste [osht] *f.* host (*mil.*).
hóstia [osh'tee-ă] *f.* Host (*relig.*).
hostil [ohsh-teel'] *adj.* hostile.
hostilidade [ohsh-tee-lee-dahd'] *f.* hostility, enmity.
hotel [oh-tel'] *m.* hotel.
hoteleiro [oh-tĕ-lay'ee-roo] *m.* hotel-keeper, -proprietor.
hulha [oo'lyă] *f.* coal.
humanidade [oo-mă-nee-dahd'] *f.* humanity, mankind, human race; humanity, mercy, humaneness; human nature; *pl.* humanities (*acad.*).
humanitário [oo-mă-nee-tah'ree-oo] *m/adj.* humanitarian.
humanizar [oo-mă-nee-zar'] *va.* to humanize; to make more human, tractable.
humano [oo-mă'noo] *adj.* human; humane, kindly.
humedecer [oo-mĕ-dĕ-sayr'] *va.* to moisten, damp, wet.
humidade [oo-mee-dahd'] *f.* humidity, moisture, dampness.
húmido [oo'mee-doo] *adj.* damp, wet, humid.
humildade [oo-meel-dahd'] *f.* humility, meekness.
humilde [oo-meeld'] *adj.* humble, meek; lowly, modest.
humilhar [oo-mee-lyar'] *va.* to humiliate, humble, degrade.
humor [oo-mohr'] *m.* humour, mood, temper; bom —, good humour; mau —, bad temper.
humorismo [oo-moo-reezh'moo] *m.* humour, comedy.
humorístico [oo-moo-reesh'tee-koo] *adj.* humorous, comical.
húngaro [oo*n*'gă-roo] *m/adj.* Hungarian.

I

iate [yat] *m.* yacht.
ibérico [ee-bair'ee-koo] *adj.* Iberian.
ibero [ee-bair'oo] *m.* Iberian.
içar [ee-sar'] *va.* to hoist, lift.
icterícia [eek-tĕ-ree'see-ă] *f.* jaundice (*med.*).
ida [ee'dă] *f.* going, departure; bilhete de —, single ticket;

bilhete de — e volta, return ticket.
idade [ee-dahd'] *f.* age; period, epoch; — **média**, Middle Ages; **certidão de** —, birth certificate.
ideal [ee-dee-al'] *adj.* ideal, perfect; imaginary; *m.* ideal.
idealizar [ee-dee-ă-lee-zar'] *va.* to idealize.
idear [ee-dee-ar'] *va.* to imagine; to devise, conceive.
idéia [ee-de'yă] *f.* idea; plan, scheme; belief, notion; **fazer** —, to imagine; **não faço** —, I can't imagine. [same.
idem [ee'den] *pr.* ditto, the
idêntico [ee-den'tee-koo] *adj.* identical.
identidade [ee-den-tee-dahd'] *f.* identity.
identificação [ee-den-ti-fee-kă-sown'] *f.* identification.
ideologia [ee-dee-oo-loo-zhee'ă] *f.* ideology.
idílio [ee-dee'lee-oo] *m.* idyll.
idioma [ee-dee-oh'mă] *m.* language.
idiota [ee-dee-o'tă] *m.* idiot, fool; *adj.* idiotic.
idiotia [ee-dee-oo-tee'ă] *f.* idiocy. [silliness.
idiotice [ee-dee-oo-tees'] *f.*
idiotismo [ee-dee-oo-teezh'-moo] *m.* idiocy (*med.*); idiom, idiomatic expression (in language).
idólatra [ee-do'lă-tră] *adj.* idolatrous; *m.* idolater, idol-worshipper.
idolatrar [ee-doo-lă-trar'] *va.* to idolize, worship.
idolatria [ee-doo-lă-tree'ă] *f.* idolatry.
ídolo [ee'doo-loo] *m.* idol.
idoneidade [ee-do-nay-ee-dahd'] *f.* suitability, fitness; capacity.
idóneo [ee-do'nee-oo] *adj.* suitable, fit; capable; apt.
idoso [ee-doh'zoo] *adj.* old, aged, elderly.
ignaro [eeg-nah'roo] *adj.* ignorant, unlettered.
ignavo [eeg-nah'voo] *adj.* lazy, indolent; cowardly, weak.
igneo [eeg'nee-oo] *adj.* fiery; igneous (rocks).
ignição [eeg-nee-sown'] *f.* ignition.
ignominia [eeg-noo-mee'nee-ă] *f.* ignominy, dishonour.
ignominioso [eeg-noo-mee-nee-oh'zoo] *adj.* dishonourable, disgraceful, ignominious.
ignorado [eeg-noo-rah'doo] *adj.* unknown; obscure.
ignorância [eeg-noo-ran'see-ă] *f.* ignorance.
ignorante [eeg-noo-rant'] *adj.* ignorant; *m.* ignorant person, ignoramus.
ignorar [eeg-noo-rar'] *va.* not to know; to be unaware of.
ignoto [eeg-no'too] *adj.* unknown; hidden.
igreja [ee-gray'zhă] *f.* church.
igual [ee-gwal'] *adj.* equal; similar, the same, identical; even, level; *m.* equal.
igualar [ee-gwă-lar'] *va.* to equalize, make equal; to level, make even; *vn.* to equal, be equal to.
igualdade [ee-gwal-dahd'] *f.* equality; parity.
igualha [ee-gwal'yă] *f.* (equal social) class; **não é da minha** —, he is not of my class.
iguaria [ee-gwă-ree'ă] *f.* delicacy (food).
ilação [ee-lă-sown'] *f.* inference, deduction.
ilegal [ee-lĕ-gal'] *adj.* illegal, unlawful.
ilegitimo [ee-lĕ-zhee'tee-moo] *adj.* illegitimate; spurious.
ilegível [ee-lĕ-zhee'vel] *adj.* illegible. [unharmed,
ileso [ee-le'zoo] *adj.* unhurt.

ilha [ee'lyă] *f.* island; isle.
ilharga [ee-lyar'gă] *f.* flank, side; **de —**, sideways; on one's side.
ilícito [ee-lee'see-too] *adj.* illicit, unlawful.
ilimitado [ee-lee-mee-tah'doo] *adj.* unlimited, boundless.
ilógico [ee-lo'zhee-koo] *adj.* illogical, irrational.
iludir [ee-loo-deer'] *va.* to deceive, delude; to evade (the law); *vr.* to deceive oneself.
iluminação [ee-loo-mee-nă-sow*n*'] *f.* illumination, lighting.
iluminar [ee-loo-mee-nar'] *va.* to illuminate, light up; to enlighten (the understanding).
iluminura [ee-loo-mee-noo'-ră] *f.* illumination (of book, etc. with coloured lettering).
ilusão [ee-loo-zow*n*'] *f.* illusion; delusion.
ilusório [ee-loo-zo'ree-oo] *adj.* illusory; deceptive.
ilustração [ee-loosh-tră-sow*n*'] *f.* illustration; picture; learning.
ilustrado [ee-loosh-trah'doo] *adj.* cultured, well-read, educated; enlightened; illustrated.
ilustrar [ee-loosh-trar'] *va.* to illustrate (with pictures); to elucidate; to enlighten (the mind); to make illustrious.
ilustre [ee-loosh'trĕ] *adj.* illustrious, distinguished, famous.
imã [ee'ma*n*] *m.* magnet.
imaculado [ee-mă-koo-lah'-doo] *adj.* immaculate.
imagem [ee-mah'zhe*n*] *f.* image; likeness; figure, symbol; reflection.
imaginação [ee-mă-zhee-nă-sow*n*'] *f.* imagination; conception, notion, mental image; fantasy, fancy.
imaginar [ee-mă-zhee-nar'] *va.* to imagine, picture; to conceive; to devise; to suppose.
imaginário [ee-mă-zhee-nah'-ree-oo] *adj.* imaginary, unreal, fancied.
imaginativo [ee-mă-zhee-nă-tee'voo] *adj.* imaginative.
imaturo [ee-mă-too'roo] *adj.* immature; unripe; premature.
imbecil [ee*n*-bĕ-seel'] *m/adj.* imbecile.
imbecilidade [ee*n*-bĕ-see-lee-dahd'] *f.* imbecility, feeble-mindedness, stupidity.
imberbe [ee*n*-bairb'] *adj.* beardless; young.
imbricar [ee*n*-bree-kar'] *va.* to overlap.
imbuir [ee*n*-boo-eer'] *va.* to imbue.
imediações [ee-mĕ-dee-ă-soy*n*sh'] *f.pl.* vicinity, surrounding area.
imediato [ee-mĕ-dee-ah'too] *adj.* immediate; instantaneous; next, adjoining; *m.* first mate, chief officer (*naut.*); second-in-command; chief assistant.
imensidade [ee-me*n*-see-dahd'] *f.* immensity, vastness.
imenso [ee-me*n*'soo] *adj.* immense, vast, boundless, huge.
imerecido [ee-mĕ-rĕ-see'doo] *adj.* undeserved, unmerited.
imigração [ee-mee-gră-sow*n*'] *f.* immigration.
imigrante [ee-mee-gra*n*t'] *m.* immigrant.
iminente [ee-mee-ne*n*t'] *adj.* imminent, impending.
imiscuir-se [ee-meesh-kweer'sĕ] *vr.* to meddle, interfere in.
imitação [ee-mee-tă-sow*n*'] *f.* imitation, copy.
imitar [ee-mee-tar'] *va.* to imitate, copy; to mimic.
imobiliário [ee-moo-bee-lee-ah'ree-oo] *adj.* fixed, immovable (property); **bens —s**, real estate.
imobilidade [ee-moo-bee-lee-dahd'] *f.* immobility; fixity.

imoderado [ee-moo-dĕ-rah'-doo] *adj.* immoderate, unrestrained.
imolar [ee-moo-lar'] *va.* to immolate, sacrifice.
imoral [ee-moo-ral'] *adj.* immoral.
imorredouro [ee-moo-rĕ-doh'roo] *adj.* immortal, undying, imperishable.
imortal [ee-moor-tal'] *adj.* immortal, everlasting, eternal.
imortalizar [ee-moor-tă-lee-zar'] *va.* to immortalize.
imóvel [ee-mo'vel] *adj.* motionless, steady, immovable.
impaciência [ee*n*-pă-see-e*n*'-see-ă] *f.* impatience, restlessness, impetuosity.
impaciente [ee*n*-pă-see-e*n*t'] *adj.* impatient; impetuous, restless, fidgety.
impagável [ee*n*-pă-gah'vel] *adj.* priceless, invaluable; comical; absurd.
impalpável [ee*n*-pal-pah'vel] *adj.* intangible, impalpable
impar [ee*n*'par] *adj.* odd (number); unmatched.
imparcial [ee*n*-păr-see-al'] *adj.* impartial, fair, unbiassed.
imparcialidade [ee*n*-păr-see-ă-lee-dahd'] *f.* impartiality.
impassível [ee*n*-pă-see'vel] *adj.* impassive; insensitive; unmoved, unruffled; expressionless.
impávido [ee*n*-pa'vee-doo] *adj.* fearless, dauntless, brave.
impecável [ee*n*-pĕ-kah'vel] *adj.* impeccable, faultless, sinless.
impedido [ee*n*-pĕ-dee'doo] *m.* (officer's) batman, servant (*mil.*); *adj.* impeded, hindered; closed (to traffic); interrupted.
impedimento [ee*n*-pĕ-dee-me*n*'too] *m.* obstacle, obstruction, impediment.
impedir [ee*n*-pĕ-deer'] *va.* to obstruct, hinder, impede.
impelir [ee*n*-pĕ-leer'] *va.* to impel, drive, push (on).
impenetrável [ee*n*-pĕ-nĕ-trah'vel] *adj.* impenetrable; unfathomable; impervious.
impenitente [ee*n*-pĕ-nee-te*n*t'] *adj.* unrepentant, obdurate.
impensado [ee*n*-pe*n*-sah'doo] *adj.* unexpected, unforeseen; unpremeditated.
imperador [ee*n*-pĕ-ră-dohr'] *m.* emperor.
imperar [ee*n*-pĕ-rar'] *vn.* to reign, rule, be in control.
imperativo [ee*n*-pĕ-ră-tee'-voo] *adj.* imperative, peremptory.
imperatriz [ee*n*-pĕ-ră-treesh'] [*f.* empress.
imperceptível [ee*n*-pĕr-se-tee'vel] *adj.* imperceptible; faint, slight, very small.
imperdoável [ee*n*-pĕr-doo-ah'vel] *adj.* unforgiveable, inexcusable.
imperecedouro [ee*n*-pĕ-rĕ-sĕ-doh'roo] *adj.* imperishable.
imperfeição [ee*n*-pĕr-fay-ee-sow*n*'] *f.* imperfection, defect, fault, flaw.
imperfeito [ee*n*-pĕr-fay'ee-too] *adj.* imperfect, faulty; unfinished, incomplete; *m.* imperfect (grammatical tense).
imperial [ee*n*-pĕ-ree-al'] *adj.* imperial; *f.* upper deck, top (of vehicle).
imperialismo [ee*n*-pĕ-ree-ă-leezh'moo] *m.* imperialism.
imperícia [ee*n*-pĕ-ree'see-ă] *f.* awkwardness, lack of skill.
império [ee*n*-pair'ee-oo] *m.* empire; state; domination.
imperioso [ee*n*-pĕ-ree-oh'-zoo] *adj.* imperious, arrogant; urgent, pressing (need, etc.).
imperito [ee*n*-pĕ-ree'too] *adj.* unskilled.

impermeável [een-pĕr-mee-ah'vel] *adj.* impervious, impermeable; waterproof; *m.* raincoat.

impertérrito [een-pĕr-te'ree-too] *adj.* dauntless, fearless.

impertinência [een-pĕr-tee-nen'see-ă] *f.* impertinence.

impertinente [een-pĕr-tee-nent'] *adj.* impertinent, insolent; petulant, cross; irrelevant, inappropriate.

imperturbabilidade [een-pĕr-toor-bă-bee-lee-dahd'] *f.* imperturbability, calm, steadiness.

imperturbável [een-pĕr-toor-bah'vel] *adj.* imperturbable, calm, unruffled, cool, nonchalant.

impessoal [een-pĕ-soo-al'] *adj.* impersonal.

ímpeto [een'pĕ-too] *m.* impetus; violence, fury; impulse; momentum.

impetrar [een-pĕ-trar'] *va.* to entreat.

impetuosidade [een-pĕ-too-oo-zee-dahd'] *f.* impetuousness, vehemence, rashness.

impetuoso [een-pĕ-too-oh'-zoo] *adj.* impetuous, hasty, violent, rash.

impiedade [een-pee-ĕ-dahd'] *f.* irreverence; godlessness, atheism; cruelty, ruthlessness.

impigem [een-pee'zhen] *f.* rash, impetigo, skin trouble.

impingir [een-peen-zheer'] *va.* to inflict (on); to foist (on).

ímpio [een'pee-oo] *adj.* wicked; godless, blasphemous.

implacável [een-plă-kah'vel] *adj.* implacable, relentless, unforgiving.

implicar [een-plee-kar'] *va.* to implicate, involve; to imply, indicate, to include; **— -se com,** to pick a quarrel with.

implícito [een-plee'see-too] *adj.* implicit.

implorar [een-ploo-rar'] *va.* to implore, entreat, beseech, beg.

imponderado [een-pon-dĕ-rah'doo] *adj.* thoughtless, rash.

imponente [een-poo-nent'] *adj.* imposing, impressive, majestic.

impopular [een-poo-poo-lar'] *adj.* unpopular.

impor [een-pohr'] *va.* to impose; to levy (taxes); to inflict (penalties); *vr.* to impose oneself; to make one's influence felt.

importação [een-poor-tă-sown'] *f.* importing, importation; imports, imported goods.

importância [een-poor-tan'-see-ă] *f.* importance, significance; amount, sum (of money); cost; **não tem —,** it doesn't matter; it's not important.

importante [een-poor-tant'] *adj.* important; essential; weighty, serious.

importar [een-poor-tar'] *va.* to import; to introduce, bring in; *vn.* to matter; to be of importance, concern; *vr.* **— com,** to concern oneself with.

importe [een-port'] *m.* total, amount; cost.

importunar [een-poor-too-nar'] *va.* to pester, bother, annoy, importune.

importuno [een-poor-too'-noo] *adj.* troublesome, wearisome, annoying, importunate.

imposição [een-poo-zee-sown'] *f.* imposition.

impossibilidade [een-poo-si-bee-lee-dahd'] *f.* impossibility.

impossibilitar [een-poo-si-bee-lee-tar'] *va.* to disable, incapacitate; to make impossible; to preclude, prevent.

impossível [een-poo-see'vel] *adj.* impossible, impracticable.
imposto [een-pohsh'too] *m.* tax; duty; — de rendimento, income tax; *adj.* imposed.
impostura [een-poosh-too'ră] *f.* imposture, fraud, hoax.
impotente [een-poo-tent'] *adj.* impotent, powerless, weak.
impraticável [een-pră-tee-kah'vel] *adj.* impracticable; impassable (road).
imprecação [een-prĕ-kă-sown'] *f.* curse, imprecation.
impregnar [een-prĕg-nar'] *va.* to impregnate, fill, saturate.
imprensa [een-pren'să] *f.* (printing-)press; printing.
imprescindível [een-prĕsh-seen-dee'vel] *adj.* essential, indispensable.
impressão [een-prĕ-sown'] *f.* impression, effect; imprint, mark; printing.
impressionante [een-prĕ-see-oo-nant'] *adj.* moving, touching; impressive.
impressionar [een-prĕ-see-oo-nar'] *va.* to impress; to move, touch, thrill.
impressivo [een-prĕ-see'voo] *adj.* impressive, striking.
impresso [een-pre'soo] *m.* printed work, printed matter; leaflet; form; *adj.* printed.
impressor [een-prĕ-sohr'] *m.* printer.
impreterível [een-prĕ-tĕ-ree'vel] *adj.* unavoidable, inevitable.
imprevidente [een-prĕ-vee-dent'] *adj.* improvident, careless, lacking in foresight.
imprevisto [een-prĕ-veesh'too] *adj.* unforeseen, unexpected.
imprimir [een-pri-meer'] *va.* to print; to stamp; to inculcate; to leave an imprint on; — movimento, to set in motion.
improbabilidade [een-proo-bă-bee-lee-dahd'] *f.* improbability.
ímprobo [een-proh'boo] *adj.* dishonest; laborious, arduous (toil).
improcedente [een-proo-sĕ-dent'] *adj.* groundless, unfounded, unjustified.
improdutivo [een-proo-doo-tee'voo] *adj.* unproductive.
improficiente [een-proo-fee-see-ent'] *adj.* incompetent, inefficient, unskilled.
improfícuo [een-proo-fee'koo-oo] *adj.* useless, fruitless, ineffective.
impropério [een-proo-pair'-ee-oo] *m.* curse, bad language; insult.
impropriedade [een-proo-pree-ĕ-dahd'] *f.* impropriety, unseemliness; unsuitability.
impróprio [een-prop'ree-oo] *adj.* unsuitable; incorrect; improper, unseemly.
improvável [een-proo-vah'-vel] *adj.* improbable, unlikely.
improvidência [een-proo-vee-den'see-ă] *f.* improvidence, thriftlessness, carelessness.
improvidente [een-proo-vee-dent'] *adj.* improvident, careless, thriftless.
improvisação [een-proo-vee-ză-sown'] *f.* improvisation.
improvisado [een-proo-vee-zah'doo] *adj.* improvised; makeshift; extempore.
improvisar [een-proo-vee-zar'] *va.* to improvise; to extemporize.
improviso [een-proo-vee'zoo] *m.* impromptu speech, composition, etc.; *adj.* sudden; de —, on the spur of the moment; suddenly.

imprudência [een-proo-den'-see-ă] *f.* imprudence, indiscretion, rashness.
imprudente [een-proo-dent'] *adj.* imprudent, indiscreet, rash, unwise.
impudência [een-poo-den'-see-ă] *f.* shamelessness, indecency; insolence, impudence.
impudente [een-poo-dent'] *adj.* indecent, shameless.
impudico [een-poo-dee'koo] *adj.* indecent, shameless, lewd.
impugnar [een-poog-nar'] *va.* to contest, oppose, impugn.
impulsar [een-pool-sar'] *va.* to thrust, drive forward.
impulsionar [een-pool-see-oo-nar'] *va.* to impel, thrust forward; to incite, stimulate.
impulso [een-pool'soo] *m.* impulse, impetus; thrust, push, drive.
impune [een-poon'] *adj.* unpunished, with impunity.
impunidade [een-poo-nee-dahd'] *f.* impunity.
impureza [een-poo-ray'ză] *f.* impurity.
impuro [een-poo'roo] *adj.* [impure.
imputação [een-poo-tă-sown'] *f.* imputation, accusation.
imputar [een-poo-tar'] *va.* to impute; to charge with, blame for.
imputável [een-poo-tah'vel] *adj.* attributable.
imundícia [ee-moon-dee'see-ă] *f.* filth, dirt; refuse, garbage.
imundo [ee-moon'doo] *adj.* dirty, filthy; obscene.
imunidade [ee-moo-nee-dahd'] *f.* immunity; exemption.
imunizar [ee-moo-nee-zar'] *va.* to immunize.
imutável [ee-moo-tah'vel] *adj.* fixed, unchangeable, immutable.
inabalável [ee-nă-bă-lah'vel] *adj.* unshakeable, indomitable.
inábil [ee-na'beel] *adj.* unskilful, clumsy; incapable.
inabilidade [ee-nă-bee-lee-dahd'] *f.* inability; incapacity; incompetence.
inabilitar [ee-nă-bee-lee-tar'] *va.* to disqualify; to incapacitate.
inabitável [ee-nă-bee-tah'vel] *adj.* uninhabitable.
inacção [ee-nah-sown'] *f.* inactivity, inertia.
inaceitável [ee-nă-say-ee-tah'vel] *adj.* unacceptable.
inacessível [ee-nă-sĕ-see'vel] *adj.* inaccessible.
inactividade [ee-nah-tee-vee-dahd'] *f.* lethargy, sluggishness; inactivity; passar à —, to retire from active service; estar na —, to be off the active list.
inactivo [ee-nah-tee'voo] *adj.* inactive; inert; dormant, quiescent.
inadequado [ee-nă-dĕ-kwah'-doo] *adj.* inadequate; unsuitable.
inadmissível [ee-năd-mĕ-see'vel] *adj.* inadmissible, unacceptable.
inadquirível [ee-năd-ki-ree'-vel] *adj.* unobtainable.
inadvertência [ee-năd-vĕr-ten'see-ă] *f.* oversight; carelessness, inadvertence.
inadvertido [ee-năd-vĕr-tee'-doo] *adj.* inadvertent; unintentional. [inhaler.
inalador [ee-nă-lă-dohr'] *m.*
inalar [ee-nă-lar'] *va.* to inhale.
inalterável [ee-nal-tĕ-rah'vel] *adj.* unchangeable, firm, imperturbable.
inanição [ee-nă-nee-sown'] *f.* exhaustion.
inanimado [ee-nă-nee-mah'-doo] *adj.* inanimate, lifeless.
inaptidão [ee-nap-tee-down']

f. unsuitability; incapacity, lack of aptitude.
inapto [ee-nap'too] *adj.* unfit(ted), unsuitable, unqualified, incapable.
inatacável [ee-nă-tă-kah'vel] *adj.* unassailable; unimpeachable (source, etc.).
inatingível [ee-nă-teen-zhee'vel] *adj.* unattainable; inaccessible; incomprehensible.
inato [ee-nah'too] *adj.* innate, inborn.
inaudito [ee-now-dee'too] *adj.* unheard of, unprecedented.
inauguração [ee-now-goo-ră-sow*n*'] *f.* inauguration, opening.
inaugurar [ee-now-goo-rar'] *va.* to inaugurate, open.
incalculável [een-kal-koo-lah'vel] *adj.* incalculable, innumerable, untold.
incandescente [een-kan-dĕsh-sent'] *adj.* incandescent; (*fig.*) fiery.
incansável [een-kan-sah'vel] *adj.* tireless, indefatigable.
incapacidade [een-kă-pă-see-dahd'] *f.* incapacity, inability; incompetence.
incapacitar [een-kă-pă-see-tar'] *va.* to disable, incapacitate; to disqualify.
incapaz [een-kă-pash'] *adj.* unable; incapable, incompetent; unfit.
inçar [een-sar' *va.* to infest; to infect.
incauto [een-kow'too] *adj.* careless, thoughtless; unwary, incautious.
incendiar [een-sen-dee-ar'] *va.* to set fire to; (*fig.*) to inflame, incense.
incendiário [een-sen-dee-ah'-ree-oo] *m/adj.* incendiary; *m.* firebrand, agitator.
incêndio [een-sen'dee-oo] *m.* fire, conflagration.
incenso [een-sen'soo] *m.* incense; (*fig.*) flattery.
incentivo [een-sen-tee'voo] *m.* incentive, stimulus.
incerteza [een-sĕr-tay'ză] *f.* uncertainty, doubt.
incerto [een-sair'too] *adj.* uncertain, doubtful, unsettled, unreliable.
incessante [een-sĕ-sant'] *adj.* unceasing, incessant, ceaseless.
inchar [een-shar'] *va.* to swell (out, up), inflate, puff out.
incidente [een-see-dent'] *m.* incident, event.
incinerar [een-see-nĕ-rar'] *va.* to incinerate; to cremate (corpse).
incipiente [een-see-pee-ent'] *adj.* incipient.
incisão [een-see-zow*n*'] *f.* cut, gash; (*med.*) incision.
incisivo [een-si-zee'voo] *adj.* incisive, penetrating, biting; *m.* incisor (tooth).
incitamento [een-see-tă-men'too] *m.* incitement, stimulus.
incitar [een-see-tar'] *va.* to incite, rouse, urge on.
incivil [een-sĕ-veel'] *adj.* ill-mannered, discourteous.
inclemência [een-klĕ-men'-see-ă] *f.* severity, rigour, harshness, inclemency.
inclemente [een-klĕ-ment'] *adj.* severe, harsh, inclement.
inclinação [een-klee-nă-sow*n*'] *f.* inclination, tendency, preference; incline, slope (of ground); tilt.
inclinar [een-klee-nar'] *va.* to incline, influence, induce; to tilt (an object); to bend (head); *vn.* to slope; to tend; *vr.* to bow, stoop; to incline towards.
ínclito [een'klee-too] *adj.* illustrious, renowned.
incluir [een-kloo-eer'] *va.* to include; to contain; to enclose.

inclusão [een-kloo-zown'] *f.* inclusion.
inclusive [een-kloo-zee've] *adv.* inclusive(ly).
incluso [een-kloo'zoo] *adj.* included; enclosed, herewith (in letter).
incoerente [een-koo-ě-rent'] *adj.* incoherent.
incógnito [een-kog'nee-too] *adj.* unknown; incognito.
incolor [een-koo-lohr'] *adj.* colourless.
incólume [een-ko'loom] *adj.* safe and sound, unharmed.
incomensurável [een-koo-men-soo-rah'vel] *adj.* immeasurable, immense.
incomodar [een-koo-moo-dar'] *va.* to disturb, inconvenience, trouble; to annoy; *vr.* to bother, put oneself out; to worry.
incómodo [een-ko'moo-doo] *adj.* troublesome, irksome; inconvenient; uncomfortable; *m.* annoyance, nuisance; trouble; inconvenience.
incomparável [een-kon-pă-rah'vel] *adj.* incomparable, matchless.
incompatibilidade [een-kon-pă-ti-bee-lee-dahd'] *f.* incompatibility.
incompatível [een-kon-pă-tee'vel] *adj.* incompatible, uncongenial; discordant.
incompetência [een-kon-pĕ-ten'see-ă] *f.* incompetence.
incompetente [een-kon-pĕ-tent'] *adj.* incompetent, incapable; unfitted.
incompleto [een-kon-ple'too] *adj.* incomplete; unfinished; defective.
incompreensível [een-kon-pree-en-see'vel] *adj.* incomprehensible.
incomunicável [een-koo-moo-nee-kah'vel] *adj.* incommunicable; incommunicado (of prisoners); unsociable.
inconcebível [een-kon-sĕ-bee'vel] *adj.* inconceivable.
inconciliável [een-kon-see-lee-ah'vel] *adj.* irreconcilable, incompatible.
inconcludente [een-kon-kloo-dent'] *adj.* inconclusive.
inconcusso [een-kon-koo'soo] *adj.* firm, unshakable.
incondicional [een-kon-dee-see-oo-nal'] *adj.* unconditional.
inconfesso [een-kon-fe'soo] *adj.* unconfessed; without having made one's confession; unrevealed.
inconfidência [een-kon-fee-den'see-ă] *f.* disloyalty, treason; abuse of confidence, breach of trust, perfidy.
inconfundível [een-kon-foon dee'vel] *adj.* unmistakable distinct.
incongruente [een-kon-groo-ent'] *adj.* incongruous; inconsistent with.
inconsciente [een-konsh-see-ent'] *adj.* unconscious; unaware of; unwitting.
inconsequente [een-kon-sĕ-kwent'] *adj.* inconsistent; irrelevant; inconsequent.
inconsiderado [een-kon-see-dĕ-rah'doo] *adj.* thoughtless, inconsiderate.
inconsistente [een-kon-seesh-tent'] *adj.* inconsistent; unstable, inconstant.
inconsolável [een-kon-soo-lah'vel] *adj.* inconsolable.
inconstante [een-konsh-tant'] *adj.* changeable, fickle, variable, inconstant.
incontestável [een-kon-tĕsh-tah'vel] *adj.* indisputable, unquestionable, incontestable.
incontinente [een-kon-tee-nent'] *adj.* incontinent; licentious; unrestrained.

inconveniência [een-kon-vě-nee-en'see-ă] *f.* impropriety, improper act *or* expression.
inconveniente [een-kon-vě-nee-ent'] *adj.* improper, rude, unseemly; *m.* difficulty, obstacle; inconvenience; drawback.
incorporar [een-koor-poo-rar'] *va.* to incorporate; *vr.* to join.
incorrecção [een-koo-re-sown'] *f.* inaccuracy; impropriety.
incorrecto [een-koo-re'too] *adj.* incorrect, faulty.
incorrer [een-koo-rayr'] *vn.* to incur, fall into.
incorrigível [een-koo-ri-zhee'vel] *adj.* incorrigible.
incorruptível [een-koo-roo-tee'vel] *adj.* incorruptible.
incredulidade [een-krě-doo-lee-dahd'] *f.* incredulity, unbelief.
incrédulo [een-kre'doo-loo] *adj.* incredulous, disbelieving; *m.* unbeliever, sceptic.
incremento [een-krě-men'-too] *m.* increase; development.
increpar [een-krě-par'] *va.* to rebuke, denounce.
incrível [een-kree'vel] *adj.* incredible, hard to believe; amazing.
incubar [een-koo-bar'] *va.* to incubate, hatch.
inculcar [een-kool-kar'] *va.* to point out, indicate; to inculcate, impress on; *vr.* to push oneself forward, make oneself prominent.
inculpado [een-kool-pah'doo] *adj.* blameless, innocent; inculpated, accused.
inculpar [een-kool-par'] *va.* to accuse; to blame.
inculto [een-kool'too] *adj.* uncultivated (land); uneducated; uncouth.
incumbir [een-koon-beer'] *va/vn.* to charge, entrust (with a task); *vr.* to undertake, take upon oneself.
incurável [een-koo-rah'vel] *adj.* incurable.
incúria [een-koo'ree-ă] *f.* carelessness, negligence.
incursão [een-koor-sown'] *f.* incursion, raid, attack.
incutir [een-koo-teer'] *va.* to instil, inculcate.
indagação [een-dă-gă-sown'] *f.* investigation, inquiry, search.
indagar [een-dă-gar'] *va.* to investigate, examine, inquire into.
indecente [een-dě-sent'] *adj.* indecent, obscene, shameless.
indeciso [een-dě-see'zoo] *adj.* undecided; vague, uncertain.
indefectível [een-dě-fek-tee'-vel] *adj.* unfailing.
indefenso [een-dě-fen'soo] *adj.* defenceless, unprotected.
indeferido [een-dě-fě-ree'doo] *adj.* rejected, refused.
indefesso [een-dě-fe'soo] *adj.* indefatigable, tireless.
indefinido [een-dě-fi-nee'-doo] *adj.* indefinite, vague, undefined.
indelével [een-dě-le'vel] *adj.* indelible.
indelicado [een-dě-lee-kah'-doo] *adj.* indelicate, coarse.
indemnização [een-dem-nee-ză-sown'] *f.* indemnity, compensation.
indemnizar [een-dem-nee-zar'] *va.* to compensate, indemnify.
independência [een-dě-pen-den'see-ă] *f.* independence.
independente [een-dě-pen-dent'] *adj.* independent, free.
indicação [een-dee-kă-sown'] *f.* indication, evidence, sign, hint.
indicar [een-dee-kar'] *va.* to point out; to indicate, hint.

índice [een'dees] *m.* index; table of contents.
indício [een-dee'see-oo] *m.* sign, indication; clue.
indiferença [een-dee-fĕ-ren'-să] *f.* indifference; unconcern; apathy.
indiferente [een-dee-fĕ-rent'] *adj.* indifferent; unconcerned; é-me —, I don't mind.
indígena [een-dee'zhĕ-nă] *mf.* native; *adj.* indigenous, native.
indigência [een-dee-zhen'see-ă] *f.* poverty, penury, destitution.
indigestão [een-dee-zhĕsh-town'] *f.* indigestion.
indigesto [een-dee-zhesh'too] *adj.* indigestible; undigested; (*fig.*) confused, badly arranged.
indignação [een-deeg-nă-sown'] *f.* indignation; anger, resentment.
indignado [een-deeg-nah'doo] *adj.* indignant; angry.
indignar [een-deeg-nar'] *va.* to anger, provoke, shock, incense; *vr.* to resent, be indignant at.
indignidade [een-deeg-nee-dahd'] *f.* insult, indignity.
indigno [een-deeg'noo] *adj.* unworthy; disgraceful, mean, despicable.
índio [een'dee-oo] *m/adj.* Indian.
indirecto [een-dee-re'too] *adj.* indirect; implied (attitude, etc.); round-about (procedure).
indiscreto [een-dish-kre'too] *adj.* indiscreet, injudicious, foolish, unwise.
indiscrição [een-dish-kree-sown'] *f.* lack of discretion; tactlessness; cometer uma —, to make a blunder.
indiscutível [een-dish-koo-tee'vel] *adj.* indisputable, undeniable.
indispensável [een-dish-pen-sah'vel] *adj.* indispensable, essential, vital, necessary.
indisponível [een-dish-poo-nee'vel] *adj.* unavailable; inalienable.
indispor [een-dish-pohr'] *va.* to upset, irritate; to set (somebody) at variance with; *vr.* to fall out with (somebody).
indisposição [een-dish-poo-zee-sown'] *f.* indisposition, slight ailment; annoyance.
indisposto [een-dish-pohsh'-too] *adj.* indisposed, ill, out of sorts; reluctant, unwilling; ill-disposed.
indistinto [een-dish-teen'too] *adj.* indistinct, vague, obscure.
individual [een-di-vee-doo-al'] *adj.* individual, particular.
indivíduo [een-di-vee'doo-oo] *m.* individual; person; (*pop.*) fellow, chap.
indiviso [een-di-vee'zoo] *adj.* undivided.
indizível [een-di-zee'vel] *adj.* unspeakable, unutterable.
indócil [een-do'seel] *adj.* unruly, unmanageable.
índole [een'dool] *f.* temperament, character, disposition, nature, inclination, bent.
indolência [een-doo-len'see-ă] *f.* indolence, idleness, laziness.
indomável [een-doo-mah'vel] *adj.* indomitable, invincible; untameable.
indómito [een-do'mee-too] *adj.* wild, untamed, unbroken; unconquerable.
indulgência [een-dool-zhen'-see-ă] *f.* forbearance, leniency, indulgence.
indulto [een-dool'too] *m.* dispensation (*eccl.*); pardon, amnesty; special favour.
indumento [een-doo-men'too] *m.* dress, costume, attire; outer covering, integument.
indústria [een-doosh'tree-ă] *f.*

industry; work, toil, diligence; cavalheiro de —, trickster.
industrioso [een-doosh-tree-oh'zoo] *adj.* industrious; skilful.
induzir [een-doo-zeer'] *va.* to induce, persuade; to cause; to lead (into error).
inédito [ee-ne'dee-too] *adj.* unpublished, unknown; inedited.
inefável [ee-nĕ-fah'vel] *adj.* ineffable, indescribable.
ineficaz [ee-nĕ-fee-kash'] *adj.* ineffective, useless, unavailing.
inegável [ee-nĕ-gah'vel] *adj.* undeniable.
inelutável [ee-nĕ-loo-tah'vel] *adj.* unavoidable, inevitable.
inépcia [ee-nep'see-ă] *f.* ineptitude, folly, stupidity.
inepto [ee-nep'too] *adj.* inept, clumsy; stupid.
inequívoco [ee-nĕ-kee'voo-koo] *adj.* clear, straightforward, unmistakable.
inércia [ee-nair'see-ă] *f.* inertia; sluggishness, inactivity.
inerente [ee-nĕ-re*n*t'] *adj.* inherent.
inerme [ee-nairm'] *adj.* defenceless, unarmed.
inerte [ee-nairt'] *adj.* inert; inactive; torpid, sluggish.
inesgotável [ee-nĕzh-goo-tah'vel] *adj.* inexhaustible, boundless, abundant.
inesperado [ee-nĕsh-pĕ-rah'doo] *adj.* unexpected.
inesquecível [ee-nesh-ke-see'vel] *adj.* unforgettable.
inevitável [ee-nĕ-vee-tah'vel] *adj.* inevitable, unavoidable.
inexactidão [ee-nĕ-zah-tee-dow*n*'] *f.* inaccuracy.
inexpugnável [ee-nĕsh-poog-nah'vel] *adj.* impregnable; stubborn, invincible.
infalível [ee*n*-fă-lee'vel] *adj.* infallible; inevitable.
infamar [ee*n*-fă-mar'] *va.* to libel, slander, defame.
infame [ee*n*-fahm'] *adj.* infamous, vile, despicable.
infâmia [ee*n*-fă'mee-ă] *f.* dishonour, infamy; infamous (disgraceful) action.
infância [ee*n*-fa*n*'see-ă] *f.* infancy; childhood.
infantaria [ee*n*-fa*n*-tă-ree'ă] *f.* infantry.
infante [ee*n*-fa*n*t'] *m.* prince; infant, baby; foot-soldier.
infatigável [ee*n*-fă-tee-gah'vel] *adj.* indefatigable.
infausto [ee*n*-fowsh'too] *adj.* unfortunate, unlucky, ill-omened.
infecção [ee*n*-fe-sow*n*'] *f.* infection; contamination.
infectar [ee*n*-fek-tar'] *va.* to infect, pollute, contaminate.
infelicidade [ee*n*-fĕ-lee-see-dahd'] *f.* unhappiness, misery, distress; misfortune.
infeliz [ee*n*-fĕ-leesh'] *adj.* unhappy, wretched; unfortunate; unlucky.
inferior [ee*n*-fĕ-ree-ohr'] *adj.* inferior; subordinate; lower.
inferioridade [ee*n*-fĕ-ree-oo-ree-dahd'] *f.* inferiority.
inferir [ee*n*-fĕ-reer'] *va.* to infer, deduce.
inferno [ee*n*-fair'noo] *m.* hell.
infestar [ee*n*-fesh-tar'] *va.* to infest.
inficionar [ee*n*-fee-see-oo-nar'] *va.* to contaminate, corrupt, infect.
infidelidade [ee*n*-fee-dĕ-lee-dahd'] *f.* infidelity, faithlessness; disbelief.
infiel [ee*n*-fee-el'] *adj.* unfaithful, disloyal; *m.* unbeliever, infidel.
ínfimo [ee*n*'fee-moo] *adj.* lowest; meanest, worst.
infinidade [ee*n*-fi-nee-dahd'] *f.* infinity; endless number.

infinito [een-fi-nee'too] *adj.* infinite, endless; *m.* infinite.
inflação [een-flă-sown'] *f.* inflation; swelling; pomposity.
inflamar [een-flă-mar'] *va.* to inflame, set on fire.
inflar [een-flar'] *va.* to inflate, blow up; to make conceited.
inflexível [een-flek-see'vel] *adj.* inflexible, rigid, unbending.
infligir [een-flee-zheer'] *va.* to inflict, impose (punishment).
influência [een-floo-en'see-ă] *f.* influence.
influenciar [een-floo-en-see-ar'] *va.* to influence.
influente [een-floo-ent'] *adj.* influential.
influir [een-floo-eer'] *va.* to induce, inspire, infuse; *vn.* to influence.
influxo [een-flook'soo] *m.* influx, inflow; influence.
informação [een-foor-mă-sown'] *f.* information, report, account; enquiry.
informante [een-foor-mant'] *m.* informant; informer.
informar [een-foor-mar'] *va.* to inform, tell, report; *vr.* to enquire about.
informe [een-form'] *adj.* shapeless; misshapen; *m.* report, statement.
infortúnio [een-foor-too'nee-oo] *m.* misfortune.
infracção [een-frah-sown'] *f.* breach, infringement.
infringir [een-freen-zheer'] *va.* to break, infringe (a law, etc.).
infrutuoso [een-froo-too-oh'zoo] *adj.* fruitless, unfruitful; vain, useless.
infundado [een-foon-dah'doo] *adj.* baseless, unfounded.
infundir [een-foon-deer'] *va.* to infuse, instil in; to steep, soak.
ingente [een-zhent'] *adj* (*poet.*) tremendous, enormous, prodigious.
ingenuidade [een-zhĕ-noo-ee-dahd'] *f.* innocence, candour, frankness; simplicity, naïvety, ingenuousness.
ingénuo [een-zhe'noo-oo] *adj.* open, unsophisticated, simple, ingenuous, naïve.
ingerência [een-zhĕ-ren'see-ă] *f.* interference; intervention.
ingerir [een-zhĕ-reer'] *va.* to swallow; *vr.* to interfere in.
inglês [een-glaysh'] *adj.* English; *m.* Englishman; English (language).
ingratidão [een-gră-tee-down'] *f.* ingratitude.
ingrato [een-grah'too] *adj* ungrateful; unpleasant, disagreeable; barren (soil, subject, etc.).
ingrediente[een-grĕ-dee-ent'] *m.* ingredient.
íngreme [een'grĕm] *adj.* steep.
ingressar [een-grĕ-sar'] *vn.* to enter, join (a society, group, etc.).
ingresso [een-gre'soo] *m.* entry, entrance; right of entrance.
inhame [ee-nyăm'] *m.* yam.
inibir [ee-ni-beer'] *va.* to forbid; to inhibit, restrain.
inicial [ee-nee-see-al'] *adj* original, first, initial; *f.* initial (letter).
iniciar [ee-nee-see-ar'] *va* to begin, start, inaugurate; to initiate.
iniciativa [ee-nee-see-ă-tee'vă] *f.* initiative.
inimigo [ee-ni-mee'goo] *m.* enemy; *adj.* enemy, hostile.
inimizade [ee-ni-mee-zahd'] *f.* enmity, hatred.
iníquo [ee-nee'kwoo] *adj.* iniquitous, wicked, unjust.

injecção [een-zhe-sown'] *f.* injection.
injectado [een-zhe-tah'doo] *adj.* injected; olhos —s, bloodshot eyes.
injúria [een-zhoo'ree-ă] *f.* insult, slander; abuse, curse.
injuriar [een-zhoo-ree-ar'] *va.* to curse; to slander; to insult.
injurioso [een-zhoo-ree-oh'-zoo] *adj.* insulting, offensive.
injustiça [een-zhoosh-tee'să] *f.* injustice, unfairness.
injusto [een-zhoosh'too] *adj.* unjust, unfair.
inocência [ee-noo-sen'see-ă] *f.* innocence; simplicity.
inocente [ee-noo-sent'] *adj.* innocent, blameless; harmless; simple. [to inoculate.
inocular [ee-noo-koo-lar'] *va.*
inofensivo [ee-noo-fen-see'-voo] *adj.* inoffensive; harmless.
inópia [ee-no'pee-ă] *f.* poverty, penury, indigence.
inoportuno [ee-noo-poor-too'-noo] *adj.* inopportune, inconvenient.
inóspito [ee-nosh'pee-too] *adj.* inhospitable.
inovação [ee-noo-vă-sown'] *f.* innovation.
inquebrantável [een-kĕ-bran-tah'vel] *adj.* unyielding, inflexible, unbreakable.
inquérito [een-ke'ree-too] *m.* inquiry, investigation; inquest.
inquietação [een-kee-e-tă-sown'] *f.* unrest, restlessness; disquiet, uneasiness.
inquietar [een-kee-e-tar'] *va.* to disturb, upset, trouble; *vr.* to worry.
inquieto [een-kee-e'too] *adj.* anxious, worried; restless, turbulent. [tenant.
inquilino [een-ki-lee'noo] *m.*
inquirição [een-ki-ree-sown'] *f.* inquiry, investigation, examination, interrogation.
inquirir [een-ki-reer'] *va.* to inquire, look into, examine; to interrogate.
inquisição [een-ki-zee-zown'] *f.* inquisition (*eccl.*).
inquisidor [een-ki-zee-dohr'] *m.* inquisitor.
insaciável [een-să-see-ah'vel] *adj.* insatiable.
insalubre [een-să-loo'brĕ] *adj.* unhealthy.
insânia [een-să'nee-ă] *f.* madness, insanity, folly.
inscrever [eensh-krĕ-vayr'] *va.* to inscribe; to register, note down; *vr.* to enrol, register, put one's name down (in a list).
inscrição [eensh-kree-sown'] *f.* inscription; registration.
insecticida [een-sek-ti-see'-dă] *m.* insecticide. [sect.
insecto [een-sek'too] *m.* in-
insegurança [een-sĕ-goo-ran'să] *f.* insecurity.
insensatez [een-sen-să-taysh'] *f.* stupidity, foolishness.
insensato [een-sen-sah'too] *adj.* stupid, crazy, foolish.
insensibilidade [een-sen-si-bee-lee-dahd'] *f.* insensibility; insensitiveness, callousness.
insensível [een-sen-see'vel] *adj.* insensible, unconscious; insensitive, unresponsive.
inseparável [een-sĕ-pă-rah'-vel] *adj.* inseparable.
inserir [een-sĕ-reer'] *va.* to insert, introduce.
insidioso [een-see-dee-oh'zoo] *adj.* insidious, sly, wily.
insigne [een-seeg'nĕ] *adj.* eminent, distinguished.
insígnia [een-seeg'nee-ă] *f.* badge; *pl.* insignia.
insignificante [een-sig-nee-fee-kant] *adj.* insignificant.
insinuação [een-see-noo-ă-sown'] *f.* insinuation, innuendo; suggestion, hint.
insinuante [een-see-noo-ant']

adj. ingratiating; attractive, pleasant.
insinuar [een-see-noo-ar′] *va.* to insinuate, hint; *vr.* to ingratiate oneself with, worm one's way into.
insípido [een-see′pee-doo] *adj.* insipid, flat, tasteless; dull, drab.
insistir [een-sish-teer′] *vn.* to insist; to persist.
insofrido [een-soo-free′doo] *adj.* impatient, restless.
insolação [een-soo-lă-sown′] *f.* sunstroke.
insolência [een-soo-len′see-ă] *f.* insolence, impudence.
insolente [een-soo-lent′] *adj.* insolent, impudent.
insólito [een-so′lee-too] *adj.* unusual, extraordinary.
insolúvel [een-soo-loo′vel] *adj.* insoluble; inextricable.
insolvência [een-sohl-ven′-see-ă] *f.* insolvency.
insondável [een-son-dah′vel] *adj.* unfathomable.
insónia [een-so′nee-ă] *f.* insomnia.
insosso [een-soh′soo] *adj.* tasteless, insipid; unsalted.
inspecção [eensh-pe-sown′] *f.* inspection, examination, survey.
inspeccionar [eensh-pe-see-oo-nar′] *va.* to inspect, examine.
inspector [eensh-pe-tohr′] *m.* inspector; supervisor.
inspiração [eensh-pee-ră-sown′] *f.* inspiration; inhalation (*anat.*).
inspirar [eensh-pee-rar′] *va.* to inspire; to inhale (*anat.*).
instalação [eensh-tă-lă-sown′] *f.* installation; apparatus, plant, fitting, equipment.
instalar [eensh-tă-lar′] *va.* to instal; to set up; *vr.* to settle.
instância [eensh-tan′see-ă] *f.* urgent (insistent), request; (legal) proceeding; tribunal **de primeira —**, (*approx.*) court of summary jurisdiction, magistrates' court; **em última —**, in the last resort; **ceder às —s de**, to yield to the pleas of.
instantâneo [eensh-tan-tă′-nee-oo] *adj.* instantaneous; *m.* snapshot, snap (*photo.*).
instante [eensh-tant′] *m.* moment, instant; *adj.* urgent, pressing.
instar [eensh-tar′] *vn.* to insist; to be pressing (danger, etc.).
instaurar [eensh-tow-rar′] *va.* to institute, establish.
instável [eensh-tah′vel] *adj.* unstable.
instigar [eensh-tee-gar′] *va.* to instigate, provoke, urge.
instinto [eensh-teen′too] *adj.* instinct.
instituição [eensh-tee-too-ee-sown′] *f.* institution.
instituir [eensh-tee-too-eer′] *va.* to institute, establish.
instituto [eensh-tee-too′too] *m.* institute.
instrucção [eensh-troo-sown′] *f.* education, teaching, training; instruction, explanation; order, command.
instruído [eensh-troo-ee′doo] *adj.* educated, well-read.
instruir [eensh-troo-eer′] *va.* to instruct, teach; to drill (*mil.*).
instrumento [eensh-troo-men′too] *m.* instrument; tool, implement.
insubordinação [een-soo-boor-dee-nă-sown′] *f.* insubordination, mutiny (*mil.*).
insubordinar-se [een-soo-boor-dee-nar′sĕ] *vr.* to mutiny.
insuficiência [een-soo-fee-see-en′see-ă] *f.* insufficiency; inadequacy.

insuficiente [een-soo-fee-see-ent'] *adj.* insufficient, inadequate; incompetent.
insuflar [een-soo-flar'] *va.* to blow (air) into, inflate.
insulano [een-soo-lă'noo] *adj.* island, insular; *m.* islander; native of the Azores *or* Madeira.
insular [een-soo-lar'] *va.* to isolate; *adj.* insular.
insulso [een-sool'soo] *adj.* savourless, flat, insipid.
insultar [een-sool-tar'] *va.* to insult.
insulto [een-sool'too] *m.* insult; affront; — **cardíaco**, heart attack.
insuperável [een-soo-pĕ-rah'-vel] *adj.* insuperable.
insuportável [een-soo-poor-tah'vel] *adj.* intolerable, unbearable.
insurgente [een-soor-zhent'] *m/adj.* insurgent.
insurgir-se [een-soor-zheer'-sĕ] *vr.* to revolt, rebel.
insurreição [een-soo-ray-ee-sown'] *f.* rebellion, revolt, insurrection.
insuspeito [een-soosh-pay'ee-too] *adj.* unsuspected; trustworthy, reliable.
insustentável [een-soosh-ten-tah'vel] *adj.* untenable.
intacto [een-tak'too] *adj.* undamaged, unharmed; intact, whole.
intangível [een-tan-zhee'vel] *adj.* intangible.
integral [een-tĕ-gral'] *adj.* integral, total.
integrante [een-tĕ-grant'] *adj.* integral, constituent, component.
integrar [een-tĕ-grar'] *va.* to integrate.
integridade [een-tĕ-gree-dahd'] *f.* integrity; honesty.
integro [een'tĕ-groo] *adj* upright, honest; complete.
inteirar [een-tay-ee-rar'] *va.* to inform; to complete; *vr.* to get to know, find out.
inteireza [een-tay-ray'ză] *f.* entirety, integrity, probity.
inteiro [een-tay'ee-roo] *adj.* whole, entire; complete; unbroken, undamaged.
intelecto [een-tĕ-le'too] *m.* intellect, understanding.
intelectual [een-tĕ-le-too-al'] *m/adj.* intellectual.
inteligência [een-tĕ-lee-zhen'see-ă] *f.* intelligence; intellect.
inteligente [een-tĕ-lee-zhent'] *adj.* intelligent, clever.
inteligível [een-tĕ-lee-zhee'-vel] *adj.* intelligible.
intemerato [een-tĕ-mĕ-rah'-too] *adj.* unsullied, undefiled.
intemperança [een-ten-pĕ-ran'să] *f.* intemperance.
intempérie [een-ten-pair'ee-ĕ] *f.* bad weather.
intenção [een-ten-sown'] *f.* intention, purpose; **segunda** —, ulterior motive.
intencionado [een-ten-see-oo-nah'doo] *adj.* **bem** —, well disposed, well meaning.
intencional [een-ten-see-oo-nal'] *adj.* intentional, deliberate.
intendente [een-ten-dent'] *m.* manager, superintendent.
intensidade [een-ten-see-dahd'] *f.* intensity.
intenso [een-ten'soo] *adj.* intense; intensive.
intentar [een-ten-tar'] *va.* to attempt, try; — **uma acção, um processo**, to bring an action, to sue (*leg.*).
intento [een-ten'too] *m.* aim, purpose, intention.
intercalar [een-tĕr-kă-lar'] *va.* to insert, intercalate.
interceder [een-tĕr-sĕ-dayr'] *vn.* to intercede.

interceptar [een-tĕr-sep-tar'] *va.* to intercept.
intercessão [een-tĕr-se-sown'] *f.* intercession.
interdito [een-tĕr-dee'too] *adj.* forbidden, prohibited; *m.* (*eccl.*) interdict; prohibition.
interessado [een-tĕ-rĕ-sah'-doo] *m.* interested party.
interessante [een-tĕ-rĕ-sant'] *adj.* interesting; attractive.
interessar [een-tĕ-rĕ-sar'] *va.* to interest; *vr.* to take an interest in.
interesse [een-tĕ-rays'] *m.* interest; concern; benefit, advantage.
interesseiro [een-tĕ-rĕ-say'-ee-roo] *adj.* self-seeking.
interferência [een-tĕr-fĕ-ren'see-ă] *f.* interference.
interino [een-tĕ-ree'noo] *adj.* temporary, provisional, interim.
interior [een-tĕ-ree-ohr'] *adj.* interior, inside,i nner, internal; *m.* inside; interior; hinterland (*geog.*); ministro do —, Home Secretary (in U.K.); Minister for Internal Affairs.
interjeição [een-tĕr-zhay-ee-sown'] *f.* interjection.
intermediário [een-tĕr-mĕ-dee-ah'ree-oo] *m.* mediator, intermediary; middleman (*com.*).
intermédio [een-tĕr-me'dee-oo] *adj.* intermediate; *m.* mediator, intermediary; por — de, by means of, through, by, through the medium of.
interminável [een-tĕr-mee-nah'vel] *adj.* endless, interminable.
intermissão [een-tĕr-mee-sown'] *f.* interval.
intermitente [een-tĕr-mee-tent'] *adj.* intermittent.
internacional [een-tair-nă-see-oo-nal'] *adj.* international.
internado [een-tĕr-nah'doo] *m.* inmate (e.g. of a residential home); in-patient (of hospital); internee.
internar [een-tĕr-nar'] *va.* to intern; *vr.* to go deeper into, penetrate.
internato [een-tĕr-nah'too] boarding school; orphanage.
interno [een-tair'noo] *adj.* internal; inner, inside; *m.* boarder (in school); (in hospital) house-surgeon, intern (U.S.A.).
interpelar [een-tĕr-pĕ-lar'] *va.* to question, interpellate; to interrupt.
interpolar [een-tĕr-poo-lar'] *va.* to interpolate, insert.
interpor [een-tĕr-pohr'] *va/vr.* to interpose, place between, intervene.
interpretação [een-tĕr-prĕ-tă-sown'] *f.* interpretation, explanation, elucidation.
interpretar [een-tĕr-prĕ-tar'] *va.* to interpret.
intérprete [een-tair'prĕt] *m.* interpreter.
interrogação [een-tĕ-roo-gă-sown'] *f.* interrogation; ponto de —, question mark.
interrogar [een-tĕ-roo-gar'] *va.* to interrogate, question.
interromper [een-tĕ-ron-payr'] *va.* to interrupt, break off, stop; to break in on.
interrupção [een-tĕ-roop-sown'] *f.* interruption; stoppage.
interruptor [een-tĕ-roop-tohr'] *m.* switch (*elect.*); interrupter.
intersecção [een-tĕr-sek-sown'] *f.* intersection.
interstício [een-tĕrsh-tee'see-oo] *m.* interstice, crack.
interurbano [een-tĕr-oor-bă'noo] *m.* trunks, long dis-

tance telephone; *adj.* interurban. [interval.
intervalo [een-těr-va'loo] *m.*
intervir [een-těr-veer'] *vn.* to intervene; to participate in.
intestado [een-těsh-tah'doo] *adj.* intestate.
intestino [een-těsh-tee'noo] *m.* intestine.
intimar [een-tee-mar'] *va.* to notify; to summon (*leg.*); to order, require, enjoin.
intimidade [een-ti-mee-dahd'] *f.* close acquaintance, friendship, intimacy.
intimidar [een-ti-mee-dar'] *va.* to intimidate, overawe.
íntimo [een'tee-moo] *adj.* innermost, inmost (feelings, etc.); intimate, close (friendship, link, etc.); private (life, etc.); *m.* intimate (close) friend; no —, at heart.
intitular [een-tee-too-lar'] *va.* to entitle.
intolerância [een-too-lě-ran'-see-ă] *f.* intolerance.
intolerável [een-too-lě-rah'-vel] *adj.* intolerable.
intoxicação [een-tok-see-kă-sown'] *f.* poisoning.
intraduzível [een-tră-doo-zee'vel] *adj.* untranslatable.
intransigência [een-tran-zee-zhen'see-ă] *f.* inflexibility; intolerance.
intransigente [een-tran-zee-zhent'] *adj.* intransigent, uncompromising, intolerant.
intransitável [een-tran-zee-tah'vel] *adj.* impassable.
intransmissível [een-tranzh-mi-see'vel] *adj.* non-transferable.
intratável [een-tră-tah'vel] *adj.* intractable, unapproachable, difficult, unsociable.
intrepidez [een-trě-pee-daysh'] *f.* boldness, courage, fearlessness.
intrépido [een-tre'pee-doo] *adj.* intrepid, dauntless, daring.
intriga [een-tree'gă] *f.* plot, intrigue.
intrigar [een-tree-gar'] *va.* to embroil (in a plot); to intrigue, rouse the curiosity of; *vn.* to plot, intrigue.
intrincado [een-treen-kah'-doo] *adj.* intricate.
intrínseco [een-treen'zě-koo] *adj.* intrinsic.
introdução [een-troo-doo-sown'] *f.* introduction.
introduzir [een-troo-doo-zeer'] *va.* to introduce, bring in; *vr.* to get in(to); to penetrate.
intrometer [een-troo-mě-tayr'] *va.* to insert; *vr.* to interfere, meddle in.
intrometido [een-troo-mě-tee'doo] *adj.* interfering, meddlesome, (*pop.*) nosey; *m.* busybody, (*pop.*) nosey-parker.
intrujão [een-troo-zhown'] *m.* trickster.
intrujar [een-troo-zhar'] *va.* to trick, take in, swindle.
intruso [een-troo'zoo] *m.* intruder; outsider; *adj.* intrusive.
intuição [een-too-ee-sown'] *f.* intuition.
intuito [een-twee'too] *m.* aim, purpose, intention.
inumano [ee-noo-mă'noo] *adj.* inhuman, cruel.
inumerável [ee-noo-mě-rah'-vel] *adj.* innumerable, countless.
inundação [ee-noon-dă-sown'] *f.* flood, inundation.
inundar [ee-noon-dar'] *va.* to flood, inundate, deluge.
inútil [ee-noo'teel] *adj.* useless.
inutilidade [ee-noo-ti-lee-dahd'] *f.* uselessness.
inutilizar [ee-noo-ti-lee-zar'] *va.* to make useless; to incapa-

citate; to put out of action; to invalidate, cancel.
invadir [een-vă-deer'] *va.* to invade.
inválido [een-va'lee-doo] *adj.* invalid, sick, disabled; not valid.
invariável [een-vă-ree-ah'-vel] *adj.* invariable, unchanging.
invasão [een-vă-zown'] *f.* invasion.
invasor [een-vă-zohr'] *m.* invader.
invectiva [een-ve-tee'vă] *f.* invective.
inveja [een-ve'zhă] *f.* envy, jealousy.
invejar [een-vĕ-zhar'] *va.* to envy; to grudge.
invejoso [een-vĕ-zhoh'zoo] *adj.* envious.
invenção [een-ven-sown'] *f.* invention; contrivance, device; (inventive *or* imaginative) power, force.
invencível [een-ven-see'vel] *adj.* invincible, unconquerable.
inventar [een-ven-tar'] *va.* to invent; to devise; to fabricate.
inventariar [een-ven-tă-ree-ar'] *va.* to list, catalogue, make an inventory of.
inventário [een-ven-tah'ree-oo] *m.* inventory.
inventiva [een-ven-tee'vă] *f.* inventiveness.
inventor [een-ven-tohr'] *m.* inventor.
inverno [een-vair'noo] *m.* winter.
inverosímil [een-vĕ-roo-zee'-meel] *adj.* unlikely, improbable.
inversão [een-vĕr-sown'] *f.* reversal; inversion.
inverso [een-vair'soo] *m/adj.* inverse; reverse; ao — de, contrary to.
inverter [een-vĕr-tayr'] *va.* to reverse; to turn upside down, invert; to invest (money).
invés [een-vesh'] *m.* wrong side; ao —, on the contrary.
investigação [een-vĕsh-tee-gă-sown'] *f.* investigation.
investigar [een-vĕsh-tee-gar'] *va.* to investigate, look into.
investir [een-vĕsh-teer'] *va.* to attack, assault; to invest (with authority, etc.; money).
inveterado [een-vĕ-tĕ-rah'-doo] *adj.* inveterate, persistent.
invicto [een-veek'too] *adj.* unconquered, unvanquished.
inviolável [een-vee-oo-lah'vel] *adj.* inviolable.
invisível [een-vi-zee'vel] *adj.* invisible.
invocar [een-voo-kar'] *va.* to invoke, implore, call on.
invólucro [een-vo'loo-kroo] *m.* covering, envelope, wrapper, case.
involuntário [een-voo-loon-tah'ree-oo] *adj.* involuntary, unintentional; unwilling.
invulnerável [een-vool-nĕ-rah'vel] *adj.* invulnerable.
iodo [ee-o'doo] *m.* iodine.
ir [eer] *vn.* to go; to proceed; to travel; — **a pé**, to walk; — **a cavalo**, to ride; — **buscar**, to fetch; — **de carro**, to go by car; *vr.*—**(embora)**, to go away, off.
ira [ee'ră] *f.* anger, fury, wrath.
iracundo [ee-ră-koon'doo] *adj.* irritable, irascible; angry.
íris [ee'reesh] *m.* iris (*bot.*, *anat.*); arco —, rainbow.
irlandês [eer-lan-daysh'] *adj.* Irish; *m.* Irishman.
irmã [eer-man'] *f.* sister.
irmanar [eer-mă-nar'] *va.* to link together, pair.
irmandade [eer-man-dahd'] *f.* brotherhood, fraternity; friendship.
irmão [eer-mown'] *m.* brother; — **de leite**, — **colaço**, foster brother; — **consanguíneo**, half-brother.

ironia [ee-roo-nee'ă] *f.* irony.
irónico [ee-ro'nee-koo] *adj.* ironical.
irra [ee'ră] *interj.* damn!
irracional [ee-ră-see-oo-nal'] *adj.* irrational.
irreflexão [ee-rě-fle-sow*n*'] *f.* rashness, thoughtlessness.
irrefragável [ee-rě-fră-gah'-vel] *adj.* irrefutable, undeniable.
irregular [ee-rě-goo-lar'] *adj.* [irregular.
irremediável [ee-rě-mě-dee-ah'vel] *adj.* irremediable, irreparable.
irremissível [ee-rě-mi-see'-vel] *adj.* unpardonable.
irreparável [ee-rě-pă-rah'vel] *adj.* irreparable.
irrequieto [ee-rě-kee-e'too] *adj.* restless; fidgety.
irresistível [ee-rě-zish-tee'-vel] *adj.* irresistible.
irresoluto [ee-rě-zoo-loo'too] *adj.* hesitant, undecided, irresolute.
irresponsável [ee-rěsh-po*n*-sah'vel] *adj.* irresponsible.
irrigar [ee-ree-gar'] *va.* to irrigate, water.
irrisório [ee-ree-zo'ree-oo] *adj.* ridiculous, ludicrous, derisive.
irritação [ee-ree-tă-sow*n*'] *f.* irritation; exasperation.
irritar [ee-ree-tar'] *va.* to irritate, annoy, anger; *vr.* to get angry, annoyed.
irrupção [ee-roop-sow*n*'] *f.* irruption; incursion, raid.
isca [eesh'kă] *f.* bait; fried liver.
isenção [ee-ze*n*-sow*n*'] *f.* exemption; independence; disinterestedness.
isentar [ee-ze*n*-tar'] *va.* to exempt, free from.
isento [ee-ze*n*'too] *adj.* exempt, free from.
isolamento [ee-zoo-lă-me*n*'too] *m.* isolation; insulation (*elect.*).
isolar [ee-zoo-lar'] *va.* to isolate; to insulate (*elect.*).
isqueiro [ish-kay'ee-roo] *m.* cigarette lighter.
istmo [eesht'moo] *m.* isthmus.
italiano [ee-tă-lee-ă'noo] *m/adj.* Italian.
itálico [ee-ta'lee-koo] *m.* italics (*print.*).
iterar [ee-tě-rar'] *va.* to repeat.
itinerário [ee-tee-ně-rah'ree-oo] *m.* itinerary, route; guidebook.

J

já [zhah] *adv.* already; now; immediately; — **não**, no longer; **desde** —, immediately, straightaway, right now; — **que**, now that, seeing that; — **se vê**, of course, naturally; **até** —, cheerio!, good-bye!, see you soon!; — **esteve em . . .?** have you ever been in . . .?
jacaré [zhă-kă-re'] *m.* alligator.
jacente [zhă-se*n*t'] *adj.* lying, situated; *m.* girder (of bridge); *m.pl.* shoals, shallows.
jacinto [zhă-see*n*'too] *m.* hyacinth.
jactância [zhăk-ta*n*'see-ă] *f.* boasting, bragging; conceit.
jactar-se [zhăk-tar'sě] *vr.* to boast, brag (about).
jacto [zhak'too] *m.* jet, stream, gush; (**avião de**) —, jet (plane).
jaez [zhă-aysh'] *m.* harness, trappings; (*fig.*) kind, sort.
jaguar [zhă-gwar'] *m.* jaguar.
jaleco [zhă-le'koo] *m.* jacket.
jamais [zhah-mȳsh'] *adv.* never; ever, at any time.
janeiras [zhă-nay'ee-răsh] *f. pl.* New Year's gifts *or* carols.
janeiro [zhă-nay'ee-roo] *m.* January.

janela [zhă-ne'lă] *f.* window.
jangada [zhan-gah'dă] *f.* raft.
janota [zhă-no'tă] *m.* dandy, swell, (*sl.*) toff.
jantar [zhan-tar'] *m.* dinner; *vn.* to dine, have dinner.
japonês [zhă-poo-naysh'] *m/adj.* Japanese.
jaqueta [zhă-kay'tă] *f.* jacket.
jardim [zhăr-deen'] *m.* garden; — zoológico, zoo.
jardineiro [zhăr-dee-nay'ee-roo] *m.* gardener.
jarra [zha'ră] *f.* vase (for flowers).
jarretar [zhă-rĕ-tar'] *va.* to hamstring, cripple.
jarro [zha'roo] *m.* jar, pot, jug (for water); arum lily (*bot.*).
jasmim [zhăzh-meen'] *m.* jasmine.
jaula [zhow'lă] *f.* cage.
javali [zhă-vă-lee'] *m.* wild boar.
jazer [zhă-zayr'] *vn.* to lie.
jazigo [zhă-zee'goo] *m.* tomb, grave, resting place; field, deposit (*min.*).
jeito [zhay'ee-too] *m.* skill, knack, flair, aptitude; appearance; habit; way, manner.
jeitoso [zhay-ee-toh'zoo] *adj.* handy, skilful.
jejuar [zhĕ-zhoo-ar'] *vn.* to fast.
jejum [zhĕ-zhoon'] *m.* fast, fasting.
jerarquia [zhĕ-rar-kee'ă] *f.* class, hierarchy.
jesuíta [zhĕ-zoo-ee'tă] *m.* Jesuit; intriguer, crafty fellow; hypocrite.
jibóia [zhee-boy'ă] *f.* boa constrictor.
joalharia [zhoo-ă-lyă-ree'ă] *f.* jeweller's (shop); jewellery.
jocoso [zhoo-koh'zoo] *adj.* jocular, humorous, cheerful.
joeira [zhoo-ay'ee-ră] *f.* sieve, riddle.
joelho [zhoo-ay'lyoo] *m.* knee; de —s, kneeling.
jogador [zhoo-gă-dohr'] *m.* player; gambler.
jogar [zhoo-gar'] *va.* to play; to gamble.
jogo [zhoh'goo] *m.* game; play; gambling; movement (*mech.*); — franco, fair play; — de palavras, play on words.
joguete [zhoo-gayt'] *m.* plaything; dupe; laughing-stock.
jóia [zhoy'ă] *f.* jewel, gem.
jornada [zhoor-nah'dă] *f.* (day) trip; journey.
jornal [zhoor-nal'] *m.* newspaper; daily wage.
jornaleiro [zhoor-nă-lay'ee-roo] *m.* day-labourer.
jornalista [zhoor-nă-leesh'tă] *m.* journalist.
jorrar [zhoo-rar'] *vn.* to spurt out, gush, flow; to jut out, bulge.
jorro [zhoh'roo] *m.* torrent, flood, rush.
jovem [zho'ven] *adj.* young; *m.* young man, youth; *f.* girl, young lady.
jovial [zhoo-vee-al'] *adj.* jovial, cheerful, jolly.
juba [zhoo'bă] *f.* mane.
jubilação [zhoo-bee-lă-sown'] *f.* retirement (on pension); jubilation, rejoicing.
júbilo [zhoo'bee-loo] *m.* joy, rejoicing, jubilation.
judeu [zhoo-day'oo] *adj.* Jewish; *m.* Jew.
judia [zhoo-dee'ă] *f.* Jewish woman, Jewess.
judiaria[zhoo-dee-ă-ree'ă] *f.* ghetto.
judicatura [zhoo-dee-kă-too'ră] *f.* judicature.
judicial [zhoo-dee-see-al'] *adj.* judicial, legal.
judicioso [zhoo-dee-see-oh'zoo] *adj.* judicious, wise.
jugo [zhoo'goo] *m.* yoke.

juiz [zhoo-eesh'] *m.* judge, magistrate.
juízo [zhoo-ee'zoo] *m.* judgement; (common)sense, intelligence; opinion.
julgamento [zhool-gă-me*n*'too] *m.* judgement, sentence; trial.
julgar [zhool-gar'] *va.* to judge; to deliver judgement on; to think, believe.
julho [zhoo'lyoo] *m.* July.
jumento [zhoo-me*n*'too] *m.* ass, donkey.
junco [zhoo*n*'koo] *m.* rush; junk (Chinese ship).
jungir [zhoo*n*-zheer'] *va.* to yoke.
junho [zhoo'nyoo] *m.* June.
júnior [zhoo'nee-or] *adj.* junior.
junta [zhoo*n*'tă]. *f.* council, board, assembly; joint (*anat.*); yoke of oxen; junction.
juntar [zhoo*n*-tar'] *va.* to join, fasten together.
junto [zhoo*n*'too] *adj.* joined, united; — **de, a,** near, adjoining.
juntura [zhoo*n*-too'ră] *f.* [joint; juncture.
jurado [zhoo-rah'doo] *m.* juror, member of a jury, juryman; inimigo —, sworn enemy.
juramento [zhoo-ră-me*n*'too] *m.* oath.
jurar [zhoo-rar'] *va*/*vn.* to swear, take an oath, vow; to curse.
júri [zhoo'ree] *m.* jury; (board of) adjudicators.
jurídico [zhoo-ree'dee-koo] *adj.* legal, juridical, judicial.
jurisconsulto [zhoo-reesh-ko*n*-sool'too] *m.* jurist.
jurisdição [zhoo-reezh-dee-sow*n*'] *f.* jurisdiction, authority.
jurisprudência [zhoo-reesh-proo-de*n*'see-ă] *f.* jurisprudence, law.
jurista [zhoo-reesh'tă] *m.* jurist; money-lender.
juro [zhoo'roo] *m.* interest (on money).
justeza [zhoosh-tay'ză] *f.* exactness, correctness.
justiça [zhoosh-tee'să] *f.* justice; fairness.
justiçar [zhoosh-tee-sar'] *va.* to execute.
justiceiro [zhoosh-tee-say'ee-roo] *m.* just, impartial; inflexible, severe.
justificação [zhoosh-tee-fee-kă-sow*n*'] *f.* justification.
justificar [zhoosh-tee-fee-kar'] *va.* to justify; *vr.* to vindicate oneself.
justo [zhoosh'too] *adj.* just, fair; exact, accurate; tight.
juvenil [zhoo-vĕ-neel'] *adj.* juvenile, youthful.
juventude [zhoo-ve*n*-tood'] *f.* youth; young people.

L

lá [lah] *adv.* there, in that place.
lã [la*n*] *f.* wool.
labareda [lă-bă-ray'dă] *f.* flame, blaze.
labéu [lă-be'oo] *m.* blot, stain, disgrace.
lábio [lah'bee-oo] *m.* lip.
labirinto [lă-bĕ-ree*n*'too] *m.* labyrinth, maze.
laboratório [lă-boo-ră-to'ree-oo] *m.* laboratory.
laborioso [lă-boo-ree-oh'zoo] *adj.* hard-working; laborious.
labrego [lă-bray'goo] *adj.* rustic; uncouth; *m.* lout, yokel, country bumpkin.
labuta [lă-boo'tă] *f.* toil, hard work, drudgery.
labutar [lă-boo-tar'] *vn.* to toil, work hard.
laca [lah'kă] *f.* lacquer.
lacaio [lă-kȳ'oo] *m.* lackey, footman.

laço [lah'soo] *m.* bow, knot; noose, snare; **—s de amizade,** ties of friendship.
lacónico [lă-ko'nee-koo] *adj.* laconic, terse; brief.
lacrar [lă-krar'] *va.* to seal.
lacre [lak'rĕ] *m.* sealing-wax.
lacrimoso [lă-kree-moh'zoo] *adj.* tearful, lachrymose.
lácteo [lak'tee-oo] *adj.* milky; **via —a,** Milky Way.
lacticínio [lăk-ti-see'nee-oo] *m.* milk product, milk food *or* preparation.
lacuna [lă-koo'nă] *f.* gap, omission, lacuna.
ladainha [lă-dă-ee'nyă] *f.* litany; (*fig.*) rigmarole; (long, tiresome) tale, yarn.
ladear [lă-dee-ar'] *va.* to flank; to stand beside; to accompany; to evade.
ladeira [lă-day'ee-ră] *f.* slope; hillside.
ladino [lă-dee'noo] *adj.* crafty, wily, sly; sharp, clever.
lado [lah'doo] *m.* side; direction, way; **ao — de,** beside, next to; **por outro —,** on the other hand.
ladrão [lă-drown'] *m.* thief, robber.
ladrar [lă-drar'] *vn.* to bark.
ladrilho [lă-dree'lyoo] *m.* tile; brick.
lagar [lă-gar'] *m.* wine press; olive press.
lagarto [lă-gar'too] *m.* lizard.
lago [lah'goo] *m.* lake.
lagoa [lă-goh'ă] *f.* (small) lake, tarn; lagoon, pool.
lagosta [lă-gohsh'tă] *f.* crayfish; lobster.
lagostim [lă-goosh-teen'] *m.* prawn.
lágrima [lag'ree-mă] *f.* tear; drop.
laguna [lă-goo'nă] *f.* lagoon.
laia [lȳ'ă] *f.* kind, sort, type.
laivo [lȳ'voo] *m.* stain, spot, blemish; *pl.* smattering, slight knowledge.
laje [lahzh] *f.* **lájea, laja,** paving-stone, flagstone.
lajear [lă-zhee-ar'] *va.* to pave.
lama [lă'mă] *f.* mud.
lamaçal [lă-mă-sal'] *m.* mire, bog, quagmire.
lamacento [lă-mă-sen'too] *adj.* muddy.
lambareiro [lan-bă-ray'ee-roo] *adj.* greedy; having a sweet tooth.
lambaz [lan-bash'] *m.* mop, swab.
lamber [lan-bayr'] *va.* to lick.
lameiro [lă-may'ee-roo] *m.* marsh, swamp.
lamentação [lă-men-tă-sown'] *f.* lamentation, lament; wail, plaint.
lamentar [lă-men-tar'] *va.* to lament, regret; to mourn.
lamentável [lă-men-tah'vel] *adj.* lamentable, deplorable.
lamento [lă-men'too] *m.* lament, wail, moan.
lâmina [lă'mee-nă] *f.* thin plate, sheet (of metal); blade (of knife, etc.).
lâmpada [lan'pă-dă] *f.* lamp.
lampejar [lan-pĕ-zhar'] *vn.* to flash.
lampião [lan-pee-own'] *m.* lantern; street-lamp.
lampreia [lan-pray'yă] *f.* lamprey.
lamúria [lă-moo'ree-ă] *f.* lamentation, wail(ing); whine.
lança [lan'să] *f.* lance, spear.
lançadeira [lan-să-day'ee-ră] *f.* shuttle.
lançamento [lan-să-men'too] *m.* throwing; launching (of ship); dropping (of bombs).
lançar [lan-sar'] *va.* to throw, hurl; to launch (ship).
lance [lans] *m.* event, incident; emergency, crisis; **de um —,** all at once.
lanceta [lan-say'tă] *f.* lancet.
lancha [lan'shă] *f.* launch.

lanche [la*n*sh] *m.* snack; picnic.
lanço [la*n*'soo] *m.* throw(ing); bid (at auction); — **de escadas**, flight of stairs; — **de olhos**, glance.
lande [la*n*d] *f.* acorn.
languescer [la*n*-gĕsh-sayr'] *vn.* to languish.
languidez [la*n*-gee-daysh'] *f.* languor, listlessness.
lânguido [la*n*'gee-doo] *adj.* languid, listless; weary.
lanho [lă'nyoo] *m.* cut, slash.
lanifícios [lă-nee-fee'see-oosh] *m. pl.* woollen goods.
lanterna [la*n*-tair'nă] *f.* lantern.
lanugem [lă-noo'zhe*n*] *f.* [down, fluff.
lapa [lah'pă] *f.* cave, den; limpet.
lapela [lă-pe'lă] *f.* lapel.
lápida [la'pee-dă] *f.* or **lápide**, tablet; tombstone.
lapidar [lă-pee-dar'] *va.* to stone (to death); to polish, cut (precious stones); *adj.* clear, well-expressed (style, etc.); stone, lapidary (inscriptions).
lápis [lahpsh] *m.* pencil.
lapiseira [lă-pee-zay'ee-ră] *f.* propelling pencil; pencil case.
lapso [lap'soo] *m.* lapse.
lar [lar] *m.* hearth, fireside; home.
laranja [lă-ra*n*'zhă] *f.* orange.
laranjada [lă-ra*n*-zhah'dă] *f.* orangeade.
laranjal [lă-ra*n*-zhal'] *m.* orange grove.
laranjeira [lă-ra*n*-zhay'ee-ră] *f.* orange tree.
larápio [lă-rah'pee-oo] *m.* pilferer, sneak thief.
lareira [lă-ray'ee-ră] *f.* hearth; fireside.
larga [lar'gă] *f.* liberty, freedom; **à** —, generously; **viver à** —, to live on a lavish scale; **dar** —**s a**, to give free rein to.
largar [lăr-gar'] *va.* to let go, drop; to let out (a laugh, etc.); *vn.* to sail, put to sea; *vr.* to escape.
largo [lar'goo] *adj.* wide, broad; **ao** —, in the offing (*naut.*); **fazer-se ao** —, to put to sea.
largueza [lăr-gay'ză] *f.* liberality, generosity.
largura [lăr-goo'ră] *f.* width, breadth.
laringe [lă-ree*n*zh'] *f.* larynx.
lasca [lash'kă] *f.* chip, piece; splinter; slice.
lascívia [lăsh-see'vee-ă] *f.* lasciviousness.
lascivo [lăsh-see'voo] *adj.* lascivious, lewd, bawdy.
lassidão [lă-see-dow*n*'] *f.* lassitude, weariness.
lasso [la'soo] *adj.* weary, exhausted; slack, limp.
lástima [lash'tee-mă] *f.* pity, compassion; pitiful state (person, thing, event).
lastimar [lăsh-tee-mar'] *va.* to deplore; to pity; to grieve, hurt; *vr.* to complain; to weep.
lastimoso [lăsh-tee-moh'zoo] [*adj.* pitiful.
lastro [lash'troo] *m* ballast.
lata [lah'tă] *f.* tin, can; tinplate; (wooden) lath; (*sl.*) face, 'mug'; cheek, impudence.
latada [lă-tah'dă] *f.* trellis.
latão [lă-tow*n*'] *m.* brass.
látego [la'tĕ-goo] *m.* whip.
latejar [lă-tĕ-zhar'] *vn.* to throb, beat, pulsate.
latejo [lă-tay'zhoo] *m.* beating (of heart), throbbing, pulsation.
lateral [lă-tĕ-ral'] *adj.* side, lateral.
latente [lă-tent'] *adj.* latent, [concealed.
latido [lă-tee'doo] *m.* bark(ing), yelp(ing).

latim [lă-teen'] *m.* Latin.
latino [lă-tee'noo] *adj.* Latin; vela —a, lateen sail.
latinório [lă-tee-no'ree-oo] *m.* (speech in) dog Latin.
latir [lă-teer'] *vn.* to bark, yelp.
latitude [lă-tee-tood'] *f.* latitude; scope, extent.
lato [lah'too] *adj.* broad, wide.
latoeiro [lă-too-ay'ee-roo] *m.* tinsmith.
latrocínio [lă-troo-see'nee-oo] *m.* armed robbery.
laudatório [low-dă-to'ree-oo] *adj.* laudatory.
laureado [low-ree-ah'doo] *adj.* honoured, decorated; awarded (a prize, an honour).
laurel [low-rel'] *m.* laurel crown; *pl.* honours.
lauto [low'too] *adj.* sumptuous.
lava [lah'vă] *f.* lava.
lavabo [lă-vah'boo] *m.* wash-basin; lavabo (*eccl.*).
lavadeira [lă-vă-day'ee-ră] *f.* washerwoman, laundress.
lavadoiro [lă-vă-doh'ee-roo] *m.* washing-place; wash-house; wash-tub.
lavagante [la-vă-gant'] *m.* lobster.
lavagem [lă-vah'zhen] *f.* [washing.
lava-louça [lah'vă loh'să] *f.* (kitchen) sink.
lavandaria [lă-van-dă-ree'ă] *f.* laundry.
lavar [lă-var'] *va.* to wash.
lavatório [lă-vă-to'ree-oo] *m.* wash-stand,-basin.
lavor [lă-vohr'] *m.* needle-work, embroidery; work, labour.
lavoura [lă-voh'ră] *f.* ploughing, tilling; farming.
lavra [lav'ră] *f.* ploughing, tilling; mining; production, work.
lavradeira [lăv-ră-day'ee-ră] *f.* woman farmworker, peasant woman; needlewoman.
lavradio [lăv-ră-dee'oo] *adj* arable.
lavrador [lav-ră-dohr'] *m.* farm-hand, -labourer; farmer.
lavrar [lăv-rar'] *va.* to plough, till; to carve, chisel, plane, shape (wood); to cut, polish (stones); to draw up (document).
laxante [lak-sant'] *m/adj.* [laxative.
lazareto [lă-ză-ray'too] *m.* quarantine station.
lazeira [lă-zay'ee-ră] *f.* lazi-ness; starvation; misery.
leal [lee-al'] *adj.* loyal, faithful.
lealdade [lee-al-dahd'] *f.* loyalty, fidelity; sincerity.
leão [lee-own'] *m.* lion.
lebre [leb'rĕ] *f.* hare.
leccionar [le-see-oo-nar'] *va.* to teach.
lectivo [le-tee'voo] *adj.* academic, scholastic; ano —, academic year, school year.
ledo [lay'doo] *adj.* gay, joyful, cheerful.
legação [lĕ-gă-sown'] *f.* lega- [tion.
legado [lĕ-gah'doo] *m.* legate, envoy; legacy.
legal [lĕ-gal'] *adj.* legal, lawful.
legalidade [lĕ-gă-lee-dahd'] *f.* legality, lawfulness.
legalizar [lĕ-gă-lee-zar'] *va.* to legalise.
legar [lĕ-gar'] *va.* to bequeath; to transmit.
legatário [lĕ-gă-tah'ree-oo] *m.* [legatee.
legenda [lĕ-zhen'dă] *f.* inscription; title, heading; sub-title (in film).
legião [lĕ-zhee-own'] *f.* legion.
legislação [lĕ-zheezh-lă-sown'] *f.* legislation, law.
legislar [lĕ-zheezh-lar'] *vn.* to legislate.
legitimar [lĕ-zhee-tee-mar'] *va.* to legitimize, legalize.
legítimo [lĕ-zhee'tee-moo] *adj.* legitimate, lawful; genuine; justifiable, valid.

legível [lĕ-zhee'vel] *adj.* legible, readable.
légua [le'gwă] *f.* league (*approx. 3 miles in Port., approx. 4 in Braz.*).
legume [lĕ-goom'] *m.* vegetable.
lei [lay'ee] *f.* law; statute; act; projeto de —, bill.
leigo [lay'ee-goo] *adj.* lay, secular; not expert, unlearned, ignorant; *m.* layman; ignoramus.
leilão [lay-ee-lown'] *m.* auction.
leitão [lay-ee-town'] *m.* sucking-pig.
leitaria [lay-ee-tă-ree'ă] *f.* dairy.
leite [lay'eet] *m.* milk.
leito [lay'ee-too] *m.* bedstead; bed; couch; — **de rio**, river bed.
leitor [lay-ee-tohr'] *m.* reader; (*acad.*) lecturer.
leitorado [lay-ee-too-rah'doo] *m.* lectureship.
leitura [lay-ee-too'ră] *f.* reading.
leiva [lay'ee-vă] *f.* ploughed land; ridge (between furrows).
lema [lay'mă] *m.* motto, device.
lembrança [len-bran'să] *f.* memory, remembrance, recollection; souvenir; *pl.* greetings.
lembrar [len-brar'] *va.* to remind; to recall; *vr.* to remember.
leme [lem] *m.* helm; rudder.
lenço [len'soo] *m.* handkerchief; scarf.
lençol [len-sol'] *m.* sheet.
lenda [len'dă] *f.* legend, story.
lendário [len-dah'ree-oo] *adj.* legendary.
lêndea [len'dee-ă] *f.* nit.
lenha [lĕ'nyă] *f.* (fire)wood.
lenhador [lĕ-nyă-dohr'] *m.* woodcutter.
lenho [lĕ'nyoo] *m.* log (of wood); (*poet.*) boat, ship; Santo —, Holy Cross.
lenitivo [lĕ-nee-tee'voo] *adj.* soothing; *m.* palliative; soothing remedy.
lente [lent] *f.* lens; *m.* professor, lecturer.
lentidão [len-tee-down'] *f.* slowness, sluggishness.
lentilha [len-tee'lyă] *f.* lentil.
lento [len'too] *adj.* slow, tardy; sluggish; moist.
leoa [lee-oh'ă] *f.* lioness.
leopardo [lee-oo-par'doo] *m.* leopard.
lépido [le'pee-doo] *adj.* cheerful, sprightly, lively.
lepra [le'pră] *f.* leprosy; (*fig.*) corruption, rot.
leproso [lĕ-proh'zoo] *m.* leper; *adj.* leprous; (*fig.*) loathsome, corrupt.
leque [lek] *m.* fan.
ler [layr] *va.* to read.
lerdo [layr'doo] *adj.* sluggish; dull, stupid.
lés [lesh] *m.* de — a —, from one side to the other, right across, right through; — nordeste, east north-east.
lesão [lĕ-zown'] *f.* lesion; injury.
lesar [lĕ-zar'] *va.* to injure, damage.
lesma [layzh'mă] *f.* slug; (*fig.*) sluggard, stick-in-the-mud.
leso [le'zoo] *adj.* hurt, injured; —a majestade, high treason.
leste [lesht] *m.* east.
lesto [lesh'too] *adj.* quick, alert, brisk.
letargo [lĕ-tar'goo] *m.* lethargy; apathy.
letra [lay'tră] *f.* letter (of alphabet); handwriting; type (*print.*); bill, promissory note (*com.*); **à (ao pé da)** —, literally; exactly; *pl.* learning; letters, literature; licenciado em —, (*abbrev.* lic. em l.).

Bachelor of Arts (B.A.); primeiras —, elementary schooling, the three Rs.
letrado [lĕ-trah'doo] *adj.* learned; *m.* man of letters.
letreiro [lĕ-tray'ee-roo] *m.* inscription, lettering, sign.
léu [le'oo] *m.* idleness, opportunity; ao —, aimlessly; **cabeça ao —**, bareheaded.
leva [le'vă] *f.* weighing (anchor); levy, group (of soldiers, convicts); mustering, levying (of troops).
levada [lĕ-vah'dă] *f.* watercourse; mill stream; sluice.
levadiço [lĕ-vă-dee'soo] *adj.* movable; **ponte —a**, drawbridge.
levantamento [lĕ-va*n*-tă-me*n*'too] *m.* (up)rising, revolt; raising, lifting; survey.
levantar [lĕ-va*n*-tar'] *va.* to lift (up), raise (up); to stir up, rouse; to prepare (document); to terminate (meeting); **— vôo**, to take off (aeroplane); **— a mesa**, to clear the table; *vr.* to rise, stand up, get up, get out of bed.
levante [lĕ-va*n*t'] *m.* east, orient; Levant.
levar [lĕ-var'] *va.* to carry (off); to take (away); to charge (a price); **— a mal**, to take amiss; **— a cabo**, to carry through; **— uma vida feliz**, to lead a happy life; **— em conta**, to take into account; **— tempo**, to take time.
leve [lev] *adj.* light; slight.
levedura [lĕ-vĕ-doo'ră] *f.* yeast.
leviandade [lĕ-vee-a*n*-dahd'] *f.* frivolity, levity.
leviano [lĕ-vee-ă'noo] *adj.* frivolous, thoughtless; fickle.
léxico [lek'see-koo] *m.* dictionary, vocabulary.
lezíria [lĕ-zee'ree-ă] *f.* meadowland.
lhaneza [lyă-nay'ză] *f.* plainness; sincerity; friendliness, homeliness.
lhano [lyă'noo] *adj.* sincere; unpretentious; friendly, homely.
lia [lee'ă] *f.* lees, dregs.
liaça [lee-ah'să] *f.* straw-packing.
liame [lee-ahm'] *m.* tie, bond.
libelo [lee-be'loo] *m.* formal charge (*leg.*); lampoon.
libélula [lee-be'loo-lă] *f.* dragon-fly.
liberal [lee-bĕ-ral'] *m.* Liberal; *adj.* liberal; generous.
liberalidade [lee-bĕ-ră-lee-dahd'] *f.* liberality, generosity.
liberalismo [lee-bĕ-ră-leezh'-moo] *m.* Liberalism.
liberar [lee-bĕ-rar'] *va.* to settle (debt); to release (from obligation).
liberdade [lee-bĕr-dahd'] *f.* freedom, liberty.
libertador [lee-bĕr-tă-dohr'] *m.* liberator.
libertar [lee-bĕr-tar'] *va.* to free, liberate, set free.
libertino [lee-bĕr-tee'noo] *m.* rake, libertine; *adj.* loose-living, dissolute.
libidinoso [li-bee-dee-noh'-zoo] *adj.* lecherous, lustful.
libra [lee'bră] *f.* pound (money; weight); **— esterlina**, pound sterling.
liça [lee'să] *f.* lists.
lição [lee-sow*n*'] *f.* lesson; lecture; example.
licença [lee-se*n*'să] *f.* permission, authorization; permit, licence; leave, furlough; **com —**, excuse me; **dá-me —**, may I (come in, interrupt, etc.).?
licenciado [lee-se*n*-see-ah'-

doo] *m.* graduate; Bachelor of Arts, B.A. (in England).
licenciar [lee-see*n*-see-ar′] *va.* to allow, license; to discharge; *vr.* to graduate (*acad.*).
licenciatura [lee-se*n*-see-ă-too′ră] *f.* degree (*acad.*); conferring of a degree.
licencioso [lee-se*n*-see-oh′zoo] *adj.* licentious.
liceu [lee-say′oo] *m.* secondary school, grammar school.
licitar [lee-see-tar′] *vn.* to bid (at auction); *va.* to (put up for) auction.
lícito [lee′see-too] *adj.* permitted, permissible; lawful.
licor [lee-kohr′] *m.* liquid, liquor; liqueur.
licoroso [lee-koo-roh′zoo] *adj.* strong and sweet (wine).
lida [lee′dă] *f.* toil; drudgery.
lidar [lee-dar′] *vn.* to strive, struggle; to toil.
liga [lee′gă] *f.* league; garter; alloy (metals).
ligação [lee-gă-sow*n*′] *f.* connection, link.
ligadura [lee-gă-doo′ră] *f.* bandage; ligature.
ligar [lee-gar′] *va.* to bind, tie; to connect, join; to fasten; to turn on, switch on (radio, light, etc.); — **importância a,** to attach importance to; — **para,** to (tele)phone to.
ligeireza [lee-zhay-ray′ză] *f.* lightness; quickness, agility; levity, thoughtlessness.
ligeiro [lee-zhay′ee-roo] *adj.* light; quick, swift; agile; flighty.
lilás [lee-lash′] *m.* lilac.
lima [lee′mă] *f.* file; lime (fruit).
limão [lee-mow*n*′] *m.* lemon.
limar [lee-mar′] *va.* to file; to polish.
limeira [lee-may′ee-ră] *f.* lime-tree.
limiar [lee-mee-ar′] *m.* threshold, entrance.
limitação [lee-mee-tă-sow*n*′] *f.* limitation, restriction.
limitar [lee-mee-tar′] *va.* to limit, restrict.
limite [lee-meet′] *m.* limit; boundary.
limo [lee′moo] *m.* (river, pond weed; scum, slime.
limoal [lee-moo-al′] lemon grove.
limoeiro [lee-moo-ay′ee-ro] *m.* lemon tree.
limonada [lee-moo-nah′dă] *f.* lemonade.
limpar [lee*n*-par′] *va.* to clean (up); *vn.* to clear up (weather).
limpeza [lee*n*-pay′ză] *f.* cleaning; cleanliness; purity.
limpo [lee*n*′poo] *adj.* clean; neat, tidy; clear; **passar a —,** to make a fair copy; **tirar a —,** to find out the truth.
lince [leens] *m.* lynx.
linchar [lee*n*-shar′] *va.* to lynch.
lindeira [lee*n*-day′ee-ră] *f.* lintel.
lindo [lee*n*′doo] *adj.* lovely, beautiful, pretty, elegant.
lineamentos [lee-nee-ă-me*n*′-toosh] *m.pl.* lineaments.
linfa [lee*n*′fă] *f.* lymph.
língua [lee*n*′gwă] *f.* tongue; language; strip (of land); **má —,** slanderer; *m.* interpreter (*archaic*).
linguado [lee*n*-gwah′doo] *m.* sole (fish); sheet (of paper, metal).
linguagem [lee*n*-gwah′zhe*n*] *f.* language, speech; style.
linguareira [lee*n*-gwă-ray′ee-ră] *f.* chatterbox, gossip, scandalmonger.
lingueta [lee*n*-gway′tă] *f.* pointer (of scales); catch (of lock).
linguista [lee*n*-gweesh′tă] *mf.* linguist.
linguística [lee*n*-gweesh′tee-kă] *f.* linguistics.
linha [lee′nyă] *f.* line; thread

; string; row, rank; [illegible]ry. [seed.
linhaça [lee-nyah'să] *f.* lin-
linhagem [lee-nyah'zhe*n*] *f.* lineage, ancestry, pedigree.
linho [lee'nyoo] *m.* linen; flax.
linóleo [lee-no'lee-oo] *m.* linoleum.
líquen [lee'ke*n*] *m.* lichen.
liquidação [lee-kee-dă-sow*n*'] *f.* liquidation; clearance sale.
liquidar [lee-kee-dar'] *va.* to liquidate; to settle; to wind up (business).
líquido [lee'kee-doo] *m.* liquid, fluid; *adj.* liquid; net (profits, etc.).
lira [lee'ră] *f.* lyre.
lírica [lee'ree-kă] *f.* lyric poetry, lyric poems.
lírico [lee'ree-koo] *adj.* lyric(al); *m.* lyric poet.
lírio [lee'ree-oo] *m.* lily, iris.
lirismo [lee-reezh'moo] *m.* lyricism; high-flown, *or* sentimental, expressions.
lisboeta [leezh-boo-ay'tă] *adj.* (of) Lisbon; *mf.* native of Lisbon.
liso [lee'zoo] *adj.* smooth, even, flat; easy to get on with, sincere, straightforward; **cabelo —**, straight hair.
lisonja [lee-zo*n*'zhă] *f.* flattery; blandishment.
lisonjear [lee-zo*n*-zhee-ar'] *va.* to flatter.
lisonjeiro [lee-zo*n*-zhay'ee-roo] *adj.* flattering; gratifying; *m.* flatterer.
lista [leesh'tă] *f.* list; catalogue; telephone book, directory; menu; stripe; strip (of paper).
listra [leesh'tră] *f.* stripe.
liteira [lee-tay'ee-ră] *f.* litter.
literário [lee-tĕ-rah'ree-oo] *adj.* literary.
literato [lee-tĕ-rah'too] *m.* man of letters, writer.
literatura [lee-tĕ-ră-too'ră] *f.* literature.
litigar [lee-tee-gar'] *vn.* to go to law; to contend.
litígio [li-tee'zhee-oo] *m.* litigation; lawsuit.
litoral [lee-too-ral'] *m.* coast(line), seaboard; *adj.* coastal.
litro [lee'troo] *m.* litre (1¾ pints).
lívido [lee'vee-doo] *adj.* livid.
livramento [lee-vră-me*n*'too] *m.* deliverance, release.
livrar [lee-vrar'] *va.* to release, deliver, set free; *vr.* to escape from, free oneself from; to get rid of; **Deus me livre!** Heaven forbid!; **livra-te de . . .!**, watch out (if, that) . . .!
livraria [lee-vră-ree'ă] *f.* bookshop.
livre [lee'vrĕ] *adj.* free; clear, open (field, space, etc.); **ao ar —**, in the open air.
livreiro [lee-vray'ee-roo] *m.* bookseller.
livro [lee'vroo] *m.* book; **— de consulta**, reference book; **— de facturas**, invoice book; **— mestre**, *or* **razão**, ledger; **— de mortalhas**, packet of cigarette-papers.
lixa [lee'shă] *f.* sandpaper.
lixo [lee'shoo] *m.* rubbish, garbage, refuse, litter.
loas [loh'ăsh] *f.* hymns, carols; praises; (lying) tales, fibs.
lobisomem [loo-bee-zo'me*n*] *m.* werewolf.
lobo [loh'boo] *m.* wolf; **— do mar**, sea-dog (i.e. old sailor); seal.
lôbrego [loh'brĕ-goo] *adj.* gloomy, dismal; fearful.
lobrigar [loo-bree-gar'] *va.* to catch sight of, a glimpse of; to see (far off, in the distance).
lóbulo [lo'boo-loo] *m.* lobe.
locação [loo-kă-sow*n*'] *f.* lease.

local [loo-kal'] *m.* site; premises; *adj.* local.
localidade [loo-kă-lee-dahd'] *f.* locality, district, place.
localizar [loo-kă-lee-zar'] *va.* to localize, place.
loção [loo-sown'] *f.* lotion; hair-lotion.
locatário [loo-kă-tah'ree-oo] *m.* tenant, lessee.
locomoção [loo-koo-moo-sown'] *f.* locomotion.
locomotiva [loo-koo-moo-tee'-vă] *f.* (railway-) engine, locomotive.
locução [loo-koo-sown'] *f.* phrase, idiom, locution.
locutório [loo-koo-to'ree-oo] *m.* visiting room (in convent, monastery), locutory.
lodo [loh'doo] *m.* mud.
lógica [lo'zhee-kă] *f.* logic.
lógico [lo'zhee-koo] *adj.* logical; *m.* logician.
logo [lo'goo] *adv.* immediately; presently, soon; *conj.* therefore, then, so; **desde —**, at once; naturally, of course; **— que**, as soon as; **até —**, cheerio!, see you later!
logradoiro [loo-gră-doh'ee-roo] *m.* common (-land).
lograr [loo-grar'] *va.* to manage to, succeed in; to obtain; to attain, achieve; to enjoy (the possession of, fruits of); to deceive, trick, swindle.
logro [loh'groo] *m.* possession, enjoyment; fraud, trick, hoax, trap.
loiro [loh'ee-roo] *adj.* fair, blond; golden, yellow.
loja [lo'zhă] *f.* shop; (masonic) lodge.
lojista [loo-zheesh'tă] *mf.* shopkeeper.
lomba [lon'bă] *f.* ridge, brow.
lombada [lon-bah'dă] *f.* long ridge; back (of ox); back, spine (of book).
lombo [lon'boo] *m.* loin; back.
lona [loh'nă] *f.* canvas.
londrino [lon-dree'noo] *adj.* (of) London; *m.* Londoner.
longe [lonzh] *adv.* far, far off; *adj.* far, distant, remote; **— de mim**, far be it from me; **— disso**, far from it; **ao —**, far off, far away, in the distance; **de — em —**, at long intervals; *m. pl.* background (paint.); distances; touches, hints (of irony, etc.).
longevidade [lon-zhĕ-vee-dahd'] *f.* longevity.
longínquo [lon-zheen'kwoo] *adj.* distant, far-off, remote.
longitude [lon-zhee-tood'] *f.* longitude; distance.
longo [lon'goo] *adj.* long; **ao — de**, along.
lontra [lon'tră] *f.* otter.
loquaz [loo-kwash'] *adj.* talkative, garrulous, loquacious.
lorpa [lohr'pă] *adj.* stupid, idiotic; boorish; *m.* simpleton, idiot; lout.
lotação [loo-tă-sown'] *f.* (holding) capacity; (*naut.*) tonnage; estimate; blending (of wines); **— esgotada**, all seats booked; house full (*theat.*).
lotaria [loo-tă-ree'ă] *or* **loteria**, *f.* lottery.
lote [lot] *m.* lot; portion; batch; **— de terreno**, plot of land; building lot.
louça [loh'să] *f.* pottery; china; earthenware; **lavar a —**, to wash up, wash the dishes.
louçania [loh-să-nee'ă] *f.* freshness, elegance; finery, show, display.
louco [loh'koo] *adj.* mad, crazy; *m.* madman, lunatic.
loucura [loh-koo'ră] *f.* madness, folly, lunacy.
loureiro [loh-ray'ee-roo] *m.* laurel tree, bay tree.
louro [loh'roo] *m.* laurel.

mandato [man-dah'too] *m.* mandate; order.
mandíbula [man-dee'boo-lă] *f.* jaw.
mandinga [man-deen'gă] *f.* witchcraft, magic.
mandioca [man-dee-o'kă] *f.* manioc; cassava; tapioca.
mando [man'doo] *m.* command; authority, power.
mandrião [man-dree-own'] *m.* lazybones, lazy fellow, idler; *adj.* lazy.
maneio [mă-nay'yoo] *m.* manipulation, handling; management (of money, etc.).
maneira [mă-nay'ee-ră] *f.* way, manner, mode; style, fashion; custom; *pl.* manners.
manejar [mă-nĕ-zhar'] *va.* to handle; to manage.
manejável [mă-nĕ-zhah'vel] *adj.* manageable, tractable.
manejo [mă-nay'zhoo] *m.* handling; management; *pl.* intrigues.
manequin [mă-nĕ-keen'] *m.* dummy; model.
maneta [mă-nay'tă] *adj.* one-armed; one-handed.
manga [man'gă] *f.* sleeve; mango (fruit).
mangar [man-gar'] *vn.* to joke, tease.
mangra [man'gră] *f.* mildew.
mangual [man-gwal'] *m.* flail.
mangue [man'gĕ] *m.* mangrove; mangrove swamp.
mangueira [man-gay'ee-ră] *f.* mango-tree; hose, tube.
manha [mă'nyă] *f.* craftiness, slyness; trick, bad habit.
manhã [mă-nyan'] *f.* morning.
manhoso [mă-nyoh'zoo] *adj.* crafty, artful.
mania [mă-nee'ă] *f.* mania; craze, obsession.
maniatar [mă-nee-ă-tar'] *va.* to manacle, handcuff.
manicómio [mă-nee-ko'mee-oo] *m.* (lunatic) asylum mental home.
manicura [mă-nee-koo'ră] *f.* manicure.
manifestação [mă-nee-fĕsh-tă-sown'] *f.* manifestation, display; demonstration.
manifestar [mă-nee-fĕsh-tar'] *va.* to show, manifest, display; to declare, express.
manifesto [mă-nee-fesh'too] *m.* manifesto, declaration; (ship's) manifest.
manilha [mă-nee'lyă] *f.* bracelet; shackle, manacle.
manipular [mă-nee-poo-lar'] *va.* to manipulate.
manivela [mă-nee-ve'lă] *f.* crank, handle.
manjar [man-zhar'] *m.* food; titbit, delicacy.
manjedoira [man-zhĕ-doh'ee-ră] *f.* manger, crib.
manjericão [man-zhĕ-ree-kown'] *m.* basil (*bot.*).
mano [mă'noo] *m.* (*pop.*) brother.
manobra [mă-no'bră] *f.* manœuvre; ruse; trick.
manobrar [mă-noo-brar'] *vn.* to manœuvre; to work, function; *va.* to handle; to manage; to manœuvre.
manquejar [man-kĕ-zhar'] *vn.* to limp.
mansão [man-sown'] *f.* dwelling-place, residence.
mansidão [man-see-down'] *f.* gentleness, meekness.
manso [man'soo] *adj.* meek, gentle, mild; tame.
manta [man'tă] *f.* blanket; travelling-rug.
manteiga [man-tay'ee-gă] *f.* butter.
mantel [man-tel'] *m.* table-cloth.
manter [man-tayr'] *va.* to maintain, sustain, support, uphold.

mantilha [man-tee'lyă] *f.* head scarf, veil.
mantimento [man-tee-men'-too] *m.* maintenance; sustenance; *pl.* provisions.
manto [man'too] *m.* cloak.
manual [mă-noo-al'] *m.* handbook, manual; *adj.* manual.
manufactura [mă-noo-fak-too'ră] *f.* manufacture.
manuscrito [mă-noosh-kree'-too] *m.* manuscript.
manusear [mă-noo-zee-ar'] *va.* to handle; to leaf through (a book).
manutenção [mă-noo-ten-sown'] *f.* maintenance.
mão [mown] *f.* hand; paw; coat (of paint); **— -de-obra,** labour, labour force; handicraft; **feito à —,** hand-made; **de —s dadas,** hand in hand; **lançar — de,** to lay hold of; **segunda —,** second-hand; **ter entre —s,** to be working on something, to have (some work) in hand.
mapa [ma'pă] *m.* map. chart.
maquilhagem [mă-kee-lyah'-zhen] *f.* make-up.
máquina [ma'kee-nă] *f.* machine; engine; **— fotográfica,** camera; **— de escrever,** typewriter.
maquinação [mă-kee-nă-sown'] *f.* machination, plot.
maquinal [mă-kee-nal'] *adj.* mechanical; automatic.
máquinaria [mă-kee-nă-ree'-ă] *f.* machinery.
maquinista [mă-kee-neesh'-tă] *m.* machinist; mechanic; engineer; engine-driver (train).
mar [mar] *m.* sea; **— largo,** open sea; **— alto,** high seas; **beira- —,** seashore, seaside.
maracujá [mă-ră-koo-zhah'] *m.* passion-flower, -fruit.
maranha [mă-ră'nyă] *f.* tangle; (*fig.*) plot, scheme.
marasmo [mă-razh'moo] *m.* wasting away, emaciation; apathy.
maravilha [mă-ră-vee'lyă] *f.* wonder, marvel; **à —, às mil —s,** wonderfully, marvellously.
maravilhar [mă-ră-vee-lyar'] *va.* to amaze, astound; *vr.* to marvel at, wonder at.
maravilhoso [mă-ră-vee-lyoh'zoo] *adj.* marvellous, wonderful.
marca [mar'kă] *f.* mark; make, brand (*com.*); stamp; limit, boundary.
marcação [măr-kă-sown'] *f.* demarcation; **— de lugares,** booking (reservation) of seats; **— errada,** wrong number (on telephone).
marçano [măr-să'noo] *m.* shop-boy.
marcar [măr-kar'] *va.* to mark; to stamp; to fix (a time); to book, reserve (seats); to dial (a telephone number).
marceneiro [măr-sĕ-nay'ee-roo] *m.* cabinet-maker.
marcha [mar'shă] *f.* march; course, progress.
marchar [măr-shar'] *vn.* to go, move (on), proceed; to march; to walk.
marchetado [măr-shĕ-tah'-doo] *adj.* inlaid; *m.* inlaid work.
marco [mar'koo] *m.* boundary mark; **— miliário,** milestone; **— postal,** pillar-box.
março [mar'soo] *m.* March
maré [mă-re'] *f.* tide; **— cheia,** high tide.
mareante [mă-ree-ant'] *m.* seaman; mariner.
marear [mă-ree-ar'] *va.* to steer, sail; to sicken, nauseate; to tarnish; *vn.* to be seasick; to sail, go to sea; **carta de —,** sea-chart.

marechal [mă-rě-shal'] *m.* marshal.
marfim [măr-feen'] *m.* ivory.
margarida [măr-gă-ree'dă] *f.* daisy. [margarine.
margarina [măr-gă-ree'nă] *f.*
margem [mar'zhen] *f.* edge, side; (river) bank; margin; dar — a, to give an opportunity for. [band.
marido [mă-ree'doo] *m.* hus-
marinha [mă-ree'nyă] *f.* navy; seascape (*paint.*); salt-pan.
marinheiro [mă-ree-nyay'ee-roo] *m.* seaman, sailor.
marinho [mă-ree'nyoo] *adj.* sea, marine.
mariola [mă-ree-o'lă] *m.* scoundrel, rogue.
mariposa [mă-ree-poh'ză] *f.* butterfly. [shellfish.
marisco [mă-reesh'koo] *m.*
marítimo [mă-ree'tee-moo] *adj.* maritime, marine; seafaring.
marmelada [măr-mě-lah'dă] *f.* quince jam; (*sl.*) 'cinch'.
marmelo [măr-me'loo] *m.* quince.
marmita [măr-mee'tă] *f.* pan; mess-tin (*mil.*). [ble.
mármore [mar'moor] *m.* mar-
marmóreo [măr-mo'ree-oo] *adj.* (of) marble; marmoreal.
maroto [mă-roh'too] *m.* scoundrel, rogue.
marquês [măr-kaysh'] *m.* marquis.
marquesa [măr-kay'ză] *f.* marchioness.
marroquim [mă-roo-keen'] *m.* morocco leather.
marroquino [mă-roo-kee'-noo] *adj.* Moroccan.
marte [mart] *m.* Mars.
martelar [măr-tě-lar'] *va.* to hammer. [mer.
martelo [măr-te'loo] *m.* ham-
mártir [mar'teer] *m.* martyr.
martírio [măr-tee'ree-oo] *m.* martyrdom; passion flower.
marujo [mă-roo'zhoo] *m.* sailor.
marulho [mă-roo'lyoo] *m.* surge (of sea).
mas [măsh] *conj.* but.
mascar [măsh-kar'] *va.* to chew.
máscara [mash'kă-ră] *f.* mask.
mascarada [măsh-kă-rah'dă] *f.* masquerade.
mascote [măsh-kot'] *m.* mascot, lucky charm.
masculino [măsh-koo-lee'-noo] *adj.* masculine.
masmorra [măzh-moh'ră] *f.* dungeon.
massa [ma'să] *f.* mass, volume; paste; dough; (*sl.*) money, 'dough'.
massacrar [mă-să-krar'] *va.* to massacre. [massage.
massagem [mă-sah'zhen] *f.*
massudo [mă-soo'doo] *adj.* bulky, massive; dull (speech, etc.).
mastigar [măsh-tee-gar'] *va.* to chew; to mumble, mutter.
mastro [mash'troo] *m.* mast.
mata [ma'tă] *f.* forest, wood.
mata-bicho [ma'tă bee'shoo] *m.* drop, spot, tot (of alcohol).
mata-borrão [ma'tă boo-rown'] *m.* blotting-paper.
matadouro [mă-tă-doh'roo] *m.* slaughterhouse.
matagal [mă-tă-gal'] *m.* (dense) undergrowth, thicket.
matança [mă-tan'să] *f.* slaughter; massacre.
matar [mă-tar'] *va.* to kill; to quench (thirst).
mate [maht] *m.* checkmate; (*bot.*) yerba-mate; *adj.* dull, mat (colour).
matemática [mă-tě-ma'tee-kă] *f.* mathematics.
matemático [mă-tě-ma'tee-koo] *m.* mathematician.

matéria [mă-tair'ee-ă] *f.* matter; substance; material; subject (*acad.*).
material [mă-tĕ-ree-al'] *m/adj.* material.
materno [mă-tair'noo] *adj.* maternal; motherly, affectionate; **língua —a,** mother tongue.
matias [mă-tee'ăsh] *m.* simpleton, Simple Simon.
matilha [mă-tee'lyă] *f.* pack (of hounds).
matinal [mă-tee-nal'] *adj.* morning, early.
matiz [mă-teesh'] *m.* shade, tint, hue; nuance; blend (of colours).
matizar [mă-tee-zar'] *va.* to mingle, blend (colours); to colour, tinge.
mato [ma'too] *m.* undergrowth, brushwood; woodland, bush.
matraca [mă-tra'kă] *f.* rattle.
matreiro [mă-tray'ee-roo] *adj.* artful, cunning.
matrícula [mă-tree'koo-lă] *f.* register, list; registration; registration (matriculation) fee.
matrimónio [mă-tree-mo'-nee-oo] *m.* marriage; matrimony.
matriz [mă-treesh'] *f.* womb, matrix; origin, source; die, mould (*mech.*); register; **igreja —,** mother church.
maturidade [mă-too-ree-dahd'] *f.* maturity.
matutino [mă-too-tee'noo] *adj.* early, early-morning.
mau [mow] *adj.* bad, evil, wicked, harmful.
mavioso [mă-vee-oh'zoo] *adj.* gentle, tender; sweet, soft.
maxila [măk-see'lă] *f.* jaw (-bone).
máxima [ma'see-mă] *f.* maxim.
máxime [ma'see-me] *adv.* especially.
máximo [ma'see-moo] *adj.* greatest; maximum.
mazela [mă-ze'lă] *f.* sore, sore spot; (*fig.*) blemish, stain.
meada [mee-ah'dă] *f.* hank, skein (of yarn); (*fig.*) intrigue.
meado [mee - ah'doo] *m.* middle.
mealheiro [mee-ă-lyay'ee-roo] *m.* money-box; savings.
mecânica [mĕ-kă'nee-kă] *f.* mechanics.
mecânico [mĕ-kă'nee-koo] *adj.* mechanical; *m.* mechanic, fitter, engineer.
mecanismo [mĕ-kă-neezh'-moo] *m.* mechanism.
mecha [me'shă] *f.* wick; fuse.
medalha [mĕ-da'lyă] *f.* medal.
média [me'dee-ă] *f.* average.
medianeiro [mĕ-dee-ă-nay'-ee-roo] *m.* mediator, intermediary.
mediano [mĕ-dee-ă'noo] *adj.* medium, middle.
mediante [mĕ-dee-ant'] *prep.* by means of, with the aid of, through; *m.* interval.
mediar [mĕ-dee-ar'] *vn.* to mediate; to intervene, follow, (of time); to lie between (two places, etc.).
medicação [mĕ-dee-kă-sown'] *f.* (medical) treatment.
medicamento [mĕ-dee-kă-men'too] *m.* medicine; remedy.
medição [mĕ-dee-sown'] *f.* measurement.
medicina [mĕ-di-see'nă] *f.* medicine.
médico [me'dee-koo] *m.* doctor, physician.
medida [mĕ-dee'dă] *f.* measure, measurement; **à — que,** as, while.
médio [me'dee-oo] *adj.* middle; average.

mediocridade [mĕ-dee-oo-kree-dahd'] *f.* mediocrity.
medir [mĕ-deer'] *va.* to measure; to estimate.
meditabundo [mĕ-dee-tă-boon'doo] *adj.* pensive.
meditar [mĕ-dee-tar'] *va.* to consider, meditate on, ponder; *vn.* to meditate, muse.
mediterrâneo [mĕ-dee-tĕ-ră'nee-oo] *m/adj.* Mediterranean.
medium [me'dee-oon] *m.* (spiritualist) medium.
medo [may'doo] *m.* fear, dread; **ter —**, to be afraid.
medonho [mĕ-doh'nyoo] *adj.* dreadful, frightful, terrible.
medrar [mĕ-drar'] *vn.* to thrive, flourish.
medroso [mĕ-droh'zoo] *adj.* timid, frightened.
medula [mĕ-doo'lă] *f.* marrow; (*fig.*) heart, essence.
meia [may'yă] *f.* stocking; *pl.* halves, half-shares; **ir a —s**, to go halves.
meia-noite [may'yă noh'eet] *f.* midnight.
meigo [may'ee-goo] *adj.* gentle, tender, sweet.
meiguice [may-ee-gees'] *f.* gentleness, tenderness; *pl.* endearments, caresses.
meio [may'yoo] *m.* middle; environment; medium; way, means, method, expedient; *pl.* resources; means; *adj.* half; middle; **por — de**, by means of; **deixar em —**, to leave unfinished.
meio-dia [may'yoo dee'ă] *m.* midday, noon; south.
mel [mel] *m.* honey.
melaço [mĕ-la'soo] *m.* molasses.
melancia [mĕ-lan-see'ă] *f.* water-melon.
melancólico [mĕ-lan-ko'lee-koo] *adj.* melancholy, sad.
melão [mĕ-lown'] *m.* melon.
melena [mĕ-lay'nă] *f.* long (dishevelled) hair; mop of hair.
melhor [mĕ-lyor'] *adj.* better; best; **quanto mais —**, the more the better; **tanto —**, so much the better.
melhora [mĕ-lyo'ră] *f.* improvement, amelioration; **estimo as suas —s**, I hope you will be better (in health).
melhoramento [mĕ-lyoo-ră-men'too] *m.* improvement.
melhorar [mĕ-lyoo-rar'] *va/vn.* to improve; *vn.* to get better.
meliante [mĕ-lee-ant'] *m.* scoundrel, scamp.
melindrar [mĕ-leen-drar'] *va.* to offend, hurt (feelings); *vr.* to be offended, take offence.
melindroso [mĕ-leen-droh'zoo] *adj.* touchy; affected; delicate, gentle; precarious, difficult, 'tricky'.
melodia [mĕ-loo-dee'ă] *f.* melody.
melro [mel'roo] *m.* blackbird.
membro [men'broo] *m.* limb; member.
membrudo [men-broo'doo] *adj.* robust, big.
memória [mĕ-mo'ree-ă] *f.* memory; remembrance; recollection; fame; report; *pl.* memoirs.
menção [men-sown'] *f.* mention, reference.
mencionar [men-see-oo-nar'] *va.* to mention.
mendicidade [men-dee-see-dahd'] *f.* begging.
mendigar [men-dee-gar'] *va.* to beg.
mendigo [men-dee'goo] *m.* [beggar.
menear [mĕ-nee-ar'] *va.* to shake, wag, toss; *vr.* to sway.
meneio [mĕ-nay'yoo] *m.* shaking, swaying; gesture; nod.

menina [mĕ-nee'nă] *f.* girl; young lady, miss.
menino [mĕ-nee'noo] *m.* boy, (*pop.*) lad; child.
menor [mĕ-nor'] *adj.* smaller, smallest; lesser, least; minor, inferior; *m.* minor.
menos [may'noosh] *adj/adv/prep.* less, least; except; minus; pelo (ao) —, at least; — mal, not too bad.
mensageiro [me*n*-să-zhay'ee-roo] *m.* messenger.
mensagem [me*n*-sah'zhe*n*] *f.* message.
mensal [me*n*-sal'] *adj.* monthly.
mensalidade [me*n*-să-lee-dahd'] *f.* monthly payment.
mente [me*n*t] *f.* mind, understanding; **de boa —**, willingly.
mentecapto [me*n*-tĕ-kap'too] *adj.* mad, insane; crazy.
mentir [me*n*-teer'] *vn.* to lie.
mentira [me*n*-tee'ră] *f.* lie, falsehood.
mentiroso [me*n*-tee-roh'zoo] *adj.* lying; *m.* liar.
mento [me*n*'too] *m.* chin.
mercado [mĕr-kah'doo] *m.* market; market-place; — negro, black market.
mercador [mĕr-kă-dohr'] *m.* merchant, trader.
mercadoria [mĕr-kă-doo-ree'ă] *f.* merchandise; *pl.* goods; **comboio de —s**, goods train.
mercante [mĕr-ka*n*t'] *adj.* merchant.
mercê [mĕr-say'] *f.* reward; favour; mercy; **à — de**, at the mercy of; at the discretion of.
mercearia [mĕr-see-ă-ree'ă] *f.* grocer's (shop), grocery store; *pl.* groceries.
merceeiro [mĕr-see-ay'ee-roo] *m.* grocer.
mercenário [mĕr-sĕ-nah'ree-oo] *m/adj.* mercenary.
mercúrio [mĕr-koo'ree-oo] *m.* mercury, quicksilver.
merecer [mĕ-rĕ-sayr'] *va.* to deserve, merit.
merecimento [mĕ-rĕ-see-me*n*'too] *m.* merit, worthiness, worth.
merenda [mĕ-re*n*'dă] *f.* snack, light lunch; picnic.
mergulhar [mĕr-goo-lyar'] *vn.* to plunge, dive; *va.* to immerse, plunge.
meridional [mĕ-ree-dee-oo-nal'] *adj.* southern.
mérito [me'ree-too] *m.* merit, worth.
mero [mair'oo] *adj.* mere.
mês [maysh] *m.* month.
mesa [may'ză] *f.* table; **pôr a —**, to lay the table; **levantar a —**, to clear the table.
meseta [mĕ-zay'tă] *f.* (small) plateau, table-land.
mesma [mayzh'mă] *f.* the same condition *or* state.
mesmo [mayzh'moo] *adj.* same, identical; **eu —**, I myself; **nem —**, not even; **— assim**, even so; **isso —!**, exactly!; **hoje —**, this very day.
mesquinho [mĕsh-kee'nyoo] *adj.* mean, miserly; wretched, poor.
mesquita [mĕsh-kee'tă] *f.* mosque.
messias [mĕ-see'ăsh] *m.* Messiah.
mestiço [mesh-tee'soo] *m/adj.* half-caste; *adj.* hybrid, crossbred.
mestra [mesh'tră] *f.* schoolmistress, teacher; **chave —**, master-key.
mestre [mesh'trĕ] *m.* master; teacher; **— de bordo**, boatswain; **golpe de —**, masterstroke.
mestria [mesh-tree'ă] *f.* mastery, skill.
mesura [mĕ-zoo'ră] *f.* bow.

meta [me'tă] *f.* (winning-) post; goal; limit.
metade [mě-tahd'] *f.* half; minha cara —, my better half.
metal [mě-tal'] *m.* metal; pitch (of voice); *pl.* brass (*mus.*); — sonante, hard cash. [meteor.
meteoro [mě-te-o'roo] *m.*
meter [mě-tayr'] *va.* to put, place, insert, introduce; *vr.* to get involved in.
metódico [mě-to'dee-koo] *adj.* methodical.
método [me'too-doo] *m.* method; manner.
metralhadora [mě-tră-lyă-doh'ră] *f.* machine-gun.
métrico [me'tree-koo] *adj.* metric; metrical.
metro [me'troo] *m.* metre; underground (railway).
metrópole [mě-tro'pool] *f.* metropolis; capital (city); home country; Portugal (as distinct from her overseae possessions).
metropolitano [mě-troo-poo-lee-tă'noo] *adj.* metropolitan; *m.* metropolitan bishop; underground railway.
meu [may'oo] *adj.* my; *pr.* mine.
mexediço [mě-shě-dee'soo] *adj.* restless, fidgety.
mexedor [mě-shě-dohr'] *m.* mixer (utensil); busybody.
mexer [mě-shayr'] *va.* to stir; to move; to shake; *vn.* to touch; *vr.* to move, budge, stir; to get a move on.
mexericar [mě-shě-ree-kar'] *vn.* to carry tales, gossip.
mexeriqueiro [mě-shě-ree-kay'ee-roo] *m.* mischief-maker, tale-carrier, busy-body, gossip.
mexido [mě-shee'doo] *adj.* active, lively; restless; mixed; ovos —s, scrambled eggs.
mexilhão [mě-shee-lyow*n*'] *m.* mussel; meddler, busybody.
mezinha [me-zee'nyă] *f.* home-made remedy.
miar [mee-ar'] *vn.* to miaow (cat). [microbe.
micróbio [mee-kro'bee-oo] *m.*
microfone [mee-kro-fon'] *m.* microphone.
microscópio [mee-kroosh-ko'pee-oo] *m.* microscope.
mictório [meek-to'ree-oo] *m.* urinal.
migalha [mee-ga'lyă] *f.* crumb; *pl.* scraps, leavings.
migar [mee-gar'] *va.* to crumble.
migração [mee-gră-sow*n*'] *f.* migration. [urinate.
mijar [mee-zhar'] *vn.* to
mil [meel] *adj.* a thousand.
milagre [mee-la'grě] *m.* miracle; ex-voto.
milagroso [mee-lă-groh'zoo] *adj.* miraculous. [dew.
míldio [meel'dee-oo] *m.* mil-
milenário [mee-lě-nah'ree-oo] *adj.* age-old; millenary.
milha [mee'lyă] *f.* mile.
milhafre [mee-lya'frě] *m.* or **milhano**, kite (bird).
milhão [mee-lyow*n*'] *m.* million. [sand.
milhar [mee-lyar'] *m.* thou-
milharal [mee-lyă-ral'] *m.* maize field; (U.S.A.) corn-field.
milho [mee'lyoo] *m.* maize, Indian corn; (*sl.*) money, 'dough'.
milícia [mee-lee'see-ă] *f.* militia; military force.
milionário [mee-lee-oo-nah'-ree-oo] *m.* millionaire.
militar [mee-lee-tar'] *adj.* military; *m.* soldier; *vn.* to serve as a soldier; to fight; to militate against; to tell in favour of.
mim [mee*n*] *pr.* me.

mimar [mee-mar'] *va.* to spoil, pet, make a fuss over; to mimic.
mimo [mee'moo] *m.* caress, petting; grace, delicacy; gift; (*theat.*) mime.
mimoso [mee-moh'zoo] *adj.* delicate, dainty, exquisite; soft; tender, loving; *m.* favourite.
mina [mee'nă] *f.* mine; spring.
minar [mee-nar'] *va.* to mine; to undermine, sap.
mineiro [mee-nay'ee-roo] *m.* miner; inhabitant of Minas Gerais (*Braz.*); *adj.* mining; of Minas Gerais.
mineral [mee-nă-ral'] *m/adj.* mineral.
minério [mee-nair'ee-oo] *m.* ore (*min.*).
míngua [meen'gwă] *f.* want, scarcity, lack, need; **à — de**, for want of.
minguante [meen-gwant'] *adj.* waning; *m.* wane; decline.
minguar [meen-gwar'] *vn.* to decrease, decline, diminish, wane; to be lacking.
minha [mee'nyă] *adj.* my; *pr.* mine.
minhoca [mee-nyo'kă] *f.* [(earth)worm.
minhoto [mee-nyoh'too] *adj.* of the (province of) Minho (*Port.*).
miniatura [mee-nee-ă-too'ră] *f.* miniature; illuminated capital letter.
mínimo [mee'nee-moo] *adj.* least, slightest; *m.* minimum.
ministério [mi-neesh-tair'ee-oo] *m.* ministry; cabinet.
ministro [mi-neesh'troo] *m.* minister; diplomatic representative.
minorar [mee-noo-rar'] *va.* to diminish, reduce.
minoria [mee-noo-ree'ă] *f.* minority.
minucioso [mee-noo-see-oh'-zoo] *adj.* meticulous, detailed.
minúsculo [mee-noosh'koo-loo] *adj.* minute, tiny; (letra) **—a**, small letters.
minuta [mee-noo'tă] *f.* minute, note; rough draft.
minuto [mee-noo'too] *m.* minute.
miolo [mee-oh'loo] *m.* core, pith, kernel; *pl.* brains; sense.
míope [mee'oop] *adj.* short-sighted, myopic.
miopia [mee-oo-pee'ă] *f.* short-sightedness.
mira [mee'ră] *f.* sight (of gun); aim, purpose.
miradouro [mee-ră-doh'roo] *m.* terrace (commanding a fine view).
miragem [mee-rah'zhen] *f.* [mirage.
miramar [mee-ră-mar'] *m.* balcony, terrace (overlooking the sea).
mirar [mee-rar'] *va.* to gaze at, look at; to aim at.
mirrar [mee-rar'] *vn.* to wither, waste away, dry up.
mirto [meer'too] *m.* myrtle.
miscelânea [meesh-sĕ-lă'nee-ă] *f.* miscellany.
miserável [mee-zĕ-rah'vel] *adj.* miserable, wretched; miserly.
miséria [mee-zair'ee-ă] *f.* poverty, misery, wretchedness, squalor; pittance.
misericórdia [mee-zĕ-ree-kor'dee-ă] *f.* mercy, compassion.
missa [mee'să] *f.* Mass; **— do galo**, midnight Mass (on Christmas Eve); **— cantada**, High Mass.
missão [mee-sown'] *f.* mission.
missionário [mee-see-oo-nah'ree-oo] *m.* missionary.
mister [meesh-tair'] *m.* office, task; need; **ser —**, to be necessary.

mistério [meesh-tair'ee-oo] *m.* mystery.
místico [meesh'tee-koo] *m/adj.* mystic.
mistifório [meesh-tee-fo'ree-oo] *m.* mix-up, jumble.
misto [meesh'too] *m.* mingling, mixture; *adj.* mixed; **comboio —**, passenger and goods train.
mistura [meesh-too'ră] *f.* mixture, blend, compound.
misturar [meesh-too-rar'] *va.* to mix, mingle.
mitigar [mee-tee-gar'] *va.* to mitigate, alleviate.
mito [mee'too] *m.* myth.
miudeza [mee-oo-day'ză] *f.* minuteness; *pl.* details; odds and ends; (animal) giblets.
miúdo [mee-oo'doo] *adj.* very small, tiny, minute; precise; *m.* youngster, child; *m.pl.* small change; **a —**, frequently; **arraia —a**, mob, rabble; **dinheiro —**, small change; **por —**, in precise detail.
mixórdia [mee-shor'dee-ă] *f.* mix-up, mess-up, jumble.
mó [mo] *f.* millstone; grindstone (for knives, etc.).
moagem [moo-ah'zhen] *f.* grinding, milling; flour trade.
mobilar [moo-bee-lar'] *va.* to furnish.
mobilia [moo-bee'lee-ă] *f.* furniture.
mobiliário [moo-bee-lee-ah'-ree-oo] *m.* furnishings.
mobilizar [moo-bee-lee-zar'] *va.* to mobilize.
moça [moh'să] *f.* girl; servant-girl.
moção [moo-sown'] *f.* motion, proposal; movement.
mochila [moo-shee'lă] *f.* pack, knapsack, haversack.
mocho [moh'shoo] *m.* owl; *adj.* polled, cropped.
mocidade [moo-see-dahd'] *f.* youth; young people.
moço [moh'soo] *m.* youth, (*pop.*) lad; servant; *adj.* young; inexperienced; **— de câmara**, cabin-boy; **— de fretes**, porter.
moda [mo'dă] *f.* fashion, style, mode; **da —**, fashionable; **fora de —**, old-fashioned, out of fashion.
modelo [moo-day'loo] *m.* model, pattern.
moderado [moo-dĕ-rah'doo] *adj.* moderate, judicious.
moderar [moo-dĕ-rar'] *va.* to moderate; to restrain; to cut down (speed); *vr.* to calm down. [modern.
moderno [moo-dair'noo] *adj.*
modéstia [moo-desh'tee-ă] *f.* modesty; simplicity.
modesto [moo-desh'too] *adj.* modest, unassuming, unpretentious.
módico [mo'dee-koo] *adj.* moderate, modest.
modificar [moo-dee-fee-kar'] *va.* to modify, alter.
modismo [moo-deezh'moo] *m.* idiom, colloquialism.
modista [moo-deesh'tă] *f.* dressmaker.
modo [mo'doo] *m.* manner, way, mode; mood (in grammar); *pl.* manners; **de — nenhum**, not at all; **por nenhum —**, by no means; **de qualquer —**, by some means or other; **de — que**, so that.
modorra [moo-doh'ră] *f.* drowsiness; lethargy.
moeda [moo-e'dă] *f.* coin; money; **— corrente**, currency; **papel-—**, paper money; **casa da —**, the Mint.
moer [moo-ayr'] *va.* to grind, crush, pound; to batter, beat.
mofar [moo-far'] *vn.* to mock at.

mofo [moh'foo] *m.* mould, mustiness.
mogno [mog'noo] *m.* mahogany.
moinho [moo-ee'nyoo] *m.* mill.
moita [moh'ee-tă] *f.* thicket, undergrowth.
mola [mo'lă] *f.* spring.
moldar [mohl-dar'] *va.* to mould.
molde [mold] *m.* mould; *adv.* de —, suitably, appropriately.
mole [mol] *f.* (huge) mass; *adj.* soft; flabby; easy-going.
moleiro [moo-lay'ee-roo] *m.* miller.
molestar [moo-lĕsh-tar'] *va.* to annoy, bother, trouble.
moléstia [moo-lesh'tee-ă] *f.* disease; trouble, annoyance.
molesto [moo-lesh'too] *adj.* troublesome, annoying.
molhar [moo-lyar'] *va.* to soak, wet, moisten.
molhe [mo'lyĕ] *m.* pier, wharf, mole.
molho [mo'lyoo] *m.* bunch, bundle; sheaf (of wheat).
molho [moh'lyoo] *m.* sauce; gravy.
momentâneo [moo-me*n*-tă'-nee-oo] *adj.* momentary.
momento [moo-me*n*'too] *m.* moment; importance; momentum; de —, at the moment; suddenly.
monarca [moo-nar'kă] *m.* monarch, sovereign.
monarquia [moo-năr-kee'ă] *f.* monarchy.
monástico [moo-nash'tee-koo] *adj.* monastic.
monção [mo*n*-sow*n*'] *f.* monsoon.
monco [mo*n*'koo] *m.* (nasal) mucus.
mondar [mon-dar'] *va.* to weed; to root out; to prune (trees).
monge [mo*n*'zhĕ] *m.* monk.
monja [mo*n*'zhă] *f.* nun.
mono [moh'noo] *m.* monkey, ape.
monopólio [moo-noo-po'lee-oo] *m.* monopoly.
monótono [moo-no'too-noo] *adj.* monotonous.
monstro [mo*n*sh'troo] *m.* monster.
monta [mo*n*'tă] *f.* total, sum; worth; de pouca —, of little importance.
montado [mo*n*-tah'doo] *m.* oak wood (where pigs feed).
montagem [mo*n*-tah'zhe*n*] *f.* assembly (of mechanical parts); erection, setting up.
montanha [mo*n*-tă'nyă] *f.* mountain; — russa, switchback (railway), (U.S.A.) roller-coaster.
montanhês [mo*n*-tă-nyaysh'] *adj.* mountain, highland; *m.* mountain-dweller, highlander.
montanhoso [mo*n*-tă-nyoh'-zoo] *adj.* mountainous.
montante [mo*n*-ta*n*t'] *m.* total amount, sum; (*arch.*) broadsword; *adj.* rising; a —, upstream.
montão [mo*n*-tow*n*'] *m.* heap, pile.
montar [mo*n*-tar'] *va.* to mount, ride (horse); to set up; *vn.* to come to (amount).
montaria [mo*n*-tă-ree'ă] *f.* hunting.
monte [mo*n*t] *m.* hill; pile, heap; — pio, (*approx.*) friendly society, insurance fund.
montra [mo*n*'tră] *f.* shop window.
monumento [moo-noo-me*n*'-too] *m.* monument, memorial.
mor [mor] *adj.* chief, principal; altar —, high altar.
morada [moo-rah'dă] *f.* residence, home, dwelling-place.
morador [moo-ră-dohr'] *m.* resident, inhabitant; *adj.* residing.

moral [moo-ral'] *adj.* moral; *f.* morals, ethics.
morango [moo-ra*n*'goo] *m.* strawberry.
morar [moo-rar'] *vn.* to live, reside.
mórbido [mor'bee-doo] *adj.* unhealthy, sickly.
morcego [moor-say'goo] *m.* bat.
morcela [moor-se'lă] *f.* black pudding.
mordaça [moor-dah'să] *f.* gag, muzzle.
mordaz [moor-dash'] *adj.* biting, caustic, sarcastic.
mordedura [moor-de-doo'ră] *f.* bite.
morder [moor-dayr'] *va.* to bite, gnaw; to corrode.
moreno [moo-ray'noo] *adj.* dark (-skinned); *f.* brunette.
morfina [moor-fee'nă] *f.* morphia, morphine.
morgado [mor-gah'doo] *m.* heir; eldest son; estate.
moribundo [moo-ree-boo*n*'-doo] *adj.* dying, moribund.
morigerado [moo-ree-zhĕ-rah'doo] *adj.* well-behaved, exemplary, upright.
mormente [mor-me*n*t'] *adv.* chiefly, especially.
mormo [mohr'moo] *m.* glanders.
morno [mohr'noo] *adj.* lukewarm, tepid; listless.
moroso [moo-roh'zoo] *adj.* slow, sluggish, dilatory.
morrão [moo-row*n*'] *m.* fuse.
morrer [moo-rayr'] *vn.* to die, perish; to fade.
morro [moh'roo] *m.* hill, hillock.
mortadela [moor-tă-de'lă] *f.* (Italian) sausage.
mortalha [moor-ta'lyă] *f.* shroud.
mortalidade [moor-tă-lee-dahd'] *f.* mortality; death-rate.
mortandade [moor-ta*n*-dahd'] *f.* slaughter.
morte [mort] *f.* death.
mortiço [moor-tee'soo] *adj.* dying; lifeless, dull.
mortífero [moor-tee'fĕ-roo] *adj.* deadly, death-dealing.
mortificar [moor-tee-fee-kar'] *va.* to annoy, trouble; to mortify (the flesh); to deaden (part of body).
morto [mohr'too] *adj.* dead; *m.* dead person; **estar — por**, to be dying to (know something, etc.); **estar — de**, to be dying of (jealousy, etc.).
mosaico [moo-zȳ'koo] *m.* mosaic.
mosca [mohsh'kă] *f.* fly; *m.* apanha- ——s, fly-catcher; mata- —s, fly-swat.
mosqueiro [moosh-kay'ee-roo] *m.* fly-trap; (wire) cover (for foodstuffs).
mosquiteiro [moosh-kee-tay'-ee-roo] *m.* mosquito-net.
mosquito [moosh-kee'too] *m.* mosquito; gnat.
mossa [mo'să] *f.* dent; (*fig.*) impression.
mostarda [moosh-tar'dă] *f.* mustard.
mosteiro [moosh-tay'ee-roo] *m.* monastery.
mosto [mohsh'too] *m.* grape juice.
mostra [mosh'tră] *f.* display; sign, indication; *pl.* gestures; **dar —s de**, to give signs of.
mostrador [moosh-tră-dohr'] *m.* face, dial (of clock); glass counter.
mostrar [moosh-trar'] *va.* to show; to prove.
mostrengo [moosh-tre*n*'goo] *m.* lout; monster.
mote [mot] *m.* motto; theme.
motejar [moo-tĕ-zhar'] *vn.* to jeer at, make fun of.
motejo [moo-tay'zhoo] *m.* jeer, mockery, derision.

motim [moo-teen'] *m.* riot, mutiny.
motivar [moo-tee-var'] *va.* to cause, give rise to.
motivo [moo-tee'voo] *m.* motive, cause, reason; theme, motif (*mus.*).
motocicleta [moo-too-see-kle'tă] *f.* motor-cycle.
motor [moh-tohr'] *m.* motor, engine. [*m.* driver.
motorista [moh-toh-reesh'tă]
motriz [moh-treesh'] *adj.* motive, driving.
mouco [moh'koo] *adj.* deaf, hard of hearing.
movediço [moh-vĕ-dee'soo] *adj.* shifting; movable; changeable, unstable; **areia —a**, quicksand.
móvel [mo'vel] *adj.* movable; *m.* motive; piece of furniture; *pl.* **móveis**, furniture; **bens —**, personal property; goods and chattels.
mover [moh-vayr'] *va.* to move; to provoke.
movimento [moo-vee-men'-too] *m.* movement; motion.
muar [moo-ar'] *mf.* mule.
muco [moo'koo] *m.* mucus.
muçulmano [moo-sool-mă'-noo] *m/adj.* Moslem, Muslim.
mudança [moo-dan'să] *f.* change; alteration; removal.
mudar [moo-dar'] *va.* to change, alter; to moult (of feathers); **— de casa**, to move (house); **— de roupa**, to change (clothes).
mudo [moo'doo] *adj.* dumb, mute; silent; **surdo- —**, deaf and dumb; a deaf-mute.
mugir [moo-zheer'] *vn.* to moo, low; to bellow, roar.
muito [mween'too] *adj.* a lot of, much; *pl.* many; *adv.* very; too; much, a great deal, a lot; **quando —**, at most; **ter em —**, to have a high opinion of; **há — tempo,** a long time ago.
mula [moo'lă] *f.* mule.
muleta [moo-lay'tă] *f.* crutch; (*fig.*) support. [wife.
mulher [moo-lyair'] *f.* woman;
mulherão [moo-lyĕ-rown'] *m.* big, strong woman.
multa [mool'tă] *f.* fine.
multar [mool-tar'] *va.* to fine.
multidão [mool-tee-down'] *f.* crowd; multitude.
multiplicar [mool-tee-plee-kar'] *va.* to multiply.
mundano [moon-dă'noo] *adj.* worldly.
mundial [moon-dee-al'] *adj.* world, world-wide.
mundo [moon'doo] *m.* world; earth; **todo o —**, everybody.
mungir [moon-zheer'] *va.* to milk.
munição [moo-nee-sown'] *f.* munitions; ammunition; supplies.
município [moo-nee-see'pee-oo] *m.* town, borough, municipality.
munir [moo-neer'] *va.* to provide, supply.
muralha [moo-ra'lyă] *f.* wall, rampart.
murchar [moor-shar'] *va/vn.* to wither, shrivel up, wilt, fade.
murmulho [moor-moo'lyoo] *m.* rustle (of leaves); rippling (of waves).
murmuração [moor-moo-ră-sown'] *f.* muttering; backbiting.
murmurar [moor-moo-rar'] *vn.* to murmur, whisper; to complain, grumble.
murmúrio [moor-moo'ree-oo] *m.* murmur; whisper; rustle.
muro [moo'roo] *m.* wall.
murro [moo'roo] *m.* punch, blow, thump.
murta [moor'tă] *f.* myrtle.

músculo [moosh'koo-loo] *m.* muscle.
museu [moo-zay'oo] *m.* museum; art gallery.
musgo [moozh'goo] *m.* moss.
música [moo'zee-kă] *f.* music.
músico [moo'zee-koo] *m.* musician; *adj.* musical.
mutação [moo-tă-sow*n*'] *f.* mutation, alteration; change (of scenery in theatre); fickleness.
mutilado [moo-tee-lah'doo] *adj.* mutilated; disabled; — **de guerra,** disabled ex-service man.
mutilar [moo-tee-lar'] *va.* to mutilate, disable, maim.
mutuar [moo-too-ar'] *va.* to exchange.
mútuo [moo'too-oo] *adj.* mutual, reciprocal.

N

nabo [nah'boo] *m.* turnip.
nação [nă-sow*n*'] *f.* nation; country.
nácar [na'kar] *m.* mother-of-pearl; pink (colour).
naco [na'koo] *m.* piece, slice; chunk.
nada [nah'dă] *m.* nothing; nothingness; a trifle; **antes de mais —,** first of all; **de —!,** not at all!
nadador [nă-dă-dohr'] *m.* swimmer.
nadar [nă-dar'] *vn.* to swim.
nádegas [na'dĕ-găsh] *f.pl.* buttocks.
nado [nah'doo] **a —,** *adv.* (by) swimming.
naipe [nȳp] *m.* suit (of playing cards).
namorada [nă-moo-rah'dă] *f.* sweetheart, girl-friend.
namorado [nă-moo-rah'doo] *m.* sweetheart, boy-friend.
namoro [nă-moh'roo] *m.* courtship; love-making; love affair.
não [now*n*] *adv.* not; no; **pois —!,** certainly!
narciso [nar-see'zoo] *m.* daffodil; narcissus.
narcótico [năr-ko'tee-koo] *m/adj.* narcotic.
narigudo [nă-ree-goo'doo] *adj.* with a big nose.
nariz [nă-reesh'] *m.* nose; **torcer o —,** to turn up one's nose.
narração [nă-ră-sow*n*'] *f.* account, report, narration.
narrar [nă-rar'] *va.* to narrate, recount, tell.
narrativa [nă-ră-tee'vă] *f.* narrative, tale, story; narration.
nasal [nă-zal'] *f/adj.* nasal.
nasalação [nă-ză-lă-sow*n*'] *f.* nasalization.
nascença [năsh-se*n*'să] *f.* birth; origin; beginning.
nascente [năsh-se*n*t'] *f.* source; spring; *m.* East; *adj.* nascent; budding.
nascer [năsh-sayr'] *vn.* to be born; to shoot up, sprout.
nascido [năsh-see'doo] *adj.* born; **recém- —,** new-born.
nascimento [năsh-see-me*n*'-too] *m.* birth; origin.
nata [nah'tă] *f.* cream; custard; (*fig.*) the cream, the best.
natação [nă-tă-sow*n*'] *f.* swimming.
natal [nă-tal'] *m.* Christmas; *adj.* natal; native; **terra —,** birthplace; **país —,** native land.
natalício [nă-tă-lee'see-oo] *adj.* **aniversário —,** birthday; *m.* birthday.
natalidade [nă-tă-lee-dahd'] *f.* birth-rate.
natividade [nă-tee-vee-dahd'] *f.* nativity.
nativo [nă-tee'voo] *adj.* native, innate.

nato [nah'too] *adj.* born; inborn, innate; natural.
natural [nă-too-ral'] *adj.* natural; plain; life-like; *m.* native; disposition, tendency; filho —, illegitimate son.
naturalizar [nă-too-ră-lee-zar'] *va.* to naturalize.
natureza [nă-too-ray'ză] *f.* nature; — **morta**, still life (painting).
nau [now] *f.* ship, vessel.
naufragar [now-fră-gar'] *vn.* to be shipwrecked; to collapse, come to naught, be ruined.
naufrágio [now-frah'zhee-oo] *m.* shipwreck; (*fig.*) collapse, ruin, failure.
náufrago [now'fră-goo] *m.* shipwrecked person, castaway.
náusea [now'zee-ă] *f.* sickness, seasickness, nausea; disgust, loathing.
nauseabundo [now-zee-ă-boo*n*'doo] *adj.* nauseating, disgusting, nasty.
náutico [now'tee-koo] *adj.* nautical, naval.
naval [nă-val'] *adj.* naval.
navalha [nă-va'lyă] *f.* (large) pocket-knife; — **(de barba)**, razor.
nave [nahv] *f.* nave (in church).
navegação [nă-vĕ-gă-sow*n*'] *f.* navigation; sailing; voyage; shipping.
navegador [nă-vĕ-gă-dohr'] *m.* or **navegante**, *m.* navigator.
navegar [nă-vĕ-gar'] *vn.* to sail, steer, navigate.
navio [nă-vee'oo] *m.* ship, boat; — **de guerra**, warship; — **mercante**, merchant-ship; — **petroleiro**, oil tanker.
neblina [nĕ-blee'nă] *f.* mist; fog.
nebulosa [nĕ-boo-lo'ză] *f.* [nebula (*astr.*).
nebuloso [nĕ-boo-loh'zoo] *adj.* cloudy, misty; (*fig.*) obscure, indistinct.
necessário [nĕ-sĕ-sah'ree-oo] *adj.* necessary, requisite.
necessidade [nĕ-sĕ-see-dahd'] *f.* necessity, need, want.
necessitado [nĕ-sĕ-see-tah'-doo] *adj.* poor, needy, indigent.
necessitar [nĕ-sĕ-see-tar'] *va.* to need, require, want.
necrologia [nĕ-kroo-loo-zhee'ă] *f.* obituary notice; deaths column.
nédio [ne'dee-oo] *adj.* sleek, plump, glossy.
neerlandês [nee-ĕr-la*n*-daysh'] *adj.* Dutch; *m.* Dutchman.
nefando [nĕ-fa*n*'doo] *adj.* heinous, nefarious, atrocious.
nefas [ne'făsh], **por fas ou por** —, by hook or by crook, by fair means or foul.
nefasto [nĕ-fash'too] *adj.* ominous; fatal; tragic.
negaça [nĕ-ga'să] *f.* bait, lure.
negação [nĕ-gă-sow*n*'] *f.* negation, denial.
negar [nĕ-gar'] *va.* to deny; to refuse; *vr.* to refuse.
negativa [nĕ-gă-tee'vă] *f.* negative; refusal; denial.
negativo [nĕ-gă-tee'voo] *adj.* negative.
negligência [nĕ-glee-zhe*n*'see-ă] *f.* negligence, carelessness, neglect.
negligente [nĕ-glee-zhe*n*t'] *adj.* negligent, careless.
negociação [nĕ-goo-see-ă-sow*n*'] *f.* negotiation.
negociante [nĕ-goo-see-a*n*t'] *m.* trader, merchant, businessman.
negociar [nĕ-goo-see-ar'] *va.* to negotiate; to trade, deal.
negociável [nĕ-goo-see-ah'-vel] *adj.* negotiable.
negócio [nĕ-go'see-oo] *m.* business; transaction, deal;

matter; homem de —s, businessman.
negreiro [nĕ-gray'ee-roo] *m.* slave-trader.
negro [nay'groo] *adj.* black; *m.* negro.
negrura [nĕ-groo'ră] *f.* blackness, darkness.
nem [ne*n*] *conj.* nor, neither; *adv.* not.
nenhum [nĕ-nyoo*n*'] *adj/pr.* no; none.
nenúfar [nĕ-noo'far] *m.* water-lily.
neófito [nee-o'fee-too] *m.* novice, beginner.
nervo [nayr'voo] *m.* nerve; strength.
nervosidade [nĕr-voo-zee-dahd'] *f.* nervous energy; vigour; nervousness.
nervosismo [nĕr-voo-zeezh'-moo] *m.* nervousness; excitability, nervous irritability.
nervoso [nĕr-voh'zoo] *adj.* nervous, highly strung, excitable; vigorous.
nervudo [nĕr-voo'doo] *adj.* robust, sinewy.
nêspera [naysh'pĕ-ră] *f.* loquat (fruit).
neta [ne'tă] *f.* grand-daughter.
neto [ne'too] *m.* grandson.
neutral [nay-oo-tral'] *adj.* neutral.
neutralidade [nay-oo-tră-lee-dahd'] *f.* neutrality.
neutro [nay'oo-troo] *adj.* neuter; neutral.
nevar [nĕ-var'] *vn.* to snow.
neve [nev] *f.* snow.
névoa [ne'voo-ă] *f.* fog, mist.
nevoeiro [nĕ-voo-ay'ee-roo] *m.* (thick) fog.
nevralgia [nĕ-vral-zhee'ă] *f.* neuralgia.
nevrose [nĕ-vrohz'] *f.* neurosis.
nexo [nek'soo] *m.* connexion, link; sem —, incoherent.
nicho [nee'shoo] *m.* niche.
nimbo [nee*n*'boo] *m.* halo.
nímio [nee'mee-oo] *adj.* excessive.
ninguém [nee*n*-ge*n*'] *pr.* nobody, no one.
ninhada [nee-nyah'dă] *f.* brood, nest(ful).
ninharia [nee-nyă-ree'ă] *f.* trifle.
ninho [nee'nyoo] *m.* nest; home.
niquento [nee-ke*n*'too] *adj.* fussy, niggling.
nitidez [nee-tee-daysh'] *f.* clarity, brightness, polish.
nítido [nee'tee-doo] *adj.* clear, clear-cut, polished, bright.
nível [nee'vel] *m.* level; — de vida, standard of living; passagem de —, level crossing.
nivelar [nee-vĕ-lar'] *va.* to level, flatten.
níveo [nee'vee-oo] *adj.* snow-white.
nó [no] *m.* knot; tie; corredio, slip-knot; —s dos dedos, knuckles, finger-joints; — na garganta, a lump in the throat.
nobilitar [noo-bee-lee-tar'] *va.* to ennoble.
nobre [no'brĕ] *m/adj.* noble.
nobreza [noo-bray'ză] *f.* nobility; nobleness.
noção [noo-sow*n*'] *f.* notion, idea; *pl.* rudiments.
nocivo [noo-see'voo] *adj.* harmful, injurious, noxious.
noctâmbulo [nok-ta*n*'boo-loo] *m.* sleepwalker; street-roamer (at night).
nocturno [no-toor'noo] *adj.* nocturnal, night.
nódoa [no'doo-ă] *f.* stain, spot, blemish.
nogueira [noo-gay'ee-ră] *f.* walnut-tree; walnut (wood).
noitada [noh-ee-tah'dă] *f.* a whole night; a night out; a sleepless night.
noite [noh'eet] *f.* night; **à (de)** —, at *or* by night.

noiva [noh'ee-vă] *f.* fiancée; bride.
noivado [noh-ee-vah'doo] *m.* wedding; engagement.
noivo [noh'ee-voo] *m.* fiancé; bridegroom; *pl.* engaged couple; bridal pair, bride and bridegroom.
nojento [noo-zhen'too] *adj.* nauseating, disgusting.
nojo [noh'zhoo] *m.* nausea; loathing; mourning.
nome [nohm] *m.* name; reputation; noun (in grammar); — **de baptismo**, Christian name; — **de família**, surname; **de** —, by name.
nomeação [noo-mee-ă-sown'] *f.* appointment; nomination.
nomeadamente [noo-mee-ah-dă-ment'] *adv.* in particular, specially, by name.
nomear [noo-mee-ar'] *va.* to appoint; to nominate; to name.
nono [noh'noo] *adj.* ninth.
nora [no'ră] *f.* daughter-in-law; water-wheel.
nordeste [nor-desht'] *m.* north-east.
norma [nor'mă] *f.* standard, rule, model.
normal [nohr-mal'] *adj.* normal; **escola** —, training college.
normalizar [nohr-mă-lee-zar'] *va.* to normalize; *vr.* to return to normal.
noroeste [nor-wesht'] *m.* north-west.
nortada [nor-tah'dă] *f.* cold north wind.
norte [nort] *m.* north; (*fig.*) guidance, direction.
norte-americano [nort-ă-mĕ-ree-kă'noo] *m/adj.* North-American, American.
norueguês [nor-wĕ-gaysh'] *m/adj.* Norwegian.
nostalgia [noosh-tal-zhee'ă] *f.* nostalgia, homesickness
nota [no'tă] *f.* note; annotation; mark (in exam.).
notabilidade [noo-tă-bee-lee-dahd'] *f.* notability.
notar [noo-tar'] *va.* to note, observe, notice; to note down; **é de** —, it is worth noting.
notário [noo-tah'ree-oo] *m.* notary public, commissioner for oaths.
notável [noo-tah'vel] *adj.* remarkable; notable.
notícia [noo-tee'see-ă] *f.* (item, piece of) news; report; *pl.* news.
noticiar [noo-tee-see-ar'] *va.* to announce, make known.
noticiário [noo-tee-see-ah'ree-oo] *m.* news bulletin (radio); news reel (cinema); news section (in papers).
notificação [noo-tee-fee-kă-sown'] *f.* notification.
notificar [noo-tee-fee-kar'] *va.* to notify; to inform.
notório [noo-to'ree-oo] *adj.* well-known, evident.
nova [no'vă] *f.* item of news; *pl.* news.
novato [noo-vah'too] *m.* novice, beginner; freshman, 'fresher' (*acad.*); *adj.* inexperienced, raw.
nove [nov] *adj.* nine.
novela [noo-ve'lă] *f.* (short) novel; story.
noveleiro [noo-vĕ-lay'ee-roo] *adj.* tale-carrier, mischief-maker; *m.* story-teller, -writer. [novelist.
novelista [noo-vĕ-leesh'tă] *mf.*
novelo [noo-vay'loo] *m.* ball of thread *or* yarn; (*fig.*) plot, intrigue.
novembro [noo-ven'broo] *m.* November. [ninety.
noventa [noo-ven'tă] *adj.*
noviciado [noo-vee-see-ah'-

doo] *m.* novitiate (*eccl.*); apprenticeship.
noviço [noo-vee'soo] *m.* novice (*eccl.*); apprentice, beginner.
novidade [noo-vee-dahd'] *f.* novelty; (item of) news; crop (of fruit, etc.); strange incident; mishap; sem —, without incident; *pl.* news.
novilha [noo-vee'lyă] *f.* heifer.
novilho [noo-vee'lyoo] *m.* young bull.
novo [noh'voo] *adj.* new; young; de —, again, anew.
noz [nosh] *f.* nut, walnut; — moscada, nutmeg.
nu [noo] *adj.* naked, bare, nude.
nublado [noo-blah'doo] *adj.* cloudy, overcast.
nuca [noo'kă] *f.* nape (back) of the neck.
núcleo [noo'klee-oo] *m.* nucleus; core, kernel.
nudez [noo-daysh'] *f. or* **nudeza**, *f.* nakedness, nudity.
nulidade [noo-lee-dahd'] *f.* nullity, invalidity; nonentity (person).
nulo [noo'loo] *adj.* null, void.
numeração [noo-mĕ-ră-sow*n*'] *f.* numbering.
numerar [noo-mĕ-rar'] *va.* to number; to enumerate.
numerário [noo-mĕ-rah'ree-oo] *m.* cash, specie.
numérico [noo-me'ree-koo] *adj.* numerical.
número [noo'mĕ-roo] *m.* number; figure, numeral; — redondo, round figure.
numeroso [noo-mĕ-roh'zoo] *adj.* numerous; (*poet.*) harmonious, melodious.
nunca [noo*n*'kă] *f.* never; — mais, never again.
núpcias [noop'see-ăsh] *f.pl.* marriage, wedding.
nutrição [noo-tree-sow*n*'] *f.* nutrition.
nutrido [noo-tree'doo] *adj.* well-nourished; plump; robust; fogo —, heavy fire.
nutrimento [noo-tree-me*n*'-too] *m.* nourishment, food.
nutrir [noo-treer'] *va.* to nourish, feed; to cherish (hopes, etc.).
nutritivo [noo-tree-tee'voo] *adj.* nourishing, nutritious.
nuvem [noo've*n*] *f.* cloud; throng, crowd; elevar às —s, to praise to the skies; cair das —s, to be astounded; to turn up unexpectedly.

O

oásis [oo-ah'zeesh] *m.* oasis.
obcecação [ohb-sĕ-kă-sow*n*'] *f.* obduracy; obfuscation.
obcecar [ohb-sĕ-kar'] *va.* to blind (*fig.*).
obduração [ohb-doo-ră-sow*n*'] *f.* obduracy.
obedecer [oh-bĕ-dĕ-sayr'] *vn.* to obey, comply with.
obediência [oh-bĕ-dee-e*n*'see-ă] *f.* obedience, submission.
obediente [oh-bĕ-dee-e*n*t'] *adj.* obedient, submissive.
obesidade [oh-bĕ-zee-dahd'] *f.* obesity, corpulence.
óbice [o'bees] *m.* obstacle.
óbito [o'bee-too] *m.* death.
objecção [ohb-zhe-sow*n*'] *f.* objection.
objectivo [ohb-zhe-tee'voo] *m/adj.* objective.
objecto [ohb-zhe'too] *m.* object, thing, article; purpose.
objurgação [ohb-zhoor-gă-sow*n*'] *f.* reproof, objurgation.
oblíquo [oh-blee'kwoo] *adj.* oblique, slanting; lopsided.
obliterar [oh-blee-tĕ-rar'] *va.* to obliterate; to blot out from memory.
óbolo [o'boo-loo] *m.* mite, small contribution.

obra [o'bră] *f.* work, — **prima**, masterpiece; **em —s**, under repair; **pôr em —**, to put into effect; — **de**, about.
obrar [oh-brar'] *vn.* to act, work.
obreiro [oh-bray'ee-roo] *m.* worker, workman.
obrigação [oh-bree-gă-sow*n*'] *f.* obligation, duty; debenture, bond (*com.*).
obrigado [oh-bree-gah'doo] *adj.* obliged, compelled; grateful; *interj.* thank you.
obrigar [oh-bree-gar'] *va.* to compel, force, oblige; *vr.* to undertake.
obrigatório [oh-bree-gă-to'-ree-oo] *adj.* compulsory, obligatory.
obsceno [ohbsh-say'noo] *adj.* obscene, lewd.
obscurecer [ohbsh-koo-rĕ-sayr'] *va.* to obscure, darken.
obscuridade [ohbsh-koo-ree-dahd'] *f.* obscurity.
obscuro [ohbsh-koo'roo] *adj.* dark; (*fig.*) obscure.
obsequiar [ohb-zĕ-kee-ar'] *va.* to favour; to present with; to show kindness to.
obséquio [ohb-ze'kee-oo] *m.* favour, kindness; **faz —**, please.
obsequioso [ohb-zĕ-kee-oh'-zoo] *adj.* obliging, polite.
observação [ohb-sĕr-vă-sow*n*'] *f.* observation; comment, remark.
observador [ohb-sĕr-vă-dohr'] *m.* observer.
observância [ohb-sĕr-va*n*'-see-ă] *f.* observance.
observar [ohb-sĕr-var'] *va.* to observe.
observatório [ohb-sĕr-vă-to'ree-oo] *m.* observatory.
obsessão [ohb-sĕ-sow*n*'] *f.* obsession, mania, fixed idea.
obstáculo [ohbsh-ta'koo-loo] *m.* obstacle, hindrance, snag.
obstante [ohbsh-ta*n*t'] *prep.* **não —**, despite, notwithstanding.
obstar [ohbsh-tar'] *va.* to hinder, oppose.
obstinação [ohbsh-tee-nă-sow*n*'] *f.* obstinacy.
obstinado [ohbsh-tee-nah'-doo] *adj.* obstinate, stubborn.
obstinar-se [ohbsh-tee-nar'-sĕ] *vr.* to persist in, be obdurate.
obstrução [ohbsh-troo-sow*n*'] *f.* obstruction.
obstruir [ohbsh-troo-eer'] *va.* to obstruct, block up; to hinder.
obtenção [ohb-te*n*-sow*n*'] *f.* obtainment.
obter [ohb-tayr'] *va.* to obtain, get.
obturar [ohb-too-rar'] *va.* to plug, stop up; to fill (tooth).
obtuso [ohb-too'zoo] *adj.* obtuse.
obviar [ohb-vee-ar'] *va.* to obviate, prevent; to oppose.
óbvio [ob'vee-oo] *adj.* obvious.
ocasião [oh-kă-zee-ow*n*'] *f.* occasion; opportunity.
ocasionar [oh-kă-zee-oo-nar'] *va.* to cause, give rise to.
ocaso [oh-kah'zoo] *m.* setting, sunset; decline, end; west.
oceano [oh-see-ă'noo] *m.* ocean.
ocidental [oh-see-de*n*-tal'] *adj.* western.
ocidente [oh-see-de*n*t'] *m.* west.
ócio [o'see-oo] *m.* leisure time; idleness; leisurely diversion.
ociosidade [oh-see-oo-zee-dahd'] *f.* idleness.
ocioso [oh-see-oh'zoo] *adj.* idle, indolent, empty.
oco [oh'koo] *adj.* hollow.
ocorrência [oh-koo-re*n*'see-ă] *f.* incident, event.
ocorrer [oh-koo-rayr'] *vn.* to happen, occur; to come to

mind, occur; to meet (needs, etc.). [ochre.
ocre [o'krĕ] *m.* *or* **ocra,** *f.*
ocular [oh-koo-lar'] *adj.* ocular; testemunha —, eyewitness.
oculista [oh-koo-leesh'tă] *m.* optician, oculist.
óculo [o'koo-loo] *m.* spy-glass, telescope; *pl.* spectacles, glasses.
ocultar [oh-kool-tar'] *va.* to hide, conceal.
oculto [oh-kool'too] *adj.* concealed, hidden, secret; occult.
ocupação [oh-koo-pă-sow*n*'] *f.* occupation; business, profession.
ocupado [oh-koo-pah'doo] *adj.* busy; occupied, taken.
ocupar [oh-koo-par'] *va.* to occupy; *vr.* to busy oneself with.
odiar [oh-dee-ar'] *va.* to hate.
ódio [o'dee-oo] *m.* hatred, hate.
odioso [oh-dee-oh'zoo] *adj.* hateful, detestable, odious.
odorífero [oh-doo-ree'fĕ-roo] *adj.* fragrant, sweet-smelling.
odre [oh'drĕ] *m.* wineskin.
oeste [wesht] *m.* west.
ofegante [oh-fĕ-ga*n*t'] *adj.* breathless, panting, out of breath.
ofegar [oh-fĕ-gar'] *vn.* to pant, puff, gasp for breath.
ofender [oh-fe*n*-dayr'] *va.* to offend, hurt, insult; to injure.
ofensa [oh-fe*n*'să] *f.* insult, affront; (bodily) injury.
ofensiva [oh-fe*n*-see'vă] *f.* offensive.
ofensivo [oh-fe*n*-see'voo] *adj.* offensive, rude; aggressive.
oferecer [oh-frĕ-sayr'] *va.* to offer, present, proffer; *vr.* to occur; to volunteer.
oferta [oh-fair'tă] *f.* offer; gift; offering (*relig.*).
oficial [oh-fee-see-al'] *m.* officer (*mil.*); official; *adj.* official; — de serviço, duty officer.
oficialidade [oh-fee-see-ă-lee-dahd'] *f.* officers (as a group).
oficina [oh-fee-see'nă] *f.* workshop.
ofício [oh-fee'see-oo] *m.* occupation, business, trade, craft; service (*relig.*); official letter; Santo —, Inquisition; bons —s, good offices.
oficioso [oh-fee-see-oh'zoo] *adj.* obliging; unofficial.
ofuscar [oh-foosh-kar'] *va.* to darken; to dazzle.
oiro [oh'ee-roo] *or* **ouro** [oh'roo] *m.* gold; *pl.* diamonds (cards).
oitavo [oh-ee-tah'voo] *adj.* eighth. [eighty.
oitenta [oh-ee-te*n*'tă] *m/adj.*
oito [oh'ee-too] *m/adj.* eight.
olá [o-lah'] *interj.* hello!
olaia [oh-lah'yă] *f.* Judas-tree.
olaria [oh-lă-ree'ă] *f.* pottery (-works). [skin.
oleado [oh-lee-ah'doo] *m.* oil-
oleiro [oh-lay'ee-roo] *m.* pottery-worker, potter.
óleo [o'lee-oo] *m.* oil; pintura a —, oil painting.
oleoso [oh-lee-oh'zoo] *adj.* oily; greasy.
olfacto [ohl-fah'too] *m.* sense of smell. [look.
olhada [oh-lyah'dă] *f.* glance,
olhar [oh-lyar'] *va.* to look (at), gaze (at); to consider; — por, to look after; *m.* look, expression.
olheiras [oh-lyay'ee-răsh] *f.pl.* (dark) rings round the eyes.
olho [oh'lyoo] *m.* eye; dar uma vista de —s, to glance at, over; num abrir e fechar de —s, in the twinkling of an eye, in a flash; a —s vistos, visibly; ver com bons —s, to approve of; farto até aos

—s, fed up to the teeth; — pisado, black eye.
olival [oh-lee-val'] *m. or* **olivedo**, olive-grove.
oliveira [oh-lee-vay'ee-ră] *f.* olive-tree. [elm.
olmo [ohl'moo] *m. or* **olmeiro**,
olor [oh-lohr'] *m.* perfume, scent, odour.
oloroso [oh-loo-roh'zoo] *adj.* fragrant, scented.
olvidar [ohl-vee-dar'] *va.* to forget.
ombreira [*on*-bray'ee-ră] *f.* door-post; shoulder pad (in coat).
ombro [*on*'broo] *m.* shoulder; **encolher os —**, to shrug one's shoulders; **meter —s à obra**, to put one's shoulder to the wheel. [omelette.
omeleta [ohm-lay'tă] *f.*
ominoso [oh-mee-noh'zoo] *adj.* ominous.
omissão [oh-mee-sow*n*'] *f.* omission; neglect.
omisso [oh-mee'soo] *adj.* remiss, neglectful; omitted.
omitir [oh-mee-teer'] *va.* to omit, leave out; to neglect.
omoplata [oh-moh-plah'tă] *f.* shoulder-blade.
onça [*on*'să] *f.* ounce (weight); lynx, snow leopard, puma.
onda [*on*'dă] *f.* wave; **comprimento de —**, wavelength.
onde [*on*d] *adv.* where; **— quer que**, wherever.
ondear [*on*-dee-ar'] *vn.* to wave, undulate.
ondulação [*on*-doo-lă-sow*n*'] *f.* undulation; waviness; — **permanente**, permanent wave, (*pop.*) 'perm'.
ondulante [*on*-doo-la*n*t'] *adj.* waving, undulating.
onerar [oh-nĕ-rar'] *va.* to burden (with taxes).
ontem [*on*'te*n*] *adv.* yesterday; **— à noite**, last night.
onze [*on*z] *m/adj.* eleven.
onzeneiro [*on*-zĕ-nay'ee-roo] *m.* usurer, miser.
opaco [oh-pah'koo] *adj.* opaque; dark.
opção [op-sow*n*'] *f.* option, choice.
ópera [o'pĕ-ră] *f.* opera; **— bufa**, comic opera.
operação [oh-pĕ-ră-sow*n*'] *f.* operation; transaction (*com.*).
operador [oh-pĕ-ră-dohr'] *m.* operator.
operar [oh-pĕ-rar'] *va.* to produce (an effect, etc.); to operate on (*med.*); *vn.* to function.
operário [oh-pĕ-rah'ree-oo] *m.* worker, workman.
opimo [oh-pee'moo] *adj.* rich, abundant.
opinar [oh-pee-nar'] *vn.* to be of the opinion; to believe, consider, think, decide.
opinião [oh-pee-nee-ow*n*'] *f.* opinion, view.
ópio [o'pee-oo] *m.* opium.
opíparo [oh-pee'pă-roo] *adj.* sumptuous, splendid.
oponente [oh-poo-ne*n*t'] *m.* opponent; *adj.* opposing.
opor [oh-pohr'] *va.* to oppose; to resist; to face.
oportunidade [oh-poor-too-nee-dahd'] *f.* opportunity.
oportuno [oh-poor-too'noo] *adj.* opportune, timely, appropriate, suitable.
oposição [oh-poo-zee-sow*n*'] *f.* opposition; contrast.
oposto [oh-pohsh'too] *adj.* opposite; facing; contrary; opposed, antagonistic.
opressão [oh-prĕ-sow*n*'] *f.* oppression, tyranny; pressure.
opressivo [oh-prĕ-see'voo] *adj.* oppressive.
oprimir [oh-pree-meer'] *va.* to oppress.

opróbrio [oh-pro'bree-oo] *m.* infamy, disgrace, shame.
optar [op-tar'] *va.* to opt for, choose.
óptico [o'tee-koo] *m.* optician; *adj.* optic(al).
óptimo [o'tee-moo] *adj.* excellent, splendid.
opulência [oh-poo-len'see-ă] *f.* wealth, affluence, opulence.
opúsculo [oh-poosh'koo-loo] *m.* pamphlet, booklet.
ora [o'ră] *interj.* oh!, well!; — essa!, the very idea!; not at all! (i.e. no need to thank me); — bem, well now!; *conj.* but; *adv.* now, sometimes.
oração [o-ră-sown'] *f.* prayer; sentence, clause; discourse, oration; sermon.
oráculo [oh-ra'koo-loo] *m.* oracle.
orador [oh-ră-dohr'] *m.* orator, speaker.
orago [oh-rah'goo] *m.* patron [saint.
oral [oh-ral'] *adj.* oral.
orate [oh-raht'] *m.* madman; casa de —s, madhouse.
orbe [orb] *m.* orb, globe, sphere.
órbita [or'bee-tă] *f.* orbit.
orçamento [ohr-să-men'too] *m.* budget; estimate.
ordeiro [ohr-day'ee-roo] *adj.* orderly, peaceable, law-abiding.
ordem [or'den] *f.* order; arrangement; command; por —, in order; às suas —s, at your service.
ordenação [ohr-dě-nă-sown'] *f.* ordering, classification; ordination (*eccl.*); ordinance, decree.
ordenado [ohr-dě-nah'doo] *m.* salary.
ordenança [ohr-dě-nan'să] *f.* orderly (*mil.*); regulation.
ordenar [ohr-dě-nar'] *va.* to arrange, classify, put in order; to order, command; to ordain (*eccl.*).
ordenhar [ohr-dě-nyar'] *va.* to milk.
ordinário [ohr-dee-nah'ree-oo] *adj.* ordinary; common, rough.
orelha [oh-ray'lyă] *f.* ear.
órfã [or'fan] *f.* orphan.
orfanato [ohr-fă-nah'too] *m.* orphanage.
órfão [or'fown] *m.* orphan.
orfeão [ohr-fee-own'] *m.* choral society.
organismo [ohr-gă-neezh'-moo] *m.* organism; institution, body.
organista [ohr-gă-neesh'tă] *m.* organist.
organização [ohr-gă-nee-ză-sown'] *f.* organization.
organizar [ohr-gă-nee-zar'] *va.* to organize.
órgão [or'gown] *m.* organ.
orgia [ohr-zhee'ă] *f.* orgy; spree.
orgulho [ohr-goo'lyoo] *m.* pride, arrogance.
orgulhoso [ohr-goo-lyoh'zoo] *adj.* proud, haughty.
orientação [oh-ree-en-tă-sown'] *f.* direction, orientation; guidance.
orientar [oh-ree-en-tar'] *va.* to orientate, direct, guide; *vr.* to get one's bearings; to take stock of (a situation).
oriente [oh-ree-ent'] *m.* East, Orient; Extremo —, Far East.
orifício [oh-ree-fee'see-oo] *m.* hole, aperture.
origem [oh-ree'zhen] *f.* origin; source.
original [oh-ree-zhee-nal'] *adj.* original; odd, strange.
originar [oh-ree-zhee-nar'] *va.* to originate, start, create.
originário [oh-ree-zhee-nah'-ree-oo] *adj.* native of; primary.

oriundo [oh-ree-oo*n*'doo] *adj.* native of; deriving from.
orla [or'lă] *f.* edge, border; fringe; hem (of skirt, etc.).
orlar [ohr-lar'] *va.* to edge; to (sew a) hem (on).
ornamentar [ohr-nă-me*n*-tar'] *va.* to adorn, decorate.
ornamento [ohr-nă-me*n*'too] *m.* adornment, ornament, decoration.
ornar [ohr-nar'] *va.* to adorn.
ornato [ohr-nah'too] *m.* ornament, adornment.
orquestra [ohr-kesh'tră] *f.* orchestra.
ortodoxo [ohr-too-dok'soo] *adj.* orthodox.
ortografia [ohr-too-gră-fee'ă] *f.* spelling, orthography.
orvalho [ohr-val'yoo] *m.* dew.
oscilar [ohsh-see-lar'] *vn.* to sway, oscillate, swing; to hesitate.
ósculo [osh'koo-loo] *m.* (ceremonial) kiss; — **de paz**, kiss of peace.
osso [oh'soo] *m.* bone.
ossudo [oh-soo'doo] *adj.* big-boned; bony.
ostensivo [ohsh-te*n*-see'voo] *adj.* ostensible, apparent.
ostentação [ohsh-te*n*-tă-sow*n*'] *f.* ostentation, show.
ostentar [ohsh-te*n*-tar'] *va.* to display, vaunt, parade.
ostentoso [ohsh-te*n*-toh'zoo] *adj.* ostentatious.
ostra [ohsh'tră] *f.* oyster.
ou [oh] *conj.* or; either.
ouriço [oh-ree'soo] *m.* hedgehog.
ourives [oh-reevsh'] *m.* goldsmith.
ourivesaria [oh-reev-ză-ree'ă] *f.* goldsmith's art; jeweller's shop.
ouropel [oh-roo-pel'] *m.* tinsel; (*fig.*) sham, pretence.
ousadia [oh-ză-dee'ă] *f.* daring, audacity; impertinence.
ousar [oh-zar'] *va.* to dare.
outeiro [oh-tay'ee-roo] *m.* hill.
outono [oh-toh'noo] *m.* autumn; (U.S.A.) fall.
outorgar [oh-toor-gar'] *va.* to grant, concede.
outrem [oh'tre*n*] *pr.* somebody else, another person, other people.
outro [oh'troo] *adj.* other; another; — **tanto**, as much again; the same thing.
outrora [oh-tro'ră] *adv.* formerly; a long time ago.
outrossim [oh-troo-see*n*'] *adv.* also, besides.
outubro [oh-too'broo] *m.* October.
ouvido [oh-vee'doo] *m.* ear; (sense of) hearing; **de** —, by ear.
ouvinte [oh-vee*n*t'] *m.* listener.
ouvir [oh-veer'] *va.* to hear; to listen to; — **dizer que**, to hear (it said) that; — **falar de**, to hear of.
ovação [oh-vă-sow*n*'] *f.* ovation; enthusiastic reception.
ovelha [oh-vay'lyă] *f.* sheep; ewe.
ovo [oh'voo] *m.* egg; — **estrelado**, fried egg; — **mexido**, scrambled egg; — **cozido**, boiled egg; — **escalfado**, poached egg.
oxalá [o-shă-lah'] *interj.* let's hope!, would that!, God grant!
oxigenar [ok-see-zhĕ-nar'] *va.* to oxygenate; to bleach (hair).
oxigénio [ok-see-zhe'nee-oo] *m.* oxygen.

P

pá [pah] *f.* shovel; blade (of oar, propeller); *m.* (*sl.*) chum, pal, buddy.
pábulo [pa'boo-loo] *m.* mater-

ial (for gossip, etc.); (*poet.*) food.
pacato [pă-kah'too] *m.* quiet, peaceable.
pachorrento [pă-shoo-ren'-too] *adj.* slow, sluggish; easy-going.
paciência [pă-see-en'see-ă] *f.* patience; resignation; *interj.* we'll have to put up with it!; tenha —!, I'm sorry! (but it's not my fault).
paciente [pă-see-ent'] *m/adj.* patient.
pacificação [pă-see-fee-kă-sown'] *f.* pacification.
pacificar [pă-see-fee-kar'] *va.* to pacify; *vr.* to grow calm.
paço [pah'so] *m.* palace; —s do Concelho, Town Hall.
pacote [pă-kot'] *m.* parcel, packet.
pacto [pak'too] *m.* pact.
pactuar [pak-too-ar'] *va.* to arrange (a pact, etc.); *vn.* to make a pact *or* agreement.
padaria [pa-dă-ree'ă] *f.* bakery; bread-shop.
padecer [pă-dĕ-sayr'] *va.* to suffer.
padecimento [pă-dĕ-see-men'too] *m.* suffering.
padeiro [pa-day'ee-roo] *m.* baker.
padrão [pă-drown'] *m.* stone pillar, monument; standard, model, pattern; standard measure, gauge.
padrasto [pă-drash'too] *m.* stepfather.
padre [pah'drĕ] *m.* priest; father (*eccl.*); — -nosso, Lord's prayer.
padrinho [pă-dree'nyoo] *m.* godfather; best man (at wedding); second (in duel).
padroado [pă-droo-ah'doo] *m.* patronage (*eccl.*).
padroeiro [pă-droo-ay'ee-roo] *m.* patron saint; patron.
paga [pah'gă] *f.* payment; return.
pagamento [pă-gă-men' too] *m.* payment.
pagão [pă-gown'] *m/adj.* pagan.
pagar [pă-gar'] *va.* to pay (for); to retaliate; to reward; — de contado, to pay in cash.
página [pa'zhee-nă] *f.* page.
pago [pah'goo] *adj.* paid; *m.* pay.
pai [pȳ] *m.* father; *pl.* parents.
painel [pȳ-nel'] *m.* panel; painting.
paio [pȳ'oo] *m.* (thick) sausage.
paiol [pȳ-ol'] *m.* store-room (*naut.*); powder-magazine (*naut. & mil.*).
pairar [pȳ-rar'] *vn.* to hover; to tack (*naut.*); to heave to (*naut.*).
pais [pă-eesh'] *m.* country, land, nation.
paisagem [pȳ-zah'zhen] *f.* landscape, countryside, scenery.
paisano [pȳ-ză'noo] *adj.* civilian; *m.* fellow-countryman; civilian.
paixão [pȳ-shown'] *f.* passion.
pajem [pah'zhen] *m.* page (attendant).
pala [pa'lă] *f.* eye-shade; peak (of cap).
palácio [pă-la'see-oo] *m.* palace.
paladar [pă-lă-dar'] *m.* palate; taste.
paladino [pă-lă-dee'noo] *m.* champion, paladin.
palanque [pă-lank'] *m.* stand.
palavra [pă-lav'ră] *f.* word; speech; *interj.* honestly!; de —, by word of mouth; pedir a —, to ask permission to speak; usar da —, to speak; o dom da —, the gift of fluent speech, (*sl.*) gift of the gab.
palavrear [pă-lă-vree-ar'] *vn.* to chatter, babble.

palavreador [pă-lă-vree-ă-dohr'] *adj.* talkative; *m.* chatterbox, talker.
palco [pal'koo] *m.* stage.
palerma [pă-lair'mă] *adj.* stupid, silly; *m.* fool, nincompoop. [chat.
palestra [pă-lesh'tră] *f.* talk;
paleta [pă-lay'tă] *f.* palette.
paletó [pă-lĕ-to'] *m.* (over-) coat.
palha [pa'lyă] *f.* straw.
palhaço [pă-lya'soo] *m.* clown.
palheiro [pă-lyay'ee-roo] *m.* barn; haystack.
palhoça [pă-lyo'să] *f.* poor straw-thatched cottage, hut; straw cape.
paliativo [pă-lee-ă-tee'voo] *m/adj.* palliative.
paliçada [pă-lee-sah'dă] *f.* palisade, stockade.
palidez [pă-lee-daysh'] *f.* paleness, pallor. [pallid.
pálido [pa'lee-doo] *adj.* pale,
pálio [pa'lee-oo] *m.* canopy; pallium. [pick.
palito [pă-lee'too] *m.* tooth-
palma [pal'mă] *f.* palm (of hand); palm (*bot.*); **bater —s**, to clap, applaud.
palmada [pal-mah'dă] *f.* slap, smack; **dar — nas costas**, to clap on the back.
palmar [pal-mar'] *m.* palm-grove; *adj.* obvious, clear.
palmeira [pal-may'ee-ră] *f.* palm-tree.
palmo [pal'moo] *m.* span (of hand); (*approx.*) 8 inches; **— de terra**, bit of land; **— a —**, inch by inch.
palpável [pal-pah'vel] *adj.* palpable, obvious.
pálpebra [pal'pĕ-bră] *f.* eyelid.
palpitante [pal-pee-tant'] *adj.* palpitating; (*fig.*) vital; thrilling, exciting, sensational.
palpitar [pal-pee-tar'] *vn.* to palpitate, throb, quiver; to surmise, have a presentiment.
palrar [pal-rar'] *vn.* to chatter, prattle, gabble.
paludismo [pă-loo-deezh'-moo] *m.* malaria.
paludoso [pă-loo-doh'zoo] *adj.* marshy, swampy.
palustre [pă-loosh'trĕ] *adj.* marshy; marsh-dwelling (birds, etc.); **febres —s**, malaria.
pâmpano [pan'pă-noo] *m.* vine-shoot. [belly.
pança [pan'să] *f.* paunch,
pancada [pan-kah'dă] *f.* blow, knock, bang; **— de água**, downpour.
pançudo [pan-soo'doo] *adj.* potbellied, fat.
pândega [pan'dĕ-gă] *f.* high jinks, merrymaking, spree.
pandeireta [pan-day-ray'tă] *f.* tambourine.
panela [pă-ne'lă] *f.* pot, pan.
panfleto [pan-flay'too] *m.* pamphlet. [fright.
pânico [pă'nee-koo] *m.* panic,
paninho [pă-nee'nyoo] *m.* fine cotton cloth.
pano [pă'noo] *m.* cloth; curtain (*theat.*); sails (*naut.*); **a todo o —**, under full sail, with all sails set.
panorama [pă-noo-ră'mă] *m.* panorama; view.
pântano [pan'tă-noo] *m.* marsh, swamp, bog.
pantanoso [pan-tă-noh'zoo] *adj.* marshy, swampy.
panteísmo [pan-te-eezh'moo] *m.* pantheism.
pantomima [pan-too-mee'-mă] *f.* dumb-show, mime.
pão [pown] *m.* bread; loaf; **— de ló**, sponge cake.
pãozinho [pown-zee'nyoo] *m.* roll.
papa [pah'pă] *m.* Pope; *f.pl.* mushy food; gruel, porridge;

não ter —s na lingua, to be outspoken. [Papacy.
papado [pă-pah'doo] *m.*
papagaio [pă-pă-gȳ'oo] *m.* parrot; kite (plaything).
papa-léguas [pa'pă le'gwăsh] *m.* great *or* fast walker.
papalvo [pă-pal'voo] *m.* simpleton, gullible fellow.
paparicos [pă-pă-ree'koosh] *m.pl.* dainty morsels; pampering; caresses, petting.
papeira [pă-pay'ee-ră] *f.* mumps; goitre.
papel [pă-pel'] *m.* paper; part, role (*theat.*); function, duty; *pl.* documents; — **moeda**, paper-money; — **de seda**, tissue paper; **fazer um** —, to play a part.
papelada [pă-pĕ-lah'dă] *f.* pile of papers; (bureaucratic) red tape.
papelão [pă-pĕ-lown'] *m.* cardboard, pasteboard.
papelaria [pă-pĕ-lă-ree'ă] *f.* stationer's (shop).
papelinho [pă-pĕ-lee'nyoo] *m.* scrap of paper; *pl.* confetti.
papo [pah'poo] *m.* (bird's) crop, craw; double chin.
papoila [pă-poh'ee-lă] *f.* poppy.
paquete [pă-kayt'] *m.* steamship; errand boy.
par [par] *adj.* equal; even (number); *m.* couple, pair; peer; partner (in dance); **de — em** —, wide open; **sem** —, unrivalled, unequalled; **estar a — de**, to be well informed about.
para [pă'ră] *prep.* for; to; towards; in order to; — **quê?** why?, what for?; — **onde?** where to?; **estar** —, to be about to, on the point of; to intend, be disposed to.
parabéns [pă-ră-bensh'] *m.pl.* congratulations.
parábola [pă-ra'boo-lă] *f.* parable; parabola (geometry).
pára-brisas [pa'ră bree'zăsh] *m.* windscreen.
pára-choques [pa'ră shoksh] *m.* bumper (of car); buffer.
parada [pă-rah'dă] *f.* parade (*mil.*); stake (in gambling); stop, halt; pause.
paradeiro [pă-ră-day'ee-roo] *m.* whereabouts, location; stopping-place.
paradoxo [pă-ră-dok'soo] *m.* paradox.
paráfrase [pă-ra'frăz] *f.* paraphrase, free rendering; exposition.
parafuso [pă-ră-foo'zoo] *m.* screw; bolt; **chave de** —, screwdriver.
paragem [pă-rah'zhen] *f.* stop, stopping-point; location, place; stoppage.
parágrafo [pă-rag'ră-foo] *m.* paragraph.
paraíso [pă-ră-ee'zoo] *m.* paradise; garden of Eden.
paralelo [pă-ră-le'loo] *m/adj.* parallel.
paralisar [pă-ră-lee-zar'] *va.* to paralyse.
paralisia [pă-ră-lee-zee'ă] *f.* paralysis.
paramento [pă-ră-men'too] *m.* ornament; *pl.* (priest's) vestments; curtains, hangings (e.g. in church).
parapeito [pă-ră-pay'ee-too] *m.* parapet; — **de janela**, window-sill.
pára-quedas [pa'ră ke'dash] *m.* parachute.
pára-quedista [pa'ră kedeesh'ta] *m.* paratrooper (*mil.*); parachutist.
parar [pă-rar'] *vn/va.* to stop, halt; — **em**, to come to, end up in.
pára-raios [pa'ră rȳ'oosh] *m.* lightning-conductor, -rod.

parasita [pă-ră-zee'tă] *m.* parasite. [partner.
parceiro [păr-say'ee-roo] *m.*
parcela [păr-se'lă] *f.* piece, fragment; item; plot (of land).
parceria [păr-sĕ-ree'ă] *f.* partnership, association.
parcial [păr-see-al'] *adj.* partial; biassed, prejudiced.
parcialidade [păr-see-ă-lee-dahd'] *f.* partiality, bias.
parcimónia [păr-see-mo'nee-ă] *f.* carefulness (in saving money).
parcimonioso [păr-see-moo-nee-oh'zoo] *adj.* careful, thrifty (in money matters).
parco [par'koo] *adj.* thrifty, frugal, sparing.
pardal [păr-dal'] *m.* sparrow.
pardieiro [păr-dee-ay'ee-roo] *m.* dilapidated old house.
pardo [par'doo] *adj.* grey, dull.
parecer [pă-rĕ-sayr'] *vn.* to seem, appear; *vr.* to look like, resemble; **que lhe parece?** what do you think?; **ao —, ao que parece,** apparently; *m.* opinion; appearance.
parecido [pă-rĕ-see'doo] *adj.* like, similar; **bem —,** good-looking.
parede [pă-rayd'] *f.* wall.
parelha [pă-ray'lyă] *f.* pair (of horses, mules).
parente [pă-re*n*t'] *m.* relative, relation. [relations.
parentela [pă-re*n*-te'lă] *f.*
parentesco [pă-re*n*-taysh'-koo] *m.* relationship.
parêntese [pă-re*n*'tĕz] *m. or* **parêntesis,** *m.* parenthesis; brackets (signs).
pária [par'ee-ă] *m.* pariah, outcast.
paridade [pă-ree-dahd'] *f.* parity; similarity.
parir [pă-reer'] *va.* to give birth to.
parlamentar [păr-lă-me*n*-tar'] *adj.* parliamentary; *m.* parliamentarian; *vn.* to parley, treat.
parlamento [păr-lă-me*n*t'oo] *m.* parliament.
pároco [pa'roo-koo] *m.* parish priest.
parodiar [pă-roo-dee-ar'] *va.* to parody. [parish.
paróquia [pă-ro'kee-ă] *f.*
paroquiano [pă-roo-kee-ă'-noo] *m.* parishioner.
paroxismo [pă-rook-seezh'-moo] *m.* fit, attack; *pl.* death throes.
parque [park] *m.* park.
parra [pa'ră] *f.* vine-leaf.
parreira [pă-ray'ee-ră] *f.* trellised vine.
parricida [pă-ree-see'dă] *mf.* parricide.
parte [part] *f.* part, portion, section; side; place; rôle; communication; **pôr de —,** to set aside; **dar —,** to notify; **por toda a —,** everywhere.
parteira [păr-tay'ee-ră] *f.* midwife.
participação [păr-tee-see-pă-sow*n*'] *f.* participation, sharing; announcement.
participante [păr-tee-see-pa*n*t'] *m.* participant, partaker; *adj.* participating.
participar [păr-tee-see-par'] *vn.* to share, participate in; *va.* to announce, notify.
particípio [păr-tee-see'pee-oo] *m.* participle.
particular [păr-tee-koo-lar'] *adj.* private; particular, special; *m.* private individual; *m.pl.* particulars, details; **em —,** in private; **casa —,** private house.
partida [păr-tee'dă] *f.* departure; game, match; shipment (*com.*); party, meeting; (armed) gang; trick; **perder a**

—, to lose, fail; —s simples, single entry (*com.*); —s dobradas, double entry (*com.*).
partidário [păr-tee-dah'ree-oo] *m.* supporter, partisan.
partido [păr-tee'doo] *adj.* divided; broken; *m.* party (*polit.*); decision; advantage; handicap (in game); tomar o — de, to side with; um bom —, a good match (marriage).
partilha [păr-tee'lyă] *f.* share, division.
partilhar [păr-tee-lyar'] *va.* [to share.
partir [păr-teer'] *vn.* to leave, depart; *va.* to divide; to break.
parto [par'too] *m.* birth, childbirth; (*fig.*) product.
parvo [par'voo] *adj.* stupid, simple, daft; *m.* fool, ass, nitwit.
parvoice [păr-voo-ees'] *m.* stupidity, imbecility; nonsense.
pascer [păsh-sayr'] *va*/*vn.* to [graze, feed.
páscoa [pash'kwă] *f.* Easter; cara de —, cheerful face.
pasmado [păzh-mah'doo] *adj.* astounded, amazed.
pasmar [păzh-mar'] *vn.* to be amazed.
pasmoso [păzh-moh'zoo] *adj.* astounding, astonishing.
pasquim [păsh-keen'] *m.* lampoon.
passa [pa'să] *f.* raisin.
passadeira [pă-să-day'ee-ră] *f.* stair-, corridor-carpet.
passadiço [pă-să-dee'soo] *m.* passage-way.
passado [pă-sah'doo] *adj.* past; amazed; dried (fruit); cooked, roasted (meat); ano —, last year.
passador [pă-să-dohr'] *m.* strainer, colander; person who receives and uses false coins; swindler.
passageiro [pă-să-zhay'ee-roo] *m.* passenger; *adj.* passing, ephemeral, momentary.
passagem [pă-sah'zhen] *f.* passage; (act of) passing, crossing; fare; de —, in passing; passing through; — para peões, pedestrian crossing.
passajar [pă-să-zhar'] *va.* to darn, mend, stitch.
passaporte [pa-să-port'] *m.* passport.
passar [pă-sar'] *va*/*vn.* to pass; to spend (time); to cross; *vr.* to happen; — o (no) exame, to pass the examination; — a ferro, to iron, press; — por alto, to overlook; não — de, to be no more than, be only; — pelas armas, to execute, shoot; — de largo, to pass by; — sem, to do without; — por uma casa, to call at a house, drop in; passou bem? hello, how are you?
pássaro [pa'să-roo] *m.* bird; — bisnau, sly bird, wily old bird(person).
passatempo [pă-să-ten'poo] *m.* pastime, recreation, hobby.
passe [pas] *m.* pass, permit.
passear [pă-see-ar'] *vn.* to (take a) walk, stroll.
passeio [pă-say'yoo] *m.* walk, stroll; trip; pavement, (U.S.A.) sidewalk; dar um —, to go for a walk; um — de automóvel, a (car) ride, drive.
passivo [pă-see'voo] *adj.* passive; *m.* liabilities (*com.*).
passo [pa'soo] *m.* step, pace; stride; gait; dar um —, to take a step; marcar —, to mark time; ao — que, while.
pasta [pash'tă] *f.* paste; briefcase; portfolio, (ministerial) post, appointment; ministro

sem —, minister without portfolio.
pastagem [păsh-tah'zhen] *f.* pasture(-land).
pastar [păsh-tar'] *vn.* to graze.
pastel [păsh-tel'] *m.* pie; pastel drawing (*art*).
pastelaria [păsh-tĕ-lă-ree'ă] *f.* confectioner's (shop); cake shop; (art of) confectionery, pastry-making.
pastilha [păsh-tee'lyă] *f.* pastille, lozenge.
pasto [pash'too] *m.* pasture; food, nourishment; **vinho de —**, table wine; **casa de —**, cheap restaurant.
pastor [păsh-tohr'] *m.* shepherd; (*eccl.*) pastor; **cão de —**, sheepdog.
pata [pa'tă] *f.* paw, foot (of animals); duck.
pataco [pă-ta'koo] *m.* (old Portuguese) coin (of low value); *pl.* (*pop.*) cash, money.
patada [pă-tah'dă] *f.* kick.
patamar [pă-tă-mar'] *m.* landing (on stairs).
patear [pă-tee-ar'] *vn.* to stamp one's feet (in disapproval); to fail, 'flop'; *va.* to receive with disapproval.
patente [pă-tent'] *adj.* evident, obvious; *f.* patent; (*mil.*) commission; **altas — do exército**, high-ranking Army officers.
patentear [pă-ten-tee-ar'] *va.* to reveal, expose, show; to throw open.
paterno [pă-tair'noo] *adj.* paternal; **casa —a**, family home.
pateta [pă-te'tă] *mf.* idiot, blockhead, simpleton; *adj.* crazy, stupid.
patético [pă-te'tee-koo] *adj.* pathetic, moving, sad.
patíbulo [pă-tee'boo-loo] *m.* gallows, scaffold.
patife [pă-teef'] *m.* scoundrel, rogue.
patim [pă-teen'] *m.* skate; **— de rodas**, roller-skate.
patinar [pă-tee-nar'] *vn.* to skate.
patinhar [pă-tee-nyar'] *vn.* to splash about, paddle.
pátio [pa'tee-oo] *m.* yard; court(yard); quadrangle.
pato [pa'too] *m.* drake, duck.
patranha [pă-tră'nyă] *f.* lie, (*sl.*) yarn, 'whopper'.
patrão [pă-trown'] *m.* master, owner, boss, chief.
pátria [pa'tree-ă] *f.* native land, motherland.
patriarca [pă-tree-ar'kă] *m.* patriarch.
património [pă-tree-mo'nee-oo] *m.* inheritance, heritage; **— do Estado** *or* **nacional**, Government (*or* State) property.
patriota [pă-tree-o'tă] *mf.* patriot.
patrioteiro [pă-tree-oo-tay'-ee-roo] *adj.* jingoistic, chauvinistic.
patriótico [pă-tree-o'tee-koo] *adj.* patriotic.
patriotismo [pă-tree-oo-teezh'moo] *m.* patriotism.
patroa [pă-troh'ă] *f.* lady of the house; landlady; owner; boss's wife; (*pop.*) the 'missus'.
patrocinar [pă-troo-see-nar'] *va.* to support, sponsor.
patrocínio [pă-troo-see'nee-oo] *m.* patronage, sponsorship, support.
patrulha [pă-troo'lyă] *f.* patrol.
patuscada [pă-toosh-kah'dă] *f.* revelry, merrymaking, spree, carousal.
pau [pow] *m.* stick, cudgel; wood; tree; beam; *pl.* clubs (cards); **— de bandeira**, flagstaff; **a meio —**, at half-mast.
paul [pă-ool'] *m.* marsh, swamp, bog.

paulada [pow-lah'dă] *f.* blow (with stick).
paulatinamente [pow-lă-tee-nă-ment'] *adv.* slowly, gradually.
paupérrimo [pow-pe'ree-moo] *adj.* very poor.
pausa [pow'ză] *f.* pause, rest.
pausado [pow-zah'doo] *adj.* slow, deliberate, unhurried.
pauta [pow'tă] *f.* list, register; ruled paper, paper with lines; guiding lines; staff (*mus.*).
pavão [pă-vown'] *m.* peacock.
pavilhão [pă-vee-lyown'] *m.* pavilion; tent; canopy; flag; — de honra, grandstand.
pavimento [pă-vee-men'too] *m.* floor; paving.
pavio [pă-vee'oo] *m.* wick; de fio a —, from beginning to end.
pavoa [pă-voh'ă] *f.* pea-hen.
pavonear-se [pă-voo-nee-ar'-sĕ] *vr.* to strut, swagger; to show off.
pavor [pă-vohr'] *m.* dread, terror, fear.
pavoroso [pă-voo-roh'zoo] *adj.* awful, dreadful, terrible.
paz [pash] *f.* peace; quietness.
pé [pe] *m.* foot; leg (of chair, etc.); stem; support, base; pretext; state of affairs; ao — de, near, close to; de —, standing; a —, on foot; a —s juntos, emphatically; — de vento, gust of wind, squall.
peanha [pee-ă'nyă] *f.* stand, pedestal.
peão [pee-own'] *m.* pedestrian; pawn (chess).
peça [pe'să] *f.* piece; play.
pecado [pĕ-kah'doo] *m.* sin; vice.
pecaminoso [pĕ-kă-mee-noh'-zoo] *adj.* sinful.
pecar [pĕ-kar'] *vn.* to sin; to wither (fruit).
pechincha [pĕ-sheen'shă] *f.* bargain; godsend.
peco [pay'koo] *adj.* withered, blighted; (*fig.*) stupid.
peçonha [pĕ-soh'nyă] *f.* poison.
pecuário [pĕ-koo-ah'ree-oo] *adj.* relating to cattle.
peculiar [pĕ-koo-lee-ar'] *adj.* particular, special, characteristic.
pecúlio [pĕ-koo'lee-oo] *m.* savings; private fortune; wealth.
pedaço [pĕ-da'soo] *m.* piece, bit, fragment.
pedal [pĕ-dal'] *m.* pedal.
pedante [pĕ-dant'] *m.* pedant.
pedantesco [pĕ-dan-taysh'-koo] *adj.* pedantic.
pederneira [pĕ-dĕr-nay'ee-ră] *f.* flint.
pedestal [pĕ-dĕsh-tal'] *m.* pedestal.
pedicuro [pĕ-dee-koo'roo] *m.* chiropodist.
pedido [pĕ-dee'doo] *m.* request; demand.
pedinchar [pĕ-deen-shar'] *va/vn.* to beg (persistently).
pedir [pĕ-deer'] *va.* to ask (for), request; — desculpa, to apologize; — emprestado, to borrow; — licença, to ask permission.
pedra [pe'dră] *f.* stone; — angular, corner-stone; — de toque, touchstone; — de amolar, grindstone; — -pomes, pumice stone.
pedregal [pĕ-drĕ-gal'] *m.* stony ground.
pedregoso [pĕ-drĕ-goh'zoo] *adj.* stony, rocky.
pedreira [pĕ-dray'ee-ră] *f.* (stone-)quarry.
pedreiro [pĕ-dray'ee-roo] *m.* stonemason; bricklayer; — livre, freemason.
pedrisco [pĕ-dreesh'koo] *m.* hail.
pega [pe'gă] *f.* handle; catching, holding; quarrel.

pega [pay'gă] *f.* magpie; (*fig.*) chatterbox.
pegada [pe-gah'dă] *f.* footprint, track.
pegadiço [pĕ-gă-dee'soo] *adj.* sticky, adhesive, contagious.
pegar [pĕ-gar'] *va.* to stick, attach; to seize, grab, take hold of; *vn.* to take root; to catch on; to start (of machine); — **fogo**, to catch fire; — **fogo a**, to set fire to.
pego [pe'goo] *m.* deepest part of river *or* sea; abyss.
peia [pay'yă] *f.* fetter, shackle.
peitilho [pay-ee-tee'lyoo] *m.* shirt-front.
peito [pay'ee-too] *m.* chest; breast; bosom; (*fig.*) heart; valour, courage.
peitoril [pay-ee-too-reel'] *m.* window-sill; parapet.
peixe [pay'eesh] *m.* fish.
peixeiro [pay-shay'ee-roo] *m.* fishmonger.
pejar [pĕ-zhar'] *va.* to fill; to clog; *vn.* to be pregnant; *vr.* to be ashamed.
pejo [pay'zhoo] *m.* shyness, bashfulness; shame; **ter** —, to be ashamed.
pejorativo [pĕ-zhoo-ră-tee'voo] *adj.* pejorative.
pelado [pĕ-lah'doo] *adj.* hairless; bare.
pélago [pe'lă-goo] *m.* ocean, open sea; abyss.
pelar [pĕ-lar'] *va.* to skin; to peel; to scrape the hair *or* fur off; (*fig.*) to fleece, skin; *vr.* to be very fond of, crazy about; to long for.
pele [pel] *f.* skin; hide (of animals); *pl.* fur(s).
peleja [pĕ-lay'zhă] *f.* fight, battle; quarrel, squabble.
pelejar [pĕ-lĕ-zhar'] *vn.* to fight, struggle.
pelica [pĕ-lee'kă] *f.* kid (leather).
pelicano [pĕ-lee-kă'noo] *m.* pelican.
pelico [pĕ-lee'koo] *m.* (shepherd's) sheepskin coat.
película [pĕ-lee'koo-lă] *f.* film; thin skin.
pelintra [pĕ-leen'tră] *mf.* shabby but conceited and unscrupulous person; shabby-genteel person.
pelo [pay'loo] *m.* hair; fur; coat (animals); **em** —, stark naked; **montar em** —, to ride bareback.
pelotão [pĕ-loo-town'] *m.* platoon, squad.
pelourinho [pĕ-loh-ree'nyoo] *m.* pillory; decorative column (in public square).
pelúcia [pĕ-loo'see-ă] *f.* plush.
peludo [pĕ-loo'doo] *adj.* hairy, shaggy; touchy, distrustful.
pena [pay'nă] *f.* pity; grief, pain; punishment; pen; feather; **valer a** —, to be worth(while); **ter** — **de**, to be sorry for; **é (uma)** —!, it is a pity!; **sob** — **de**, on pain of; — **de morte**, death sentence, capital punishment.
penacho [pĕ-na'shoo] *m.* plume, bunch of feathers.
penal [pĕ-nal'] *adj.* penal.
penalidade [pĕ-nă-lee-dahd'] *f.* penalty.
penar [pĕ-nar'] *vn.* to suffer, grieve.
pendência [pen-den'see-ă] *f.* quarrel, dispute, feud.
pendente [pen-dent'] *adj.* hanging, suspended; pending (action, etc.); *m.* pendant.
pender [pen-dayr'] *vn.* to hang, be suspended; to droop; to sag; to be inclined to, tend to.
pêndulo [pen'doo-loo] *m.* pendulum.
pendurar [pen-doo-rar'] *va.* to hang, suspend.
penedo [pĕ-nay'doo] *m.* rock, boulder.

f.
r'] *va.*
waddle.
trä-sown']
sight, dis-
ně-trant'] *adj.*
ercing, keen.
-ně-trar'] *va.* to
penetra... pierce.

penha [pay'nyă] *f.* rock, cliff; rocky hill.

penhasco [pě-nyash'koo] *m.* (big) rock, crag, cliff.

penhor [pě-nyohr'] *m.* pledge, bond; deposit; **casa de —es**, pawnshop; **dar de (em, como) —**, to pawn.

penhorado [pě-nyoo-rah'doo] *adj.* distrained, seized; (*fig.*) grateful, obliged, indebted.

penhorante [pě-nyoo-rant'] *adj.* obliging, charming.

penhorar [pě-nyoo-rar'] *va.* to seize, distrain, confiscate (goods); to put in someone's debt, under an obligation.

penhorista [pě-nyoo-reesh'tă] *m.* pawnbroker.

península [pě-neen'soo-lă] *f.* peninsula.

peninsular [pě-neen-soo-lar'] *adj.* peninsular.

penitência [pě-nee-ten'see-ă] *f.* penance, penitence.

penitenciária [pě-nee-ten-see-ah'ree-ă] *f.* penitentiary, prison.

penitente [pě-nee-tent'] *adj.* penitent, contrite.

penoso [pě-noh'zoo] *adj.* painful; laborious.

pensado [pen-sah'doo] *adj.* deliberate, intentional.

pensador [pen-să-dohr'] *m.* thinker.

pensamento [pen-să-men'too] *m.* thought, idea; mind.

pensão [pen-sown'] *f.* boarding-house; board and lodging; allowance, pension; (*fig.*) burden, drudgery; **— completa**, full board.

pensar [pen-sar'] *va/vn.* to think; to believe; to imagine; to intend; **— em**, to think about; *va.* to dress (a wound, etc.).

pensativo [pen-să-tee'voo] *adj.* thoughtful, pensive.

pensionista [pen-see-oo-neesh'tă] *mf.* boarder (in school); pensioner.

penso [pen'soo] *m.* dressing (for wound).

pente [pent] *m.* comb.

penteado [pen-tee-ah'doo] *m.* coiffure, hair style; (*pop.*) hair-do.

pentear [pen-tee-ar'] *va.* to [comb.

pentecostes [pen-tě-kosh'těsh] *m.* Whitsuntide, Pentecost.

penugem [pě-noo'zhen] *f.* down, fluff.

penúltimo [pě-nool'tee-moo] *adj.* penultimate, last but one, next to the last.

penumbra [pě-noon'bră] *f.* penumbra, shade, shadow.

penúria [pě-noo'ree-ă] *f.* penury, poverty.

pepino [pě-pee'noo] *m.* cucumber.

pepita [pě-pee'tă] *f.* gold nugget.

pequenez [pě-kě-naysh'] *f.* smallness.

pequeno [pě-kay'noo] *adj.* small, little.

pêra [pay'ră] *f.* pear.

peralta [pě-ral'tă] *m.* dandy, fop.

perante [pě-rant'] *prep.* in the presence of, before.

percalço [pěr-kal'soo] *m.* drawback, disadvantage; difficulty, hitch.

perceber [pěr-sě-bayr'] *va.* to

understand, see, perceive; to draw (salary), receive (fee).
percentagem [pĕr-sen-tah'-zhen] *f.* percentage.
percepção [pĕr-se-sown'] *f.* perception, understanding.
percevejo [pĕr-sĕ-vay'zhoo] *m.* (bed)bug; drawing pin.
percorrer [pĕr-koo-rayr'] *va.* to travel through, all over; to investigate, explore; to glance over, peruse.
percurso [pĕr-koor'soo] *m.* course, track, distance covered; **fazer o — entre,** to travel (ply) between.
percussão [pĕr-koo-sown'] *f.* percussion; collision.
percutir [pĕr-koo-teer'] *va.* to strike; to tap.
perda [payr'dă] *f.* loss; waste; damage.
perdão [pĕr-down'] *m.* pardon, forgiveness; **(peço) —!,** I'm sorry; I beg your pardon.
perder [pĕr-dayr'] *va.* to lose; to ruin; to miss (train); **— de vista,** to lose sight of; *vr.* to get lost.
perdição [pĕr-dee-sown'] *f.* perdition, ruin; **votar à —,** to damn.
perdigão [pĕr-dee-gown'] *m.* partridge.
perdigueiro [pĕr-dee-gay'ee-roo] *m.* pointer, setter (dog).
perdiz [pĕr-deesh'] *f.* partridge.
perdoar [pĕr-doo-ar'] *va.* to forgive, pardon, excuse.
perdulário [pĕr-doo-lah'ree-oo] *adj.* wasteful, prodigal; *m.* spendthrift.
perdurar [pĕr-doo-rar'] *vn.* to last, endure.
perecedouro [pĕ-rĕ-sĕ-doh'-roo] *adj.* perishable.
perecer [pĕ-rĕ-sayr'] *vn.* to perish.
peregrinação [pĕ-rĕ-gree-nă-sown'] *f.* p[...]
peregrinar [...] *vn.* to go on a [...] travel.
peregrino [pĕ-rĕ-gr[...] pilgrim.
pereira [pĕ-ray'ee-ră] *f.* [...]
peremptório [pĕ-ren-to'r[...]oo] *adj.* decisive, categorical.
perene [pĕ-ren'] *adj.* perennial, perpetual.
perfazer [pĕr-fă-zayr'] *va.* to complete; to make up (to required number, etc.).
perfeição [pĕr-fay-ee-sown'] *f.* perfection.
perfeito [pĕr-fay'ee-too] *adj.* perfect; complete.
perfídia [pĕr-fee'dee-ă] *f.* perfidy, treachery.
pérfido [pair'fee-doo] *adj.* perfidious, treacherous.
perfil [pĕr-feel'] *m.* profile, outline.
perfilar [pĕr-fee-lar'] *va.* to draw in profile; to line up (soldiers, etc.); *vr.* to stand up straight, stand to attention.
perfumar [pĕr-foo-mar'] *va.* to perfume, scent.
perfume [pĕr-foom'] *m.* perfume, scent.
perfurador [pĕr-foo-ră-dohr'] [*m.* drill.
perfurar [pĕr-foo-rar'] *va.* to perforate, pierce, drill a hole.
pergaminho [pĕr-gă-mee'-nyoo] *m.* parchment, vellum.
pergunta [pĕr-goon'tă] *f.* question; query; **fazer uma —,** to ask a question.
perguntar [pĕr-goon-tar'] *va.* to ask, enquire; to interrogate, question.
perícia [pĕ-ree'see-ă] *f.* skill.
periferia [pĕ-ree-fĕ-ree'ă] *f.* periphery.
perífrase [pĕ-ree'frăz] *f.* periphrasis, circumlocution.
perigo [pĕ-ree'goo] *m.* danger, peril, risk.

pessoa [pĕ-soh'ă] *f.* person; individual.
pessoal [pĕ-soo-al'] *adj.* personal; *m.* staff, personnel.
pestana [pĕsh-tă'nă] *f.* eyelash; queimar as —s, to burn the midnight oil.
pestanejar [pĕsh-tă-nĕ-zhar'] *vn.* to blink.
peste [pesht] *f.* plague, epidemic; pest (person); a — negra, the Black Death.
pestífero [pĕsh-tee'fĕ-roo] *adj.* pestilential, pernicious, noxious.
pestilência [pĕsh-tee-len'see-ă] *f.* pestilence, plague.
peta [pay'tă] *f.* fib, lie.
pétala [pe'tă-lă] *f.* petal.
petição [pĕ-tee-sown'] *f.* petition; request.
peticionário [pĕ-tee-see-oo-nah'ree-oo] *m.* petitioner.
petiscar [pĕ-teesh-kar'] *va.* to peck at, nibble at (food); *vn.* to eat choice snacks.
petiscos [pĕ-teesh'koosh] *m. pl.* snacks, savouries.
petiz [pĕ-teesh'] *m.* child.
peto [pay'too] *m.* woodpecker.
petrechos [pĕ-tray'shoosh] *m. pl.* (*mil.*) stores; tools; equipment.
petrificar [pĕ-tree-fee-kar'] *va.* to petrify.
petroleiro [pĕ-troo-lay'ee-roo] *m.* incendiary; navio —, oil-tanker.
petróleo [pĕ-tro'lee-oo] *m.* petroleum; paraffin (for lamps, etc.).
petulância [pĕ-too-lan'see-ă] *f.* insolence, impertinence, brazenness.
petulante [pĕ-too-lant'] *adj.* impudent, insolent; shameless, brazen.
peúga [pee-oo'gă] *f.* sock.
pevide [pĕ-veed'] *f.* pip, seed (of apple, orange, etc.).
pez [paysh] *m.* pitch.
pia [pee'ă] *f.* trough; sink; — baptismal, font; — de água benta, holy water stoup, font.
piada [pee-ah'dă] *f.* joke; (*sl.*) (wise)crack.
pianista [pee-ă-neesh'tă] *mf.* pianist.
piano [pee-ă'noo] *m.* piano; — de cauda, grand piano.
pião [pee-own'] *m.* top (toy).
piar [pee-ar'] *vn.* to chirp, cheep; to hoot (owls); to croak (ravens).
picada [pee-kah'dă] *f.* prick (of needle, etc.); sting, bite (of insect); puncture (with hypodermic needle); (nose-) dive (of aeroplane).
picadeira [pee-kă-day'ee-ră] *f.* pick-axe.
picadela [pee-kă-de'lă] *f.* sting, bite; prick (of needle).
picado [pee-kah'doo] *adj.* pricked, stung, bitten; (pock-) marked; choppy (sea); (*fig.*) piqued; *m.* minced meat, mince.
pica-flor [pee'kă flohr] *m.* humming bird.
picanço [pee-kan'soo] *m.* woodpecker.
picante [pee-kant'] *adj.* spicy, highly seasoned (food); sharp (flavour); pungent, piquant; malicious.
picão [pee-kown'] *m.* pick.
pica-pau [pee'kă pow] *m.* woodpecker.
pica-peixe [pee'kă paysh] *m.* kingfisher.
picar [pee-kar'] *va.* to prick; to sting; to pierce, puncture; to peck; to mince, chop up fine; *vr.* to be offended; to prick oneself.
picaresco [pee-kă-raysh'koo] *adj.* ludicrous; picaresque.
pícaro [pee'kă-roo] *adj.* crafty, cunning; base, mean.
piçarra [pee-sa'ră] *f.* shale.

pico [pee'koo] *m.* peak, summit; sharp point; **e —**, and a bit, and a little over, approximately, about.
pictórico [peek-to'ree-koo] *adj.* pictorial.
piedade [pee-ĕ-dahd'] *f.* piety; pity, mercy.
piedoso [pee-ĕ-doh'zoo] *adj.* pious, devout; merciful, compassionate.
piegas [pee-e'găsh] *mf.* stupid, silly person; 'soft', 'soppy' person, 'softy'.
pieguice [pee-e-gees'] *f.* silliness, 'softness', 'soppiness'.
pífaro [pee'fă-roo] *m.* fife.
pigarro [pee-ga'roo] *m.* phlegm (in throat), (*pop.*) croak.
pigmento [peeg-me*n*'too] *m.* pigment. [pigmy.
pigmeu [peeg-may'oo] *m.*
pilão [pee-low*n*'] *m.* heavy pestle; ram, crusher (*mech.*); pylon.
pilar [pee-lar'] *va.* to pound, crush; *m.* pillar, column.
pilha [pee'lyă] *f.* pile, heap; battery (*elect.*).
pilhagem [pee-lyah'zhe*n*] *f.* pillage; plunder.
pilhar [pee-lyar'] *va.* to pillage, plunder, loot; to rob, pilfer. [joke, jest.
pilhéria [pee-lyair'ee-ă] *f.*
pilotagem [pee-loo-tah'zhe*n*] *f.* piloting; pilotage.
pilotar [pee-loo-tar'] *va.* to pilot. [(first-)mate.
piloto [pee-loh'too] *m.* pilot;
pílula [pee'loo-lă] *f.* pill.
pimenta [pee-me*n*'tă] *f.* pepper.
pimenteira [pee-me*n*-tay'ee-ră] *f.* pepper-plant.
pimenteiro [pee-men-tay'ee-roo] *m.* pepper-pot.
pimpão [pee*n*-pow*n*'] *m.* show-off, bully; dandy.
pimpolho [pee*n*-poh'lyoo] *m.* young shoot, sprig; youngster.
pináculo [pee-na'koo-loo] *m.* pinnacle, summit.
pinça [pee*n*'să] *f.* pincers.
píncaro [pee*n*'kă-roo] *m.* pinnacle, summit, peak; **pôr nos —s da lua**, to praise to the skies.
pincel [pee*n*-sel'] *m.* (small, paint-)brush; **— de barba**, shaving-brush.
pincelada [pee*n*-sĕ-lah'dă] *f.* brush-stroke.
pinchar [pee*n*-shar'] *va.* to hurl out, heave up; *vn.* to leap.
pinga [pee*n*'gă] *f.* drop (of liquid, especially wine).
pingadeira [pee*n*-gă-day'ee-ră] *f.* dripping pan; (*fig.*) steady source of income, lucrative 'line'.
pingar [pee*n*-gar'] *vn.* to drip; to yield small but steady profits; to begin to rain. [ear-ring.
pingente [pee*n*-zhe*n*t'] *m.*
pingo [pee*n*'goo] *m.* drop.
pingue [pee*n*'gĕ] *adj.* rich, profitable, substantial.
pinguim [pee*n*-gwee*n*'] *m.* penguin.
pinha [pee'nyă] *f.* pine-cone; crowd (of people).
pinhal [pee-nyal'] *m.* pine wood. [pine(-tree).
pinheiro [pee-nyay'ee-roo] *m.*
pino [pee'noo] *m.* top, topmost point; **a —**, upright; **no — do inverno**, in the depth of winter; **no — do verão**, at the height of summer.
pinta [pee*n*'tă] *f.* spot; appearance, (*sl.*) cut of his jib.
pintar [pee*n*-tar'] *va.* to paint; to describe; *vr.* to make up (face); **— a manta**, to paint the town red; **vir ao —**,

to arrive just at the right time.
pintarroxo [peen-tă-roh'-shoo] *m.* robin (-redbreast).
pinto [peen'too] *m.* chicken; old Portuguese coin.
pintor [peen-tohr'] *m.* painter.
pintura [peen-too'ră] *f.* painting; picture; — a óleo, oil painting.
pio [pee'oo] *m.* cheep (of chickens); chirping (of sparrows, etc.); hooting, screech (of owl); **nem** —!, not a squeak!
piolho [pee-oh'lyoo] *m.* louse.
pioneiro [pee-oo-nay'ee-roo] *m.* pioneer. [worst.
pior [pee-or'] *adj/adv.*worse,
piorar [pee-oo-rar'] *vn.* to grow (get) worse; *va.* to make worse.
pipa [pee'pă] *f.* cask, barrel.
piparote [pee-pă-rot'] *m.* flick.
pique [peek] *m.* pike (*mil.*); ir a —, to sink; a —, vertically, steeply; a — de, on the verge of. [pyramid.
pirâmide [pee-ră'meed] *f.*
piranga [pee-ran'gă] *adj.* shabby; hard-up, poor.
pirata [pee-rah'tă] *m.* pirate.
pirataria [pee-ră-tă-ree'ă] *f.* piracy.
pirenaico [pee-rĕ-nȳ'koo] *adj.* Pyrenean.
pires [pee'rĕsh] *m.* saucer.
pirilampo [pee-ree-lan'poo] *m.* glow-worm, firefly.
piroga [pee-ro'gă] *f.* canoe.
pirotécnia [pee-roo-tek'nee-ă] *f.* pyrotechnics; art of making fireworks.
pirueta [pee-roo-ay'tă] *f.* pirouette. [step, track.
pisada [pee-zah'dă] *f.* foot-
pisar [pee-zar'] *va.* to tread, trample, crush.
pisca [peesh'kă] *f.* speck; cigarette end.
piscar [peesh-kar'] *va.* to wink; to blink.
piscatório [peesh-kă-to'ree-oo] *adj.* fishing.
piscina [peesh-see'nă] *f.* swimming-pool, baths.
piso [pee'zoo] *m.* walk, gait; ground; floor.
pista [peesh'tă] *f.* track, trail; clue; runway (at aerodrome).
pistão [peesh-town'] *m.* piston.
pistola [peesh-to'lă] *f.* pistol.
pitada [pee-tah'dă] *f.* pinch (of snuff, salt, etc.).
pitoresco [pee-too-raysh'koo] *adj.* picturesque.
placa [plah'kă] *f.* plate, sheet (of metal); plaque; decoration, medal.
placidez [plă-see-daysh'] *f.* placidity, serenity.
plácido [pla'see-doo] *adj.* placid, calm.
plagiar [plă-zhee-ar'] *va.* to plagiarize.
plagiato [plă-zhee-ah'too] *m.* or **plágio**, *m.* plagiarism.
plaina [plȳ'nă] *f.* plane.
plana [plă'nă] *f.* category.
planador [plă-nă-dohr'] *m.* glider.
planalto [plă-nal'too] *m.* tableland, plateau.
planar [plă-nar'] *vn.* to glide.
planear [plă-nee-ar'] *va.* to plan. [planet.
planeta [plă-nay'tă] *m.*
plangente [plan-zhent'] *adj.* plaintive, mournful.
planície [plă-nee'see-ĕ] *f.* plain; prairie.
planificar [plă-nee-fee-kar'] *va.* to plan out, draw up a plan.
plano [plă'noo] *adj.* level, flat, even, smooth; *m.* plan, diagram; plane (of projection, etc.); **primeiro** —, foreground.
planta [plan'tă] *f.* plant; plan; sole (of foot).

plantação [pla*n*-tă-sow*n*'] *f.* plantation; planting.
plantar [pla*n*-tar'] *va.* to plant; to set up, fix; to implant, establish.
planura [plă-noo'ră] *f.* tableland; plain.
plasmar [plăzh-mar'] *va.* to model, mould, shape.
plástica [plash'tee-kă] *f.* art of moulding; figure, shape.
plástico [plash'tee-koo] *adj.* plastic; pliable, supple; *m.pl.* plastics.
plataforma [pla-tă-for'mă] *f.* platform; terrace; — **giratória**, turntable.
plátano [pla'tă-noo] *m.* plane-tree.
plateia [plă-te'yă] *f.* stalls, pit (*theat.*).
platina [plă-tee'nă] *f.* platinum.
plausível [plow-zee'vel] *adj.* plausible, reasonable; praiseworthy.
plebe [pleb] *f.* common people; mob, rabble, common herd.
plebeu [plĕ-bay'oo] *adj.* common, vulgar, plebeian.
plebiscito [plĕ-bish-see'too] *m.* plebiscite.
pleitear [play-tee-ar'] *va.* to plead, argue (*leg.*).
pleito [play'ee-too] *m.* lawsuit, case, action.
plenário [plĕ-nah'ree-oo] *adj.* plenary, full.
plenilúnio [ple-nee-loo'nee-oo] *m.* full moon.
plenipotenciário [ple-nee-poo-te*n*-see-ah'ree-oo] *m/adj.* plenipotentiary.
plenitude [ple-nee-tood'] *f.* fullness, completeness.
pleno [play'noo] *adj.* full, complete; plenary; **em — dia**, in broad daylight; **em — verão**, in the middle of summer.
pleurisia [play-oo-ree-zee'ă] *f.* pleurisy.
pluma [ploo'mă] *f.* plume, feather.
plumagem [ploo-mah'zhe*n*] *f.* plumage.
plúmbeo [ploo*n*'bee-oo] *adj.* leaden.
plural [ploo-ral'] *m/adj.* [plural.
plutocrata [ploo-to-krah'tă] *m.* plutocrat; *adj.* plutocratic.
pluvial [ploo-vee-al'] *adj.* rainy, pluvial; *m.* cope (*eccl.*).
pneumático [pnay-oo-ma'tee-koo] *m.* (*abbrev.* **pneu**) tyre; *adj.* pneumatic.
pneumonia [pnay-oo-moo-nee'ă] *f.* pneumonia.
pó [po] *m.* powder; dust; — **de arroz**, face powder; —**s dentifricos**, tooth powder.
pobre [po'brĕ] *adj.* poor; needy; wretched; **um — de pedir**, beggar.
pobreza [poh-bray'ză] *f.* poverty, penury, want, destitution.
poça [poh'să] *f.* pool, pond; puddle; — **de sangue**, pool of blood.
poção [poo-sow*n*'] *f.* dose, draught, potion.
pocilga [poo-seel'gă] *f.* pigsty.
poço [poh'soo] *m.* well; mine shaft.
poda [po'dă] *f.* pruning; **fazer a — a alguém**, to take somebody down a peg.
podadeira [poo-dă-day'ee-ră] *f.* pruning-knife, -hook.
podão [poo-dow*n*'] *m.* billhook, pruning-hook.
podagra [poo-dag'ră] *f.* gout.
podar [poo-dar'] *va.* to prune, lop off, trim.
poder [poo-dayr'] *va.* to be able to; to be capable of; to have the power to; to be allowed to; can, may; **até**

mais não —, to the utmost; não — ver, to be unable to stand, tolerate (someone); *m.* power; authority; competence; em meu —, in my possession.
poderio [poo-dĕ-ree'oo] *m.* power, authority.
poderoso [poo-dĕ-roh'zoo] *adj.* powerful, mighty, forceful; todo —, almighty.
podre [poh'drĕ] *adj.* rotten, decayed, putrid; ser — de rico, to have pots of money.
podridão [poo-dree-down'] *f.* rottenness, decay.
poedeira [poo-ee-day'ee-ră] *adj.* egg-laying; galinha —, good layer (hen).
poeira [poo-ay'ee-ră] *f.* dust.
poeirento [poo-ay-ee-ren'too] *adj.* dusty.
poema [poo-ay'mă] *m.* poem.
poente [poo-ent'] *m.* west; sol —, setting sun.
poesia [poo-ĕ-zee'ă] *f.* poetry; verse; (short) poem, lyric.
poeta [poo-e'tă] *m.* poet.
poético [poo-e'tee-koo] *adj.* poetic(al).
poetisa [poo-ĕ-tee'ză] *f.* (woman-)poet, poetess.
poial [poh-yal'] *m.* stone bench; stone slab.
pois [poh'eesh] *conj.* because, since, seeing that; so, then; — sim, é, yes; of course; that's right; — não, of course!, certainly!; — bem, well then.
polaco [poo-lah'koo] *adj.* Polish; *m.* Pole; Polish (language).
polainas [poo-lȳ'năsh] *f.pl.* gaiters; leggings.
polar [poo-lar'] *adj.* polar; estrela —, Pole star.
poldra [pohl'dră] *f.* filly; *pl.* stepping-stones.
poldro [pohl'droo] *m.* colt.
polegada [pohl-gah'dă] *f.* inch.
polegar [pohl-gar'] *m.* thumb; big toe.
poleiro [poo-lay'ee-roo] *m.* perch.
polémica [poo-le'mee-kă] *f.* controversy, polemics.
pólen [po'len] *m.* pollen.
polichinelo [poo-lee-sheene'loo] *m.* Punch; puppet, clown.
polícia [poo-lee'see-ă] *f.* police, *m.* policeman; comandante de —, chief constable; commissioner of police; comissário de —, police inspector; police superintendent; esquadra de —, police-station; agente de —, police constable.
policial [poo-lee-see-al'] *adj.* police; romance —, detective story.
polidez [poo-lee-daysh'] *f.* good manners, refinement, polish.
polido [poo-lee'doo] *adj.* polite, well-bred, refined; glossy, polished, shiny.
poliglota [poo-lee-glo'tă] *m/adj.* polyglot.
polimento [poo-lee-men'too] *m.* polishing; polish (courtesy).
poliomielite [po-lee-o-mee-ĕ-leet'] *f.* poliomyelitis, (*abbrev.*) polio; infantile paralysis.
polir [poo-leer'] *va.* to polish.
política [poo-lee'tee-kă] *f.* politics; policy; astuteness.
político [poo-lee'tee-koo] *adj.* political; *m.* politician; estar — com, to be at odds with.
politiqueiro [poo-lee-teekay'ee-roo] *m.* petty politician.
pólo [po'loo] *m.* pole; polo (game).
polpa [pohl'pă] *f.* pulp, soft *or* fleshy part.
poltrão [pohl-trown'] *m.*

coward, poltroon; *adj.* cowardly, craven.
poltrona [pohl-troh'nă] *f.* armchair. [pollution.
poluição [poo-loo-ee-sown'] *f.*
poluir [poo-loo-eer'] *va.* to pollute, defile.
polvilhar [pohl-vee-lyar'] *va.* to sprinkle, powder.
polvilho [pohl-vee'lyoo] *m.* tapioca; fine powder.
polvo [pohl'voo] *m.* octopus.
pólvora [pol'voo-ră] *f.* gunpowder.
pomada [poo-mah'dă] *f.* ointment; hair cream; — **de calçado**, shoe polish.
pomar [poo-mar'] *m.* orchard.
pomba [pon'bă] *f.* dove; pigeon.
pombal [pon-bal'] *m.* dovecote; pigeon-loft.
pombo [pon'boo] *m.* pigeon; dove; — **correio**, homing-, carrier-pigeon; — **bravo**, wood-pigeon.
pomo [poh'moo] *m.* apple; (*poet.*) breast; — **de discórdia**, bone of contention.
pompa [pon'pă] *f.* pomp, pageantry, display.
pomposo [pon-poh'zoo] *adj.* stately, majestic; bombastic, pompous. [cheekbone.
pómulo [po'moo-loo] *m.*
ponderação [pon-dĕ-ră-sown'] *f.* consideration.
ponderado [pon-dĕ-rah'doo] *adj.* judicious, sober, well-considered.
ponderar [pon-dĕ-rar'] *va.* to consider, weigh (up), think over; *vn.* to meditate, ponder.
ponderoso [pon-dĕ-roh'zoo] *adj.* weighty, unwieldy, ponderous; important.
ponta [pon'tă] *f.* end, edge; tip, point; — **de cigarro**, cigarette end; **na — dos pés**, on tiptoe; **trazer alguém de —**, to be ill-disposed towards somebody. [toon.
pontão [pon-town'] *m.* pon-
pontapé [pon-tă-pe'] *m.* kick.
pontaria [pon-tă-ree'ă] *f.* aiming; aim; **fazer —**, to take aim.
ponte [pont] *f.* bridge; — **levadiça**, drawbridge; — **suspensa**, suspension bridge; — **de barcas**, pontoon bridge.
pontear [pon-tee-ar'] *va.* to dot; to stitch.
ponteiro [pon-tay'ee-roo] *m.* hand (of clock, watch); pointer (rod); chisel; plectrum (*mus.*); **vento —**, headwind.
pontiagudo [pon-tee-ă-goo'-doo] *adj.* sharp (-pointed).
pontificado [pon-ti-fee-kah'-doo] *m.* pontificate.
pontífice [pon-tee'fees] *m.* pontiff, Pope; archbishop, bishop.
pontilhar [pon-tee-lyar'] *va.* to dot, mark with dots; **linha pontilhada**, dotted line.
pontinha [pon-tee'nyă] *f.* bit; touch (of chill, of jealousy, etc.); **nas —s dos pés**, on tiptoe.
pontinho [pon-tee'nyoo] *m.* dot; small, fine stitch; *pl.* dots (ellipsis); **ser todo —s**, to be extremely punctilious.
ponto [pon'too] *m.* point; dot; stitch; aim, object; subject; place, spot; prompter (*theat.*); register; *pl.* points, score (in games); **em —**, prompt, exactly; **a — de**, on the point of; — (**final**), full stop; — **e vírgula**, semi-colon; — **de interrogação**, question mark; **dois —s**, colon.
pontuação [pon-too-ă-sown'] *f.* punctuation.
pontual [pon-too-al'] *adj.*

punctual, prompt, accurate, reliable.
pontualidade [po*n*-too-ă-lee-dahd'] *f.* punctuality; preciseness.
popa [poh'pă] *f.* stern; à —, aft; de vento em —, before the wind; (*fig.*) flourishing.
popelina [po-pĕ-lee'nă] *f.* poplin.
populaça [poo-poo-lah'să] *f.* mob, rabble.
população [poo-poo-lă-sow*n*'] *f.* population.
popular [poo-poo-lar'] *adj.* popular; of the people, people's; common, current (language, usage, etc.).
popularizar [poo-poo-lă-ree-zar'] *va.* to popularize; *vr.* to become general; to become popular.
populoso [poo-poo-loh'zoo] *adj.* populous, thickly inhabited.
por [poor] *prep.* by; through; for; during; — aqui, this way; around here; — detrás, behind; estar — fazer, still to be done; — isso, therefore, so; — mais fácil que, however easy; — cento, per cent; — dia, per day, a day; — assim dizer, so to speak; — Deus!, for heaven's sake!; — escrito, in writing.
pôr [pohr] *va.* to put, place, set; to bet; to lay (eggs); to put on (dress); — casa, to set up house; — de lado, to set aside; *vr.* to set (sun); — de pé, to stand up; — a caminho, to set out, start off.
porão [poo-row*n*'] *m.* hold (*naut.*).
porca [por'kă] *f.* sow; nut [(*mech.*).
porção [poor-sow*n*'] *f.* portion, part, piece; uma — de, a good number of (people, etc.).
porcaria [poor-kă-ree'ă] *f.* filth, filthiness; filthy (disgusting, swinish) act *or* state; foul language; slovenly mess; rubbish.
porcelana [poor-sĕ-lă'nă] *f.* porcelain, china.
porcionista [poor-see-oo-neesh'tă] *mf.* boarder (in school).
porco [pohr'koo] *m.* pig, hog; (carne de) —, pork; *adj.* dirty, filthy.
porco-espinho [pohr'koo ish-pee'nyoo] *m.* porcupine.
porco-montês [pohr'koo mo*n*-taysh'] *m.* wild boar.
porém [poo-re*n*'] *conj.* however, but, yet.
porfia [poor-fee'ă] *f.* obstinacy, stubbornness; pertinacity; dispute, wrangle; à —, rivalling one another, in competition with one another.
porfiado [poor-fee-ah'doo] *adj.* stubborn; pertinacious; hard-fought, hotly-contested (struggle).
porfiar [poor-fee-ar'] *vn.* to contend, dispute; to persist.
pormenor [poor-mĕ-nohr'] *m.* detail; small point.
pormenorizar [poor-mĕ-noo-ree-zar'] *va.* to relate in detail, give full details of.
poro [poh'roo] *m.* pore.
poroso [poo-roh'zoo] *adj.* porous.
porquanto [poor-kwa*n*'too] *conj.* seeing that, since.
porque [poor'kĕ] *conj.* because, as, since; *adv.* why.
porquê [poor-kay'] *adv.* why; *m.* reason, motive.
porqueiro [poor-kay'ee-roo] *m.* swineherd.
porta [por'tă] *f.* door; gateway; entrance; — traseira, back door; — principal, front door, main door; —

falsa, trap-door; —s a dentro, indoors; vão de —, doorway.
porta-aviões [por'ta-vee-oynsh] *m.* aircraft carrier.
portada [poor-tah'dă] *f.* portal; frontispiece (of book).
portador [poor-tă-dohr'] *m.* bearer; — de bilhete, ticket-holder; — de acções, share-holder.
portagem [poor-tah'zhen] *f.* toll; toll-gate.
portal [poor-tal'] *m.* portal, doorway.
portaló [poor-tă-lo'] *m.* gang-way.
porta-moedas [por'tă moo-e'dăsh] *m.* purse.
portanto [poor-tan'too] *conj.* so, therefore, consequently.
portão [poor-town'] *m.* large gate; front entrance.
portar-se [poor-tar'sĕ] *vr.* to behave, conduct oneself.
portaria [poor-tă-ree'ă] *f.* main entrance; vestibule; (government) decree, order, edict.
portátil [poor-ta'teel] *adj.* portable, easily carried; light (luggage, etc.); pocket-size (book, etc.).
porta-voz [por'tă vosh] *m.* spokesman, representative; megaphone.
porte [port] *m.* carriage, trans-port; freight charge; postage; capacity, tonnage (*naut.*); bearing, deportment, de-meanour; — pago, carriage paid.
porteiro [poor-tay'ee-roo] *m.* porter, doorman, janitor.
portento [poor-ten'too] *m.* wonder, prodigy, marvel.
portentoso [poor-ten-toh'zoo] *adj.* marvellous, prodigious.
pórtico [por'tee-koo] *m.* por-tico, porch.
portinhola [poor-tee-nyo'la] *f.* (carriage) door; fly (of trousers).
porto [pohr'too] *m.* port, harbour; port wine; Oporto; — de escala, port of call; — franco, free port; — exterior, outer harbour; capitão do —, harbour master.
portuense [poor-too-ens'] *adj.* of Oporto; *mf.* inhabitant of Oporto.
português [poor-too-gaysh'] *m/adj.* Portuguese.
porventura [poor-ven-too'ră] *f.* perhaps; by any chance.
porvir [poor-veer'] *m.* future.
pós-escrito [poz-ish-kree'too] *m.* postscript, P.S.
posição [poo-zee-sown'] *f.* position; state, circum-stances; rank, standing; posture, stance.
positivo [poo-zee-tee'voo] *adj.* positive, certain, sure.
possante [poo-sant'] *adj.* powerful, mighty, strong.
posse [pos] *f.* possession; tenure; tomar — de, to take over; to assume office; *pl.* wealth, means; strength, capacity; ability.
possessão [poo-sĕ-sown'] *f.* possession, dominion.
possesso [poo-se'soo] *adj.* possessed (by the devil), crazed, bewitched.
possibilidade [poo-see-bee-lee-dahd'] *f.* possibility; *pl.* (financial) means.
possibilitar [poo-see-bee-lee-tar'] *va.* to make possible, facilitate.
possível [poo-see'vel] *adj.* pos-sible, feasible; fazer todo o —, to do one's best, do every-thing possible.
possuidor [poo-soo-ee-dohr'] *m.* possessor, owner, holder.
possuir [poo-soo-eer'] *va.* to possess, have; to own.

posta [posh'tă] *f.* slice, piece, portion; post, mail; — restante, poste restante.
postal [poosh-tal'] *m.* post-card; — ilustrado, picture postcard; *adj.* postal; marco —, pillar-box.
poste [posht] *m.* post, pole; — de iluminação, lamp-post.
postergar [poosh-tĕr-gar'] *va.* to postpone, put off; to neglect, disregard.
posteridade [poosh-tĕ-ree-dahd'] *f.* posterity; future generations; offspring, descendants.
posterior [poosh-tĕ-ree-ohr'] *adj.* later, subsequent; back, hind (part); *m.* posterior, buttocks.
posteriormente [poosh-tĕ-ree-ohr-me*n*t'] *adv.* subsequently, later.
postiço [poosh-tee'soo] *adj.* artificial, false; dentes —s, false teeth.
postigo [poosh-tee'goo] *m.* spy-hole, peep-hole, shutter, hatch; wicket-gate.
posto [pohsh'too] *adj.* put, placed; ao sol —, at sunset; bem —, well dressed, well groomed; — que, although; *m.* post, place, position; job; — de socorros, first-aid post.
postremo [poosh-tre'moo] *adj.* last, final, ultimate.
postulado [poosh-too-lah'doo] *m.* axiom, postulate, principle.
póstumo [posh'too-moo] *adj.* posthumous.
postura [poosh-too'ră] *f.* posture, position, pose; attitude; (municipal) by-law, ordinance; — de ovos, number of eggs laid.
potassa [poo-ta'să] *f.* potash.
potável [poo-tah'vel] *adj.* drinkable; água —, drinking water.
pote [pot] *m.* jug, jar, pot; (of person) tub.
potência [poo-te*n*'see-ă] *f.* power; ability; strength; Great Power (nation).
potencial [poo-te*n*-see-al'] *adj.* potential.
potente [poo-te*n*t'] *adj.* powerful, strong, mighty.
potro [poh'troo] *m.* colt, young horse; rack (for torture).
pouca-vergonha [poh'kă vĕr-goh'nyă] *f.* disgrace, scandal, shameful behaviour, shame.
pouco [poh'koo] *adj.* little; *pl.* few; *adv.* little, not much; a bit, rather; not very; *m.* a little; há — tempo, a short time ago; — depois, soon afterwards; — a —, gradually, bit by bit; por —, almost, nearly; —as vezes, rarely, seldom.
poucochinho [poh-koo-shee'nyoo] *adv.* very little; *m.* a little bit.
poupado [poh-pah'doo] *adj.* thrifty, careful.
poupar [poh-par'] *va.* to save, economize; *vr.* to spare oneself (no trouble, effort, etc.).
pousada [poh-zah'dă] *f.* inn, hotel.
pousar [poh-zar'] *va.* to put, place, set down; *vn.* to perch; to rest.
pousio [poh-zee'oo] *m.* fallow land.
povo [poh'voo] *m.* people; common people, ordinary folk.
póvoa [po'voo-ă] *f.* (small) village.
povoação [poo-voo-ă-sow*n*'] *f.* village; small town; settlement; population; colonization, peopling.
povoado [poo-voo-ah'doo] *m.* village; settlement; *adj.* populated.
povoar [poo-voo-ar'] *va.* to people; to colonize; to stock with (fish, shrubs, etc.).

praça [prah'să] *f.* square; market; fortress; private soldier; — **de touros,** bull-ring; **vender em —,** to sell by auction; assentar —, to enlist.
prado [prah'doo] *m.* meadow, field.
praga [prah'gă] *f.* curse; plague; pest, nuisance.
pragmática [prag-ma'tee-kă] *f.* rules (for official ceremonies), etiquette.
praguejar [pră-gĕ-zhar'] *va/vn.* to curse. [seaside.
praia [prȳ'ă] *f.* beach, shore;
prancha [pran'shă] *f.* plank; gang-plank (*naut.*).
prantear [pran-tee-ar'] *va.* to mourn, lament; *vn.* to weep.
pranto [pran'too] *m.* weeping.
prata [prah'tă] *f.* silver.
prateado [pră-tee-ah'doo] *adj.* silver-plated; silvery.
prateleira [pră-tĕ-lay'ee-ră] *f.* shelf.
prática [pra'tee-kă] *f.* practice; experience; exercise; habit; short sermon *or* address.
praticante [pră-tee-kant'] *adj.* practising; *m.* apprentice, probationer, assistant.
praticar [pră-tee-kar'] *va.* to perform, do; to commit (a crime); to practise.
praticável [pră-tee-kah'vel] *adj.* practicable, feasible; passable, negotiable (way, etc.).
prático [pra'tee-koo] *adj.* practical; *m.* pilot (*naut.*); expert, experienced man.
prato [prah'too] *m.* plate; dish (food); course (at meals); scale (of balance); *pl.* cymbals (*mus.*).
praxe [prash] *f.* custom, tradition; rule.
prazenteiro [pră-zen-tay'ee-roo] *adj.* cheerful, affable, jolly, pleasant.
prazer [pră-zayr'] *m.* pleasure; delight; **muito — (em conhecê-lo),** how do you do? (on being introduced).
prazo [prah'zoo] *m.* period of time, time limit, fixed time; **a longo —,** at long term; **a curto —,** at short term *or* notice.
pré [pre] *m.* daily pay (*mil.*); praça de —, private (soldier).
preâmbulo [pree-an'boo-loo] *m.* preamble, preface, introduction.
prebenda [prĕ-ben'dă] *f.* (Canon's) stipend; canonry; (*fig.*) sinecure.
precário [prĕ-kah'ree-oo] *adj.* precarious, insecure, uncertain.
precatado [prĕ-kă-tah'doo] *adj.* wary, cautious.
precatar-se [prĕ-kă-tar'sĕ] *vr.* to be careful, take care; **quando mal se precata,** when least expected.
precaução [prĕ-kow-sown'] *f.* precaution, forethought.
precaver [prĕ-kă-vayr'] *va.* to forewarn, caution; *vr.* to be on one's guard. [(to God).
prece [pres] *f.* prayer; plea
precedência [prĕ-sĕ-den'see-ă] *f.* precedence, priority.
preceder [prĕ-sĕ-dayr'] *va.* to precede.
preceito [prĕ-say'ee-too] *m.* precept, rule; injunction.
preceituar [prĕ-say-ee-too-ar'] *va.* to ordain, lay down precepts.
preceptor [prĕ-sep-tohr'] *m.* tutor, master.
preciosidade [prĕ-see-oo-zee-dahd'] *f.* preciousness, worth; treasure; preciosity; **que —!** what a lovely thing *or* scene!.
preciosismo [prĕ-see-oo-zeezh'moo] *m.* preciosity, affectation.
precioso [prĕ-see-oh'zoo] *adj.*

precious, valuable; affected, over-refined; lovely.
precipício [prĕ-see-pee'see-oo] *m.* precipice.
precipitação [prĕ-see-pee-tă-sow*n*'] *f.* haste, rashness; precipitation.
precipitado [prĕ-see-pee-tah'-doo] *adj.* precipitate, hurried, hasty, headlong; rash.
precipitar [prĕ-see-pee-tar'] *va.* to hurl down; to hasten (on), precipitate.
precipitoso [prĕ-see-pee-toh'-zoo] *adj.* steep, precipitous.
precisão [prĕ-see-zow*n*'] *f.* necessity, need; accuracy, precision.
precisar [prĕ-see-zar'] *va.* to need, want; to specify, particularize, give in detail.
preciso [prĕ-see'zoo] *adj.* wanted, needed, necessary; precise, accurate; **é —**, it is necessary.
preclaro [prĕ-klah'roo] *adj.* illustrious, famous.
preço [pray'soo] *m.* price, cost; value; **— tabelado**, official (controlled) price; **— por atacado**, wholesale price; **— a retalho**, retail price.
precoce [prĕ-kos'] *adj.* premature, early; precocious (talent).
precocidade [prĕ-koo-see-dahd'] *f.* premature (early) development; precociousness.
preconceito [prĕ-ko*n*-say'ee-too] *m.* prejudice, preconception.
preconizar [prĕ-koo-nee-zar'] *va.* to commend publicly, extol.
precursor [prĕ-koor-sohr'] *m.* precursor, forerunner; herald.
predatório [prĕ-dă-to'ree-oo] *adj.* predatory, plundering.
predecessor [prĕ-dĕ-sĕ-sohr'] *m.* predecessor.
predestinado [prĕ-dĕsh-tee-nah'doo] *adj.* predestined, foreordained.
predial [prĕ-dee-al'] *adj.* pertaining to buildings *or* land; **crédito —**, mortgage loan; **contribuição —**, land-tax, property tax.
predição [prĕ-dee-sow*n*'] *f.* prediction, forecast.
predilecção [prĕ-dee-le-sow*n*'] *f.* preference, predilection, liking.
predilecto [prĕ-dee-le'too] *m/adj.* favourite; *adj.* favoured (by), loved (by).
prédio [pre'dee-oo] *m.* building; house; land; property.
predispor [prĕ-deesh-pohr'] *va.* to predispose.
predizer [prĕ-dee-zayr'] *va.* to predict, foretell.
predominar [prĕ-doo-mee-nar'] *vn.* to predominate, prevail.
predomínio [prĕ-doo-mee'-nee-oo] *m.* predominance, preponderance.
preeminência [pree-mee-ne*n*'see-ă] *f.* pre-eminence, distinction; authority.
preeminente [pree-mee-ne*n*t'] *adj.* pre-eminent, distinguished, outstanding.
preencher [pree-e*n*-shayr'] *va.* to fill (up); to fulfil, accomplish, perform.
prefácio [prĕ-fa'see-oo] *m.* preface, introduction.
prefeito [prĕ-fay'ee-too] *m.* prefect.
preferência [prĕ-fĕ-re*n*'see-ă] *f.* preference; choice; priority; **de —**, preferably.
preferir [prĕ-fĕ-reer'] *va.* to prefer.
prega [pre'gă] *f.* fold, pleat.
pregadeira [prĕ-gă-day'ee-ră] *f.* pin cushion.
pregador [pre-gă-dohr'] *m.* preacher.

pregão [prĕ-gown'] *m.* street-cry; public proclamation; *pl.* banns (of marriage).
pregar [pre-gar'] *va/vn.* to preach; to proclaim aloud.
pregar [prĕ-gar'] *va.* to nail; to fix, sew on, pin on; — **uma partida**, to play a trick; — **um bofetão**, to give a slap; — **os olhos em**, to fix (rivet) one's eyes on; **não — olho**, not to sleep a wink.
prego [pre'goo] *m.* nail; **pôr no —**, to pawn.
pregoeiro [prĕ-goo-ay'ee-roo] *m.* town-crier; auctioneer.
preguiça [prĕ-gee'să] *f.* laziness, idleness; tardiness; (*zool.*) sloth.
preguiçoso [prĕ-gee-soh'zoo] *adj.* lazy, idle.
preia-mar [pray'yă mar] *f. or* **preamar** high tide, high water.
preito [pray'ee-too] *m.* homage; token of respect.
prejudicar [prĕ-zhoo-dee-kar'] *va.* to damage, harm, prejudice.
prejuízo [prĕ-zhoo-ee'zoo] *m.* injury, damage, loss; prejudice, bias.
prelado [prĕ-lah'doo] *m.* prelate.
prelecção [prĕ-le-sow*n*'] *f.* lecture.
preliminar [prĕ-lee-mee-nar'] *adj.* preliminary.
prelo [pre'loo] *m.* (printing-) press.
prelúdio [prĕ-loo'dee-oo] *m.* prelude; overture.
prematuro [prĕ-mă-too'roo] *adj.* premature.
premeditar [prĕ-mĕ-dee-tar'] *va.* to premeditate.
premente [prĕ-men*t*'] *adj.* pressing.
premer [prĕ-mayr'] *va. or* **premir** to press.
premiar [prĕ-mee-ar'] *va.* to award a prize to; to reward.
prémio [pre'mee-oo] *m.* prize, award; (insurance) premium.
premissa [prĕ-mee'să] *f.* premiss.
prenda [pre*n*'dă] *f.* present, gift; *pl.* talents; endowments, accomplishments; **jogo de —s**, forfeits (game).
prendado [pre*n*-dah'doo] *adj.* talented, gifted.
prender [pre*n*-dayr'] *va.* to fasten; to arrest, capture; to seize, catch.
prenhe [pray'nyĕ] *adj.* pregnant; (*fig.*) full, replete.
prensa [pre*n*'să] *f.* press; — **de lagar**, winepress; oil press.
prensar [pre*n*-sar'] *va.* to press; to squeeze.
prenúncio [prĕ-noo*n*'see-oo] *m.* (fore)warning; sign (of a coming event).
preocupação [pree-oo-koo-pă-sow*n*'] *f.* preoccupation; concern, worry, care.
preocupar [pree-oo-koo-par'] *va.* to preoccupy; to worry.
preparação [prĕ-pă-ră-sow*n*'] *f.* preparation.
preparar [prĕ-pă-rar'] *va.* to prepare, get ready.
preparativos [prĕ-pă-ră-tee'-voosh] *m. pl.* preparations.
preponderância [prĕ-po*n*-dĕ-ra*n*'see-ă] *f.* preponderance.
preposição [prĕ-poo-zee-sow*n*'] *f.* preposition.
prerrogativa [pre-roo-gă-tee'vă] *f.* prerogative, privilege.
presa [pray'ză] *f.* prize (in war), booty; prey (of animals); talon, claw; fang.
presbitia (prĕzh-bee-tee'ă] *f.* long-sightedness.
presbitério [prĕzh-bee-tair'-ee-oo] *m.* priest's house, presbytery; sanctuary.
presciência [prĕsh-see-e*n*'see-ă] *f.* prescience, foreknowledge.

presciente [prĕsh-see-*ent*'] *adj.* far-sighted, prescient.
prescindir [prĕsh-see*n*-deer'] *vn.* to do without, forego, dispense with.
prescindível [prĕsh-see*n*-dee'-vel] *adj.* dispensable.
prescrever [prĕsh-krĕ-vayr'] *va.* to prescribe.
prescrição [prĕsh-kree-sow*n*'] *f.* order, ordinance; (*leg.*) prescription.
presença [prĕ-ze*n*'să] *f.* presence; demeanour, bearing; — **de espírito**, presence of mind; **fazer acto de —**, to be present, appear.
presenciar [prĕ-ze*n*-see-ar'] *va.* to be present at, witness.
presente [prè-ze*nt*'] *m.* present, gift; present (time); present tense (of verb); *pl.* those (persons) present; *adj.* present; **o — documento**, this document; **ter —**, to remember; to bear in mind.
presentemente [prĕ-ze*n*-tĕ-me*nt*'] *adv.* at present.
presépio [prĕ-ze'pee-oo] *m.* crib, Nativity scene.
preservação [prĕ-zĕr-vă-sow*n*'] *f.* preservation.
preservar [prĕ-zĕr-var'] *va.* to preserve, protect.
presidência [prĕ-zee-de*n*'see-ă] *f.* presidency; chairmanship.
presidente [prĕ-zee-de*nt*'] *m.* president; chairman; — **do Conselho (de Ministros)**, Prime Minister.
presidiário [prĕ-zee-dee-ah'ree-oo] *m.* convict.
presídio [prĕ-zee'dee-oo] *m.* military prison; fortress.
presidir [prĕ-zee-deer'] *vn* to preside; to take the chair.
presilha [prĕ-zee'lyă] *f.* fastener, flap, loop.
preso [pray'zoo] *adj.* imprisoned; arrested; captured; tied, bound; *m.* prisoner.
pressa [pre'să] *f.* hurry, haste; **a toda a —** with all speed, post-haste; **ter (estar com) —**, to be in a hurry.
pressagiar [prĕ-să-zhee-ar'] *va.* to presage, betoken.
presságio [prĕ-sa'zhee-oo] *m.* omen, sign.
pressão [prĕ-sow*n*'] *f.* pressure; **panela de —**, pressure cooker.
pressentimento [prĕ-sen-tee-me*n*'too] *m.* presentiment, foreboding, 'a feeling'.
pressentir [prĕ-se*n*-teer] *va.* to foresee; to have a presentiment, a feeling; to surmise.
pressuposto [prĕ-soo-pohsh'-too] *m.* presupposition; pretext; intention; plan.
pressuroso [prĕ-soo-roh'zoo] *adj.* hasty, swift, quick.
prestação [prĕsh-tă-sow*n*'] *f.* instalment (payment).
prestamista [prĕsh-tă-meesh'tă] *mf.* money-lender.
prestar [prĕsh-tar'] *va.* to give, render; — **atenção**, to pay attention; — **juramento**, to take an oath; **não — (para nada)**, to be no good, of no use; *vr.* to lend oneself (itself) to; to be suitable for.
prestes [presh'tĕsh] *adj.* ready to, on the point of.
presteza [prĕsh-tay'ză] *f.* speed, alacrity; nimbleness.
prestidigitador [prĕsh-tee-dee-zhee-tă-dohr'] *m.* conjurer; juggler.
prestígio [prĕsh-tee'zhee-oo] *m.* prestige, reputation, standing.
prestigioso [prĕsh-tee-zhee-oh'zoo] *adj.* eminent, distinguished; influential.
préstimo [presh'tee-moo] *m.* use, utility; worth, value.

presumido [prĕ-zoo-mee'doo] *adj.* vain, conceited; impertinent.
presumir [prĕ-zoo-meer'] *va.* to presume, suppose; *vn.* to show off, give oneself airs.
presunção [prĕ-zoon-sown'] *f.* presumption, conjecture; conceit, presumptuousness.
presuntivo [prĕ-zoon-tee'voo] *adj.* presumptive.
presunto [prĕ-zoon'too] *m.* (smoked) ham.
pretendente [prĕ-ten-dent'] *m.* claimant, pretender; applicant; suitor.
pretender [prĕ-ten-dayr'] *va.* to claim; to apply for; to endeavour, try; to aspire to, seek to (win, possess, etc.).
pretensão [prĕ-ten-sown'] *f.* claim, pretension; *pl.* pretentiousness, airs and graces.
preterir [prĕ-tĕ-reer'] *va.* to pass over, ignore.
pretérito [prĕ-te'ree-too] *adj.* bygone, past; (in grammar) preterite, past (definite).
pretexto [prĕ-taysh'too] *m.* pretext, excuse, pretence.
pretidão [prĕ-tee-down'] *f.* blackness; darkness.
preto [pray'too] *adj.* black; dark; *m.* negro; **pôr o — no branco**, to put down in black and white.
prevalecer [prĕ-vă-lĕ-sayr'] *vn.* to prevail.
prevaricar [prĕ-vă-ree-kar'] *vn.* to betray a trust; to pervert justice.
prevenção [prĕ-ven-sown'] *f.* prevention; warning; prejudice; **estar de —**, to be on one's guard; to be alerted.
prevenido [prĕ-vĕ-nee'doo] *adj.* forewarned, prepared, on one's guard.
prevenir [prĕ-vĕ-neer'] *va.* to warn, caution; to prevent, hinder; to prepare.
preventivo [prĕ-ven-tee'voo] *adj.* preventive.
prever [prĕ-vayr'] *va.* to foresee.
previdência [prĕ-vee-den'see-ă] *f.* forethought; precaution; **— social**, social welfare.
prévio [pre'vee-oo] *adj.* prior, advance, previous.
previsão [prĕ-vee-zown'] *f.* forecast; foresight; **— meteorológica**, weather forecast.
previsto [prĕ-veesh'too] *adj.* foreseen.
prezado [prĕ-zah'doo] *adj.* esteemed; (in letters) dear.
prezar [prĕ-zar'] *va.* to prize, esteem, value highly; *vr.* to pride oneself on.
prima [pree'mă] *f.* cousin.
primacial [pree-mă-see-al'] *adj.* primatial (*eccl.*); superior; principal, leading; essential.
primado [pree-mah'doo] *m.* primacy; pre-eminence.
primário [pree-mah'ree-oo] *adj.* primary.
primavera [pree-mă-vair'ă] *f.* spring; (*bot.*) primrose.
primaz [pree-mash'] *m.* primate.
primazia [pree-mă-zee'ă] *f.* primacy; pre-eminence.
primeiro [pri-may'ee-roo] *adj.* first; principal; **— ministro**, prime minister.
primícias [pri-mee'see-ăsh] *f. pl.* first-fruits.
primitivo [pri-mee-tee'voo] *adj.* primitive; original.
primo [pree'moo] *m.* cousin; **— co-irmão**, first cousin; **— segundo**, second cousin; *adj.* prime; **obra- —a**, masterpiece.
primogénito [pree-moo-zhe'-nee-too] *adj.* first-born.
primor [pree-mohr'] *m.* perfection, excellence; beauty; **é um —**, it's perfect, marvellous.

primordial [pree-moor-dee-al'] *adj.* original, primitive, primal; fundamental.
primoroso [pree-moo-roh'-zoo] *adj.* perfect, fine, exquisite. [princess.
princesa [preen-say'ză] *f.*
principado [preen-see-pah'-doo] *m.* principality.
principal [preen-see-pal'] *adj.* principal, chief, main; *m.* head, principal; (*com.*) principal. [prince.
príncipe [preen'seep] *m.*
principiante [preen-see-pee-ant'] *m.* beginner, novice.
principiar [preen-see-pee-ar'] *va/vn.* to begin, start.
princípio [preen-see'pee-oo] *m.* beginning; principle; **a, ao, no —**, at first, in the beginning; **por —**, on principle.
prior [pree-ohr'] *m.* prior; parish-priest.
prioridade [pree-oo-ree-dahd'] *f.* priority, precedence.
prisão [pree-zown'] *f.* prison, jail (*or* gaol); arrest; imprisonment; bond; **ordem de —**, warrant (for arrest); **— preventiva**, preventive detention; **— de ventre**, constipation.
prisioneiro [pree-zee-oo-nay'-ee-roo] *m.* prisoner.
privação [pree-vă-sown'] *f.* deprivation, loss; *pl.* hardship(s), privation(s).
privado [pree-vah'doo] *m.* favourite, intimate friend; *adj.* private; deprived.
privança [pree-van'să] *f.* favour (at Court).
privar [pree-var'] *va.* to deprive; *vn.* **— com**, to associate closely with.
privativo [pree-vă-tee'voo] *adj.* peculiar to; exclusive.
privilegiado [pri-vi-lĕ-zhee-ah'doo] *adj.* privileged; exceptional, distinguished.
privilégio [pri-vi-le'zhee-oo] *m.* privilege.
pró [pro] *m.* advantage; *adv.* for, pro; **em — de**, for the benefit of; **os —s e os contras**, the pros and cons.
proa [proh'ă] *f.* prow, bows; (*fig.*) conceit; **castelo de —**, forecastle.
probabilidade [proo-bă-bee-lee-dahd'] *f.* probability, likelihood.
probidade [proo-bee-dahd'] *f.* probity, integrity.
problema [proo-blay'mă] *m.* problem. [upright.
probo [proh'boo] *adj.* honest,
procedência [proo-sĕ-den'see-ă] *f.* origin, source.
proceder [proo-sĕ-dayr'] *vn.* to proceed, go on; to act, behave; to arise from, proceed from; *m.* conduct.
procedimento [proo-sĕ-dee-men'too] *m.* behaviour, conduct; procedure.
procela [proo-se'lă] *f.* storm, tempest.
proceloso [proo-sĕ-loh'zoo] *adj.* stormy.
processar [proo-sĕ-sar'] *va.* to prosecute, proceed against.
processo [proo-se'soo] *m.* process, procedure; trial, lawsuit, proceedings (*leg.*).
proclamação [proo-klă-mă-sown'] *f.* proclamation; promulgation.
proclamar [proo-klă-mar'] *va.* to proclaim, promulgate.
procriar [proo-kree-ar'] *va.* to procreate, breed, beget.
procura [proo-koo'ră] *f.* search; (*com.*) demand; **à — de**, looking for, in search of.
procuração [proo-koo-ră-sown'] *f.* power of attorney; letter (warrant) of attorney; **casamento por —**, marriage by proxy.

procurador [proo-koo-ră-dohr'] *m.* attorney, agent, proxy.
procurar [proo-koo-rar'] *va.* to look for, search for, seek; to try to; to call on, look (a person) up.
prodigalizar [proo-dee-gă-lee-zar'] *va.* to squander, lavish.
prodígio [proo-dee'zhee-oo] *m.* prodigy.
prodigioso [proo-dee-zhee-oh'zoo] *adj.* prodigious, marvellous, amazing; huge.
pródigo [pro'dee-goo] *adj.* wasteful, extravagant, prodigal; lavish.
produção [proo-doo-sow*n*'] *f.* production; produce.
produtivo [proo-doo-tee'voo] *adj.* productive, fertile; profitable.
produto [proo-doo'too] *m.* product; produce; profits, proceeds.
produzir [proo-doo-zeer'] *va.* to produce.
proeminência [proo-ay-mee-ne*n*'see-ă] *f.* prominence; protuberance, jutting out.
proeminente [proo-ay-mee-ne*nt*'] *adj.* prominent.
proémio [proo-e'mee-oo] *m.* preface, prologue.
proeza [proo-ay'ză] *f.* heroic deed, exploit, feat.
profanar [proo-fă-nar'] *va.* to profane, desecrate, defile.
profanidade [proo-fă-nee-dahd'] *f.* profanity.
profano [proo-fă'noo] *adj.* profane; blasphemous; secular, lay (society, etc.); unlettered; *m.* the profane; layman.
profecia [proo-fĕ-see'ă] *f.* prophecy.
proferir [proo-fĕ-reer'] *va.* to utter; to pronounce (judgment); to make (a speech).
professar [proo-fĕ-sar'] *va.* to declare, avow, profess; to practise (profession); *vn.* to take religious vows.
professor [proo-fĕ-sohr'] *m.* teacher; — **catedrático,** professor (in university).
professorado [proo-fĕ-soo-rah'doo] *m.* teaching staff; teaching (as function *or* career).
profeta [proo-fe'tă] *m.* prophet.
profetizar [proo-fĕ-tee-zar'] *va.* to prophesy, predict.
proficiência [proo-fee-see-e*n*'see-ă] *f.* proficiency, skill, competence.
proficiente [proo-fee-see-e*nt*'] *adj.* proficient, competent.
profícuo [proo-fee'koo-oo] *adj.* useful, advantageous.
profissão [proo-fee-sow*n*'] *f.* profession; declaration.
profissional [proo-fee-see-oo-nal'] *adj.* professional.
prófugo [pro'foo-goo] *adj.* fugitive.
profundidade [proo-foo*n*-dee-dahd'] *f.* depth; profundity.
profundo [proo-foo*n*'doo] *adj.* very deep; profound.
profusão [proo-foo-zow*n*'] *f.* profusion.
progénie [proo-zhe'nee-ĕ] *f.* progeny, offspring; lineage.
progenitor [proo-zhĕ-nee-tohr'] *m.* progenitor; *pl.* ancestors.
prognosticar [proog-noosh-tee-kar'] *va.* to prognosticate, predict, foretell; *vn.* to make a prognosis (*med.*).
prognóstico [proog-nosh'tee-koo] *m.* prediction, prognostication; (*med.*) prognosis.
programa [proo-gră'mă] *m.* programme.
progredir [proo-grĕ-deer'] *vn.* to progress, advance, get on.
progresso [proo-gre'soo] *m.* progress.

proibição [proo-ee-bee-sown'] *f.* prohibition, ban.
proibir [proo-ee-beer'] *va.* to prohibit, forbid.
projecção [proo-zhe-sown'] *f.* projection.
projectar [proo-zhe-tar'] *va.* to project, throw; to plan.
projéctil [proo-zhe'teel] *m.* missile, projectile.
projecto [proo-zhe'too] *m.* scheme, plan, project; — de lei, bill.
projector [proo-zhe-tohr'] *m.* projector; searchlight.
prol [prol] *m.* benefit; **em** — de, for; on behalf of.
prole [prol] *f.* offspring, progeny.
proletariado [proo-lě-tă-ree-ah'doo] *m.* proletariat, working class.
prolífico [proo-lee'fee-koo] *adj.* prolific, abundant.
prolixo [proo-leek'soo] *adj.* long-winded, tedious, prolix.
prólogo [pro'loo-goo] *m.* prologue, introduction.
prolongamento [proo-lo*n*-gă-me*n*'too] *m.* prolongation, extension.
prolongar [proo-lo*n*-gar'] *va.* to extend, prolong, lengthen.
promessa [proo-me'să] *f.* promise.
prometedor [proo-mě-tě-dohr'] *adj.* promising.
prometer [proo-mě-tayr'] *va.* to promise.
promiscuidade [proo-meesh-kwee-dahd'] *f.* indiscriminate confusion, promiscuity.
promissão [proo-mee-sown'] *f.* promise; **terra da** —, Promised Land.
promoção [proo-moo-sown'] *f.* promotion, preferment.
promontório [proo-mo*n*-to'-ree-oo] *m.* promontory, headland.
promotor [proo-moo-tohr'] *adj.* for the promotion of; *m.* initiator, promoter; instigator (of riot, etc.); (*leg.*) prosecutor.
promover [proo-moo-vayr'] *va.* to promote, raise; to further, foment; to instigate, stir up.
promulgar [proo-mool-gar'] *va.* to publish, promulgate, issue.
pronome [proo-nohm'] *m.* pronoun.
prontidão [pro*n*-tee-dow*n*'] *f.* promptness, readiness.
pronto [pro*n*'too] *adj.* ready, prepared; prompt, speedy, quick.
prontuário [pro*n*-too-ah'ree-oo] *m.* handbook, reference book.
pronúncia [proo-noo*n*'see-ă] *f.* pronunciation; (*leg.*) indictment.
pronunciação [proo-noo*n*-see-ă-sow*n*'] *f.* pronunciation; utterance, enunciation.
pronunciamento [proo-noo*n*-see-ă-me*n*'too] *m.* (*mil.*) revolt, rising.
pronunciar [proo-noo*n*-see-ar'] *va.* to pronounce; to utter; *vr.* to declare oneself; to rise in revolt.
propagação [proo-pă-gă-sow*n*'] *f.* spread(ing), dissemination, propagation.
propagar [proo-pă-gar'] *va.* to propagate, spread.
propender [proo-pe*n*-dayr'] *vn.* to incline.
propenso [proo-pe*n*'soo] *adj.* (favourably) inclined.
propina [proo-pee'nă] *f.* fee(s).
propínquo [proo-pee*n*'kwoo] *adj.* near, close.
propor [proo-pohr'] *va.* to propose, suggest.

proporção [proo-poor-sown'] *f.* proportion.
proporcionado [proo-poor-see-oo-nah'doo] *adj.* proportioned; proportionate, commensurate.
proporcionar [proo-poor-see-oo-nar'] *va.* to afford, offer, provide; to adjust.
proposição [proo-poo-zee-sown'] *f.* proposition, proposal.
propósito [proo-po'zee-too] *m.* purpose, aim, intention; a —, incidentally, by the way; suitably, to the purpose; de —, on purpose; a — de, with regard (reference) to; as to.
proposta [proo-posh'tă] *f.* proposal, offer.
pròpriamente [pro-pree-ă-ment'] *adv.* properly; exactly; — dito, strictly speaking.
propriedade [proo-pree-ĕ-dahd'] *f.* property; ownership; attribute; propriety, appropriateness.
proprietário [proo-pree-ĕ-tah'ree-oo] *m.* owner, proprietor; landlord.
próprio [pro'pree-oo] *adj.* (my, his, etc.) own; proper, suitable; exact; characteristic of; o — homem, the very man; eu —, I myself; o — diabo, the devil himself.
propulsão [proo-pool-sown'] *f.* propulsion.
propulsor [proo-pool-sohr'] *adj.* propelling; *m.* propelling mechanism.
prorrogação [proo-roo-gă-sown'] *f.* prorogation; extension.
prorrogar [proo-roo-gar'] *va.* to adjourn, prorogue; to extend, prolong (licence, period of payment, etc.).
prorromper [proo-ron-payr'] *vn.* to burst out, break out (into cries, etc.).
prosa [pro'ză] *f.* prose; ter boa —, to have the gift of the gab.
prosador [proo-ză-dohr'] *m.* prose-writer.
prosaico [proo-zȳ'koo] *adj.* prosaic, dull, humdrum.
prosápia [proo-za'pee-ă] *f.* lineage; conceit.
proscénio [proosh-se'nee-oo] *m.* (front of the) stage.
proscrever [proosh-krĕ-vayr'] *va.* to banish, proscribe, outlaw.
proscrição [proosh-kree-sown'] *f.* exile, banishment; prohibition.
proscrito [proosh-kree'too] *m.* exile; outlaw, outcast.
prosélito [proo-ze'lee-too] *m.* convert, proselyte.
prospecto [proosh-pe'too] *m.* prospectus, circular; prospect, view.
prosperar [proosh-pĕ-rar'] *vn.* to prosper, thrive.
prosperidade [proosh-pĕ-ree-dahd'] *f.* prosperity, success.
próspero [prosh'pĕ-roo] *adj.* prosperous, successful, thriving; favourable.
prossecução [proo-sĕ-koo-sown'] *f.* continuation.
prosseguimento [proo-sĕ-gee-men'too] *m.* continuation.
prosseguir [proo-sĕ-geer] *va.* to continue, follow, pursue, proceed with.
prostituir [proosh-tee-too-eer'] *va.* to prostitute, debase.
prostituta [proosh-tee-too'tă] *f.* prostitute.
prostração [proosh-tră-sown'] *f.* prostration, depression.
prostrar [proosh-trar'] *va.* to lay low, overthrow, prostrate; *vr.* to prostrate oneself; to be exhausted.
protagonista [proo-tă-goo-neesh'tă] *mf.* protagonist.
protecção [proo-te-sown'] *f.*

protection; favour, patronage.
proteccionismo [proo-te-see-oo-neezh'moo] *m.* protectionism.
protector [proo-te-tohr'] *m.* protector, defender; patron.
proteger [proo-tě-zhayr'] *va.* to protect, shield, shelter.
protegido [proo-tě-zhee'doo] *m.* protégé, favourite; *adj.* protected.
proteína [pro-tay-ee'nă] *f.* protein.
protelar [proo-tě-lar'] *va.* to postpone, put off.
protestação [proo-těsh-tă-sow*n*'] *f.* assurance, protestation.
protestante [proo-těsh-ta*n*t'] *m/adj.* Protestant; protesting.
protestar [proo-těsh-tar'] *vn.* to protest, object; *va.* to assert, declare.
protesto [proo-tesh'too] *m.* protest; affirmation.
protocolo [proh-too-ko'loo] *m.* protocol; procedure.
protótipo [pro-to'tee-poo] *m.* prototype, model.
protuberância [proo-too-bě-ra*n*'see-ă] *f.* protuberance.
prova [pro'vă] *f.* proof; test, trial; sign, token; sample; (*print.*) proof; (examination) paper; **à —**, on approval; on trial; **à — de**, proof against; **à — de água**, waterproof.
provação [proo-vă-sow*n*'] *f.* trial, test; tribulation, suffering.
provar [proo-var'] *va.* to prove; to try, test; to taste, sample; to try on (clothes); **— fortuna**, to try one's luck.
provável [proo-vah'vel] *adj.* probable, likely.
provedor [proo-vě-dohr'] *m.* president of a charitable institution; provider, supplier.
proveito [proo-vay'ee-too] *m.* profit; advantage; **em — de** for the benefit of.
proveitoso [proo-vay-ee-toh'-zoo] *adj.* advantageous, profitable, useful.
proveniência [proo-vě-nee-e*n*'see-ă] *f.* source, origin.
proveniente [proo-vě-nee-e*n*t'] *adj.* coming from, originating in.
prover [proo-vayr'] *va.* to provide, supply, furnish.
provérbio [proo-vair'bee-oo] *m.* proverb, saying.
providência [proo-vee-de*n*'-see-ă] *f.* Providence; stroke of luck; forethought; **tomar —s**, to take steps, measures.
providenciar [proo-vee-de*n*-see-ar'] *va.* to arrange; *vn.* to make provision.
providente [proo-vee-de*n*t'] *adj.* provident, careful.
provido [proo-vee'doo] *adj.* provided, supplied.
próvido [pro'vee-doo] *adj.* provident.
província [proo-vee*n*'see-ă] *f.* province.
provinciano [proo-vee*n*-see-ă'noo] *adj.* provincial.
provir [proo-veer'] *vn.* to proceed from, derive from.
provisão [proo-vee-zow*n*'] *f.* provision, supply.
provisório [proo-vee-zo'ree-oo] *adj.* provisional, temporary.
provocação [proo-voo-kă-sow*n*'] *f.* provocation.
provocador [proo-voo-kă-dohr'] *adj.* *or* **provocante**, provocative, provoking.
provocar [proo-voo-kar'] *va.* to provoke, rouse; to tempt.
proximidade [pro-see-mee-dahd'] *f.* proximity; *pl.* vicinity, neighbourhood.
próximo [pro'see-moo] *adj.* near, close, adjacent; next; *m.* fellow-man, neighbour.

prudência [proo-den'see-ă] *f.* prudence, wisdom.
prudente [proo-dent'] *adj.* prudent, wise, discreet.
prumo [proo'moo] *m.* sounding lead, plummet; plumb (-line); a —, vertically, perpendicularly.
prurido [proo-ree'doo] *m.* itch; (*fig.*) hankering, yearning.
psicanálise [psee-kă-na'leez] *f.* psychoanalysis.
psicologia [psee-koo-loo-zhee'ă] *f.* psychology.
psicólogo [psee-ko'loo-goo] *m.* psychologist.
pua [poo'ă] *f.* sharp point.
publicação [poo-blee-kă-sown'] *f.* publication.
publicar [poo-blee-kar'] *va.* to publish, proclaim, announce.
publicidade [poo-blee-see-dahd'] *f.* publicity; advertising. [public.
público [poo'blee-koo] *m/adj.*
púcaro [poo'kă-roo] *m.* jug; mug, cup.
pudibundo [poo-dee-boon'-doo] *adj.* chaste, modest, shy.
pudim [poo-deen'] *m.* pudding.
pudor [poo-dohr'] *m.* bashfulness, shyness, modesty.
puerícia [poo-ĕ-ree'see-ă] *f.* boyhood, childhood.
puericultura [poo-ĕ-ree-kool-too'ră] *f.* child-care.
pueril [poo-ĕ-reel'] *adj.* childish, puerile.
puerilidade [poo-ĕ-ree-lee-dahd'] *f.* childishness; childish action, remark, etc.
pugilato [poo-zhee-lah'too] *m.* fighting, boxing.
pugilismo [poo-zhee-leezh'-moo] *m.* boxing.
pugna [poog'nă] *f.* fight, struggle.
pugnacidade [poog-nă-see-dahd'] *f.* pugnacity.
pugnar [poog-nar'] *vn.* to fight, struggle, contend.
pugnaz [poog-nash'] *adj.* pugnacious, combative.
pujança [poo-zhan'să] *f.* vigour, strength; vigorous growth; na — da idade, in the prime of life.
pujante [poo-zhant'] *adj.* vigorous, strong, powerful.
pular [poo-lar'] *vn.* to jump, leap.
pulga [pool'gă] *f.* flea.
pulha [poo'lyă] *m.* rogue, 'skunk'; repartee; *adj.* low, vulgar, coarse.
pulmão [pool-mown'] *m.* lung.
pulo [poo'loo] *m.* leap, jump, bound; dar —s de contente, to be delighted, overjoyed; aos —s, by leaps and bounds; de um —, at one bound.
púlpito [pool'pee-too] *m.* pulpit.
pulsação [pool-să-sown'] *f.* pulsation, beat(ing).
pulsar [pool-sar'] *vn.* to beat, pulsate, throb; *va.* to finger, strike (*mus.*). [bracelet.
pulseira [pool-say'ee-ră] *f.*
pulso [pool'soo] *m.* wrist; pulse; (*fig.*) vigour, strength; obra de —, work of great importance.
pulular [poo-loo-lar'] *vn.* to swarm, teem; to spring up.
pulverizar [pool-vĕ-ree-zar'] *va.* to grind (to powder), pulverize.
punção [poon-sown'] *m.* punch (*mech.*); *f.* puncture (*med.*).
pundonor [poon-doo-nohr'] *m.* sense of honour; dignity.
pungente [poon-zhent'] *adj.* painful, sharp, grievous.
pungir [poon-zheer'] *va.* to pierce; to prick; to distress, afflict. [handful.
punhado [poo-nyah'doo] *m.*
punhal [poo-nyal'] *m.* dagger.

punhalada [poo-nyă-lah'dă] *f.* stab, knife wound.
punho [poo'nyoo] *m.* fist; (shirt-)cuff; handle, hilt; **por seu próprio —**, in his own handwriting.
punição [poo-nee-sow*n*'] *f.* punishment; penalty.
punir [poo-neer'] *va.* to punish.
pupila [poo-pee'lă] *f.* pupil (of eye); ward.
pupilo [poo-pee'loo] *m.* ward.
puré [poo-re'] *m.* purée; **— de batatas**, mashed potatoes.
pureza [poo-ray'ză] *f.* purity; clarity.
purga [poor'gă] *f. or* **purgante** purgative (*med.*).
purgação [poor-gă-sow*n*'] *f.* purge, purification, purgation.
purgar [poor-gar'] *va.* to purge, cleanse, purify; to expiate (sins).
purgativo [poor-gă-tee'voo] *m/adj.* purgative.
purgatório [poor-gă-to'ree-oo] *m.* purgatory.
puridade [poo-ree-dahd'] *f.* purity; (*archaic*) secret; **escrivão da —**, secretary of state, (king's) private secretary.
purificar [poo-ree-fee-kar'] *va.* to purify, cleanse; to refine.
purista [poo-reesh'tă] *mf.* purist.
puro [poo'roo] *adj.* pure; clear; clean; chaste; complete, absolute (lie, truth, etc.).
púrpura [poor'poo-ră] *f.* purple.
purpúreo [poor-poo'ree-oo] *adj.* purple; crimson, deep-red.
purulento [poo-roo-le*n*'too] *adj.* festering, suppurating.
pusilânime [poo-zee-lă'neem] *adj.* timid, faint-hearted, cowardly.
puxador [poo-shă-dohr'] *m.* handle, knob.
puxão [poo-show*n*'] *m.* tug, pull, jerk. [draw, haul
puxar [poo-shar'] *va.* to pull'

Q

quadra [kwad'ră] *f.* four-line stanza, quatrain (*poet.*); time, period, age; room; a four (playing card, dominoes).
quadrado [kwă-drah'doo] *m/adj.* square.
quadrar [kwă-drar'] *va.* to square (*maths.*); to make square; *vn.* to square with, agree with, fit in with.
quadriculado [kwă-dree-koo-lah'doo] *adj.* squared; chequered (pattern); **papel —**, squared paper, graph paper.
quadril [kwă-dreel'] *m.* hip; haunch.
quadrilha [kwă-dree'lyă] *f.* gang (of thieves, etc.); troop; quadrille (*mus.*).
quadrilongo [kwă-dree-lo*n*'-goo] *m/adj.* oblong.
quadrimotor [kwă-dree-moh-tohr'] *adj.* four-engined.
quadro [kwad'roo] *m.* picture, painting; picture-frame; scene, spectacle; table, list; staff; **— preto**, blackboard; **— de distribuição**, switchboard; **— de reserva**, reserve list (*mil.*); **— de comando**, instrument panel.
qual [kwal] *pr.* which; **cada —**, each one; *conj.* like, as; **tal —**, just like; as; *interj.* **— história, (carapuça)**, what nonsense!
qualidade [kwă-lee-dahd'] *f.* quality; **na — de**, as; in the capacity of.
qualificação [kwă-lee-fee-kă-sow*n*'] *f.* qualification; classification.

qualificar [kwă-lee-fee-kar′] *va.* to qualify; to classify; to ennoble.
qualquer [kwal-kair′] *pr/adj.* any; either; anybody; **— dia,** some day, one day, any day; *m.* **um —,** somebody or other.
quando [kwa*n*′doo] *adv/conj.* when; if; **— muito,** at most; **de vez em —, de — em —,** now and then, from time to time; **ainda —,** even though; **a — da sua chegada,** at the time of his arrival.
quantia [kwa*n*-tee′ă] *f.* sum, amount (of money).
quantidade [kwa*n*-tee-dahd′] *f.* quantity, amount, number.
quanto [kwa*n*′too] *adj/pr.* all that, as much as; (*pl.*) all; *interrog.* how much?, (*pl.*) how many?; **— mais . . . tanto mais,** the more . . . the more; **— a,** as for, as to; **— antes,** as soon as possible; **— mais cedo, melhor,** the sooner the better; **— tempo?** how long?; **tudo —,** everything that, all that.
quão [kwow*n*] *adv.* how; **tão . . . —,** as . . . as.
quarenta [kwă-re*n*′tă] *f.* forty.
quarentena [kwă-re*n*-tay′nă] *f.* quarantine; (a group of) forty.
quaresma [kwă-rezh′mă] *f.* Lent.
quarta [kwar′tă] *f.* quarter; pitcher; **— de agulha,** point of the compass.
quarta-feira [kwar′tă fay′ee-ră] *f.* Wednesday.
quarteirão [kwăr-tay-ee-row*n*′] *m.* twenty-five; block of houses.
quartel [kwăr-tel′] *m.* quarter; barracks, quarters (*mil.*); mercy, quarter; **— general,** (general) headquarters.
quarteto [kwăr-tay′too] *m.* quartet (*mus.*).
quartilho [kwăr-tee′lyoo] *m.* pint.
quarto [kwar′too] *m.* room; quarter; watch (*mil., naut.*); **— de casal,** double-room; *adj.* fourth. [nearly.
quase [kwah′zĕ] *adv.* almost,
quatro [kwa′troo] *adj.* four.
que [kĕ] *pr.* which, who, that, whom; **o —,** what; he who; **os —,** those who; *interrog.* what; *conj.* that; because; *interj.* what a . . .!, how . . .!
quê [kay] *m.* something; complication; **tem seus —s,** it has its complications; **não tem de —,** not at all!, don't mention it!; **para —?,** why?, what for?
quebra [ke′bră] *f.* break, breach, rupture; bankruptcy.
quebra-cabeça [ke′bră kă-bay′să] *m.* problem, puzzle; worry; jigsaw puzzle.
quebrada [kĕ-brah′dă] *f.* (steep) slope; ravine, gully.
quebradiço [kĕ-bră-dee′soo] *f.* fragile, brittle.
quebrado [kĕ-brah′doo] *adj.* broken; exhausted; ruptured; bankrupt; *m.* fraction.
quebra-gelo [ke′bră zhay′-loosh] *m.* ice-breaker (*naut.*).
quebra-luz [ke′bră-loosh] *m.* lampshade.
quebra-mar [ke′bra mar] *m.* breakwater; sea-wall.
quebrantar [kĕ-bra*n*-tar′] *va.* to break; to weaken.
quebranto [kĕ-bra*n*′too] *m.* exhaustion, prostration; weakness; evil eye.
quebrar [kĕ-brar′] *va.* to break; to weaken; to interrupt; to bend; to become bankrupt.
queda [ke′dă] *f.* fall; downfall; tendency, inclination.

quedar [kĕ-dar'] *vn/vr.* to stay, stop, remain.
quedo [kay'doo] *adj.* still, quiet.
queijada [kay-ee-zhah'dă] *f.* (*approx.*) cheese-cake.
queijeira [kay-zhay'ee-ră] *f.* dairy.
queijo [kay'ee-zhoo] *m.* cheese.
queima [kay'ee-mă] *f.* burning; à —-roupa, point-blank.
queimadura [kay-ee-mă-doo-ră] *f.* burn.
queimar [kay-ee-mar'] *va.* to burn, scorch, scald; to tan; to wither, blight.
queixa [kay'ee-shă] *f.* complaint, accusation; lament.
queixada [kay-ee-shah'dă] *f.* jaw(-bone).
queixar-se [kay-ee-shar'sĕ] *vr.* to complain; to grumble.
queixo [kay'ee-shoo] *m.* chin; jaw; de — caído, crestfallen.
queixoso [kay-ee-shoh'zoo] *adj.* plaintive, doleful; querulous, complaining; *m.* plaintiff, complainant (*leg.*).
queixume [kay-ee-shoom'] *m.* lament, complaint, moan.
quem [ken] *pr.* who, whom; anybody who; de —, whose; — quer que, whoever; por — é, for pity's sake; I beg you; for heaven's sake; — me dera, if only I were; I wish I could.
quente [kent] *adj.* hot, warm; (*fig.*) fiery, ardent.
queque [kayk] *m.* (small) cake.
quer [kair] *conj.* either, or; whether; — queiras — não, whether you like it or not; onde — que, wherever.
querela [kĕ-re'lă] *f.* indictment, accusation, complaint (*leg.*); dispute; altercation; lament.
querelado [kĕ-rĕ-lah'doo] *m.* defendant, accused (*leg.*).
querelador [kĕ-rĕ-lă-dohr'] *m.* *or* **querelante** plaintiff, complainant (*leg.*).
querelar [kĕ-rĕ-lar'] *va.* to make a formal complaint *or* charge against; to sue, prosecute; *vr.* to complain.
querença [kĕ-ren'să] *f.* affection, liking.
querer [kĕ-rayr'] *va.* to want, wish, desire; — **bem a,** to be fond of, to love; — **mal a,** to bear a grudge against; to hate; — **dizer,** to mean.
querido [kĕ-ree'doo] *adj.* dear, beloved; *m.* dear, darling.
quesito [kĕ-zee'too] *m.* question, query.
questão [kĕsh-town'] *f.* point; question; inquiry; dispute, quarrel.
questionar [kĕsh-tee-oo-nar'] *vn.* to bicker, wrangle, quarrel; *va.* to controvert, question.
quezília [kĕ-zee'lee-ă] *f.* dislike, aversion.
quiçá [kee-sa'] *adv.* perhaps.
quício [kee'see-oo] *m.* hinge.
quieto [kee-e'too] *adj.* still, quiet, tranquil.
quietude [kee-e-tood'] *f.* quiet, peace, calm.
quilate [kee-lat'] *m.* carat; (*fig.*) excellence, sterling quality.
quilha [kee'lyă] *f.* keel.
quilo [kee'loo] *m.* *or* **quilograma** *m.* kilo, kilogram, kilogramme.
quilómetro [kee-lo'mĕ-troo] *m.* kilometre, kilometer.
quimera [kee-mair'ă] *f.* chimera, illusion, fancy.
química [kee'mee-kă] *f.* chemistry.
químico [kee'mee-koo] *adj.* chemical; *m.* chemist.
quina [kee'nă] *f.* corner; a five (in cards, etc.); *pl.* the

five shields on Portuguese standard.
quinhão [kee-nyow*n*'] *m.* share, portion.
quinhentista [kee-nye*n*-teesh'tă] *adj.* of the 16th century.
quinina [ki-nee'nă] *f.* quinine.
quino [kee'noo] *m.* lotto.
quinquilharias [kee*n*-kee-lyă-ree'ăsh] *f. pl.* oddments, knick-knacks, trinkets; toys.
quinta [kee*n*'tă] *f.* farm; *adj.* fifth.
quinta-feira [kee*n*'ta fay'ee-ră] *f.* Thursday; — santa, Maundy Thursday.
quintal [kee*n*-tal'] *m.* garden; yard; hundredweight.
quinteiro [kee*n*-tay'ee-roo] *m.* (tenant-)farmer.
quinto [keen'too] *adj.* fifth.
quinze [kee*n*z] *adj.* fifteen; fifteenth.
quinzena [kee*n*-zay'nă] *f.* fortnight; two weeks' wages; short coat, long jacket.
quiosque [kee-oshk'] *m.* kiosk; bookstall.
quisto [keesh'too] *m.* cyst.
quitação [kee-tă-sow*n*'] *f.* acquittance, receipt in full.
quitanda [kee-ta*n*'dă] *f.* stall, (small) shop.
quitar [kee-tar'] *va.* to release from (debt, obligation); to take away.
quite [keet] *adj.* free, clear; *pl.* quits, even.
quota [kwo'tă] *f.* quota, share; contribution.
quotidiano [kwo-tee-dee-ă'-noo] *adj.* daily.

R

rã [ran] *f.* frog.
rabada [ră-bah'dă] *f.* rump.
rabadela [ră-bă-de'lă] *f. or* **rabadilha** tail-end, rump.
rabanada [ră-bă-nah'dă] *f.* blow from the tail; (*approx.*) fritter; — de vento, gust of wind.
rabanete [ră-bă-nayt'] *m.* radish.
rabeca [ră-be'kă] *f.* fiddle, violin.
rabelo [ră-bay'loo] *m.* boat on river Douro with large rudder.
rabiça [ră-bee'să] *f.* plough handle.
rabicho [ră-bee'shoo] *m.* pigtail; crupper (of harness).
rabino [ră-bee'noo] *adj.* naughty; troublesome; restless; *m.* (Jewish) rabbi.
rabiscar [ră-beesh-kar'] *va/vn.* to scribble, scrawl.
rabo [rah'boo] *m.* tail; handle (of spade, etc.); (*pop.*) bottom, rump; — do olho, corner of the eye.
rabugem [ră-boo'zhĕn] *f. or* **rabugice** *f.* sulkiness, sullenness, peevishness; mange (disease).
rabugento [ră-boo-zhe*n*'too] *adj.* peevish, surly, cross.
raça [rah'să] *f.* race; breed; strain; de —, thoroughbred.
ração [ră-sow*n*'] *f.* ration(s), allowance, share.
racha [rah'shă] *f.* split, crack, fissure; splinter.
rachador [ră-shă-dohr'] *m.* woodcutter.
rachar [ră-shar'] *va.* to split, crack; to chop (wood); frio de —, bitter cold.
racimo [ră-see'moo] *m.* bunch, cluster.
raciocinar [ră-see-oo-see-nar'] *vn.* to reason.
raciocínio [ră-see-oo-see'nee-oo] *m.* reasoning.
racional [ră-see-oo-nal'] *adj.* rational.
racionamento [ră-see-oo-nă-me*n*'too] *m.* rationing; distribution of rations.

racionar [rǎ-see-oo-nar'] *va.* to ration.
rada [rah'dǎ] *f.* roadstead.
radiador [rǎ-dee-ǎ-dohr'] *m.* radiator.
radiante [rǎ-dee-*a*nt'] *adj.* radiant; beaming.
radical [rǎ-dee-kal'] *adj.* radical, fundamental; *m.* root, stem (of word).
radicar [rǎ-dee-kar'] *va.* to root, plant; *vr.* to take root; to be rooted.
rádio [rah'dee-oo] *f.* wireless, radio; *m.* wireless *or* radio set; radium (*chem.*); radius (*anat.*).
radiodifusão [rǎ-dee-oo-dee-foo-zow*n*'] *f.* broadcasting.
radiografia [rǎ-dee-oo-grǎ-fee'ǎ] *f.* radiography; X-ray plate *or* photograph.
radiograma [rǎ-dee-oo-grǎ'-mǎ] *m.* cablegram, radiogram.
radioso [rǎ-dee-oh'zoo] *adj.* radiant, brilliant.
rafar [rǎ-far'] *va.* to wear out.
raia [rȳ'ǎ] *f.* line, stroke, dash; boundary, border; (*zool.*) ray, skate; **tocar as —s,** to reach the limit.
raiano [rǎ-yah'noo] *adj.* bordering on.
raiar [rǎ-yar'] *vn.* to radiate; to dawn.
rainha [rǎ-ee'nyǎ] *f.* queen.
raio [rȳ'oo] *m.* ray, beam; flash (of lightning); thunderbolt; radius; spoke (of wheel); **como um —,** like (in) a flash.
raiva [rȳ'vǎ] *f.* rage, fury, anger; (*med.*) rabies.
raivoso [rȳ-voh'zoo] *adj.* furious, rabid, wild.
raiz [rǎ-eesh'] *f.* root; origin, source; **bens de —,** real estate; **lançar —es,** to strike (take) root.
rajada [rǎ-zhah'dǎ] *f.* gust, blast (of wind); burst (of eloquence, anger, gunfire).
ralador [rǎ-lǎ-dohr'] *m.* grater.
ralar [rǎ-lar'] *va.* to worry; to annoy, irritate; to crumble (bread).
ralé [rǎ-le'] *f.* mob, riff-raff, rabble; prey (of eagle, etc.); (*archaic*) stock, breed, species.
ralhar [rǎ-lyar'] *vn.* to reprimand, scold, nag.
ralo [rah'loo] *adj.* thin, sparse; *m.* nozzle, spout (of watering-can etc.); grating (in door).
rama [rǎ'mǎ] *f.* branches, foliage; **pela —,** superficially; **algodão em —,** cotton-wool.
ramada [rǎ-mah'dǎ] *f.* branches, foliage; trellis; arbour, shelter.
ramagem [rǎ-mah'zhe*n*] *f.* branches; foliage.
ramal [rǎ-mal'] *m.* branch-line (railway); branch-road; extension line.
ramalhete [rǎ-mǎ-lyayt'] *m.* bunch of flowers, bouquet.
ramificar-se [rǎ-mee-fee-kar'sě] *vr.* to branch out, spread out.
ramo [rǎ'moo] *m.* branch; section, division; bunch (of flowers); **domingo de —s,** Palm Sunday.
rampa [ra*n*'pǎ] *f.* slope, incline, ramp.
rancheiro [ra*n*-shay'ee-roo] *m.* cook (*mil.*).
rancor [ra*n*-kohr'] *m.* rancour, spite, hatred, malice.
rancoroso [ra*n*-koo-roh'zoo] *adj.* malicious, spiteful.
rançoso [ra*n*-soh'zoo] *adj.* rancid; (*fig.*) wearisome.
ranger [ra*n*-zhayr'] *vn.* to creak; **— os dentes,** to grind (gnash) one's teeth.
rangífero [ra*n*-zhee'fě-roo] *m.* reindeer.
ranho [rǎ'nyoo] *m.* mucus; 'dirt', 'snot'.
ranhoso [rǎ-nyoh'zoo] *adj.* snivelly, snotty-nosed.

ranhura [rã-nyoo'rã] *f.* groove, slot, slit.
ranúnculo [rã-noon'koo-loo] *m.* buttercup.
rapacidade [rã-pã-see-dahd'] *f.* rapacity, greed.
rapagão [rã-pã-gown'] *m.* big, strong lad.
rapapé [rã-pã-pe'] *m.* bowing and scraping, flattery.
rapar [rã-par'] *va.* to scrape; to scratch; to shave; (*sl.*) to clean up (money); **frio de —,** bitter cold.
rapariga [rã-pã-ree'gã] *f.* girl. [youth.
rapaz [rã-pash'] *m.* boy; lad;
rapaziada [rã-pã-zee-ah'dã] *f.* gang of lads; prank, trick, lark.
rapé [rã-pe'] *m.* snuff.
rapidez [rã-pee-daysh'] *f.* speed, rapidity; dispatch, quickness.
rápido [ra'pee-doo] *adj.* fast, rapid, quick, swift; *m.* express (train).
rapina [rã-pee'nã] *f.* plunder; ave de —, bird of prey.
raposa [rã-poh'zã] *f.* fox, vixen; foxy (crafty) person; **apanhar uma —,** to fail (in examination).
raposo [rã-poh'zoo] *m.* fox; foxy person.
rapsódia [rãp-so'dee-ã] *f.* rhapsody.
raptar [rãp-tar'] *va.* to kidnap, seize, abduct.
rapto [rap'too] *m.* kidnapping, abduction; ecstasy, rapture, transport.
raqueta [rã-kay'tã] *f.* racket.
raquítico [rã-kee'tee-koo] *adj.* rickety; stunted; feeble, shaky.
raquitismo [rã-kee-teezh'-moo] *m.* rickets.
rarear [rã-ree-ar'] *va.* to make scarce, thin out; *vn.* to be scarce, rare.
raridade [rã-ree-dahd'] *f.* rareness, scarcity; rarity, rare thing.
raro [rah'roo] *adj.* rare, uncommon; sparse.
rasa [rah'zã] *f.* bushel; **pôr pela —,** to discredit, slander.
rasar [rã-zar'] *va.* to level; to fill to the brim; to skim (the waves, etc.).
rascunhar [rãsh-koo-nyar'] *va.* to draft out, sketch.
rascunho [rãsh-koo'nyoo] *m.* rough draft, sketch.
rasgado [rãzh-gah'doo] *adj.* torn, ripped; spacious, open, large; **cumprimentos —s,** effusive greetings; **trote —,** full trot.
rasgão [rãzh-gown'] *m.* tear, rip, rent.
rasgar [razh-gar'] *va.* to tear, rip, rend, split.
rasgo [razh'goo] *m.* dash, stroke; burst (of eloquence, etc.); flight (of fancy, etc.); (heroic, generous, etc.) gesture; **de um —,** at one blow.
raso [rah'zoo] *adj.* flat, even, level; filled, full up; close-cropped (hair); **campo —,** open country; **soldado —,** private soldier.
rasoira [rã-zoh'ee-rã] *f.* levelling rod; (carpenter's) rasp, file. [scraping.
raspa [rash'pã] *f.* shaving,
raspadeira [rãsh-pã-day'ee-rã] *f.* scraper.
raspão [rãsh-pown'] *m.* scratch; graze; **tocar de —,** to graze.
raspar [rãsh-par'] *va.* to scrape, scratch, graze; to erase; *vr.* to clear off.
rasteiro [rãsh-tay'ee-roo] *adj.* creeping, crawling; low(-flying); servile, abject.
rastejar [rãsh-tẽ-zhar'] *vn.* to creep, crawl; *va.* to track.